The Chinese Economy Under Deng Xiaoping

The Chinese Economy Under Deng Xiaoping

Edited by
ROBERT F. ASH
Y. Y. KUEH

*new articles
see preface*

CLARENDON PRESS · OXFORD
1996

Oxford University Press, Walton Street, Oxford OX2 6DP
Oxford New York
Athens Auckland Bangkok Bombay
Calcutta Cape Town Dar es Salaam Delhi
Florence Hong Kong Istanbul Karachi
Kuala Lumpur Madras Madrid Melbourne
Mexico City Nairobi Paris Singapore
Taipei Tokyo Toronto
and associated companies in
Berlin Ibadan

Oxford is a trade mark of Oxford University Press

Published in the United States
by Oxford University Press Inc., New York

H   *Copyright © The China Quarterly, 1996*

British Library Cataloguing in Publication Data
Data available

Library of Congress Cataloging-in-Publication Data
The Chinese economy under Deng Xiaoping / edited by Robert F. Ash, Y.Y. Kueh.
(Studies on contemporary China)
Rev. versions of papers originally presented at a conference held at the Hilton Hotel,
Hong Kong Sept. 23, 1991.
Includes bibliographical references.
1. China–Economic conditions–1976–Congresses. 2. China–Economic policy–1976–Congresses.
I. Ash, Robert F. II. Kueh, Y.Y. III. Series: Studies on
contemporary China (Oxford, England) HC427.92.C4672167 1996 96-33771
338.951–dc20

ISBN 0-19-828822-0

Typeset by Best-set Typesetter Ltd., Hong Kong
Printed in Great Britain
on acid-free paper by Biddies Ltd., Guildford & King's Lynn.

Preface NA

The origins of this book lie in a workshop, jointly sponsored by the Contemporary China Institute (School of Oriental and African Studies), *The China Quarterly*, and Lingnan College, Hong Kong. It was held, under the chairmanship of the then Editor of *The China Quarterly*, Mr Brian Hook, at the Hilton Hotel, Hong Kong during 2–3 September 1991.

Revised versions of papers presented at this conference subsequently appeared in a Special Issue of *The China Quarterly* (No. 131, September 1992) under the title, "The Chinese Economy in the 1990s". For the purposes of the present volume, several of those articles have been up-dated and revised. The editors have also provided a new, extended introduction.

R.F.A.
Y.Y.K.

Contents

BK title:

Introduction

China

P27

P21

Robert F. Ash

Y. Y. Kueh

The nature, rationale and impact of China's post-1978 economic reforms are already the subject of a considerable literature. This book offers an assessment of major aspects of those reforms during their first decade and considers their implications for China's economic development during the 1990s. Each contributor has sought to review the economic achievements of the 1980s, highlighting the major problems which emerged out of them and, from the perspective of the early 1990s, to speculate on the challenges and opportunities that exist for further growth in the foreseeable future.

China's economic performance in the 1980s was certainly impressive. Quantitative indicators readily attest to the rapid growth, major structural changes and unprecedented improvements in mass living standards which took place during these years. But the record of success was by no means unqualified and some of the more negative aspects of China's development experience are a major theme of this book. A consensus view would no doubt attribute much of China's economic success to the reformist thrust of its economic policies. But those same reforms have been the source of new tensions or have left unresolved other problems inherited from the past. An awareness of such contradictions informs the economic assessments contained in subsequent chapters. It also helps explain the caution which characterizes many of the judgments of China's future economic prospects.

Economic development in the first half of the 1990s was dominated by the impact of the tour of southern China, which Deng Xiaoping undertook at the beginning of 1992.[1] In the wake of more than two years of economic retrenchment, prompted by severe inflationary pressures in 1988–89, Deng used his tour to advocate renewed reform and accelerated growth. The choice of Guangdong as his principal destination was not coincidental: this was, after all, the province most deeply affected by the reforms (especially the open door strategy) implemented in previous years. Nor was it coincidental that he should have described Guangdong as the "leading force for economic development" and urged it to emulate Taiwan, South Korea, Hong Kong and Singapore in order to become the fifth "little Asian dragon."[2]

---

[1] Deng's "southern inspection tour" (*nanxun*) during January–February 1992 included visits to Shanghai and Guangzhou, as well as Shenzhen and Zhuhai Special Economic Zones.

[2] Quoted in Robert F. Ash, "Quarterly Chronicle and Documentation," *The China Quarterly*, No. 130 (June 1992), p. 455.

Deng's highly-publicized remarks during his southern tour were a characteristic response to China's economic circumstances, entirely in keeping with his former beliefs. They demonstrated his continuing commitment to the policies of reform and opening up and reaffirmed the central importance of economic work in promoting national development. In particular, the need for *rapid* economic growth once more emerged as a clear priority, with Deng warning that ". . . low-speed development is equal to stagnation or even retrogression."[3]

Deng's calls for accelerated reform and development defined the major thrust of subsequent economic policy. At the Fourteenth National Party Congress (October 1992), they were translated into official demands for the creation of a "socialist market economic system." To many this seemed an inherently ambiguous formula. But it signalled clearly enough a determination to move even further towards reliance on prices and competitive markets in allocating resources, albeit in a context in which public ownership and macroeconomic regulation from the centre would each enjoy a continuing role.

As Table 1 suggests, accelerated growth did characterize China's domestic economic performance in the wake of Deng's southern tour. Indeed, in their own terms the figures highlight a dramatic contrast between the period of retrenchment (1989–91) and the years of renewed expansion from 1992.

Moreover, the immediate response to Deng's advocacy of an even wider open door policy was also overwhelming. In particular, in 1992 and 1993, utilized foreign direct investment (FDI) increased by some 150 per cent p.a.[4] The significance of such expansion is suggested in the fact that by 1993, foreign-funded enterprises accounted for more than 10 per cent of national GVIO and almost 35 per cent of total trade.[5]

To deny the remarkable record of China's growth performance in the first half of the 1990s would be facile. That such an enormous economy should become the fastest-growing in the world is evidence enough of the scale of that achievement.[6] But it would be naive not to recognize that the impressive quantitative indicators concealed major underlying difficulties – many of them familiar from the 1980s, or in some cases even earlier. It is noteworthy, for example, that in 1992 and 1993 the accumulation rate

---

[3] Quoted in Ash, *The China Quarterly*, No. 130, p. 456. Naughton has identified prioritization of economic development, advocacy of an open door strategy and a belief that "rapid economic growth is best" as three consistent themes which have characterized the Dengist policy ethos. See his "Deng Xiaoping: The Economist" in David Shambaugh (ed.), *Deng Xiaoping* (Oxford: Clarendon Press, 1995), pp. 83–106.

[4] FDI estimates for 1992 and 1993 can be found in *TJNJ 1994*, pp. 528–30.

[5] See *TJNJ 1994*, pp. 375 and 506; and US Central Intelligence Agency, *China's Economy in 1993 and 1994: The Search for a Soft Landing* (report submitted to the Subcommittee on Technology and National Security of the Joint Economic Committee, US Congress), p. 11.

[6] Regional growth differentials and, in particular, the emergence of a broad economic dichotomy between the coastal regions and the interior offer a significant qualification to this statement.

TABLE 1. *Selected Economic Indicators, 1989–94*

	Average annual real rate of growth (%)		
	GDP	GVIO	GVAO
1989	4.3	8.5	3.1
1990	3.9	7.8	7.6
1991	8.0	14.8	3.7
1992	13.6	27.5	6.4
1993	13.4	28.0	7.8
1994	11.8	17.4	3.5

Sources:
State Statistical Bureau (SSB), *Zhongguo tongji nianjian,
1994* [*TJNJ*] (Chinese Statistical Yearbook, 1994) (Beijing:
SSB Publishing House, 1994), pp. 34, 330 and 375. British
Broadcasting Corporation, *Summary of World Broadcasts*
[SWB], Part 3: Asia-Pacific, FE/2245, 7 March 1995.
Notes:
GDP = gross domestic product;
GVIO = gross value of industrial output;
GVAO = gross value of agricultural output.

soared to a level unequalled since the Great Leap Forward.[7] The very rapid
rates of industrial and economic growth were based on excessively high
rates of fixed asset investment;[8] they also gave rise to increasingly severe
domestic raw material shortages and infrastructural bottlenecks. In 1992,
there was a sizeable increase in the fiscal deficit (by 36 per cent), which
remained largely intact in 1993,[9] and meanwhile, the money supply (M1)
continued to expand at a high rate.[10] The buoyant trade performance concealed a deterioration in the balance of merchandise trade, which in 1993
took it into deficit for the first time since 1989.[11]

Against the background of these and other difficulties, it is not surprising
that the most severe cost of the unprecedented growth of the early 1990s
was the re-emergence of serious inflationary pressures. In the middle of
1993, a first round of measures was introduced in an effort to restrain

[7] As a proportion of national income, accumulation reached an astonishing 38.7% in 1993
(cf. 43.8% and 39.6% in 1958 and 1959) (*TJNJ 1993*, p. 43 and *TJNJ 1994*, p. 40).

[8] In nominal terms, total fixed asset investment increased by 43% and 59% in 1992
and 1993 (*TJNJ 1994*, p. 139). The rate of increase slowed to 31.4% in 1994 (*TJNJ 1995*,
p. 137).

[9] IDE Spot Survey, *Investment Risk in Post-Deng China* (Tokyo: Institute of Developing
Economies, 1995), p. 42.

[10] By 30.3%, 21.6% and 26.8% in 1992, 1993 and 1994. *Ibid.* During 1992 and 1993, the
volume of circulating cash rose by 36.4% and 35.3%, respectively – the highest increases since
1984 (IDE, 1995, p. 20).

[11] Chinese Customs data show that in the wake of surging imports, the previous surplus on
the balance of trade in merchandise goods almost halved in 1992 and was transformed into a
deficit of US$ 12.19 billion in 1993 (*TJNJ 1994*, p. 506).

inflation.[12] Their impact was positive, but short-lived, and by the end of 1994, the inflation rate was still in excess of 25 per cent. Renewed growth of fixed asset investment and consumer spending, as well as further price liberalization measures, were amongst the most important contributory factors. In the end, however, they were no more than symbols of the seminal problem, arising from the structural contradictions inherent in the transition from a planned system to a market economy. Meanwhile, as China approached the completion of its Eighth Five-Year Plan (1991–95), the search for a soft landing in the face of inflationary pressures remained as elusive as ever.

This thumbnail sketch of economic developments in China during the early 1990s serves to highlight a degree of continuity of experience, carried over from the 1980s. As such, it underlines the validity of the cautious assessment contained in much of this book's analysis. It also incidentally demonstrates the need to avoid overly sanguine expectations of China's future growth performance – a point which is also made by several of the contributors to this volume.

The macroeconomic context of China's recent development is addressed most directly by K. C. Yeh. His analysis highlights the damaging consequences of inflationary pressures, but also points to the implications for economic advancement of continuing population growth. The simple arithmetic of population growth demonstrates the threat to economic growth which the failure to meet demographic targets poses. In February 1995, China's total population exceeded 1.2 billion – a highly symbolic event, this figure having originally been set as a target for the end of the century. Population growth is unlikely to cease until at least the middle of the next century. Meanwhile, the goal for the year 2000 is that total population should not exceed 1.3 billion. In quantitative terms, this seems a modest target, its fulfilment requiring an average rate of natural increase of around 13 per thousand for the rest of the 1990s (that is, significantly below the current rate and less than the average for the entire reform period).

This apparent conservatism may, however, reflect problems associated with the implementation of family planning policies and of the reforms themselves. As Yeh shows, difficulties of these kinds already existed in the 1980s. They are likely to have increased in the 1990s, as increasing numbers of people have reached marriageable age and the large-scale migration of surplus labour has added to the "floating population" of transients, who are less susceptible to official controls.

Yeh's analysis of the sources of economic growth also highlights the critical roles which capital formation and factor productivity growth must

---

[12] These were the 16 measures, introduced by Vice-Premier Zhu Rongji at the National Financial Work Conference in June, 1993.

continue to play in the search for sustained development through the 1990s. But their fulfilment faces serious obstacles: constraints on the capacity to generate increased domestic savings, the lagging performance of state enterprises,[13] and the need to accommodate China's enormous, largely unskilled labour force.[14] The persistence of such constraints during the early 1990s lends weight to Yeh's doubts that the latest plans offer solutions to these intractable problems.

The first half of the 1980s witnessed unprecedented growth in China's agricultural sector. Subsequent stagnation in some of its major branches (notably grain) highlights the challenges and dilemmas which still confront China's planners in their efforts simultaneously to accommodate the conflicting objectives of farmers and the state, and meet agriculture's developmental demands. Indeed, one of the apparent ironies of China's economic situation in the early 1990s was the primacy of a slogan first advanced in the early 1960s to the effect that "agriculture is the foundation of the national economy." The emphasis seems surprising. After all, the conjunction of declining agricultural growth and accelerated overall expansion after 1984 suggested that agriculture has ceased to be a major constraint on the developmental momentum of the Chinese economy – still less, that economic growth was agriculture-led. Yet in the mid-1990s, agriculture was still described as "the most fundamental issue" in China's economic development[15] and senior officials warned that "without agriculture, there can be no stability; without grain, there will be chaos" (*wunong buwen; wuliang zeluan*).

Part of the concern has less to do with the economic difficulties of agriculture than with their social and political implications, evidenced by unrest – sometimes violently expressed – in the countryside.[16] Yet peasant protest is not endemic, nor have its most serious manifestations affected more than a small proportion of provinces. Farm growth and rural economic diversification in the 1980s and 1990s brought major improvements in living standards to many peasants. The most likely focus of rural economic discontent are unemployed, or under-employed farmers – especially those engaged in

[13] Notwithstanding their pivotal position in the Chinese economy, the proportion of loss-making state-owned enterprises rose from 28% (1991) to more than 40% (1994) (IDE, 1995, p. 25).

[14] China's working age population is expected to reach 660 million by the year 2000 (*SWB*, FE/2203 S1/1, 17 January 1995). As of the mid-1990s, the rate of urban unemployment is officially expected to reach around 3% – a figure which, however, seriously understates the reality by ignoring an estimated 15 million redundant employees in the state-owned enterprise sector. A State Councillor (Chen Junsheng) also predicted that by the end of the century, China's surplus rural labour force will have reached around 200 million (*SWB* FE/2227/S1/7, 14 February 1995).

[15] See *Renmin ribao* (*RMRB*) (*People's Daily*), 8 December 1994.

[16] The precipitating causes were twofold: the practice of issuing so-called "IOUs" (*baitiaozi*), instead of cash, for produce delivered by farmers to the state under contract; and the imposition on peasants of illegal exactions (*tanpai*) in order to finance non-budgetary development projects, often unrelated to the needs of agriculture.

less profitable work (above all, grain production) in poorer parts of the country.

In any case, the future direction of institutional change in agriculture, the relationship between such change and productivity-enhancing technical progress, the search for a rational effective price policy for farm products, the formulation of an effective investment policy[17] – all have continued to pose serious policy changes. It is a mere truism to argue that if the underlying dilemmas are to be resolved and agriculture is simultaneously to meet its development demands and fulfil farmers' material aspirations, clear guidelines are essential. But Robert Ash's analysis points to ambiguities and contradictions in policy pronouncements, which – even allowing for the apparent modesty of output targets contained in the Ninth Five-Year Plan (1991–95) and Ten-Year Development Programme (1991–2000) – warn against too sanguine an assessment of agriculture's future prospects.

The issue of grain has also returned to the centre-stage of policy discussions during the 1990s.[18] The performance of this sector since the mid-1980s has been extremely disappointing. Following rapid growth in the wake of early post-1978 reforms, total grain output stagnated between 1984 and 1989. A large increase in 1990 (by 9.5 per cent) took production to a new level, but thereafter no clear upward trend was discernible. Whether even the modest output targets for the year 2000 can be met remains to be seen, though Ash's analysis suggests some of the constraints which surround efforts to guarantee their fulfilment. Even if they are fulfilled, he suggests that there remains a wide gap between such targets and production levels needed to secure the "comfortably well-off" (xiaokang) living standard sought by the end of the century.

The industrial sector is Robert Michael Field's concern and a meticulous examination of relevant sources and statistics is the basis on which his analysis of China's recent industrial performance rests. It reveals an impressive, but erratic, pattern of growth during the 1980s. Annual industrial growth rates fluctuated wildly, though the expansionary trend worked more consistently to the advantage of processing industries and branches producing consumer goods. The benefits of growth were also spread unevenly amongst enterprises, the principal beneficiaries being units at and below township level.[19]

The attainment of rapid industrial growth was not, however, reflected in major improvements in productivity or efficiency. Field shows that in state

---

[17] It is no coincidence that such issues define some of the most outstanding difficulties facing agriculture during the first half of the 1990s.

[18] If agriculture is described as the "foundation of the national economy," the same slogan insists that "grain is the basis of the foundation."

[19] This is a pattern which persisted into the 1990s. During 1991–93, the average annual growth of GVIO from state-owned enterprises was consistently outstripped by that of collectively-owned enterprises. And within the latter category, township and village enterprises excelled. See *TJNJ 1994*, p. 375.

and collective sectors, increased provision of capital during the second half of the 1980s was accompanied by significant declines in the efficiency with which it was used. By 1990, both the number of loss-making enterprises and the level of their losses were greater than in the early 1980s – a situation that was particularly serious in the key state sector.[20] Field argues that in the absence of fundamental economic reform, such problems will be difficult to resolve. Even allowing for the likelihood that 1995 and 2000 targets are met, he expects that low levels of productivity and declining profits will exert downward pressure upon the rate of industrial growth during the 1990s.

Tatsu Kambara's analysis highlights energy's key role in China's economic development. He finds that disappointing output growth of oil and coal (overwhelmingly, still the chief sources of primary energy[21]) was offset by "astounding" declines in the intensity of energy use, thereby facilitating the attainment of basic balance between overall production and consumption throughout the 1980s. Whether or not such balance can be maintained during the 1990s, China's chronic energy deficiency is unlikely to disappear, especially given the uneven regional distribution of resources. Indeed, Kambara's postscript reveals that in 1992, domestic production left China short of 19.14 million tonnes (SCE) of primary energy.[22] These developments suggest that the author's original belief that investment and technological initiatives might help overcome supply constraints may have been misplaced. But they underline his contention that the formulation of an integrated plan that allows for the reform of energy prices and regulatory systems is essential if such constraints are to be eliminated altogether.

China's economic achievement since 1978 owes much to the adoption of radical initiatives affecting its external economic relations. Key aspects of this open door policy are addressed by two of the authors in this volume. Y. Y. Kueh's investigation of overseas capital flows reveals that foreign direct investment (FDI) rose on average by 30 per cent p.a. during 1985–90. The major beneficiaries were the coastal provinces – a bias which aggravated the regional economic imbalance between coast and interior in China. This rapid expansion of FDI was accompanied by a marked shift in its destination from services towards manufacturing industry. Even allowing for the unequal role of Hong Kong and the tendency to focus on small-scale, labour-intensive activities, Kueh shows that FDI's contribution to capital formation, its impact on income in priority areas (for example, Guangdong, Fujian and the Special Economic Zones in these provinces) and their ability to earn foreign exchange were very considerable. He concludes that by the beginning of the 1990s, FDI had already become a sustainable endeavour –

---

[20] See also above, footnote 13.

[21] In 1992, coal accounted for 75.7% of total energy consumption (SCE), and oil for a further 17.5% (*TJNJ 1994*, p. 193).

[22] The deficit continued into 1993, although it fell to 5.05 million tonnes (*ibid.*).

and one whose role was likely to become even more important, as ties between Taiwan and the PRC grew closer.

Attention has already been drawn in this Introduction to the extraordinary surge in FDI, which occurred in the wake of Deng Xiaoping's southern tour. At the most general level, the regional concentration of FDI in the early 1990s mirrored that of previous years: that is to say, the major destination of FDI continued to be the coastal provinces of China. But it is some interest that the *degree* of regional concentration declined significantly. By 1993, slightly less than 80 per cent of FDI inflows went to coastal regions, compared with 93 per cent in 1990.[23] Meanwhile, the share of Guangdong – consistently, the single most important beneficiary of FDI – fell sharply from 46.1 to 27.6 per cent.[24] The declining role of Guangdong in part reflects a shift in the distribution of FDI northwards along the coast to new destinations (Fujian, Jiangsu, Shanghai and Shandong seem to have been the principal beneficiaries in this respect). But the decline in the coastal region's overall share of FDI indicates a dispersion of such capital to the interior, which was previously not in evidence.

The evidence which Kueh presents in favour of the positive impact of the open door strategy is confirmed by Nicholas Lardy's analysis of Chinese foreign trade performance. During the 1980s China's rate of growth outstripped that of the rest of the world and its share of global trade, though it remained relatively small, expanded. The sources of this expansion also underwent a marked transformation. Initially, trade remained largely state-directed and biased towards the export of primary products – especially oil. The domestic energy constraints highlighted by Kambara were one factor which increasingly made such bias questionable. In addition, after 1985, decentralization permitted more flexibility and encouraged a shift towards the export of labour-intensive manufactured goods – products which maximized the use of China's most abundant resource. Lardy shows that between 1985 and 1991, the share of manufactured products in total Chinese exports rose from 50 to 78 per cent. By 1993, the corresponding figure had reached 82 per cent.[25]

Reforms affecting the domestic prices of traded goods, as well as adjustments to the exchange rate and a relaxation of exchange controls, contributed significantly to the changing patterns of China's foreign trade expansion in the 1980s. Domestic prices of imports and exports moved closer to world levels, whilst a major reduction in the real value of the *renminbi* (by almost 40 per cent between 1985 and 1990) helped promote exports and reduce import subsidies. Devaluation of China's currency continued in the early 1990s – a process that was assisted by the unification, in January 1994, of China's dual exchange rates.

---

[23] *TJNJ 1993*, p. 631; and *TJNJ 1994*, p. 530.
[24] *Ibid.*   [25] *TJNJ 1994*, p. 507.

The pattern of China's foreign trade expansion was also characterized by important sectoral and regional developments. Decentralization encouraged the emergence of rural township and village enterprises, as well as joint ventures, as the most dynamic sources of export earnings. As for Guangdong's preeminent role in the emerging picture, Lardy suggests that factors other than the region's propinquity to Hong Kong – factors related to the scale of manufacturing activities, the limited role of the state and a strong orientation towards a market economy in Guangdong – contributed significantly to its impressive trade performance.

In the final chapter of the book, Joseph Chai's concern is with the impact of economic reforms on consumption and living standards in China. If the growth of average per capita disposable income and material consumption are thought to be reliable indicators of changes in welfare, there can be no doubt that China achieved significant gains during the 1980s – though at a declining rate in the second half of the decade. Consumer satisfaction also improved and the pattern of rural consumption began to move closer to that of urban residents. International comparisons provide a useful perspective to these changes and Chai contrasts China's pattern of consumption during the latter half of the 1980s with that of Japan and Taiwan at comparable stages of development (1955–60 and the late 1960s, respectively). His findings in this regard underline the paucity of non-staple food supplies in China and point to the excessive consumption of housing and clothing relative to prevailing levels of per capita income.

According to Chai, some *qualitative* measures of welfare seem to indicate deteriorating welfare standards under the impact of reform. For example, estimates of life expectancy and adult illiteracy suggest growing inequality in access to education and health facilities. It seems likely too that economic and social security, income distribution and the quality of the environment have all been casualties of post-1978 reforms.

Overall, Chai is cautious in his judgment of the likely extent of further improvements in living standards and the ability of the Chinese government to bring real consumption to a "moderately comfortable" (*xiaokang*) level by the end of the century. Developments in the first half of the 1990s appear to have offered no basis for a revision of this assessment. Fears of accelerated population growth have, it is true, so far proved to be unfounded. But predictions of a declining rate of accumulation have been wide of the mark.[26] In addition, far from narrowing (as official projections anticipated), the urban–rural consumption gap has actually widened during the 1990s.[27] Chai also suggests that constraints on the growth of supplies of consumer durables, urban housing and non-staple foodstuffs – goods whose demand is likely to expand most rapidly during the 1990s – could impinge on future

---

[26] See above, footnote 7.

[27] In nominal terms, the ratio of consumption of urban to rural residents widened from 2.82 (1990) to 3.20 (1993) (*TJNJ 1994*, p. 256).

welfare improvements. His argument that the Chinese government might have to choose between price increases, income growth restraint or enhanced private sector production of these goods in order to overcome such constraints has lost none of its force in the context of more recent developments which have taken place.

Several common themes emerge out of this book. One is the cautious assessment of China's post-1978 record which most of the contributors make and the reservations which many of them display in appraising its future economic prospects. There is general agreement that impressive economic progress was made during the 1980s, but its unevenness – in particular, the disappointing performance after 1984–85 – also emerges clearly. If there is a prescriptive thrust to the articles, it is that China's sustained economic development in the future can best be secured through the adoption of bolder and integrated reform measures. At one point in his analysis, Yeh refers to the "compromise, ambiguities and contradictions," inherent in the proposals for the Ten-Year Development Programme (1991–2000) and the Eighth Five-Year Plan (1991–95). From the perspective of the mid-1990s, the persistence of policy dilemmas suggests the continuing validity of his words. Three years of economic retrenchment and a similar period of renewed growth have not yet demonstrated that such tensions are about to be resolved, nor that the many fundamental problems addressed in this book will readily be overcome in the foreseeable future.

Macroeconomic Issues in China in the 1990s

K. C. Yeh

In 1981 the Chinese leadership set the goal of quadrupling China's 1980 per capita GNP by the year 2000 in order to raise the people's standard of living to a "relatively comfortable level."[1] But apart from sustained growth, the Chinese planners are also very much concerned with economic efficiency and price stability. The new development strategy to attain these goals is economic reform and opening to the outside world. Over a decade has now elapsed since these goals were set. This article addresses the issues of how far the Chinese economy has advanced toward those objectives, the major challenges that lie ahead and China's economic prospects in the 1990s.[2]

The first section briefly reviews the growth record of the 1980s, and against this background raises some critical issues concerning China's economic future in the 1990s. The primary problem of controlling population is discussed in the second section, then the third examines the sources of economic growth and explores how they might accelerate or constrain growth in the next decade. The problem of inflation in the process of transition to a market-based economy is discussed in the next section, and the article concludes with some comments on the Ten-Year Programme and the Eighth Five-Year Plan.

The Growth Record

How fast did China's per capita GNP grow in the 1980s? Table 1 compares the growth rates of GNP and population in 1980–90 with those of earlier periods. The GNP growth rates are based on official statistics that are fraught with methodological problems.[3] However, despite the many statis-

---

[1] In a meeting with members of the Japanese Diet in April 1981, Deng Xiaoping stated: "China aims at increasing its GNP to U.S. $1,000 per capita. . . . Our GNP is $250 at present. We want to increase this to $500 in ten years and double it to $1,000 in the next ten years." *Mainichi shimbun*, Tokyo, 15 April 1981, p. 7. See also Deng Xiaoping, *Building Socialism with Chinese Characteristics* (Beijing, 1984), pp. 37, 40. This goal was later formally adopted by the Chinese Communist Party. Zhao Ziyang, "Advance along the road towards socialism with Chinese characteristics," *Renmin ribao* (*People's Daily*, hereafter *RMRB*), 4 November 1987, p. 2.

[2] These are very broad issues. For obvious reasons, one can only explore selected aspects. Some important issues that have not been covered here include regional economic growth patterns, income distribution and balance of payments.

[3] The problems with the Chinese national income accounts are too numerous and complex to discuss fully here. For details, see the forthcoming study by the World Bank, *China, Statistical System in Transition*. Essentially, the shortcomings of the data include, first, that the series in comparable prices for the period 1952–80 is a chain index linking the constant price

TABLE 1. *Average Annual Growth Rates, GNP and Population, 1952–90 (%)*

	GNP	Population	GNP per capita
1952–57	9.2	2.4	6.8
1951–62	2.1	0.8	1.3
1962–65	15.1	2.5	12.6
1965–70	6.9	2.7	4.2
1970–75	5.7	2.2	3.5
1975–80	6.5	1.3	5.2
1980–85	10.1	1.4	8.7
1985–90	7.8	1.6	6.2
1952–80	6.2	1.9	4.3
1980–90	8.9	1.5	7.4
1990–2000 (planned)	6.0	1.3	4.7

Sources:
   State Statistical Bureau, *Qiwu shiqi guomin jingji he shehui fazhan gaikuang (National Economic and Social Development During the Seventh Five-Year Period)* (Beijing, 1991), pp. 27, 188; State Statistical Bureau, *Zhongguo tongji nianjian 1990 (China Statistical Yearbook 1990*, hereafter *TJNJ* 1990) (Beijing, 1991), p. 5; *Beijing Review*, 2–8 October 1989, p. 20 and 6–12 May 1991, pp. 18–19.

tical shortcomings, there can be little doubt that the growth rate in the 1980s was substantially higher than in the pre-1980 period. Indeed, except for the early 1950s and the three years 1962–65, when the economy was recovering from war or economic disaster, at no time in the history of the PRC has the economy grown as fast as in the 1980s. Meanwhile, the growth of population has been slower, so that the difference between the per capita GNP growth rates in the pre-1980 and post-1980 periods is even more marked.

As economic growth has accelerated, major changes in the economic structure have occurred, as shown in Table 2. Output and employment

series for sub-periods 1952–57, 1957–70 and 1970–80. The series for 1952–80 therefore is not strictly in constant prices. More seriously, biases in the series for the sub-periods are embedded in the comparable price series. Secondly, the constant price series for each sub-period is derived by a single deflation method, assuming the price changes for inputs and outputs are proportionately the same. In some cases, such as in agriculture during 1952–57, this assumption is not valid. Thirdly, some deflators are apparently understated so that an upward bias is imparted into the output series. For example, the factory price indexes during 1984–88 given in Hu Bongding, *Zhongguo wujia nianjian 1989 (China Price Yearbook 1989)* (Beijing, 1989), pp. 413, 471, rise much faster than the implicit deflator for gross value of industrial output given in State Statistical Bureau, *Zhongguo tongji zhaiyao 1991 (A Statistical Survey of China 1991)* (Beijing, 1991), (hereafter *TJZY* 1991), pp. 9–10. In the case of rural industries, the gross output included in the constant price series has reportedly not been deflated for lack of data. All these considerations suggest that the growth rate based on official data is biased upwards.

TABLE 2. *Selected Economic Indicators 1970, 1980 and 1990 (%)*

	1970	1980	1990
Share in GDP			
Agriculture	47.4	30.4	23.2
Industry	36.0	49.0	52.7
Services	16.6	20.6	24.1
Share in employment			
Agriculture	80.8	68.9	60.0
Industry	10.2	18.5	21.4
Services	9.0	12.6	18.6
Share of employment in population	41.5	42.9	49.6
Rate of investment	26.3	31.8	37.1*
Ratio of exports to GNP	8.2	10.8	15.2*
Index of per capita consumption	71.3	100.0	169.3*
Index of GDP deflator	88.8	100.0	164.5*

Note:
 * 1989.
Sources:
 TJNJ 1990, pp. 89, 117; *TJZY* 1991, pp. 5, 14, 17; *World Tables 1991*, Washington, D.C., pp. 184–5. The shares in GDP are based on World Bank totals in 1980 prices. The percentages of investment and exports in GDP and the index of private consumption are based on totals in 1987 prices.

structures have shifted in favour of industry and services, suggesting a continuation of the industrialization process. During the 1980s the ratio of employment to population rose sharply. So did the investment rate, the export–GNP ratio, per capita private consumption and the overall price level. In each case the rate of increase was much higher in the 1980s than in the 1970s. All in all, except for the inflation rate, economic achievements in the last decade were quite impressive.

Despite the remarkable record, the prospect of continued economic success in the 1990s is by no means certain, because several fundamental problems remained unsolved and much depends on how effectively China copes with them. One is the relatively high rate of population growth from a very large base of over a billion in 1990. As Table 1 shows, the average annual growth rate dropped to 1.3 per cent in 1975–80 but began to rise again and averaged 1.5 per cent in the 1980s. However, in 1991 it fell back to 1.3 per cent, the lowest since 1984.[4] It is not yet clear whether this signifies the beginning of a declining trend or marks a temporary drop as in 1983 and 1984. If the growth rate in the next decade should remain higher than 1.3

[4] State Statistical Bureau (SSB), "Communiqué on national economic and social development in 1991," *RMRB*, 29 February 1992, p. 2.

per cent, the target of 6 per cent growth in per capita GNP will not be attained even if by the year 2000 GNP has quadrupled its 1980 level.

A second major issue is whether the high GNP growth rate is sustainable, and if so, whether it will be in the nature of intensive growth through raising factor productivity, or extensive growth through increasing factor input. In addition, the vast supply of manpower both offers opportunities of underused human resources and poses formidable problems of unemployment, education and internal migration.

A third potential problem is that of inflation. China experienced a sharp rise in the general price level in 1985 and 1988, at a time when GNP growth accelerated to unprecedented levels and when the leadership stepped up economic reforms. One may ask whether inflation will flare up again once the economy surges forward and economic reconstructuring resumes. Although population, systemic inefficiencies, inflation and unemployment are not the only macroeconomic issues confronting the Chinese leadership, they are certainly the major challenges in the next decade.

Population Growth in the 1990s

In the early 1980s the Chinese leadership planned to limit the total population to less than 1.2 billion by the year 2000.[5] To attain this goal, the average natural growth rate would have to drop sharply from 1.75 per cent per year for the decade up to 1980 to 0.98 per cent per year during the period 1980–2000. At the time the development goals were formulated this seemed attainable as the natural growth rate had fallen from 2.58 per cent in 1970 to 1.19 per cent in 1980, and a continued, moderate decline in the following two decades appeared plausible.

However, demographic trends were contrary to the leadership's expectations. Instead of a continuous decline, the natural growth rate rose to a relatively high plateau of 1.5 per cent per year during 1981–90. In both the Sixth and Seventh Five-Year Plan periods (1981–85 and 1986–90), population growth rates not only exceeded the planned targets by a considerable margin, but also accelerated in the second half of the 1980s[6]:

	1981–85	1986–90
	(Per cent per year)	
Planned	1.30	1.24
Actual	1.41	1.55

[5] Ma Bin, *Lun Zhongguo renkou wenti* (*On China's Population Problem*) (Beijing, 1987), p. 1.

[6] For the actual growth rates, see *TJZY* 1991, p. 14. For the planned growth rates, see Zhao Ziyang, "Report on the Sixth Five-Year Plan," *Guangming ribao* (*Guangming Daily*), 14 December 1982, p. 2, and State Statistical Bureau, "Economic and social development during the Seventh Five-Year Plan period in retrospect," *Liaowang* (*Outlook*), No. 47 (19 November 1990), p. 7.

By 1990, total population reached 1.14 billion, surpassing all earlier estimates.

Not surprisingly, the original goal for the year 2000 was successively revised upwards to 1.3 billion.[7] The change required that the 1980 level of GNP should more than quadruple. A more serious consideration was that the factors behind the rising trends in the 1980s might persist in the 1990s so that the projected growth rate of 1.25 per cent per year in the Ten-Year Programme would again fall short of the actual rate.[8]

A cursory examination of the crude birth and mortality rates in the 1980s suggests that the mortality rate remained fairly stable and that changes in the natural growth rate largely reflected changes in the birth rate, particularly among the rural population.[9] For convenience of discussion, the crude birth rate can be divided into two components: the relative size of the female population of childbearing age (15 to 49 years) in the total population, and the general fertility rate (the number of births per woman of childbearing age). In this case both elements contributed to the rise in the crude birth rate.

Rising share of women of reproductive age

As Table 3 shows, the relative size of the female population of childbearing age hardly changed during 1953–82. But from 1982, the trend was distinctly upward. This was the result of the upsurge in childbirths during the period 1962–75. Some 360 million people born during this period are now entering their reproductive age at the rate of about 4 million each year from 1986.[10] The significance of this echo effect is that the increase will continue into the 1990s, and there is virtually nothing the government can do to change the age composition of the population in the short term.[11]

---

[7] Qu Wei, "China's population situation and measures to cope with the problem," *Qunyan* (*Popular Tribune*), No. 4 (7 April 1989), pp. 4–10, 22. Apparently the change in population control targets had been influenced by the upward revision of population projections. For example, the projection for the year 2000 by Song Jian and others in 1982 was 1.13 billion. Song Jian, Tian Xueyuan, Yu Jingyuan and Li Guangyuan, *Renkou yuce he renkou kongzhi* (*Population Projection and Population Control*) (Beijing, 1982), p. 173. In 1986, a study by the State Council projected a total of 1.25 billion. Ma Hong (ed.), *2000 nian de Zhongguo* (*China in the year 2000*) (Beijing, 1989), p. 98. In 1990, Tian Xueyuan provided an estimate of 1.3 billion. *Guangming ribao* (*Guangming Daily*), 19 December 1990, p. 2. Similarly, demographers with the World Bank raised their projections from 1.2 billion in 1985 to 1.29 billion. World Bank, *World Development Report*, issues for 1985, 1987, and 1991 (New York, various years).

[8] "CPC Central Committee's proposals for Ten-Year Development Program and Eighth Five-Year Plan," *Beijing Review*, No. 8–9 (18 February–3 March 1991), p. 25.

[9] For crude birth rates and mortality rates since 1949, see *TJNJ* 1990, p. 90; *TJZY* 1991, p. 14; *RMRB*, 29 February 1992, p. 2.

[10] Yao Changli, "Warning: China's population exceeds 1.1 billion," *Liaowang* (*Outlook*), No. 15 (10 April 1989), p. 15.

[11] The average number of women of childbearing age during 1991–95 was estimated to be 322 million, notably larger than the 298 million for 1985–90. Li Chin, "Population control for this and the next century," *Liaowang*, No. 34 (26 August 1991), p. 39. The SSB projected a total of 340 million by the year 2000. *RMRB*, 14 April 1989, p. 5.

TABLE 3. *Share of Female Population of Reproductive and Prime Childbearing Age and Total Fertility Rate, 1953–90, Selected Years (%)*

| | Share of woman population of | | |
	Reproductive age[a]	Prime reproductive age[b]	Total fertility rate[c]
1953	23.4	32.5	6.05
1964	21.8	31.6	6.18
1981	24.5	–	2.63
1982	24.7	31.6	2.86
1983	–	–	2.42
1984	25.8	–	2.35
1985	26.2	–	2.20
1986	26.5	–	2.42
1987	26.8	33.8	2.59
1988	26.9	–	2.31
1989	26.7	35.8	2.35
1990	27.1	37.5	2.31

Notes:
[a] Ratio: woman population of age 15–49 to total population.
[b] Ratio: woman population of age 20–29 to woman population of age 15–49.
[c] Sum of age-specific birth rates of women aged 15–49.
Where no figure is given data are not available.

Source:
Columns 1 and 2: 1953, 1964, 1982, 1987 – taken from State Statistical Bureau, *Zhongguo renkou tongji nianjian 1988 (China Population Statistics Yearbook 1988)* (Beijing, 1988), pp. 54–5, 323–4, 400–1, 477–8. 1981 – based on an index of total number of women of reproductive age for 1989, 124.4% with 1981 as base, in Beijing Xinhua, 8 November 1990, reported in FBIS-CHI-90-219 (13 November 1990), p. 32, and data on woman population of reproductive age in 1989 explained below, and total population in 1981 from *TJZY* 1991, p. 14. 1984–86, 1988 – based on total numbers of women of reproductive age given in De Ming, "China's population problem remains grim," *Liaowang*, No. 17 (25 April 1988), p. 10, and total population from *TJZY* 1991, p. 14. 1989–90 – Xue Muqiao and Ma Hong (eds.), *Zhongguo jingji nianjian 1991 (Almanac of China's Economy)* (Beijing, 1991), hereafter, *JJNJ* 1991, pp. II–71, 72. Column 3: Jia Ruiguan, "China's third population birth peak is not a fertility peak," *Renkou yanjiu (Population Research)*, No. 3 (1991), p. 9; *RMRB*, 20 September 1989, p. 5; *JJNJ* 1991, p. II–71.

Rising trend in general fertility rate

The general fertility rate has also been rising slightly, or at least remained unchanged in the 1980s, as suggested by the crude birth rate growing perceptibly faster than the relative share of female population of reproductive age.[12] Underlying this trend were two salient demographic developments: a shift in the age structure of women of reproductive age favouring those of prime childbearing age (20–49), and the lack of change in the total fertility rate (the sum of age-specific birth rates at each age from 15 to 49).

As Table 3 shows, the share of women in the age group 20–29 years as a percentage of those of reproductive age rose from 31.6 per cent in 1982 to 37.5 per cent in 1990. Because the age-specific birth rates of women in the age groups 20–24 and 25–29 are markedly higher than those for other five-year age intervals,[13] a rapidly rising share of women in their prime childbearing age raises the general fertility rate, which is derived as the weighted average of the birth rates of different age groups with the relative size of these groups as weights.

Again, the current trend in the structural shift will continue into the 1990s. According to the Minister of the Family Planning Commission, 11 to 13 million young women will enter the prime childbearing age each year during 1986–97.[14] The average relative size of this group as a proportion of all women of reproductive age is projected to increase from 35.2 per cent for 1986–90 to 37.9 for 1991–95.[15]

The other factor affecting China's general fertility rate is the total fertility rate. After a dramatic decline from 5.8 for women in 1970 to 2.2 for women in 1980, the total fertility rate levelled off at about 2.5 births per woman in the 1980s.[16] Compared with the average level of 4.2 births per woman in less developed countries, China's total fertility rate is not high.[17] But its stationary trend is a cause for concern, because unlike the age structure, the fertility rate is susceptible to change through family planning, and the lack of change raises questions about the effectiveness of population control.

Early marriages and multiple births

It seems that strong undercurrents pushing for early marriages (that is below the legal age of 22 for men and 20 for women) and multiple births per couple have undermined the government's effort to control population

---

[12] The average crude birth rate rose from 21.03 for 1981–82 and 1984–85 to 22.43 per thousand in 1986–89. The relative share of women of reproductive age in the corresponding periods was 25.39 and 26.9 per cent respectively. For sources, see *TJZY* 1991, p. 14 and Table 3.

[13] For example, the birth rates for these two groups in 1981 were 146.6 and 238.7 per thousand, compared to the next highest of 86.5 per thousand for those of age 30–34. Li Chengrui, *Zhongguo renkou pucha he jieguo fenxi* (*China's Population Census and Analysis of the Results*) (Beijing, 1987), p. 144. See also data for 1989 in *TJNJ* 1990, p. 100.

[14] Peng Peiyun, "Controlling population growth to achieve economic prosperity," *Liaowang*, No. 1 (1 January 1990), p. 7.

[15] Li Chin, "Population control," p. 34.

[16] Li Chengrui, *Population Census*, p. 141.

[17] Gerald M. Meier, *Leading Issues in Economic Development*, 5th ed. (New York, 1989), p. 445.

growth. In the 1980s people were marrying younger than in earlier periods.[18] This generally results in earlier births, because in China most women give birth one year after their marriage.[19] The direct effect is an upsurge in the age-specific birth rates of women in the 15–19 age group.[20]

Meanwhile, the practice of having more than one child per family persisted in rural areas. According to a survey by the State Family Planning Commission in 1988, 93 per cent of rural women who had one child gave birth to a second; 47 per cent of those with two children gave birth to a third; and 28 per cent of those with three children had a fourth.[21] Thus, despite the one child per family policy being implemented for over a decade, slightly over one-half of the total births in 1990 were not first-born children.[22]

Several reasons for the recent trend toward early marriages and multiple births can be suggested. First, the peasants' traditional desire to have more children remains strong. In particular, they want more sons to ensure the continuity of the family tree, to support them in their old age and to have more working hands in the family.[23] These attitudes are not new, but they were largely suppressed under the commune system and were revived only after the return to household farming when the family once again became the basic economic unit. The limited social services provided by the communes are no longer available, so peasants rely on their sons for future old-age support. Moreover, agricultural production and other economic activities still depend heavily on human labour. The larger the family, the more land it can lease from the government; its labour force can also earn more than a smaller one. In contrast to the urban areas, the cost of raising children amounts to a fraction of peasants' income, and children can start working on the farm long before they reach the age of 16.[24] Not surprisingly,

[18] Indicators of this trend include a drop in the average age of first marriage from 25.5 to 23.7 for men and from 22.8 to 21.0 for women between 1982 and 1987, a rise in the proportion of early marriages in total marriages from 15 to 20% and an increase in the proportion of males aged 15–24 and women aged 15–19 who were married from 3.24% in 1982 to 4.91% in 1987. *RMRB*, 14 April 1989, p. 5; SSB, "China's population structure," *Beijing Review* (5–11 December 1988), p. 28.

[19] Yu Yunchung, *Shiyi yi ren (1.1 Billion Population* (Beijing, 1990), pp. 35–6.

[20] For example, the birth rates of this group tripled between 1982 and 1987. SSB, "China's population structure," p. 28.

[21] Sun Huaiyang, "Solving the population problem is crucial if we hope to become comparatively well off," *Zhongguo renkou bao (China's Population Bulletin)*, 9 September 1991, p. 2, translated in JPRS-CAR-91-064, 15 November 1991, p. 55.

[22] State Statistical Bureau, "Communiqué on the major statistics concerning the 1990 population census, no. 9," *Zhongguo tongji (China Statistics)*, No. 9 (1991), p. 5.

[23] See results of a survey reported in *Jingji yanjiu (Economic Research)*, hereafter *JJYJ*, No. 6 (1982) p. 56. Supporting evidence of the preference for sons can be found in the fact that the relatively large proportion (about two-thirds) of the couples that have pledged to have one child were parents of baby boys. *The Economist*, 29 January 1983, p. 4. For 1991, about 92% of all old people in the countryside depend on their children for support. Guo Shutian, "Rural population problems and countermeasures," *Zhongguo renkou bao (China's Population Bulletin)*, 7 October 1991, p. 2.

[24] For example, in 1989 the total cost of raising a child during the first 16 years was estimated at 2,909 *yuan*, of which the peasant contributed 2,542 *yuan*. *RMRB*, 29 January 1989, p. 8. The

a survey of the peasants' attitudes towards childbirth in 1988 showed that over 95 per cent of those interviewed wanted more than one child and most wanted at least one son.[25] Indeed, the urge was so strong that many defied government regulations by concealing births or fleeing to remote areas to have additional children.

A second important element affecting the fertility trend was the rapid increase in peasants' income in the wake of rural reform. Per capita income in current prices rose from 191 *yuan* in 1980 to 630 *yuan* in 1990, and accumulated household savings from 11.7 to 184.2 billion *yuan* over the same period.[26] With increased wealth, many peasants could afford the high wedding costs, support a larger family and, if necessary, pay the stiff penalties for having more children than the government allowed.[27]

A third major factor was shortcomings of the population control policy and its implementation. Some government policies actually encouraged rather than checked population growth. For example, land for farming and residential housing was leased to peasants on a per capita basis, thus motivating them to have a larger family.[28] The marriage law of 1980 lowered the minimum marriageable age to a level below that which in fact obtained at that time. The one child per family policy left open many loopholes for the peasants legitimately to have more than one child.[29] In particular, the policy

average annual cost was therefore about 159 *yuan*, or 6% of the average farm household income in 1989. *TJZY* 1991, p. 48.

[25] Ye Yangzhong, "A preliminary exploration of the peasants' concept of fertility," *Renkou yanjiu*, No. 4 (1988), pp. 29–30.

[26] *TJZY* 1991, pp. 44, 48.

[27] The experience for China, that an increase in per capita income led to more births, seems to contradict the empirical finding that in general the level of per capita income is negatively associated with the total fertility rate. For example, the total fertility rates for low-income, middle-income and high-income economies in 1989 were 3.9, 3.7 and 1.8 respectively. World Bank, *World Development Report 1991* (New York, 1991), pp. 256–7. However, the contradiction is apparent rather than real. The cross-section data on income and fertility for China actually confirms the general experience of other countries. In 1987, the average net material product per capita in Beijing, Tianjin and Shanghai was 2,000 *yuan* and that in Qinghai, Yunnan and Henan was below 700 *yuan*. The corresponding total fertility rates were 2.1 and 2.99. *RMRB*, 14 April 1989, p. 5. There is apparently a critical value of per capita income below which the total fertility rate rises with income and above which the reverse is true. The critical value has been estimated at 1,400 *yuan* per person in 1987 (*ibid.*). Elsewhere in Liaoning, it has been found that rural households with an only daughter chose not to have a second child when their per capita income reached 1,000 to 1,500 *yuan*. Cao Jingchun, "On the development of the commodity economy and rural family planning," *Renkou yu jingji* (*Population and the Economy*), No. 1 (25 February 1989), pp. 16–21, translated in JPRS-CAR-89-058, 5 June 1989, p. 29.

[28] Even though children born outside the family planning quota are not entitled to acquire land at birth, they become eligible once they reach the age of 14, a delay that many farmers find easy to accept. Meng Xiangfeng, "Difficulties in rural family planning policies," *RMRB*, 17 May 1991, p. 4.

[29] Couples were often permitted to have a second child if the first one was a girl. Consequently, the number of second children born increased from 4.6 million in 1984 to 7.8 million in 1987. Hu Angang, "Causes of losing control of China's population and countermeasures," *Liaowang*, No. 10 (6 March 1989), pp. 17–18. See also Ma Bin, *On China's Population Problem*, p. 17.

towards minorities has been quite liberal.[30] In addition, a migrant population moving from province to province, mainly in search of employment,
has been rapidly growing,[31] with large families common since family planning for a floating population is difficult to supervise.[32]

Effects of education and urbanization

Two important factors commonly associated with fertility decline – education and urbanization – are also important in China, as suggested by the
sharp differences in fertility rate between women with different levels of
education and between cities, towns and counties.[33] However, rural education had apparently not made significant headway in the 1980s, as indicated
by the lack of discernible improvements in the educational level of the rural
labour force[34]:

	1984	1989
Percentage of rural labour force		
Illiterate	20.89	22.57
Primary school	40.73	38.67
Secondary school or higher	38.38	38.76
Total	100.00	100.00

It is worth noting that the percentage of illiterate women is considerably
higher than the overall illiteracy rate.[35] In short, the educational level of the
childbearing group remained particularly low.

Despite the government's renewed effort to raise the educational level of
the rural population in recent years, school enrolment continued to drop in
the 1980s, from 128 to 97 million primary school students, and from 40 to 26

[30] The one-child policy applies only to minorities with a population exceeding 10 million.
Those with a smaller population are permitted to have two or even three children per family.
RMRB, 22 May 1988, p. 8. As a result, the average annual growth rate for minorities was 3.87%
during 1982–90, compared with 1.48% for the entire nation. *Beijing Review*, 12–18 November
1990, p. 23.
[31] By 1991, China had a transient population of 70 million. *China Daily*, September 1991,
p. 1.
[32] Yang Xiaobing, "Countering the surge in population," *Beijing Review*, 13–19 March 1989,
p. 4.
[33] See Li Chengrui, *Population Census*, p. 145; *China Daily*, 16 December 1987, p. 3; *RMRB*,
14 April 1989, p. 5; *TJNJ* 1990, pp. 101–3; Peng Xizhe, "Major determinants of China's fertility
transition," *The China Quarterly*, No. 117 (March 1989), pp. 3–37.
[34] State Council and Ministry of Agriculture, *Zhongguo nongcun jingji shehui tongji ziliao*
(*Rural Economic and Social Statistics of China*), (no place or date of publication), p. 129; SSB,
Zhongguo nongcun tongji nianjian 1990 (*China Rural Statistics Yearbook 1990*) (Beijing,
1990), p. 230.
[35] A survey in 1987 showed that 44.2% of rural women age 12 or over were illiterate,
compared with 31.5% for both sexes. Guo Shutian, "Rural population problems." See also Xin
Renzhou and Zhang Yuxian, "Causes of rural population growth and countermeasures,"
Zhongguo nongcun jingji (*China's Rural Economy*), No. 7 (20 July 1990), pp. 8–12.

million secondary school students between 1980 and 1989.[36] The decline was larger than can be explained by the reduction in the relevant age groups.[37] The peasants clearly considered that the economic return on education was lower than the opportunity cost, now that rural enterprises and other non-farm activities offered new opportunities for employment. The problem is that incentives for rural students to drop out will persist as economic reforms continue to chip away the barriers to factor mobility. Just as the sharp increase in enrolment in the aftermath of the Cultural Revolution raised the educational level of the population a decade later, the fall in rural student enrolment will have its adverse effect on the educational level of the rural population in the 1990s.

Turning to urbanization, it is noticeable that it proceeded gradually until 1978, then the pace quickened in the 1980s.[38] However, any effect the change might have had on the fertility rate was not significant enough to offset other negative effects. Perhaps this was because urbanization during this period resulted largely from population growth in small towns rather than in the cities, partly because of the broadening of the definition of township in 1984, partly as a result of government policy to restrict the inflow of population into the cities, and partly because of the rapid development of rural enterprises in small towns.[39] A good proportion of the urban population were farmers, and those engaged in non-farm activities were "detached from the soil but not from the villages."[40] They did not come

[36] State Council and Ministry of Agriculture, *Rural Economic and Social Statistics* and SSB, *Rural Statistics Yearbook*. The government remains optimistic about the educational level of the total population in the near future. By 1995, the proportion of total population that has received at least a primary education is projected to reach 93% compared with the current 72%. *China Daily*, 4 January 1992, p. 1. Given the total population in 1991, 1,158 million (*RMRB*, 29 February 1992, p. 2), and the projected total of 1,227 million for 1995 (a target for population control given by Peng Peiyun, reported by *Xinhua*, Beijing, 27 March 1992, translated in FBIS-CHI-92-069, 6 April 1992, p. 26), the total number of people having at least a primary school education would be 834 and 1,141 million respectively. The net increase in four years, 307 million, implies an annual increase of 77 million, which is more than four times the 18.6 million primary school graduates in 1990 (*JJNJ* 1991, p. VIII–129.) It seems unrealistic to project so abrupt and such a large increase in primary school graduates.

[37] World Bank, *China: Long-Term Issues and Options*, Annex A: *Issues and Prospects in Education* (Woshington, D.C., 1985), p. ii. A serious dropout problem is also noted in Guo Shutian, "Rural population problems."

[38] The urban population had remained at around 18% in the 1960s and 1970s, but it began to rise steadily from 19.4% in 1980 to 26.4% in 1990. *TJNJ* 1990, p. 89; *TJZY* 1991, p. 14. The definition of urban was changed several times by the SSB (in 1953, 1955, 1963, and 1964). See SSB, *China Population Yearbook 1988*, p. iv. Because of this the data are not always comparable. For example, urban population in 1989 is given at 51.7% in *TJNJ* 1990, p. 89, and 26.2% in *TJZY* 1991, p. 14. For a discussion of the intricacies of the Chinese urban population statistics, see Kam Wing Chan and Xueqiang Xu, "Urban population growth and urbanization in China since 1949: reconstructing a baseline," *The China Quarterly*, No. 104 (December 1985), pp. 583–613.

[39] In 1980–87, the population in towns increased by 316% and that in cities by only 94%. SSB, *China Population Yearbook 1988*, p. 206.

[40] For example, in 1987 the share of agricultural population in total urban population was 62%. *Ibid.*

under the pressure of the much higher cost of raising children in the cities. Nor, except perhaps for those living near the big cities, did they experience the change in life style associated with a decline in fertility.

To sum up, after a decade of decline, the population growth rate rose to a plateau of around 14.5 per thousand in the 1980s. The crucial question of whether it can be lowered to the planned target of 12.5 per thousand will depend on the outcome of two sets of countervailing forces. On one side, the factors that pushed the crude birth rate upwards in the last decade are likely to persist, including the echo effect of the baby boom in the 1960s and 1970s (which will continue to increase the number of marriages and births); the peasants' strong preference for sons and their financial independence built on the household farming system; and the rising tide of the floating population, the great majority of whom are of childbearing age.[41] Some of these factors are the delayed effects of past developments which the government can do little to counteract. Others are the outcome of the ongoing reforms and pose new problems of population control.

On the other side, the government will continue to tighten its family planning policies. The year 1991 actually witnessed a drop in the population growth rate to 12.98 per thousand from 14.39 per thousand in 1990. Whether this decline signifies the beginning of a downward trend or a temporary drop is hard to tell.[42] One plausible view of the intermediate future suggested by Banister is that both sets of factors counteract so that the fertility rate will not change dramatically from the level of the 1980s.[43]

If indeed China's population continues to grow at around 14 per thousand per year, it will probably have negative impacts on economic growth. The relationship between population growth and economic development is complex, and no simple generalizations can be made.[44] In China's case,

[41] According to the Minister of the Family Planning Commission, China will have the highest birth rate in the early 1990s. The annual net increase during 1991–95 will be around 16 million and the growth rate about 14 to 15 per thousand. Peng Peiyun, "The 1990s are a crucial decade for controlling population growth in China," *Liaowang*, No. 1 (1 January 1990), p. 7.

[42] According to the SSB, the decline was due mainly to the implementation of the Decision by the Party Central and the State Council to tighten population control in 1991, and partly to the people's decision to postpone having births in 1991 for superstitious reasons. *RMRB*, 29 February 1992, p. 3. If true, there is uncertainty as to what the people's decision may be in the future. For the Party Central's Decision, see *Xinhua*, Beijing, 12 June 1991, reported in FBIS-CHI-91-119, 20 June 1991, pp. 33–6. For reports of more rigorous efforts to implement population control, see *RMRB*, 29 April 1991, p. 1; *New York Times*, 16 June 1991, pp. 1, 4.

[43] Judith Banister, "China's population changes and the economy," in Joint Economic Committee, *China's Economic Dilemmas in the 1990s: The Problems of Reforms, Modernization, and Interdependence* (Washington, D.C., 1991), pp. 234–51. For other projections, see Zeng Yi and J. Vaupel, "Some problems of future demographic processes in China," *Social Sciences in China* (January 1992), pp. 43–53.

[44] For surveys of a large body of literature on the subject, see Nancy Birdsall, "Economic approaches to population growth and development," in Hollis Chenery and T.N. Srinivasan (eds.), *Handbook of Development Economics* (Amsterdam, 1988), and Allen C. Kelly, "Economic consequences of population change in the Third World," *Journal of Economic Literature*, Vol. XXVI, No. 4 (December 1988), pp. 1685–728.

however, the impact is fairly clear. Based on an extensive review of studies on the issue, Kelly identifies the conditions under which the population impact is likely to be negative:

Population's adverse impact has most likely occurred where arable land and water are particularly scarce or costly to acquire, where property rights to land and natural resources are poorly defined, and where government policies are biased against the most abundant factor of production – labor.[45]

These conditions fit China's case neatly. Rapid population growth will affect China's economic future through its impact on the dependency rates, the capital–labour ratio and the pattern of investment. But population is only one of many factors affecting China's economic growth. Its effects can be properly assessed only in a broad framework, to which this article now turns.

Sources of Economic Growth, 1980–90

Table 4 presents some rough measures of sources of growth of net material product (NMP) during the period 1952–90.[46] The data suggest interesting contrasts between the pre-1976 and post-1976 developments, with the growth of output distinctly faster in the latter period. Accelerated growth in the 1980s can be attributed largely to increases in the growth of capital stock and factor productivity. Throughout the four decades the growth of the labour force remained virtually constant so that its contribution to output growth was apparently unchanged in absolute terms and declining in its relative share. By contrast, the growth of capital stock has been continuously rising since the 1950s. The trend reflected the long-established policy

[45] Kelly, "Economic consequences of population change," pp. 1715–20.

[46] There is no reliable data on GNP, so growth rates of NMP are used here. Because services expanded rapidly in the 1980s, growth of factor productivity would probably be higher if GNP growth had been used. There are other statistical pitfalls. For example, the NMP growth rates are based on an index in comparable prices and may well be higher than if they were calculated from constant prices. The depreciation rates are generally understated so that the growth of capital stock is probably too high. The growth of labour input during the period of collectivized farming (1957–78) is probably slower than the growth of agricultural employment. But the crudeness of the data probably does not significantly change the overall picture. For other estimates of factor productivity growth, Zhang Junkuang, "A comprehensive analysis of economic effects during the Seventh Five-Year Plan period," *JJYJ*, No. 4 (1991), pp. 8–17; Li Feng, "On the role of technological advance in economic development," and Yang Jianbai, "Speed, structure and efficiency," *JJYJ*, No. 9 (1991), pp. 15–22 and 36–44; Jin Pei, "Technical progress in China's industrialization process," *Zhongguo gongye jingji yanjiu* (*China Industrial Economics Research*), No. 9 (1991), pp. 14–21; Chen Kuan, Wong Hongchang, Zheng Yuxin, Garry H. Jefferson and Thomas G. Rawski, "Productivity change in Chinese industry: 1953–85," *Journal of Comparative Economics*, No. 12 (1988), pp. 570–91; Gary H. Jefferson, Thomas G. Rawski and Yuxin Zheng, "Growth, efficiency and convergence in China's state and collective industry," *Economic Development and Cultural Change*, Vol. 40, No. 2 (January 1992), pp. 239–66; World Bank, *China: Long-Term Issues and Options, The Main Report* (Washington, D.C., 1985), p. 157.

TABLE 4. *Sources of Growth of Net Material Product, 1952–90 (% per year)*

| | | Contributions to NMP growth | | |
	Growth of NMP	Capital	Labour	Productivity
1952–57	6.61	0.84	1.67	4.10
1957–65	2.09	1.87	1.63	−1.41
1965–76	5.11	2.81	1.68	0.62
1976–85	8.78	3.30	1.69	3.79
1985–90	7.50	4.39	1.62	1.49

Sources:
  For sources of data, assumptions and method of deriving estimates for 1952–85, see Dwight H. Perkins, "Reforming China's economic system," *Journal of Economic Literature*, Vol. XXVI No. 2 (June 1988), pp. 628–9. Those for 1985–90 are estimated by the same method. See *TJNJ* 1990, p. 35; *TJZY* 1991, pp. 7–9, 15. The implicit deflator for industry in 1980–90 is lacking and is assumed to be the same as that for gross value of industrial output.

of the Chinese leadership to rely on capital accumulation as the primary source of economic growth. Unlike labour or capital, the growth of total factor productivity vacillated. In the 1950s, it rose sharply as the post-war economy rapidly recovered. The Great Leap and Cultural Revolution plunged the economy into chaos, so that there was hardly any increase in the 1960s and 1970s. It was not until the post-Mao period that factor productivity growth accelerated again. In the early 1980s, its contribution to the growth of net material product even exceeded that of capital inputs. Although growth slowed somewhat in the late 1980s, the rate was still much higher than during the 1970s.

This brief review of the sources of growth in the past points to three major economic challenges for China in the 1990s: how to sustain the growth of capital without causing inflation; how to make full use of China's enormous labour resources not only to maintain social stability but also to enhance the contribution of labour input to economic growth at a much more significant level than in the past; and, most importantly, how to accelerate and sustain the growth of factor productivity. These are fundamental problems confronting most developing countries. For China they are particularly formidable, partly because of the legacies of its past. For example, the large and growing population poses serious problems for capital formation and employment. Decades of self-imposed isolation from the outside world have left a large technological gap that makes the need for progress pressing and difficult. But more importantly, the economy is now in the process of being transformed from a command economy into a market-orientated one. Problems of economic growth are compounded by those of institutional restructuring. China's economic performance in the initial stage of this transition is no small achievement, but the basic problems have not yet been resolved and they will undoubtedly surface again in the 1990s.

Growth of capital

Growth of capital depends on investment. In the period 1980–89 real gross investment grew by 10.7 per cent per year.[47] It could have grown even faster had there been sufficient savings to finance investment growth. In the 1990s the growth of capital will be similarly constrained by inadequate savings rather than the lack of investment demand.

Indeed, the demand for investment is likely to expand further despite a lower target for GNP growth rate, because capital needs relative to GNP growth will probably rise. For decades a predominantly large share of investment was allocated to heavy industries to the neglect of other sectors. The effect of the consequent imbalance in the capital structure can no longer be ignored as bottlenecks in the neglected areas have become more severe. Problems in three such areas are particularly serious. The first is China's economic infrastructure, such as energy, transport and water supply.[48] The second is the obsolescence of the existing capital stock. In the early 1980s, about 70 per cent of China's large and medium-sized enterprises, the backbone of China's industry, had been built in the 1950s and 1960s and their equipment was worn out or had become technologically obsolete.[49] In the rural areas, many drainage and irrigation systems have remained in need of major repair.[50] The third area of neglect is the "non-productive" (non-material producing) sectors, such as residential housing, urban public facilities and environmental protection.[51] Although the pattern of investment has been restructured to divert more resources to these three areas, much more will be needed in the 1990s, not only to fill the gap left from the past but also to meet new demands created by population

[47] *World Tables 1991*, p. 185. The discussion in this section focuses on fixed investment. Because this is by far the larger component of total investment, and because working capital is closely related to fixed capital, this is also directly relevant to total investment.

[48] For a discussion of these problems, see the section on factor productivity below and the article by Kambara in this issue.

[49] Zhang Shuguang, *Jingji jiegou he jingji xiaoguo* (*Economic Structure and Economic Returns*) (Beijing, 1982), pp. 133–4; Dai Yuanchun, "Several problems concerning replacement of fixed capital," *JJYJ*, No. 10 (1982), pp. 64–70; *China Daily*, 19 December 1986, p. 4. See also Tan Xingmin and Wang Yuanjing, "Tentative comments on investment strategy for the 1990s," *Jingji cankao bao* (*Economic Information*), 21 January 1991, p. 4.

[50] *RMRB* editorial, 23 October 1991, p. 1.

[51] For reports of poor conditions in urban housing, urban public facilities and environmental protection, see *China Daily*, 27 November 1990, 12 August and 8 October 1991; *The Economist*, 18 February 1989, p. 34; *Wen hui bao*, 5 September 1990, p. 10; *Guangming ribao*, 19 January 1987, p. 2; Xiao Zhunming, "Greater effort is needed to construct urban public facilities," *Jingji ribao* (*Economic Daily*), hereafter *JJRB*, 20 October 1990, p. 2; State Environmental Protection Bureau, "Communiqué on China's environmental situation in 1990," *RMRB*, 5 June 1991, p. 3; Li Dibin, "Memorandum on China's environmental problem," *Liaowang*, No. 46 (1988), pp. 5–7.

growth, urbanization, increasing pollution, and economic reform. For example, the need to increase further the share of investment in transport and urban facilities in the 1990s has been recognized.[52] Average annual investment in urban housing construction will be raised to more than double that of 1978–90.[53] The government spent 11 billion *yuan* on environmental protection between 1986 and 1989 and plans to spend another 200 billion *yuan* over the next decade.[54] A total of 38 billion *yuan* has been planned for investment in water conservation during the period 1991–95, much more than the total investment in the entire agricultural sector in the preceding five years.[55] If investment in the recently approved Three Gorges Dam Project is added, the projected total will be even larger.[56]

A common feature of these investments is that the direct increase in output per unit of investment is small when compared with industrial investment. This is true of infrastructural investment because of the long gestation period and its capital-intensive nature. Replacement and non-productive investment does not increase productive capacity directly, although it improves the quality of life and generally enhances the technological level of the equipment. If the share of this in total investment should rise significantly, as is likely, aggregate demand for capital per unit of increase in output will be considerably greater than in the 1980s.

The rapid growth of investment in the 1980s was financed by an equally rapid growth of domestic savings. The average savings rate for the period reached 38 per cent, quite high by any standards. The marginal savings rate also increased discernibly in the late 1980s.[57] Nevertheless, new problems are emerging that tend to lower the savings rates of the three principal groups of savers.

Table 5 shows government revenue and current expenditure in 1980 and 1990. One striking feature suggested by the data is that current expenditure has been growing faster than revenue so that by 1990 government savings were negative. In the 1990s the disparity in the growth rates is likely to persist because, on the one hand, growth of budget revenues will be difficult

[52] Tan Xingmin and Wang Yuanjing, "Tentative comments."

[53] Total investment in residential housing during 1979–90 was 280 billion *yuan*, and the investment needs for 1991–2000 are projected at 495 billion *yuan*. *RMRB*, 10 and 14 October 1991.

[54] *The Economist*, 15 February 1992, p. 40.

[55] *China Daily*, 5 November 1991, p. 1; *TJZY* 1991, p. 25.

[56] The official estimate of investment cost for the project is 57 billion *yuan* at 1990 prices, or US$12 billion at the official rate of exchange. *RMRB*, 27 December 1991, p. 1. But some experts have placed the final cost as high as US$100 billion. *Far Eastern Economic Review*, 19 September 1991, p. 39.

[57] For different estimates see World Bank, *Long-Term Issues*, p. 115; Guo Shuqing, "Consumption, investment and savings," *JJYJ*, No. 4 (1990), p. 13; Yingyi Qian, "Urban and rural household saving in China," *International Monetary Fund Staff Papers* (December 1988), p. 594. The World Bank study shows a rising share of business savings in total savings whereas Guo indicates a decline during the period 1982–88, and Qian's data show no discernible trend during 1978–84.

TABLE 5. *Government Revenue and Current Expenditure, 1980 and 1990*

	1980 (billion yuan)	1990 (billion yuan)	Annual growth (%)
Total revenue	104.2	288.6	10.7
Current expenditure	55.9	309.3	18.6
Subsidies	33.8	106.3	12.1
Education, health and welfare	21.9	67.1	11.8
Administrative expenses	7.6	30.8	15.0
Defence	19.4	29.0	4.1

Sources:
    TJNJ 1990, pp. 229, 232–7; *TJNJ* 1991, pp. VIII–108, 109; Wang Yunguo, "A study of China's financial subsidies," *Xinhua wenzhai (New China Digest)*, No. 8 (1991) p. 57; *Zhongguo tongxun she* (Hong Kong) 28 January 1991, reported in FBIS-CHI-91-024 (5 February 1991), p. 38.

to accelerate as many state enterprises continue to incur losses and, on the other, the major items of current expenditure are likely to grow just as rapidly as in the recent past.

In 1991 there was a slight decline in fiscal subsidies. Any substantial reduction will, however, have to await significant improvements in the financial conditions of the state enterprises and sweeping reforms in the wage system. Government expenditure on education, science and health care will probably accelerate in order to make up for the heavy loss of human capital in the 1970s and to provide health and welfare for the growing population. Restructuring the economy will require the development of a social security system to provide a safety net for transitional unemployment. Similarly, the growth of administrative expenditure is unlikely to slow down, mainly because there is still no institutional constraint or accountability system to limit public expenditure.

The growth of military spending in the 1980s was relatively low, presumably because of the leadership's decision to defer military modernization until the economy is well on its way to sustained growth. However, there have been sizeable, consecutive increases since 1988, averaging 15 per cent per year between 1988 and 1991. The reasons for this are not known. Perhaps potential conflicts with other countries over the Spratly and Paracel Islands, the leadership's decision to maintain a military posture at the Taiwan Straits and the military's stronger role in China's political system since 1989 account for the recent rise in defence spending. If indeed these are the crucial factors, the rising trend will continue, for national security and the political power of the military are likely to remain important issues for some time to come.

Trends in business savings are hard to ascertain for lack of data. However, it seems clear that enterprises' capacity to save has increased at a declining rate, as indicated by the trend in enterprise income during 1986–90,[58] and is corroborated by the same trend in industrial profits.[59] One possible reason for the slowdown is the increase in losses due partly to the distorted price system but mainly to poor management. In addition enterprise profits are squeezed from various sources, such as the burden of support for retired and disabled workers and employees.[60] The number of retirees rapidly increased from eight to 22 million between 1980 and 1989, and will increase further as the ageing of the population accelerates in the later 1990s.[61] Another burden on enterprises is the cost of environmental protection, which increased from 0.1 to 0.4 billion *yuan* during 1978–87.[62] Because China has only just begun to control pollution this expenditure is likely to increase in the 1990s. There are also numerous levies forced upon the enterprises by local governments and departments in the form of fees, fines and donations,[63] the amount of which is increasing.[64] Central government has tried to eliminate such extortion, but the results are uncertain, mainly because this directly conflicts with the economic interests of local authorities and departments. Last, but not least, a considerable proportion of retained earnings has been used to increase bonuses and welfare payments to the workers.[65]

In the 1980s household savings increased both in absolute terms and relative to GNP. Whether this trend will continue into the 1990s will depend on a number of factors. On the positive side, the continued rise in per capita income will probably raise the savings rate, as suggested by empirical studies of the savings function in developing countries.[66] In China there is the additional factor that increases in income have largely taken the form of

[58] Estimates of enterprise income as based on its share in GDP given in SSB, *Qiwu shiqi guomin jingji he shehui fazhan gaikuang* (*National Economic and Social Development During the Seventh Five-Year Plan Period*) (Beijing, 1991), p. 30; and GDP given in YJZY 1991, p. 5.

[59] For profits of industrial enterprises including state-owned, collective and private enterprises, see SSB, *Zhongguo gongye jingji tongji nianjian 1990* (Beijing, 1990), p. 124.

[60] The burden falls almost entirely on enterprises. See *TJNJ* 1990, p. 816. See also the results of a survey of 400 industrial enterprises in 20 cities in 1986 reported in *JJRB*, 20 January 1987, p. 1.

[61] By the year 2000, the number of retirees is expected to reach 400 million and total pension payments over 100 billion *yuan*. *China Daily*, 2 March 1991, p. 1.

[62] *RMRB*, 17 August 1988, p. 2.   [63] *China Daily*, 6 November 1986, p. 3.

[64] A survey of enterprises in Shaanxi and Sichuan revealed that forced donations amounted to 5 to 15% of their annual income. *China Daily*, 11 September 1986, p. 3. Levies in Shandong came to 20% of the enterprises' retained earnings. *RMRB*, 2 April 1987, p. 3. Rural enterprises in Yunnan had to contribute payments equal to their taxes. *JJRB*, 14 May 1988, p. 1.

[65] According to one report, 70 to 80% of retained profits of many enterprises have been paid to workers as bonuses or welfare payments. *Jiefang ribao* (*Liberation Daily*), 25 December 1987, p. 1. See also Dai Yungchen and Li Hanming, "Wages squeezing profits," *JJYJ*, No. 6 (1988), pp. 3–11.

[66] Raymond F. Mikesell and James E. Zinser, "The nature of the savings function in developing countries: a survey of the theoretical and empirical literature," *Journal of Economic Literature*, Vol. XI, No. 1 (March 1973), pp. 8–10; Mark Gersovitz, "Saving and development" in Chenery and Srinivansan, *Handbook of Development Economics*, p. 416.

rises in transitory income (bonuses, payment in kind and special subsidies) which generally lead to a higher propensity to save.[67] Presumably, this trend will persist as the current reform continues to emphasize discretionary financial power of factory directors. Another positive factor is the increasing share of employment in non-state-owned enterprises (collectives, private enterprises and joint ventures). These workers do not enjoy free medical services, pension, unemployment insurance or other benefits. They tend to save more for retirement and as a hedge against illness or unemployment.[68] Again, their share in total employment is likely to become larger as reforms move forward. Finally, one can expect savings to increase as financial markets develop and more financial instruments to absorb savings become available.[69]

On the negative side, there is first the demographic factor. As noted above, a relatively high rate of population growth in the next decade is a distinct possibility. The new baby boom will raise the dependency rate and, consequently, lower the savings rate.[70] And as those born during the 1960s and early 1970s enter their twenties, the marriage rate is bound to rise, and the increase in consumption expenditure on weddings and setting up new households will have to be financed by accumulated savings or current income.[71]

A second factor adversely affecting the savings rate is the new trend towards increasing consumption as per capita income rises. A survey shows that there have been marked increases in spending on articles of daily use, books and magazines, and medicine. More importantly, with further increase in income, the consumers seek to upgrade their living standards by providing education for their children, buying high quality consumer durables and having better food.[72]

[67] Fan Gang, "Understanding the increase in savings in China during a period of economic retrenchment," *Caimao jingji* (*Economics of Finance and Trade*), No. 5 (1991), p. 5.

[68] In a national survey in 1987, the largest percentage of those interviewed listed this as a major motive to save. He Jiacheng and Zhang Ronggang, "New changes in Chinese resident's consumption and savings deposits," *RMRB*, 18 March 1988, p. 5. Surveys of residents in Beijing, Shanghai and Taiyan show similar findings. Liang Yu and Xu Peiang, "An analysis of motivations behind people's saving behaviour," *Xinhua wenzhai* (*New China Digest*), No. 1 (1991), pp. 54–5; *Jiefang ribao*, 7 August 1990, p. 5; *JJRB*, 10 June 1990, p. 2.

[69] One possible factor is income distribution. There is a hypothesis that increasing inequality of incomes increases savings. S. Kuznets, "Quantitative aspects of the economic growth of Nations. VII. The share and structure of consumption," *Economic Development and Cultural Change*, Vol. X, No. 2 (January 1962), pp. 6–8. But whether and to what extent income distribution will become less equal in China remains unclear.

[70] It has been estimated that each year 20% of the increase in net material product has to be used to support the new population. Yao Zhanli, "Warning: China's population exceeds 1.1 billion," *Liaowang*, No. 15 (10 April 1989), p. 16.

[71] Wedding costs are high in China. In 1986, the average cost amounted to three and five times the combined annual income of an average couple in the urban and rural areas respectively. *Guangming ribao*, 27 January and 30 August 1987, and *TJNJ* 1986, p. 673. For this reason, one of the strong incentives to save is to prepare for marriages of family members and funerals. He Jiacheng and Zhang Ronggang, "New changes."

[72] He Jiacheng and Zhang Ronggang, "New changes."

A third factor is the lack of a social security system in rural China. The steep decline in the birth rate in the 1970s will bring about a rise in the proportion of the elderly in the second half of the 1990s, a large number of whom will be rural residents who are not covered by social security. Their family members will have to provide old age support, thereby lowering their savings rate.

The sharp rise in household savings in the 1980s is indicated by the phenomenal growth of savings deposits.[73] But the future is unclear. Even if household savings increase, the rise may be offset by dissaving by other groups. Assuming national savings do rise, the increase will have to exceed or match the increase in investment, if inflation is to be avoided.[74]

To a limited extent, capital shortage can be alleviated by using foreign capital, as China did in the 1980s, although this may not now be so easy. As a result of foreign loans made in the last decade, China's debt service will peak during the 1990s, averaging US$9 billion a year, which is only slightly below the combined inflow of foreign loans and foreign investment (US$11 billion in 1991).[75] Furthermore with almost all members of the Commonwealth of Independent States joining the International Monetary Fund and World Bank, and with Japan shifting its investments back towards home, China will have to compete with more borrowers in a tight, world capital market. But there are also new opportunities in attracting foreign investment. The development of economic relations between China and South Korea and Taiwan has opened new channels of capital inflow. Foreign investments have increased in recent years, and the trend may well continue as rising wages in Taiwan, South Korea and Hong Kong make it attractive to move labour-intensive manufacturing facilities to China, and as reform in China accelerates.

Within China, there are two other potential sources of savings that can be tapped. The first is the potential savings derived from greater efficiency in capital formation and capital use; the other is the mobilization of China's enormous labour resources for investment in kind. The former relates to economic reform and the latter to the problem of under-employment of labour.

---

[73] One must not equate the increase in the people's bank deposits with the increase in their savings, although the two are closely related. This is because these deposits include the operating capital of individual businesses and private enterprises, and the public or private savings of profit-making and non-profit-making units. *RMRB*, 9 February 1990, p. 6; *China Daily*, 9 September 1991, p. 4. In some localities, public and private funds account for as much as 40% of the increase in saving deposits. *RMRB*, 16 September 1991, p. 2.

[74] Some are optimistic. Guo Shuqing, "Consumption, investment and savings." Others remain concerned. *China Daily*, 28 October 1985, p. 1.

[75] For an estimate of debt service, see Wu Jinglian, "Prospects for China's economic development in the 1990s," *Caimao jingji*, No. 2 (1991), p. 11. For capital inflow in 1991, see *RMRB*, 29 February 1992, p. 2.

Supply of labour

The contribution of labour as a factor input to economic growth shown in Table 4 understates its significance, because the relevant measure of labour input is the actual man-hours worked, and there are reasons to believe that labour input has expanded faster than the number of workers employed because the hours worked per worker have increased. The rise in hours worked per person is primarily the result of economic reform. The replacement of the commune system with household farming motivated farmers to work much harder than before, as the change reduced the marginal tax rate from nearly 100 per cent to virtually zero. At the same time, the increasing use of the bonus system and contract labour, and a rising share of the workers in collective and private enterprises in the labour force – presumably working longer hours than those in state enterprises – raised the man-hours worked per worker in the urban areas.[76]

Looking ahead, it seems safe to say that labour supply will not become a constraint on GNP growth, given continued population growth and a target GNP growth rate of 6 per cent per year that is substantially lower than the actual growth in the 1980s of 9 per cent. Rather it is the over-supply of labour that could cause massive unemployment and adversely affect economic growth. The root cause of the current unemployment problem lies mainly in rapid population growth during the late 1960s and early 1970s and the hidden unemployment that resulted from China's long-standing policy of "providing five jobs for the work of three," and from the effect of dwindling arable land. These factors will remain operative for some time to come.

Furthermore, there are sharp differences in labour supply and demand conditions between regions, resulting from uneven regional economic and population growth in recent years. In the coastal areas, particularly the large cities and the special economic zones, the demand for labour has been relatively strong, whereas in interior China, the reverse is the case.[77] Since regional disparities in economic and population growth are likely to persist and perhaps even widen, so too will regional differences in unemployment rates and the social and economic problems caused by these differences.

[76] According to one report, workers and employees in state enterprises and government organizations worked only 19.2 to 20 hours a week with efficiency, even though they were supposed to work 48 hours. *China Daily*, 15 March 1989, p. 4.

[77] For example, in 1986 the urban unemployment rate for the nation as a whole was 1.8%. Those for such developed areas as Shanghai, Beijing and Tianjin were 0.2, 0.4 and 0.8% respectively, whereas those for interior provinces such as Quinghai and Ningxia were 7.7 and 3.1% respectively. *Wen hui bao*, Hong Kong, 18 April 1990, p. 4. For the Chinese definition of unemployment rate, see *TJNJ* 1990, p. 149. For a comparison of the Chinese and western concepts of unemployment, see Fu Gangzhan, "Theory and statistical concepts of employment in China," *Tongji yanjiu (Statistical Research)*, No. 5 (1991), pp. 35–40.

A third cause for concern over potential unemployment is the sheer magnitude of the problem. The supply of labour in the next decade derives mainly from three sources. The first is the net increase in the number of people of working age during the period 1991–2000. According to one estimate, China's employment-age population will increase from 697 million in 1990 to 781 million by the year 2000, of which 74 million will seek employment.[78] The second is the existing stock of unemployed and under-employed labour in the urban areas. Included in this group are the 12 million unemployed at the end of 1990,[79] and about 20 million redundant workers in state enterprises, institutions and government organizations.[80] The third, and perhaps the most significant, is the redundant workers in rural areas. There is no consensus on the size of this surplus, but a median estimate is 100 million.[81] Thus, the total supply of labour from all three sources seeking employment in the next decade amounts to 200 million.

On the assumption that the elasticity of employment with respect to income in the next decade remains the same as in 1978–90, 0.33, and that the growth rate of GNP is 6 per cent per year, employment will grow at about 2 per cent per year.[82] The increase in employment in the 1990s will then be 125 million, far below the projected increase in supply.[83] If indeed massive unemployment should emerge, serious social and economic problems will follow. Large numbers of rural unemployed would leave the countryside to seek jobs in the cities. The influx would strain urban facilities, create social problems and divert scarce resources to welfare. Massive unemployment would keep the wages low, but would also delay the capital-deepening process essential to productivity growth. In addition it could retard the reform movement, as grave concerns over unemployment might prompt local authorities to set up regional barriers to protect local industries.

---

[78] Li Xizheng, "China's employment situation in the 1990s," *Jingji cankao*, 21 November 1990, p. 4. For a different estimate presumably based on a different definition, see Wang Huijiang and Li Boxi, *China Towards the Year 2000* (Beijing, 1989), p. 31.

[79] Ruan Chongwu, "Do a good job in employment work; promote social stability," *Qiushi* (*Seeking Truth*), No. 4 (1990), p. 37.

[80] Estimates of redundant workers in 1988–89 range from 15 to 30 million. *China Daily*, 21 September 1988, p. 4 and 3 March 1989, p. 1.

[81] The low estimate is that by the SSB, 60–80 million, cited in Mo Weikuang and Chen Chiyuan, "Transferring China's rural surplus labour to township enterprise Development," *Jingji daobao* (*Economic Reporter*), Hong Kong, No. 42 (1990), p. 23. A high estimate of 150–200 million is given in Wu Canping, "Quantity and quality of China's rural population in connection with industrial restructuring," *Zhongguo nongcun jingji* (*Chinese Rural Economy*), No. 2 (1989), pp. 15–19, 35, translated in JPRS-CAR-89-058 (5 June 1989), p. 25. For other estimates ranging from 100–50 million see *Wen hui bao*, 10 December 1990, p. 2; *China Daily*, 5 December 1990, p. 4; Kao Chang, *An Estimation of Labour Surplus in Rural Mainland China* (Taipei, 1983).

[82] For data used to calculate elasticity, see *TJZY* 1991, pp. 5, 15.

[83] Some projections put the rural surplus labour alone at 200 to 350 million. Wang Linjin, "My views on the absorption of rural surplus labour," *JJRB*, 14 April 1990, p. 2; Song Boqin, "Guided relocation: a new approach to resolving the problem of surplus agricultural population," *Jingji cankao*, 23 July 1990, p. 4.

Further delay in implementing the bankruptcy law for fear of creating more unemployment might also ensue.

There are, however, major opportunities to put the surplus labour to productive use. One such outlet is the continued development of rural enterprises in industry, construction and transport. Others are the development of services, the direct export of labour, and rural investment in kind, such as construction and repair of irrigation networks, opening up waste land and building roads. There was rapid development in the first three of these areas in the 1980s, but there still appears to be substantial potential for further expansion. Economic reform could further these developments. For example, the realignment of prices might encourage peasants to invest more in the land, while the establishment of labour markets would make it easier to use workers in sectors where there is demand, and the expansion of domestic trade could stimulate rural industries and employment, as in the case of Wenzhou.

Factor productivity growth

Table 4 above shows that productivity growth was distinctly higher in the 1980s than in the preceding decades but that this was slowing down towards the end of the period. Why was the growth rate higher? Was the slowdown a transient development or the beginning of a downward trend? The limited information available does not permit an in-depth analysis, so only some plausible hypotheses can be suggested here.

For convenience of discussion, three sets of factors affecting China's productivity growth can be distinguished. The first is changes in the quality of capital stock and labour. The quality of capital stock improves as the technology embodied in the equipment advances. Since new technologies are generally incorporated in new equipment, changes in the average life of capital stock roughly indicate improvements or deterioration of the quality of the capital.[84] According to the 1985 industrial census, China's industrial capital was relatively young: 38.9 per cent had been built in the 1980s, 43 per cent in the 1970s and only 18.1 per cent before 1970.[85] However, in China's case, this may not be a reliable indicator of quality. Although the bulk of equipment is relatively new, it does not embody up-to-date technology. Equipment built in the 1970s actually uses technology of the 1950s, and also the quality of machinery produced during the Cultural Revolution was rather poor. Consequently, only one-third of the equipment was technologically advanced, with two-thirds obsolete.[86] It therefore appears that the

[84] Richard N. Nelson, "Aggregate production functions and medium range growth projections," *American Economic Review* (September 1964), pp. 575–606.

[85] Zhong Pengyong, "Idle resources and China's macro-economic policies," *Xinhua wenzhai* (*New China Digest*), No. 3 (1991), p. 55.

[86] *Ibid.* See also Ma Hong (ed.), *Zhongguo gongye jingji wenti yanjiu* (*Studies in Problems of China's Industrial Economy*) (Beijing, 1983), pp. 203–6. About one-half of the industrial

quality of capital stock improved somewhat but not sufficiently to make a difference to its contribution to output growth.

Among the many factors that affect the quality of labour, two are particularly relevant to present-day China: the educational level, and the average age of the work force. The 1982 census data show that the educational level of workers was low. About 28 per cent were illiterate, 34 per cent were educated to primary school level, 26 per cent to junior high school, 11 per cent to senior high school, and those with college education constituted less than 1 per cent.[87] Substantial effort was made in the 1980s to improve and expand the education system,[88] so that there was a rise in the educational level of the total population between 1982 and 1990.[89] The effect of this was clearly positive, but its significance is hard to ascertain for various reasons. First, the educational system did not directly address the needs of economic construction. For example, in the current transition to a market-oriented economy management expertise is greatly needed. Yet China's schools and colleges were ill-prepared for this task.[90] The rural educational system also put more emphasis on training students for university entrance than the technical training that was badly needed for agricultural modernization.[91] Secondly, the rate of return on education varied. Per capita incomes of better-educated peasants were markedly higher,[92] but there was hardly any variation between the wages of workers and employees with different levels of education. In some cases, those with less education but working in blue-collar jobs earned more.[93]

Looking ahead, one detects some disturbing signs. As Table 6 shows, the share of educational expenditure in GNP declined after the mid-1980s. School enrolment fell steadily throughout the 1980s. This may perhaps be because of the relatively low returns on education compared with those of work experience.[94] The negative effect of the decline in the accumulation of human capital in the last decade will be felt in the 1990s.

equipment in the early 1980s should have been scrapped. *Liaowang*, No. 12 (25 March 1991), p. 15.

[87] Li Chengrui, *Population Census*, p. 118.

[88] Zhao Wei, "China's education surges forward in the new epoch," *Liaowang*, No. 11 (18 March 1991), pp. 28–9.

[89] *Beijing Review*, 12–18 November 1990, p. 23. For improvements in the educational level of the rural labour force in 1985 and 1989, see Wen Jianwu, "A quantitative analysis of the relationship between the peasants' income and their educational level," *Tongji yanjiu* (*Statistical Research*), No. 4 (1991), p. 27.

[90] He Boquan, "Ten great crises in China's education in the future," *Weilai yu fazhan* (*Future and Development*), No. 4 (1985), p. 26.

[91] Cai Hong, "Education is the key out of poverty," *China Daily*, 5 January 1991, p. 4.

[92] Wen Jianwu, "A quantitative analysis," p. 28.

[93] Wang Xianyi, "On the effect of income differentials on family intellectual investment," *Renkou yu jingji* (*Population and Economics*), No. 2 (1991), p. 37.

[94] Raymond P. Byron and Evelyn Manaloto, "Returns to education in China," *Economic Development and Cultural Change*, Vol. 38, No. 4 (July 1990), pp. 783–96. *RMRB*, 13 November 1990, p. 5 reported that most of the dropouts left school to work.

TABLE 6. *Education and Research, Selected Indicators, 1980–90*

	School enrolment (1,000)	Share in GNP		R&D* personnel (1,000)	Major R&D achieved (no.)	Major inventions (no.)
		Education (%)	R&D (%)			
1980	204	2.6	1.4	323	2,687	109
1981	195	2.6	1.3	337	3,371	123
1982	188	2.7	1.3	372	4,186	153
1983	183	2.8	1.4	328	5,397	212
1984	186	2.8	1.4	335	10,615	264
1985	186	3.0	1.2	336	10,476	185
1986	187	3.1	1.2	366	14,915	26
1987	184	2.8	1.0	314	11,800	225
1988	180	2.6	0.8	307	16,552	217
1989	176	2.5	–	297	20,278	150
1990	175	2.0	0.7	291	26,829	224

Note:
   * Includes those in natural sciences in government sector only.
Source:
   TJNJ 1986, p. 768; *TJNJ* 1990, pp. 33, 238, 276, 264; *TJNJ* 1983, p. 90, 1984, p. 104, 1986, p. 117, 1987, p. 112, 1990, p. 107; State Statistical Bureau, 1991, pp. 114, 238; *Guangming ribao (Guangming Daily)*, 18 March 1991, p. 1; *JJNJ* 1991, p. VIII–134; *RMRB*, 27 March 1991, p. 2.

Technological progress is another major source of productivity growth. Notable achievements in R&D have been made in China since 1980, although its contribution to output growth appears to have been quite limited. R&D funding as a percentage of GNP was relatively low by international standards and declined from 1.4 per cent in 1980 to 0.7 per cent in 1990.[95] Table 6 also shows that the technical manpower engaged in R&D was in decline from 1986. However, despite the slow growth of inputs, the system has been productive and the rate of increase in the number of major R&D achievements far exceeds that of its funding. The results are remarkable in view of the many problems plaguing the R&D system. As a result of rigid compartmentalization into five independent branches (the Chinese Academy of Science, the military R&D system, universities, research institutes of government ministries, and research institutes under local governments and private research organizations), technical manpower and equipment have been under-used, research projects duplicated and functional specialization virtually non-existent.[96] Institutional reforms have re-

   [95] The shares for Japan, South Korea and India were 2.8, 1.8 and 1.2% respectively. Fan Xian, "Open wide the channels for funding science and technology," *JJRB*, 27 August 1990, p. 3.
   [96] Qiu Chengli and Yang Lincun, "An exploratory analysis of optimal restructuring of

cently taken place, such as the employment of the technology contract system, the establishment of science funds and the transfer of military technology to civilian use. These changes have apparently somewhat improved the efficient use of R&D resources.

However, as far as the effect of technology on growth is concerned, applying available technology to production is more important than creating new technology.[97] Yet application and diffusion of new technology remain the weakest links in the innovation process in China. As recently as 1990, less than 15 per cent of the new technologies have been applied and popularized.[98] The main reason for the low application rate is the lack of co-ordination between the R&D and production systems, which historically developed separately and independently of each other. Managers of industrial enterprises are not interested in introducing new products or adopting new technologies, because their primary concern is to fulfil quotas for production, and the profits and taxes contributed to the state (the most important criteria by which their performances are evaluated). Transferring a new technology from laboratory to factory generally involves substantial costs in terms of intermediate tests, the design of new equipment, the establishment of pilot plants and trial production. It also takes two to three years before the new technology generates profits.[99] Thus, as long as traditional products sell, managers are unwilling to take risks. And if new technology really is needed to make a profit, as in the case of some consumer durables, they rely on imported technology. At the same time, the government has done little to channel the technological achievements into the production system. There are no special funds to facilitate commercialization of research results. Nor are firms rewarded for taking risks in developing new products.[100]

In recent years, some effort has been made to reverse the trend. One measure was the development of technology markets, embracing technology sales, job contracting, technical consulting and other services. The volume of technology trade has increased at an average annual rate of 60 per cent, to reach 7.5 billion *yuan* in 1990.[101] Another important measure is transfer from abroad. During the last decade, China imported more than 7,000 items of technology costing US$29.85 billion.[102] The increasing vol-

China's research organizations," *Liaowang*, No. 29 (22 July 1991), pp. 26–27; and K. C. Yeh, *Industrial Innovation in China* (Santa Monica, 1985).

   [97] Henry Ergas, "Does technology policy matter?" in Bruce R. Guile and Harvey Brooks (eds.), *Technology and Global Industry* (Washington, D.C., 1987), pp. 191–245.
   [98] Lu Siliang, "Mobilize all social forces to popularize science and technology results," *Liaowang*, No. 33 (19 August 1991), p. 3.
   [99] Xi Mi, "Researchers, business must co-operate," *China Daily*, 21 January 1992, p. 4.
   [100] *China Daily* (Business Weekly), 21 December 1987, p. 3, 5 August 1991, p. 4.
   [101] *China Daily*, 26 April 1991, p. 1. See also Wang Zhengrong, "An analysis of the characteristics and trends in the development of China's technology markets," *Zhongguo keji luntan* (*Forum on Science and Technology in China*), No. 4 (1991), pp. 56–57, 64.
   [102] *China Daily*, 26 April 1991, p. 1 and *Business Weekly*, 29 April 1991, p. 1.

TABLE 7. *Shares of Output and Employment by Three Major Sectors, 1980 and 1990*

	1980	1990
Shares in GDP (%)		
Agriculture	30.4	27.5
Industry	49.0	45.3
Services	20.6	27.2
Shares in total employment (%)		
Agriculture	68.7	60.0
Industry	18.3	21.4
Services	13.0	18.6
Ratio: output share to employment share		
Agriculture	0.4	0.5
Industry	2.7	2.1
Services	1.6	1.5

Source:
TJZY 1991, pp. 5, 17.

ume of domestic and external transfers, albeit still limited, should contribute to the upgrading of industrial technology.

The leadership clearly intends to accelerate the development of science and technology in the next decade. A goal has been set to raise by the year 2000 the technological level of China's industry to the standards that developed countries achieved in the late 1970s or early 1980s. The application of R&D results will be increased to 60 per cent, and the share of R&D expenditures in GNP raised from 0.7 per cent in 1990 to 1 per cent in 1995 and 1.35 per cent in 2000.[103] As the foregoing discussions suggest, whether these goals will be attained depends largely on how the reforms of the R&D system and its co-ordination with the economic system progress in the future.

A third major source of productivity growth is improvement in resource allocation. It seems that it was this which generated the remarkable productivity growth in the 1980s, as well as the crucial constraints for the future. The first major development was the significant shift of resources from low to high productivity areas. Table 7 shows the shares of GDP and total employment by three major sectors: agriculture, industry (including construction) and services, in 1980 and 1990. The distinctive feature in the changing share of employment is the move from agricultural to industrial and service employment. The ratio of output share to employment share

[103] *Beijing Xinhua*, 7 April 1992, reported in FBIS-CHI-92-068 (8 April 1992), p. 33; *Jingji daobao*, Hong Kong, Nos. 1–2 (1 January 1992), p. 103; Song Jian, "Develop science and technology, vitalize China: a review of and prospects for China's science and technology activities," *Keji ribao* (*Science and Technology Daily*), 16 September 1991, pp. 1–2.

TABLE 8. *Domestic and Foreign Trade, Selected Indicators 1978 and 1990*

	1978	1990
Number of trade markets (1,000)	33.3	72.6
Volume traded in markets (billion *yuan*)	12.5	216.8
Marketing ratio of farm products (%)	39.9	48.4
Ratio: retail sales to GNP (%)	43.4	47.7
Share of labour force in trade (%)	1.9	5.0*
Ratio: exports to GNP (%)	4.7	17.2
Ratio: imports to GNP (%)	5.2	14.8

Note:
 * 1989.
Source:
 TJNJ 1990, p. 601; *TJZY* 1991, pp. 5, 15, 52, 90, 94, 97.

shows the productivity of each sector relative to that of the economy as a whole. The data indicate that relative productivities in industry and service are higher than in agriculture. A shift of employment from agriculture to the other two sectors therefore raises the overall productivity.

Another factor behind the recent productivity increase was the expansion of domestic and foreign markets, which generated substantial scale effects. Before 1978, the goal of regional and national economic self-sufficiency had high priority. The policy encouraged economic independence from the outside world and the development of small, vertically integrated, localized economies. Consequently, resource flows between regions and departments were largely blocked and foreign trade was insignificant, thus sacrificing benefits from specialization. In addition, by isolating itself from the outside world, China deprived the economy of opportunities to absorb foreign technology and capital. After 1978, an abrupt change in policy took place. The goal was now to revitalize the economy internally and open it to the outside world. As Table 8 suggests, during 1978–90 the number of free markets in rural and urban areas more than doubled. The marketing ratio for farm products, the ratio of retail sales to GNP and the share of employment in domestic trade all rose sharply. So did the share of foreign trade in GNP, which increased from 10 to 32 per cent. It is difficult to pinpoint the effects of trade expansion on productivity growth. But there is a strong presumption that trade and markets made it possible for China to shift resources from less to more productive uses, to exploit benefits from functional and regional specialization and to facilitate technological diffusion.

But as economic reform opened markets and increased foreign trade, strong undercurrents also emerged to slow the trend. These originated in the decentralization of financial power to provincial governments. The decentralization was characterized by the adoption of a fiscal responsibility system under which a province contributed a fixed amount as revenue to the state budget annually, but kept whatever the provincial government could collect above the quota. The purpose was to provide a stable source of revenue for the central government and at the same time motivate local governments to revitalize their economies. The result of decentralization was that local governments rushed to set up lucrative businesses (such as the manufacture of cigarettes, wine, textiles and colour television sets) because of their heavy dependence on industries within their locality to support their finances. To protect local industrial development, many local governments restricted the sales of products from other localities. As local industries proliferated, the battle for raw materials among the provinces became more intense. Localities fought to purchase products such as silk-worm cocoons, wool, tobacco, tea and nonferrous metals. Blockades were set up by provinces producing these raw materials in order to ensure adequate supply to their own processing plants.

Clearly, local protectionism hindered productivity growth.[104] To promote local industrial development, many localities ceased to co-operate with others and established a comprehensive industrial structure regardless of local conditions. Investment projects duplicated each other, and the growth of local factories left larger and more efficient factories idle because of shortage of raw materials. Meanwhile, local plant managers had no incentive to improve efficiency because they faced a sheltered market, and producers of raw materials had no incentive to produce more since their markets were limited to local consumption. Local governments took the opportunity to generate foreign exchange earnings for themselves by exporting at low prices materials which were in critically short supply domestically, such as petroleum products, scrap metal, sugar and nickel, while domestic users imported them at higher prices, resulting in a net loss of foreign exchange for the country as a whole.

In early 1982, the State Council issued a directive prohibiting the setting up of regional blockades,[105] but the trend towards local protectionism apparently continued. On 10 November 1990, the State Council again issued a circular calling for the removal of market barriers between regions,[106] then in early 1991 it was reported that local protectionism was escalating.[107] Once in place, regional blockades seem to breed vested interest groups that use all their political power to fight their removal. Like national tariffs, it will

---

[104] Chen Dongsheng and Wei Houkai, "Some reflections on inter-regional trade friction," *Gaige (Reform)*, No. 2 (20 March 1989), pp. 79–83; Li Shihua, "Analysis of local protectionism," *Jingji lilun yu jingji guanli (Economic Theory and Management)*, No. 4 (28 July 1991), pp. 67–9; Li Zhengyi, "Thoughts on the local blockade problem," *Caijing yanjiu (Research on Finance and Economics)*, No. 11 (3 November 1991), pp. 3–8.

[105] *RMRB*, 21 April 1982, p. 1.　　　[106] *RMRB*, 23 November 1990, p. 2.

[107] Wang Baowang, Qi Xinjian and Yan Guoming, "We must remove local protectionism," *Qunyan (Popular Forum)*, No. 2 (7 February 1991), pp. 22–3.

take a concerted effort of all members to eliminate the domestic restrictions, and co-operation and co-ordination between provinces is difficult because their economic strength and interests differ widely. If, as is likely, economic separatism should persist in the 1990s, productivity growth based on the scale effect of inter-regional division of labour will be seriously hampered.

A third factor which also generated mixed results is the changes in efficiency of resource use at the enterprise or household level. In the agricultural sector there have been marked rises in labour productivity and output per acre. The main reason for this was a major improvement in the efficiency of farm management. Under the commune system, remuneration based on egalitarian principles sapped peasants' incentives to work. Because of excessive emphasis on grain production, orchards, grazing land, sugar-cane fields and lakes were turned into grain fields even though they were more suitable for other uses. Rural reform restored household farming, opened up free markets for most farm products and offered opportunities for rural non-farm employment. Farm households now freely decide how to use their land, labour and equipment to maximize their incomes. Consequently, output and yields have soared despite a decline in state investment in agriculture. Of course these improvements cannot be attributed solely to rural reform. But there can be little doubt that privatization and development of markets have encouraged the farmers to work harder and to use their capital and land more efficiently.

The picture in the industrial enterprises is vastly different. While total factor productivity of state enterprises with independent accounting grew at 6.1 per cent per year during 1978–84, it fell to –4.2 per cent between 1984 and 1987. The number of enterprises in debt increased from 41,000 to 60,000, and their losses rose from 3.4 to 11.6 billion *yuan* over the same period.[108] According to an SSB official as recently as early 1992, conditions have not changed, and poor managerial and operational quality of the enterprises still contribute to low efficiency.[109] As may be expected, given the soft budget constraint, the enterprise managers are under no pressure to operate efficiently.

A fourth factor affecting the changing efficiency of resource allocation is the degree of distortion in the price system. Relative prices that do not reflect scarcities and preferences are likely to misguide the use of resources. Low energy prices and capital costs leading to waste are examples. In the 1980s steps were taken to reform the price system, by adjusting some prices, introducing a dual price system and freeing others.[110] But it seems fair to say

[108] Fang Lixin, "Try hard to raise economic returns: an interview with economist Zhou Shulian," *Liaowang*, No. 2 (8 January 1990), p. 31.
[109] *Beijing Xinhua*, 19 January 1992, reported in FBIS-CHI-92-028 (11 February 1992), p. 23.
[110] See Zhang Zhuyuan, "Reform of the price system," in Zhang Zhuyuan and Huang Fanzhang (eds.), *Zhongguo shinian jingji gaige lilun tansuo* (*Theoretical Explorations of China's Economic Reform in the Last Decade*) (Beijing, 1991), pp. 107–29.

that China has a long way to go before a competitive price system is firmly established.

A fifth factor, also inherited from the pre-1980 period, has been persistent bottlenecks in some critical sectors such as energy, transport and water supply. Chronic shortages of these items meant that the productive capacities of sectors dependent upon them were under-used, in turn constraining the growth of other sectors. Such shortages are likely to remain acute in the 1990s because the major sources of demand, such as population growth, expansion of foreign trade and rapid development of the coastal region, will continue to exert strong pressure on the infrastructural facilities.

Several interesting policy implications are suggested by the above observations. First, the main reasons for the remarkable growth in the 1980s were the growth of capital and factor productivity. The former will remain important in the future partly because technical progress cannot be completely independent of the growth of capital, and partly because existing bottlenecks and, more generally, imbalances in the output structure require adjustments in the capital structure.

In addition, the supply of labour is characterized by its enormous quantity and relatively poor quality. Labour has not been a major source of growth in the 1980s and will remain only a potential asset unless drastic measures are undertaken to improve the skill level of the work force, restructure the incentive systems and increase the effective use of surplus labour.

Finally, factor productivity growth has been crucial to economic growth in the 1980s. Rural reform, rapid growth of rural enterprises, private enterprises and services, and expanding domestic and foreign trade constituted the dynamic forces of productivity growth. In particular, domestic and foreign trade not only increased economies of scale but also served as a vehicle for the transfer of technical and management expertise. It is important to note that the benefits of rural reform are one-time results and that a good part of the growth due to inter-industry shifts and expanding trade represents partial economic recovery from conditions of gross inefficiency. Rapid increases in productivity in these areas are hard to duplicate. In addition, many formidable obstacles remain deep-rooted, such as regional protectionism that restricts trade expansion, price distortions that misguide the flow of resources, and poor performance of state enterprises that drains resources away from productive use. However these serious constraints may also represent potential for rapid growth, just as the dismantling of the commune system, which had inhibited productivity growth, brought significant results. The key, of course, is economic reform. The economic reform of the 1980s marked only the beginning of the transition to a market-based economy. The complexities of drastically changing people's value systems, economic behaviour and institutions are one reason for the slow progress. There have been clashes between new and old institutions, conflicts between interest groups, and a tense struggle between those who sought to hold on to the Marxist tenets and political control and others who opted for economic reform, even at the cost of political liberalization. The leadership was also divided over the model system to be developed, the pace of reform and priorities in the reform programme. Meanwhile, new problems emerged, such as corruption, social unrest and inflation, which further fuelled the dispute and disrupted the reform movement.

Inflationary Pressures in the 1990s

A serious problem faced by the Chinese leadership in the process of economic reform was that of inflation. Table 9 shows the annual rates of change in retail prices, market prices and the implicit GNP deflator in the period 1980–90. None of these indicators accurately measures changes in the general price level, either because of their limited coverage or because of shortcomings in their methods of calculation.[111] Nevertheless, it is clear that inflationary pressures made themselves felt in 1980, 1985 and 1988–89. The situation in 1988–89 was particularly serious. In 1988 market prices surged by more than 30 per cent over the preceding year. Unlike previous episodes in 1950 and 1960, inflation in the 1980s occurred in a period of rapid economic growth and restructuring, and opening to the outside world. This makes the causes of the inflation unclear, as well as the extent to which it was related to economic reform. But the same factors may exert pressure on the economy in the 1990s.

The aggregate supply–demand gap

Inflation is a complex phenomenon, particularly in China where reform caused political and economic forces to interact, generating a mixture of

[111] The retail price index is not a consumer price index, because it does not cover the prices of consumer services and does include the prices of producer goods purchased by farmers. Nor is its coverage broad enough to represent a general price index because prices of other producer goods, both wholesale and retail, are excluded, as are the prices of services such as telecommunications and transport. It is a weighted average of the prices of goods sold through the state's commercial channels and distributed through the free market, the latter about 12–15%. It therefore provides an incomplete picture of how market conditions change. The market price index is also based only on prices of consumer products and producer goods sold to farmers on the free market. It too does not accurately reflect changing supply and demand relationships partly because these markets are often regulated by the government, partly because goods sold on the free market are sometimes of a better quality than those delivered to the state, and partly because demand for goods on the free market includes some demand that the state distribution system has failed to satisfy at government regulated prices. In the case of the GNP deflator, biases originate from such sources as the use of gross output of rural enterprises in current prices as the constant price series, and the calculation of value added in constant prices by the single deflation method. See Yang Guodong, "Comments on reforming the method of compiling China's retail price index," *Jiage yuekan* (*Prices Monthly*), No. 5 (1991), pp. 36–7, 46.

TABLE 9. *Measures of Inflation, 1980–90 (% increase over preceding year)*

	Retail prices	Market prices	GNP deflator
1980	6.0	2.0	3.7
1981	2.4	6.6	2.2
1982	1.9	3.5	0
1983	1.5	4.1	1.4
1984	2.8	0.3	4.6
1985	8.8	16.9	9.0
1986	6.0	7.7	4.6
1987	7.3	15.8	5.0
1988	18.5	31.9	11.8
1989	17.8	9.7	9.2
1990	2.1	–	4.1
1991	2.9	–	–1.5

Source:
TJNJ 1990, pp. 249, 269; *TJZY* 1991, pp. 5, 38; *RMRB*, 29 February 1992, p. 2; SSB, *Zhongguo shangye waijing tongji ziliao 1952–88 (Statistics of China's Commerce and External Economic Relations 1952–88)* (Beijing, 1990), p. 401.

open and repressed inflation. Virtually all the classic elements were present: excess aggregate demand fuelled by monetary expansion, rising wages outstripping productivity increase, persistent structure imbalances and ineffective macro-economic policy. However, it appears that excess demand, rather than cost-push, was the principal cause, even though the other factors contributed to the problem.

Table 10 shows the annual growth rates of the sum of GNP and imports in constant prices in 1980–89 to approximate the percentage increase in real supply; and the annual growth rates of the sum of consumption, investment and exports in current prices to represent the percentage change in aggregate spending on final demand. Throughout the period, aggregate spending expanded faster than real supply. The difference was particularly large in 1985 and 1988, the two years with peak inflation rates. Faster growth of aggregate spending implies an aggregate supply–demand gap if there is excess or balanced demand in the initial year.[112] In this case there was an initial gap in 1980, a year with moderate inflation.

[112] The SSB has its own method of calculating the supply-demand gap. Supply and demand are defined the same way as the concepts used here, except that aggregate supply is measured in current prices, both with and without a one-year time lag. See Wu Peibin, "On the analysis and accounting of aggregate supply and demand balance," *JJYJ*, No. 10 (1991), pp. 34–9. Conceptually, aggregate supply and demand in current prices as ex-post measures cannot deviate from each other except for statistical discrepancies. They are therefore meaningless as a measure of the supply-demand gap. The gap based on the one-year lagged supply is mean-

TABLE 10. *Aggregate Supply and Demand: Annual Growth Rates, 1980–89 (%)*

	Aggregate supply	Total	Consumption	Aggregate demand Investment	Exports
1980	7.5	12.2	15.9	3.2	24.7
1981	5.6	8.2	10.2	−3.2	43.7
1982	6.0	7.8	6.1	10.5	12.3
1983	9.2	11.8	11.8	14.3	4.3
1984	14.2	21.8	17.5	27.4	36.5
1985	16.5	29.4	20.2	47.5	32.9
1986	7.1	14.5	10.9	15.6	33.1
1987	9.1	15.8	11.4	16.4	36.5
1988	11.2	22.7	24.2	21.1	20.9
1989	4.4	13.0	17.8	6.2	10.7

Source:
World Bank, *World Tables 1991*, (Washington, D.C., 1991), pp. 184–5.

At the heart of the problem was the sharp rise in investment after 1981. Because of the sizeable share of investment in aggregate demand, its contribution to the growth of aggregate spending was substantial. In 1985, growth of investment expenditures accounted for 48 per cent of the growth of aggregate spending, by far the most important factor. Even in 1988, when the growth of consumption became more important, growth in investment still contributed about one-third of the increase in aggregate demand.

To a large extent, the rapid increase in investment came from rising investment by local governments, enterprises, farm households and foreign investors with their own funds or borrowings from financial institutions. From 1981 to 1989 these categories of investment increased at an average annual rate of 23.8 per cent, compared with only 2.3 per cent growth in investments financed through the state budget.[113] A series of institutional changes set off a rapid increase in extra-budgetary investment, including the use of bank loans rather than government grants as the primary method of funding investment, decentralization of decision-making power that enabled enterprises to retain and allocate portions of their earnings, and the opening of the coastal areas to foreign investment. But it was mainly the

ingful, but the assumptions of the length of the lag and its constancy over the period need to be empirically tested.

[113] Total investment financed by funds outside the state budget increased from 99.6 billion *yuan* in 1981 to 550.7 billion *yuan* in 1989. Investment by the central government increased from 29.3 to 35.2 billion *yuan* over the same period. Total investment is derived as the sum of gross fixed investment and investment in working capital. For sources, see *TJNJ* 1990, pp. 47, 153, 236; State Statistical Bureau, *Zhongguo guding zicaitouzi tongji ziliao 1950–85 (Statistics of China's Fixed Investment 1950–85)* (Beijing, 1987), p. 8. The total investment derived from these sources is slightly different from that in *World Tables 1991*, p. 185.

strong propensity of enterprises to invest that provided the driving force behind investment growth.

In the private and rural enterprises, the predominant motive was clearly profit. For state enterprises, the emphasis remained on the growth of output as the main performance indicator, with the tendency to increase output through investment.[114] The incentive to invest was further strengthened by the relatively cheap cost of capital, the preferential treatment given to state enterprises by banks, and the enterprises' soft budget constraint, which virtually eliminated the risk of having to pay for investment failures.

The "investment hunger syndrome" of enterprises had the strong support of the local governments, because their interests coincided to a large extent. First, a larger volume of business created by new investment meant more revenue for the local governments. Moreover, more investment resulted in more jobs and social stability. There was also the possibility that economic progress in the region would enhance the political power of the local government.

The rapid rise in investment by the peasants is another story. From 1981 to 1989 their total fixed investments increased from 16.6 to 89.2 billion *yuan*,[115] of which 70 per cent was investment in residential housing. This reflected the peasants' pent-up demand for better living conditions, the rapid growth of population and the limited availability of consumer goods and services in rural areas. In addition, the peasants' fear that collectivization might some day be reinstituted deterred them from investing in farm land. As a result resources that could have contributed directly to agricultural production were concentrated in housing.

Growth of money supply

The sharp rise in aggregate demand could not have occurred without large increases in money supply. As Table 11 shows, money currently in circulation (M1), currency and demand deposits (M2) and money supply broadly defined (M3), all expanded at two-digit levels annually throughout 1979–88 – substantially above real GNP growth. Part of the increase in money supply was related to the monetization of the Chinese economy and had little to do with inflation, but it nevertheless undoubtedly played a crucial role in the inflation process.[116]

---

[114] Gross value of output has been used to evaluate performance to calculate taxes and profits, and to measure labour productivity. Ma Bin, *On China's Population Problem*, p. 65. A set of new indicators based on value added will be introduced in the second quarter of 1992, *RMRB*, 19 February 1992, p. 1.

[115] SSB, *Fixed Investment, 1950–85*, p. 16; *Fixed Investment, 1986–87*, p. 285; *TJNJ* 1990, p. 220.

[116] World Bank, 1989, p. 51. For interesting models of money supply and inflation, see Gregory Chow, *The Chinese Economy* (New York, 1985), pp. 223–7, and "Money and price level determination in China," *Journal of Comparative Economics*, No. 3 (1987), pp. 319–33.

TABLE 11. *Annual Growth Rates of Money Supply and GNP, 1979–89 (%)*

	M1	M2	M3	GNP
1979	26.3	58.8	49.2	7.1
1980	29.3	24.7	25.8	6.4
1981	14.5	17.1	18.3	4.9
1982	10.8	10.6	14.6	8.3
1983	20.6	17.5	19.7	10.0
1984	49.5	43.8	32.6	13.4
1985	24.7	20.0	35.5	12.2
1986	23.3	27.9	30.2	7.8
1987	19.4	18.5	25.3	9.8
1988	46.6	20.0	20.7	10.0
1989	9.8	6.3	18.6	3.0

Notes:
  M1 = currency in circulation.
  M2 = M1 plus demand deposits.
  M3 = M2 plus savings deposits.
Source:
  World Bank, *World Tables 1991*, pp. 184–5. GNP growth
  rates are based on totals in constant prices.

The rising demand for money derived mainly from the business sector's attempt to finance fixed investment and working capital, and from the central government's efforts to cover budget deficits. As soon as the method of financing investment changed from direct allocations of funds from the state budget to the use of bank credit in the early 1980s, growth of output, which depends heavily on investment, became closely tied to credit expansion. The motivation to expand output was strong. While capital was no longer cost-free, the debt burden was not a major consideration under soft budget constraints.[117] Hence, the demand for credit from the enterprises was also strong.[118]

From 1978, the government faced budget deficits averaging over 2 per cent of GNP every year.[119] In the early 1980s the deficit was largely financed by overdrafts from the People's Bank of China (PBC).[120] In subsequent years, overdrafts remained sizeable, although bond sales became more important. Even then, the budget deficit could still be inflationary, because

[117] The tax provision that allows enterprises to deduct loan repayments before applying the tax rate is an added incentive for enterprises to borrow. Ma Hong and Gao Shanquan, *Zhongguo tonghuo pengzhan yanjiu* (*A Study of China's Inflation*) (Beijing, 1990), p. 110.
[118] The SSB data show that in 1989, total fixed investment finance by loans accounted for only 21.1%. *TJNJ* 1990, p. 153. As explained in Ma Hong and Gao Shanquan, *China's Inflation*, p. 125, this figure understates the importance of loans, because included in "funds raised by investors themselves" are loans from non-bank financial organizations, sales of bonds and securities, and the diversion of loans for working capital to fixed investment.
[119] *TJNJ* 1990, pp. 229–32; *TJZY* 1991, p. 5, 33.   [120] World Bank, 1989, p. 147.

individuals or enterprises who bought treasury bonds with their own retained earnings could pressure the banks for credit to fund the investments.[121]

The intense demand for credit could have been checked by tight monetary policies. However, this did not happen mainly because of the weak financial system. At this stage, capital markets hardly existed, so that banks were practically the only source borrowers could turn to for capital. Yet China's banking system was still in transition from the mono-banking of the pre-1980s to one that could function as a financial intermediary and monetary authority in a market-based economy.

The responsibility of monetary management falls on the PBC. The Bank's two principal missions are to maintain price stability and support economic growth. It has so far been more successful in meeting the latter than the former objective. This is not because the PBC has no instruments to tighten credit, but rather because the government has been unwilling to apply a credit squeeze persistently enough to check monetary expansion.[122] The PBC first assumed the role of central bank in 1984, but it has not had the strong support of a powerful political constituency, an essential precondition for a central bank to assert its independence from government intervention.[123] At the same time, the local branches of the PBC and the specialized banks were politically too weak to resist the pressure from local authorities. Thus, when the central and local government demanded credit from the banks, the latter had no alternative but to acquiesce. The result was the phenomenal growth of money supply, and with it, inflation.

Structural factors

Apart from the aggregate demand–supply gap, structural imbalance was also a contributory factor in China's inflation.[124] That structural problems existed is suggested by persistent bottlenecks in some strategic sectors, monopolistic and monopsonistic market structures, and financial subsidies. Among these, perhaps most significant was the mismatching of the compositions of demand and output. Before 1978, the planners determined simultaneously what the economy should produce and what people should consume. The output structure was lopsided, reflecting planners' strong preference for heavy industries in their drive towards forced industrialization. Other sectors, particularly agriculture, consumer manufacture and the infrastructure, lagged far behind. With the limited development of markets

---

[121] Zhang Zhunbin, "Fiscal analysis of China's inflation," *Xinhua wenzhai* (*Xinhua Digest*), Nos. 7–8, (1989), p. 67.

[122] World Bank, 1989, p. 47.   [123] World Bank, 1989, p. 55.

[124] Ma Jiantang, "A structural analysis of China's inflation," *Xinhua wenzhai*, Nos. 7–8 (1989), pp. 62–5; Ma Hong and Gao Shanquan, *China's Inflation*, pp. 80–8.

in the 1980s, consumers now had some freedom to choose what they bought. As their incomes rose, pent-up demand surfaced and new tastes developed, their consumption pattern shifted toward manufactured products, better quality food, clothing and shelter, and services, all of which the pre-1978 system was ill-prepared to provide. The immediate effect of the emerging structural imbalance was a rise in the prices of commodities in short supply.[125] Price rises of individual commodities do not generally by themselves constitute inflation. However, in this case, they indirectly generated strong inflationary pressure. Chinese consumers had been accustomed to fixed prices for decades. A sharp rise in price of even a small number of commodities could cause widespread discontent. To avoid social unrest, the government either absorbed the price increase in the form of subsidies (as in the case of grain) or adjusted wages upwards to keep the workers' real income from falling. Both measures were necessarily inflationary, unless subsidies could be offset by reductions in budget expenditure on other items (or an increase in budget revenues), and wage increases were accompanied by productivity increases. As it happened, government budget expenditure rose continuously during 1980–89, and the growth of industrial productivity fell behind that of wage rates.[126]

The mismapping of demand and supply was by no means confined to consumer goods. Imbalances in the demand and supply of intermediate goods were even more serious, as evidenced by the shortages of energy, water, transport facilities and basic raw materials. The imbalances inevitably created inflationary pressure in one form or another. In the case of infrastructural facilities, prices were strictly controlled and were adjusted only intermittently. Here the inflationary pressure was suppressed, but was still present. The suppression actually tended to widen the supply–demand gap, because the artificially low prices discouraged conservation and investment in these sectors. For key producer goods, a dual price system was introduced, with planned output distributed at mandated below-market prices, and output in excess of quota sold at relatively higher negotiated or market prices. Because mobility of factors between departments, sectors and regions was still restricted, producers could not easily increase output in response to higher market prices. Supply therefore tended to remain relatively inelastic, and market prices and costs to the users relatively high. For those commodities sold only at market prices, a supply–demand imbalance naturally led to higher prices.

Price increases of individual commodities tended to spread to others, because many producers faced sellers' markets, because they enjoyed a certain degree of monopolistic power, or simply because of the conven-

---

[125] In 1980–89, the retail prices of the following rose much faster than the general retail price index: pork, beef, mutton, aquatic products, vegetables, synthetic fibre, cloth, coal and lumber, *TJNJ* 1990, pp. 250, 282.

[126] *TJZY* 1991, pp. 33, 43, 80.

tional practice of setting prices on a cost-plus basis. Sometimes the down-stream enterprises took advantage of the situation and raised their output prices more than the increase in input prices.[127]

To redress the structural imbalances, it was necessary to adjust the output structure by diverting more resources to sectors with insufficient supply. Such restructuring of investment would have to be made largely by the local governments, enterprises and farm households whose decisions were guided by their own interests and relative prices. Unfortunately, the distorted price system displayed the wrong signals. The prices of infrastructural services and basic raw materials were kept artificially low in comparison with those of processed products, which in turn lowered their profit rates per unit of capital.[128] Consequently, the bulk of investment flowed into processing industries.[129] What emerged was an industrial structure tilted towards light processing industries, instead of one emphasizing heavy producer goods. Despite recent efforts by the central government to invest more in energy, transport and agriculture, the output structure was still lopsided and was likely to remain so for some time.

The unbalanced output and investment structures clearly had unfavourable effects on the aggregate supply–demand gap. First, when bottlenecks appeared, the result was excess capacities and under-employment of labour in the downstream industries, lowering production. Secondly, sectors in need of investment, such as agriculture, were neglected, perpetuating the bottlenecks. Thirdly, in their rush to invest in the processing industries, enterprises in different provinces undertook similar projects, and the duplication gave rise to regional protectionism, as noted above. The effect of all these inefficiencies was that investment increased aggregate demand, but did not raise aggregate supply to its potential level, thus intensifying the pressure on the general price level.

Economic reform and inflation

The extent to which inflation was related to price reform, or indeed to economic reform in general, should be considered. China's approach to price reform has been to adjust the controlled prices of some commodities or services and decontrol the prices of others. Since 1978, a series of price adjustments has been made, almost all upwards by a relatively small amount. Because China's prices had been frozen for decades, the resulting

---

[127] For example, in 1988 the factory prices of products for extracting industries rose by 9.3% over 1987, those for raw materials industry by 13.5% and those for processing industry by 14.7%. Ma Hong and Gao Shanquan, *China's Inflation*, p. 110.

[128] For example the amount of profit and taxes generated per 100 *yuan* of capital was 1.28 *yuan* in coal mining, compared to 230.52 *yuan* in cigarette manufacturing in 1985, *TJNJ* 1986, p. 325.

[129] In addition to higher returns to capital, the processing industries required less capital and less time to build, and their products were in demand in the 1980s.

distortions generally required quite large adjustments. To minimize the impact, the planners made several small changes at intervals instead of a single large one. The effect of these changes has so far been mixed. Some had virtually no impact on the general price level, as in 1979 and 1990. Others triggered panic buying and led to sharply rising prices as in 1988.

The different outcomes are not difficult to understand. Price adjustments by themselves do not cause inflation. However, under certain conditions, consumers and producers facing high adjusted prices may react in a way that creates strong inflationary pressures, such as when the general public anticipates continued price increases. This was what happened in 1988. Another inflationary situation can arise when the marginal propensity to spend within the economy as a whole rises as the re-alignment of relative prices redistributes income and profits. This was apparently the case in the agricultural sector, when adjustments of agricultural prices, together with other factors, markedly increased peasants' income, and in turn led to the dramatic increase in their investment in housing construction. A third possibility is when enterprises facing adjusted prices pass on the price increase to their customers. Such practices not only spread the price increases from one industry to another, but also neutralize the effect of the reform, creating the need for another round of price adjustment. The impact of price adjustments for agricultural inputs on agricultural output prices in 1989 is a case in point.[130]

Before 1980, most prices were set by the state. By 1990, two-thirds of agricultural products, over 80 per cent of manufactured consumer goods, almost all services and one-third of producer goods were being traded at market prices.[131] Prices almost always rose once they were decontrolled. The price increases were apparent rather than real, because the controlled prices were initially set at levels below the shadow prices, and removing the control simply brought into the open the previously concealed higher prices. According to the World Bank, perhaps half the price increase during 1980–87 represented realignment of relative prices.[132] In the long run, the freeing of prices would contribute to allocative efficiency and thereby reduce the inflationary pressure caused by the distorted industrial structure.

Price reform was only one component of the reform programme. As noted above, other reform measures also affected the aggregate supply–demand balance and money supply. For example, decentralization of decision-making power had resulted in excessive spending by local governments, enterprises and farm households. However, it is important to note

---

[130] Ai Hongri, "The inevitable trend of rising prices and countermeasures," *Jiage lilun yu shijian* (*Price Theory and Practice*), No. 7 (1991), pp. 4–5; Ren Caifang, Ji Yeping and Pang Xiaolin, "Structural adjustments of current prices: an exploration," *Tongji yanjiu* (*Statistical Research*), No. 1 (1991), p. 22.

[131] *China Daily*, 23 February 1991, p. 2.

[132] World Bank, 1989, p. 39. See also Liu Guangdi, "Correctly understand the meaning of inflation," *Caimao jingji* (*Economics of Finance and Trade*), No. 3 (1988), p. 31.

that this occurred in an environment of imperfect markets, poor financial discipline and the absence of an effective macroeconomic control mechanism. In short, incoherent and incomplete reforms did create inflationary pressures. But it was not the reforms themselves that caused the difficulties but the lack of a decisive, co-ordinated programme.

Policy measures 1988–90

As inflation became rampant by mid-1988, the leadership took drastic action to check price increases: the price reform announced in June was indefinitely postponed; state investments in 1989 were to be cut by one-fifth; local authorities were told to restrain enterprises from raising wages and bonus payments; import controls were eased; there was a tightening of money supply; lending rates and bank reserve ratios were raised; the PBC's lending to the specialized banks was restricted; and the PBC would now monitor the branch banks' lending on a monthly basis.[133] By late 1989, the inflation had lost its momentum, and the retail price index fell sharply in 1990. Such success was largely the result of direct credit control and administrative regulation of investment. Perhaps equally important was the fact that the central leadership exerted strong political pressure on local authorities to implement the centre's policies. Most of the monetary policies were not very effective. The increase of the bank reserve ratio by one percentage point could not have been very significant.[134] Likewise, interest rate increases from 7.2 to 8.6 per cent for deposits and from 7.9 to 9.0 per cent for loans were inconsequential, when the retail price index was rising at 17 per cent.[135]

In 1991, the threat of inflation had all but disappeared. The general retail price index increased by only 2.9 per cent over 1990.[136] However, the very fact that price stability was achieved largely through direct controls leaves open the possibility of a vicious circle. Direct controls check inflation, making it possible to resume economic restructuring. But piecemeal reforms soon unleash inflationary forces again, necessitating the return to direct controls because of the lack of an effective monetary management mechanism. The real danger at this stage is that the fundamental factors underlying the strong propensities to spend remain deep-rooted in the system. In addition, there is the large and growing monetary overhang. The general public's financial assets at the end of 1988 have been estimated at

[133] See also Zhang Zhuyuan, "Continue to control inflation, wait for an opportunity to improve the price structure," *JJYJ*, No. 12 (1989), pp. 3–6.

[134] Besides, the specialized banks held excess reserves amounting to almost twice the required reserves, World Bank, 1989, p. 45.

[135] Apparently, the leadership was reluctant to raise interest rates by a wide margin, possibly because it might push more state-owned enterprises into the red and thus increase the state budget deficit, and also because it might fuel a cost-push inflation.

[136] *RMRB*, 29 February 1992, p. 2.

610.6 billion *yuan* – about four times the increase in money supply in 1988. Of this total, bank deposits and currency accounted for 62.5 and 28.5 per cent respectively.[137] These assets could be highly volatile. Yet the relatively low interest rate maintained by the government provides little incentive for the public to keep their savings in the bank for long periods. In view of all this, it is not at all certain that inflation will not increase again.

The Ten-Year Programme and the Eighth Five-Year Plan

A cursory perusal of the proposals for the Ten-Year Development Programme and the Eighth Five-Year Plan indicates that, in terms of planning techniques, Chinese leaders have come a long way since the 1950s when the First Five-Year Plan was formulated without a single reference to population or national income, the two most important indicators in any development plan. There are two new features in the current proposals.[138] The Eighth Five-Year Plan is set against the framework of the Ten-Year Programme. The ten-year perspective not only calls attention to the long-term problems but also ensures consistency of medium-term measures with long-term objectives. However, despite the intention of following more rigorously the guiding principles of the 1980s (balanced industrial structure, openness to the outside world and reform), the central ideas underlying the proposal represent a distinct, if subtle, move away from the liberalization programme of the early 1980s. More significantly, both plan and programme fail to address fully the major problems noted above.

The documents are marked by compromise, ambiguities and contradictions, apparently mixed products to placate diverse political groups. However, it is abundantly clear that the current leadership's overriding concern is with stability. To maintain economic stability, the GNP growth rate for the 1990s is set at 6 per cent per annum, much lower than that achieved in the 1980s, for fear that a higher growth rate might overtax the economy's capacity and generate inflation once again. To ensure political stability, the document lists as its first principle of building socialism the need to uphold the "people's democratic dictatorship," and calls for an increase in military spending and ideological education. The concern over stability is a legitimate one. No real economic progress can be made when inflation is rampant. What the proposal lacks is an understanding that central planning and state control are only temporary stop gaps. The basic causes of instability, such as widespread unemployment, growing income disparities and persistent budget deficits, remain unresolved. The proposal over-emphasizes the control of aggregate demand, but fails to address an equally (if not more

[137] Ma Hong and Gao Shanquan, *China's Inflation*, pp. 139–41; *World Tables 1991*, p. 185.
[138] "Chinese Communist Party Central Committee's proposals for the Ten-Year Development Programme and the Eighth Five-Year Plan," *RMRB*, 29 January 1991, pp. 1–4 .

important) problem – that of how to increase effective aggregate supply. It also over-emphasizes short-term at the expense of long-term stability. Specifically, it offers no constructive solutions to the problems of capital shortage and economic reform.

The proposal correctly foresees the need to allocate more resources to agriculture, basic industries, the construction of infrastructure facilities, education, and science and technology. Increased spending will help to relieve the bottlenecks, but the impact will not be felt until after the mid-1990s, because almost all such investments have long gestation periods. At the same time, the plan to develop Pudong and the Three Gorges Dam will also require enormous investments over a long time. Yet, the proposal provides no concrete suggestions about how to finance these multi-billion *yuan* projects in the face of growing budget deficits and increasing financial losses of state-owned enterprises. Instead, the current leadership intends to increase defence expenditure and rejects any foreign investment in so-called "sunset" industries.[139]

According to the proposals, economic reform will continue gradually. The goal of reform is vaguely defined: "to institute a new system of planned commodity economy and an operational mechanism that combines planning and market regulation."[140] Five main tasks for reform in 1991–95 have been specified: to develop a multi-ownership system with public ownership (the main goal); to deepen the reform of enterprises; to accelerate the pace of price reform, solve the dual-track price system and set up markets; to perfect the macroeconomic control system by revamping tax distribution and strengthening the central bank's functions; and to accelerate the reform of the social insurance and housing systems. Notwithstanding the serious intention to continue the restructuring process, it is highly uncertain whether the planned programme will contribute much to productivity growth.

First, in carrying out reform the leadership follows the same gradual, piecemeal approach which has so far proved ineffective. While the proposal calls for a variety of reforms, including that of wages, the financial system and the commercial and material supply system, its focus is on revitalizing the large and medium-sized state-owned enterprises. Yet no co-ordinated programme and no new measures have been proposed. Secondly, the thorny relationship between central government and the provinces remains unchanged. The existing contract system of revenue sharing remains intact. All the problems it created, such as regional blockades and duplicate construction projects, will continue to hinder productivity growth, because sub-optimization at the provincial level inevitably results in diseconomies of scale.

---

[139] *Asian Wall Street Journal*, 10 October 1990, p. 3.
[140] *RMRB*, 26 February 1991, p. 1; *Beijing Review*, 11–17 February 1991, p. 31.

To sum up, the 1980s witnessed unprecedented growth in GNP, and with it profound changes in the economic structure, standard of living and employment. High rates of capital formation and a sharp rise in total factor productivity have been the main sources of growth. Looking towards the 1990s, one sees many formidable obstacles to sustaining the growth of capital stock and factor productivity. Most of these have their roots in the economy of the pre-1990 period. Some the leadership can do very little about, such as the changing age structure of the population, rising marriage rate and clustering of foreign debt services in the 1990s. But there are other areas in which the choice of policy probably will make a difference. These options include the full use of idle resources, the allocation of more resources to meet the urgent demand for human capital, infrastructural capital and replacement capital and system reform.

The proposals for the Ten-Year Programme and the Eighth Five-Year Plan feature important guidelines to cope with various aspects of these problems. But they stop short of a bold and dynamic programme for reform, and planned investment in human capital is grossly inadequate. The goals are modest and can probably be attained, perhaps relying more on capital formation than on productivity growth. Barring any drastic political change, reform will continue, albeit intermittently, at a slow pace and on a piecemeal basis. The gradualist approach may be less painful and less risky in the short term. But it will not achieve major breakthroughs in China's economic modernization.

Agricultural Development in China Since 1978

Robert F. Ash

The Legacy of Reform

The diversity of China's agricultural experience during the 1980s highlights the challenges and opportunities facing the farm sector during the present decade. Until 1985 agriculture's performance was widely regarded as an unqualified success. Decollectivization and institutional initiatives provided a framework which allowed, for the majority of farmers, an unprecedented degree of independence in decision-making. Farming was once more practised on a household basis, peasants' activities increasingly geared towards the market and their economic relationship with the state defined by legal contracts. Large increases in the purchase prices of major farm products provided the material incentive for the expansion of all branches of the agricultural economy. These same increases were the source of substantial gains in income, which contained the wherewithal for large-scale investment in agricultural production.

But from 1985 the story changes. It is true that in some areas – such as animal husbandry, sidelines and aquatic production – the pattern of expansion continued unchanged. In the crop sector, however, earlier growth gave way to stagnation. Simultaneously, the decline in state and local government support for agriculture (already in evidence in the first half of the 1980s) intensified, but was still unaccompanied by any offsetting rise in indigenous investment from within the farm sector. The improvement in incentives, consequent upon the previous purchase price increases, was also increasingly eroded by much sharper rises in input prices. This discouraged crop farming and in particular led to a disinclination to engage in its least profitable, but most important, branch – grain cultivation.

During the second half of the 1980s peasant worries about the state's commitment to a de-collectivized agriculture mirrored uncertainty amongst Party and government leaders about the future direction of agricultural strategy. Some looked to more radical reform measures in order to restore peasant confidence, rekindle their enthusiasm for crop production and encourage a more active involvement in long-term investment. In some ways, the logical destination of such thinking was the privatization of land ownership, although ideological retrenchment after 1988 made it difficult to articulate this view publicly. Others, on the pretext of seeking to realize economies of scale (*guimo jingying*), were advocates of a return to a more collectivist system of agriculture. Arguments over the role and extent of further price reform were corollaries of this debate.

Public-ownership of land has remained an ideological shibboleth, which has so far proved unassailable. By contrast, the primacy of planning has weakened, although even in the mid-1990s the central authorities seek to retain a residual role in order to resolve tensions arising out of conflicting priorities of the state and individual peasant. In any case, it bears repeating that the on-going debate over agricultural policy reflects very real *economic* dilemmas confronting the Chinese government. The evolution of a farming system guided by a "household responsibility system with remuneration linked to output" (*lianchan chengbao zerenzhi*) and the demise of collective agriculture no doubt had a profound effect in releasing peasant initiative. But the experience of agriculture after the attempted elimination of the state monopoly procurement system in 1985 demonstrates that the shift from a supply-orientated to a demand-orientated structure of production contained the seeds of a basic conflict between private and public interests. The 1985 policy decision was largely prompted by the appearance of supposedly unmanageable surpluses of grain and other farm products. It is an irony that one of the consequences of that decision was quickly to renew the spectre of a food crisis, as rational income-maximizing principles encouraged peasants to abandon grain production in favour of the cultivation of cash crops (or better still, to take up economic pursuits outside crop farming). Such a response suggests that it would be facile merely to condemn advocacy of more interventionist methods as wholly lacking any rational foundation.

There is evidence too that the demise of the collective system and its replacement by household-based operations have had adverse implications for long-term infrastructural investment in agriculture and left a void which remains unfilled. The summer floods of 1991 were perhaps the most spectacular recent manifestation of the critical role of water control in China. But there is no denying that funding, and implementing, such projects has become more difficult in the new, decentralized framework of farming.[1]

Such tensions were reflected in the *Ten-Year Development Programme (10YP) and Eighth Five-Year Plan (8FYP) for National Economic and Social Development*,[2] formally adopted by the National People's Congress (NPC) on 9 April 1991. The drafting process apparently got under way early

---

[1] As the evidence of Japan shows, the establishment of cooperative associations in order to promote backward and forward linkages and to guide rural finance may command a strong economic logic.

[2] *Zhonghua renmin gongheguo guomin jingji he shehui fazhan shinian guihua he dibage wunian jihua gangyao*, (*Outline of the 10-Year Programme and Eighth Five-Year Plan for National and Social Development*), (Beijing: People's Publishing House, 1991), hereafter *Jihua Gangyao*, pp. 75–155. The text can also be found in *Renmin ribao (People's Daily)*, hereafter *RMRB*, 16 April 1991. An English translation is available in British Broadcasting Corporation, *Summary of World Broadcasts, Part 3: The Far East*, hereafter *SWB*, FE/1058, 29 April 1991.

in 1990, the intention being to bring an initial draft before a plenary session of the CCP Central Committee in October of that year. In the event, differences of opinion over the nature of future economic strategy compelled a postponement of the meeting, which was not convened until December. Indeed Deng Xiaoping was reportedly so discouraged by the excessive centralist thrust of early formulations that he rejected the first draft, drawn up by Yao Yilin under the influence of Chen Yun's economic thinking.

The final document has been described as a compromise between the reformist urge of Deng Xiaoping and the more centralist convictions of Chen Yun. The evidence suggests that the final outline of the *10YP* and *8FYP* was, however, more closely in line with Deng's philosophy. In the earlier version,[3] for example, it was argued that excessive decentralization had come to characterize many areas of production, distribution and finance and that appropriate re-centralization of material and financial resources was necessary in order to obviate current difficulties. This section was omitted from the final, published version. Such differences between the two drafts, as well as ambiguities which remain in the final document,[4] are a reminder of tensions, which have continued to surround the formulation of agricultural policy and to threaten sustained agricultural growth during the 1990s.

Growth and Structural Change in the Agricultural Sector During the 1980s

Notwithstanding the difficulties which emerged during the second half of the 1980s, the decade as a whole remains a period of impressive growth and unprecedented structural change in China's agricultural sector. The average real rate of increase of agricultural gross value-output (GVAO) during the Sixth (6FYP) and Seventh Five-Year Plan (7FYP) periods (1981–85 and 1986–90) was, for example, 6.4 per cent per annum.[5] This compares with an average annual rate of growth of 4.7 per cent during the immediately preceding decade (1971–80); and 3.05 per cent between 1952 and 1970.[6] Table 1 summarizes the growth performance of major branches of

---

[3] This was the document which the Central Committee examined on 30 December 1990. See *SWB*, FE/0958, 31 December 1990.

[4] Such ambiguity is suggested by the advocacy of measures, designed simultaneously to "enhance the strength of the collective economy" and establish a "two-tier system combining unified and decentralized management." See also below.

[5] State Statistical Bureau, *Zhongguo tongji zhaiyao 1991 (A Statistical Survey of China 1991)*, hereafter *TJZY 1991* (Beijing: Statistical Publishing House, 1991), p. 53.

[6] In constant 1970 and 1957 prices, respectively. These figures are derived from data in Ministry of Agriculture (Planning Department), *Zhongguo nongcun jingji tongji daquan, 1949–86 (Compendium of Chinese Rural Economic Statistics, 1949–86)* (Beijing: Agricultural Publishing House, 1989), pp. 106 and 108.

TABLE 1. *The Growth of Agricultural Production in the 1980s*

| | Average rate of increase of total output (% p.a.) | | | |
	6FYP 1981–85	7FYP 1986–90	1981–90	Previous best five-year record
Food grains	3.4	3.3	3.4	4.2 (1966–70)
Cotton	8.9	1.6	5.3	4.7 (1953–57)
Oil seeds	15.4	0.4	7.7	1.8 (1971–75)
Sugar	15.8	3.6	9.5	9.4 (1953–57)
Pork	7.9	6.6	7.3	
Pork, beef and mutton	7.9	7.4	7.6	8.6 (1976–80)
Aquatic production	9.4	11.9	10.6	13.3 (1953–57)

Sources:
The estimates for pork are derived from data in *TJZY 1991*, p. 59. The remaining figures are available from State Statistical Bureau, *Zhongguo tongji nianjian, 1991 (Chinese Statistical Yearbook, 1991)*, hereafter *TJNJ 1991* (Beijing: Statistical Publishing House, 1991), pp. 346–8, 357 and 363.

agricultural production during the 1980s, as well as showing their previous best performance in a five-year period.

The peculiar role of grain in China's economic development lends its performance a special significance. It is interesting that the growth record of 1981–85 was bettered during the 3FYP period (1966–70), when the average rate of increase of total cereal production exceeded 4.2 per cent p.a. But such a comparison is misleading in one important respect: the increase in total output during 1966–70 was based on a largely unchanged sown area under grain, whereas during 1981–85 some 8.4 million hectares were taken out of cultivation (a decline of over 7 per cent). In short, the more recent growth performance was entirely dependent on improvements in yields.[7]

The less impressive performance of major branches of agriculture during the 7FYP also emerges from the table, although an examination of trends between 1984 and 1989 most dramatically highlights the onset of stagnation. In 1985, for example, production of grain and cotton fell by 6.92 and 33.73 (*sic*) per cent, although oil crop output continued to rise strongly. By 1989, only grain had reattained its previous peak. In short, the fact that the growth record of the 1980s has no precedent in any previous, comparable

[7] The relevant figures are as follows:

	Grain sown area (mill. ha.)	Av grain yield (tonnes/ha.)
1965	119.63	1.635
1970	119.27	2.010
1980	117.23	2.745
1985	108.85	3.480

See *TJNJ 1991*, pp. 340 and 353.

ten-year period since 1949 is largely attributable to the extraordinary expansion of production during 1981–84 and the fine harvest of 1990.[8]

The figures for meat and fish production highlight the exceptionally rapid expansion of non-crop farming branches of the agricultural sector. They also demonstrate a more stable pattern of sustained – and in the case of aquatic products, accelerated – growth over the two five-year plan periods. It is not surprising that while average per capita consumption of grain and edible oils has shown little or no increase since 1985, that of meat and fish continued to rise quite strongly.[9]

What Table 1 does not show is the extent to which planned targets were fulfilled in the 1980s. The estimates shown in Table 2 provide that missing information.

The achievements of the Sixth Five-Year Plan (1981–85) emerge clearly enough. What the figures conceal is that so rapid was agricultural growth in the wake of the early reforms that the targets were over-fulfilled well in advance of the Plan's end-year[10] – and, in the case of cotton and grain, by even larger margins than the 1985 estimates indicate.

If anticipated levels of production in the following (Seventh) plan were based on optimistic expectations engendered by such high rates of growth, it is interesting that despite post-1984 stagnation, so many of the 1990 production targets were also over-fulfilled (although, meat and fish apart, not in advance). The important exception is of course that of oil seeds, which suffered a shortfall of more than 10 per cent.

Associated with the growth record illustrated above was a process of dramatic structural change within the agricultural sector, which is described in Table 3.

The emerging pattern is clear. The 1980s witnessed a significant realignment of agricultural activities from crop cultivation towards other farm tasks. In particular, between 1984 and 1988 the share of crop farming – already in decline since 1978 – fell by more than 5 percentage points. The principal beneficiaries were animal husbandry and fisheries, whose combined share in agricultural GVO rose from 19.95 to 24.76 per cent. Admittedly, the cropping sector partially recovered its relative position during 1989–90, but not in such a way as to affect the general trend.[11]

---

[8] Increases in total production during 1990 were as follows: grain, 9.5%; oil crops, 24.6%; cotton, 19% (*TJNJ 1994*, p. 347).

[9] Compare the following figures:

	Average per capita consumption (kg. p.a.):			
	Grain	*Edible oil*	*Pork*	*Fish*
1980	213.81	2.30	11.16	3.41
1985	251.69	5.08	13.84	4.84
1990	238.80	5.67	16.64	6.53

(*TJNJ 1991*, p. 273).

[10] In 1982 for cotton, oil seeds and sugar, and in 1983 for food grains.

[11] For a detailed analysis of changes in the structure of agricultural production, as revealed by GVAO estimates, see Robert Michael Field, "Trends in the Value of Agricultural Output"

TABLE 2. *Planned and Realized Levels of Total Production of Major Branches of Agriculture: Achievements of the Sixth and Seventh Five-year Plans (1981–85 and 1986–90)*

(a) The Sixth Five-Year Plan (1981–85)

	1985 Planned output	1985 Actual output	Actual as % planned output
Food grains	360.0	379.11	105.31
Cotton	3.6	4.15	115.19
Oil seeds	10.5	15.78	150.32
Sugar	46.7	60.47	129.48
Pork		16.54	
All meats	14.6*	17.61	
Aquatic products	5.1	7.05	138.24

(b) The Seventh Five-Year Plan (1986–90)

	1990 Planned output	1990 Actual output	Actual as % planned output
Food grains	425.00–450.00	446.24	99.16–105.0
Cotton	4.25	4.51	106.07
Oil seeds	18.25	16.13	88.39
Sugar	68.75	72.15	104.94
Pork	18.30	22.81	124.65
All meats	22.75	28.00	123.08
Aquatic products	9.00	12.37	137.44

Notes:
  All figures in million tonnes.
  * Pork, beef and mutton only
Sources:
  Actual output figures from *TJNJ, 1991*, pp. 346–8, 357 and 363; and *TJZY, 1991*, p. 59.
  Output targets for 1985 from *Zhonghua renmin gongheguo guomin jingji he hehui fazhan diliuge wunian jihua (1981–85) (The Sixth Five-Year Plan of the PRC for National Economic and Social Development)* (Beijing, People's Publishing House: 1983), pp. 35–6 and 38–9. Output targets for 1990 from State Planning Commission, *Diqige wunian nongcun fazhan zhuanti jihua (Special Topics for the Development of the Rural Economy in the Seventh Five-Year Plan)* (Beijing, Agricultural Publishing House: 1986), pp. 54 and 56.

What is more, within the cropping sector itself profound changes in the pattern of land use were under way. For example, whereas in 1980 grain accounted for 80.1 per cent of China's total sown area, by 1990 it had fallen to 76.5 per cent.[12] The area sown to economic crops meanwhile rose from

in Y. Y. Kueh and R. F. Ash (eds.), *Economic Trends in Chinese Agriculture: The Impact of Post-Mao Reforms* (Oxford: Clarendon Press, 1993), pp. 123–60.

[12] *TJNJ, 1991*, p. 340.

TABLE 3. *Structural Change in Chinese Agriculture, 1980–1990*

	GVAO (excluding side-lines)	Crops	Forestry	of which: Animal rearing	Aquatic products
1980	100.00	76.73	4.25	17.15	1.88
1981	100.00	75.84	4.65	17.26	2.24
1982	100.00	76.25	4.65	16.82	2.28
1983	100.00	76.01	4.74	16.72	2.52
1984	100.00	75.18	4.87	17.18	2.77
1985	100.00	73.43	5.01	18.37	3.19
1986	100.00	73.96	5.14	17.70	3.20
1987	100.00	72.46	5.17	19.00	3.36
1988	100.00	70.01	5.22	21.15	3.61
1989	100.00	70.96	4.95	20.74	3.35
1990	100.00	72.43	5.06	19.25	3.26

Note:
  the above percentage estimates reflect the structure of agricultural gross value-output expressed in real terms.
Source:
  TJZY 1991, pp. 52–3.

10.9 to 14.4 per cent, whilst that under vegetables, green manure, etc. remained unchanged.[13]

It is worth noting that these data take no account of the single most important structural change of all in the countryside during the 1980s: the remarkable expansion of rural township and village enterprises (*xiangzhen qiye*). Its impact on the rural sector is suggested by the finding that in 1990 the contribution of such enterprises to rural social value-output had reached 59.1 per cent.[14]

Agricultural Strategy in the 1990s: An Overview

The preceding review of agricultural development and structural change defines the context in which the plans for the 1990s have been formulated and are being implemented. Impressive as the economic record of the 1980s may have been, the starting-point of any discussion of these plans must surely be the considerable pessimism which had come to inform official comment on agriculture's situation and prospects at the start of the new decade. The following remarks are typical:

[13] *Ibid.* The same source shows that in 1985 grain and economic crops accounted, respectively, for 75.8 and 15.6 per cent of the total sown area.
[14] *TJNJ 1991*, p. 65.

... the overall [agricultural] situation remains quite grim and our tasks in the days to come will be very arduous. . . . This year's [1990] total grain output is greater than that of 1984, but the per capita amount . . . is lower than that of 1984. . . . Cotton output . . . is greater than last year, but it still cannot meet state, consumer and export needs. We still need to import some edible oil, sugar, wool and rubber every year to make up for domestic shortages. . . .[15]

... Good harvests do not prove that China's overall agricultural production capacity has definitely reached a new level. In fact, the infrastructure and basic conditions have not fundamentally improved: the ability of our agriculture to withstand natural disasters is still very weak and the basis for faster agricultural development remains inefficient.[16]

... There is a significant imbalance between the rural economy and social development, and there are still many problems and many constraints. Population growth has been excessive and the contraction in total arable area has still not been brought under effective control. Investment in agriculture is inadequate, its material and technical foundation is weak, its capacity for comprehensive production is not high, and the ability to combat natural disasters is insufficient. . . .[17]

The caution and anxiety contained in such comments were reflected in the quite modest rates of growth targeted in the 10YP and 8FYP outline (see below). No doubt they reflected the disappointing performance of major crops during the second half of the 1980s. But more than that, they appeared to underline an awareness of the technical deficiencies of Chinese agriculture – deficiencies which had not been alleviated, and may have been exacerbated, by post-1978 reforms. They also expressed an awareness of China's continuing vulnerability to the vagaries of the weather.

A striking feature of the "first decade of reform" (1979–88) was the dramatic decline in agriculture's share of total state capital construction investment, as well as other forms of farm support.[18] Recovery was already under way in 1989 and 1990, and – on any rational criteria – ought[19] to have

---

[15] Vice-Premier Tian Jiyun, the government's most senior spokesman for agricultural affairs, addressing the 16th meeting of the seventh NPC Standing Committee in October 1990. See *SWB*, FE/0908, 30 October 1990.

[16] Zou Jiahua (minister of the State Planning Commission) in a written speech to a national meeting on exchanging experience in rural economic work: see *SWB*, FE/1012, 5 March 1991. Zou's views were echoed by Song Ping, addressing the same meeting: *SWB*, FE/1024, 19 March 1991.

[17] "Zhonggong zhongyang guanyu jinyibu jiaqiang nongye he nongcun gongzuo de jueding" ("Decision of the CCP Central Committee on further strengthening agriculture and rural work"), hereafter "CCPCC 1991", adopted by the eighth plenary session of the Thirteenth CCP Central Comittee on 29 November 1991. The text can be found in *Zhenjiang ribao (Zhenjiang Daily)*, 26 December 1991. It is translated in *SWB*, FE/1268, 3 January 1992.

[18] From 11.1% (1979) to 3.0% (1988). *TJNJ 1991*, p. 156. For an analysis of state investment in agriculture and other forms of financial support, see Robert F. Ash, "The Peasant and the State," *The China Quarterly*, No. 127 (September 1991), pp. 493–526.

[19] The word is carefully chosen. In 1978 the government gave an undertaking to increase investment allocations to agriculture (from 10 to 15–18 per cent) within a few years. A year or

continued through the 1990s. The 10YP/8FYP outline itself was reticent on this aspect, but other authoritative sources made it clear that state support for agriculture – whether through the central budget, from banks and credit cooperatives or through specially created development funds – would be increased.[20]

It was axiomatic that state investment should be reserved for *large-scale* projects, related to water conservancy, infrastructural construction and the establishment of grain and cotton production bases. Irrigation and water conservancy work would be a prime focus of state investment activity, not only in order to reverse infrastructural decline and extend China's irrigated area (by 2 million hectares by 1995),[21] but also to obviate the problems associated with severe flooding, such as occurred during 1991.[22]

Smaller-scale investment projects remained the prerogative of the collective sector and individual peasants. Against the background of the remarkable growth of rural, private savings deposits during the 1980s, Song Ping's statement that "the financial strength of individual [peasant] households is quite weak"[23] seemed disingenuous. It may, however, be that *non-farming* rural residents (especially those working in local enterprises) had accounted for much of those savings – which in any case began to decline after 1984.[24] This would account for the renewed emphasis on labour mobilization as a means of enhancing agricultural investment in the 1990s,[25] as well as on the need for rural industrial subsidies to agriculture.[26]

two later, it was clear that this commitment had been abandoned (see Nicholas R. Lardy, *Agriculture in China's Modern Economic Development* (Cambridge: Cambridge University Press, 1983), pp. 191–2).

[20] "CCPCC 1991" is quite explicit on this. Thus: ". . . During the 8FYP period, state investment in . . . capital construction projects will increase each year, supplemented by the expanded use of foreign funds. Government support funds for agricultural development will also be increased. Counties' non-committed financial reserves should be used mainly for agricultural development. Agricultural development funds and other funds designated for agricultural use must be used for their proper purpose. . . .

State banks should regard loans in support of agriculture as a priority and should ensure that the expansion of such loans is greater than that of the nation's bank loans. . . . Credit cooperatives should appropriately increase deposits and extend more loans in support of agricultural production." (*Zhenjiang ribao*, p. 5.)

[21] *Jihua Gangyao*, p. 105. As of 1993, a little over 1.3 million hectares had been added to the 1990 irrigated area (*TJNJ 1994*, p. 335).

[22] Acceleration of work designed to control major rivers and lakes did in fact take place in the wake of the publication of the 10YP/8FYP document. It is noteworthy that an entire section was devoted to this issue in "CCPCC 1991."

[23] *SWB*, FE/1024, 19 March 1991.

[24] Y. Y. Kueh has shown that between 1984 and 1988, the savings ratio of Chinese peasants fell from 22.9 to 12.5 per cent. During the three years from 1985 to 1987, their marginal propensity to save was negative. See "Food consumption and peasant incomes" in Kueh and Ash (eds.), *Economic Trends in Chinese Agriculture*, especially pp. 239–42.

[25] "CCPCC 1991." In the wake of decollectivization, such activities declined greatly in the 1980s. See Ash, "The peasant and the state", p. 499.

[26] That is, through the mechanisms of *yigong bunong* ("using industry to assist agriculture") and *yigong jiannong* ("using industry for agricultural construction"): see "CCPCC 1991." Both were used at different times in the 1980s in order to inject funds into the farm sector, but with

The *institutional* thrust of agricultural strategy during the 1990s was summed up in the advocacy of the creation a "two-tier operational system" (*shuangceng jingying tizhi*), which would integrate decentralized, household-based farming with a collectively-organized "socialized service system" (*shehuihua fuwu tixi*).[27] Its economic rationale lay in the realization that notwithstanding the success of the system of contracted responsibilities in stimulating peasant initiative during the 1980s, there were many farm tasks, embracing production and distribution, which lay beyond the scope of individual households. The provision of support in these areas – whether to facilitate the development and application of better inputs, encourage infrastructural capital formation or promote the sale of farm produce – would therefore be more effectively (and cheaply) organized on a collective basis.

Even from the perspective of the mid-1990s, it remains questionable to what extent this duality of approach can be transformed into an organic whole, rather than become a divisive force in the countryside. At the beginning of the 1980s it was emphatically denied that advocacy of decentralized agricultural decision-making contained any anti-collectivist hint. Yet within a few years the collective system itself had fallen victim to the new policy. At the beginning of the 1990s there were signs that the emphasis had been reversed. Tian Jiyun was one senior figure who stressed the complementarity between collective and household responsibilities towards contracts,[28] even arguing that the 1980s had seen excessive emphasis on "separate management" to the neglect of "unified management."[29] Hence, no doubt, official encouragement of the expansion of the collective economy.[30]

But these same sources were careful to warn against collective encroachment on household operations. For example, an editorial in *People's Daily* cautioned that "... we cannot expand the collective economy by taking back land contracted to the peasants."[31] Significantly, it added that the

mixed results. See Robert F. Ash, "Agricultural Policy under the Impact of Reform" and Terry Sicular, "Ten Years of Reform: Progress and Setbacks in Agricultural Planning and Pricing", Kueh and Ash (eds.), *Economic Trends in Chinese Agriculture*.

[27] *Jihua Gangyao*, p. 102.

[28] Thus: "... Ownership of land belongs to the collective. Individuals merely possess the right of operation, but cannot sell or lease the land.... Contractors must pay taxes to the state according to law, sell farm produce to the state at prices set by the state, and deliver funds and contract fees to the collective in accordance with the terms of the contract." Tian Jiyun in *Nongmin ribao (Farmers' Daily)*, 9 October 1991, translated in *SWB*, FE/1234, 20 November 1991.

[29] *SWB*, FE/1269, 4 January 1992.

[30] For example, *Nongmin ribao*, 9 October 1991, which urged that "... our attention should be focused on expanded reproduction rather than [on] the few *mou* of peasants' land...." The same source expected that peasants who abandoned farming for industrial or tertiary occupations would release their land "to the collective for unified operation." See also *RMRB*, 22 December 1991, which stated that: "... Socialist agriculture should be based on the continuous development of the collective economy...."

[31] *Ibid.*

further development of the collective sector should be achieved on the basis of self-accumulation, not by indiscriminate levies on peasants. In short, the contractually-based household responsibility system was to be retained as a permanent feature of the institutional framework of China's agriculture.

Even allowing for flexible policies, the simultaneous advocacy of individual and collective economic activities seemed decidedly ambiguous. It is true that advocacy of extended collective operations was not incompatible with a continuing emphasis on household-based farm production. But it would be a supreme irony if – paralleling developments in the early 1980s – a revanchist emphasis on the collective economy threatened to undermine the very policies which had made such a positive contribution to increased production during those years.[32]

The conjunction of major agricultural price and output increases between 1979 and 1984 was not of course coincidental. The greater surprise is that despite even larger price rises after 1984,[33] the output of many crops did not continue to respond in the same way. One explanation is that during much of the second half of the decade, the benefits of further purchase price rises were eroded by sharp increases in the cost of inputs (especially chemical fertilizers), which lowered the net return from crop farming.[34] Circumstantial evidence supports this supposition. For example, official data show the purchase price index of farm and sideline products to have risen almost two-and-a-half times faster than that of "agricultural production materials" between 1978 and 1985; by contrast, during 1986–90 the average annual rate of increase was almost the same for both categories.[35] Moreover, from 1985 to 1990 the annual increase in the purchase price of *grain* was less than that of farm and sideline products as a whole in four out of the six years.[36] Not

[32] *RMRB*, 13 December 1991, "Several issues concerning current rural work," makes the point that in some regions of China agreed fees had been illegally increased and contracted land taken back from the peasants. For more recent evidence of trends towards re-collectivization, see *The Asian Wall Street Journal*, 13 March 1995.

[33] During 1979–84 the average annual increase in the purchase price of agricultural and sideline products was 7.62% (Hu Bangding (ed.), *Zhongguo wujia nianjian, 1990 (Chinese Price Yearbook, 1990)*, hereafter *ZGWJNJ*, (Beijing, State Price Publishing House, 1990), p. 431). During 1985–89 the corresponding figure was 13% (State Statistical Bureau, *Zhongguo wujia tongji nianjian, 1990 (Chinese Statistical Yearbook of Prices, 1990)*, hereafter *WJTJNJ 1990* (Beijing, State Statistical Publishing House, 1990), p. 113). That this pattern applied to grain is demonstrated by Claude Aubert: see his *Rural China, 1985–90: Are the Reforms Really Bogging Down?* (Chinese University of Hong Kong, Institute of Asia-Pacific Studies: Universities Service Centre Seminar Series, 1991), p. 4. Notice that these figures do not take account of changes in market prices.

[34] Aubert (*Rural China*, pp. 6–7) shows this to have been the case for both grain and cotton production.

[35] The relevant data can be found in *TJNJ 1991*, pp. 230 and 234. They should, however, be interpreted with some caution, for it seems likely that the category of "agricultural production materials" is narrowly defined and excludes certain critical agricultural inputs – notably, chemical fertilizers. Not until sufficient data are available to facilitate an analysis of price trends for a truly representative range of goods bought by farmers will it be possible to confirm that the price terms of trade did turn significantly against the farm sector during the second half of the 1980s.

[36] *WJTJNJ 1991*, p. 115.

until 1989 did an annual rise in the purchase price of grain exceed that of meat, fish, or fresh vegetables.[37]

During the 1980s *market* prices admittedly came to play an increasingly important role in the purchase of agricultural products. Such liberalization was most apparent in the meat, fish, vegetable and fruit sectors, whose output showed rapid and sustained growth throughout the decade (see Table 1 above). But elsewhere, its impact was less. In particular, in the interests of maintaining control over the supply of basic items, the state chose to retain its monopoly over cotton purchases, whilst instituting a "two-track [pricing] system" (*shuangguizhi*) for grain.

That price deregulation contributed to the vitality of the meat, fish, fruit and vegetable sectors seems undeniable. But it is as well to bear in mind that rising demand also kept the prices of these products buoyant. By contrast, in the face of the bumper harvests of 1989 and 1990, grain farmers were unable to find sufficient *state* outlets for their produce and turned to the free market. One consequence was that in 1990 excess supply seems to have been responsible for a sharp fall in the market price which they could command.[38]

Analysis of the movement of market prices for grain during the 1980s confirms the unstable production performance of the cereal sector. Between 1980 and 1985, the market price of grain fell, on average, by about 2 per cent a year; by contrast, during the second half of the decade the trend was sharply reversed, the market price *rising* by an average of 14.5 per cent p.a.[39] It is true that following four years of sharp price rises, 1990 did witness a substantial decline (by 18.6 per cent). No doubt this was partly attendant

---

[37] See *WJTJNJ 1990*, p. 113. Not since 1979 had there been such a large increase in a single year.

[38] See, for example, Tian Jiyun in *SWB*, FE/1026. Official data show that market prices of grain fell by more than 18% in 1990 (*cf.* a decline of 6.8% for grain procurement prices): *TJNJ 1991*, pp. 248 and 254. See also Aubert, *Rural China*, p. 10.

Interestingly, Liu Zhongyi (then Minister of Agriculture) commented in 1990 that sales and storage difficulties affecting grain indicated not a surfeit of production, but "incompatibility in the circulation field" (Robert F. Ash, "Quarterly Chronicle and Documentation", hereafter "QCD", *The China Quarterly*, No. 126 (June 1991), p. 663.

[39] Market prices for 1980–88 can be found in State Statistical Bureau, *Zhongguo shangye waijing tongji ziliao, 1952–1988 (Statistical Materials Relating to China's Commerce and External Economic Relations, 1952–1988)* (Beijing: State Statistical Publishing House, 1990), p. 399. Data for 1989 and 1990 are from *WJTJNJ 1991*, p. 93. It is of some interest to compare market price trends for grain with those of fresh vegetables, fish, and meat and dairy produce: the latter three categories all experienced rising prices in both the first and second halves of the 1980s, although in no case was the average annual price increase after 1985 as great as that in the grain sector. Thus:

	Average increase in market price (% p.a.)	
	1981–85	*1986–90*
Grain	– 2.0	+ 14.5
Fresh vegetables	+ 8.6	+ 8.2
Meat, poultry and eggs	+ 6.7	+ 12.2
Fish	+ 13.8	+ 10.5

upon that year's bumper harvest. But it was also the product of other factors, including reduced industrial requirements of grain, falling cereal demand associated with lay-offs of construction workers who returned to their home villages, and the inadequate storage capacity of state warehouses.[40]

In any case, the experience of the 1980s suggested that price rises and price liberalization were powerful instruments of agricultural policy. At the same time, previous experience made it clear that care was needed to ensure that the potential benefits of purchase price adjustments were not eroded by higher input costs. In this respect, it was significant that the large price rise for grain producers in 1989 had been accompanied by efforts to improve farmers' incentives. For example, new rules stipulated that supplies of subsidized chemical fertilizer were to be increased from 3 to 10–15 kilograms for every 50 kilograms of grain delivered under contract to the state.[41]

Development plans for the 1990s in fact provided little detail on pricing policy. They did, however, show an awareness of the lessons of the previous decade in their explicit commitment to raise grain purchase prices and adjust urban retail prices in order to narrow the procurement-retail price differential.[42] There was also a reference to ". . . steadily making grain purchase prices the same as retail prices during the 8FYP period."[43] In this respect, the State Council decision to raise urban retail prices of grain and edible vegetable oil (May 1991 and April 1992) was an important initiative. No doubt the adjustments were primarily designed to reduce the increasingly serious budget deficit suffered by the central government in its grain transaction in circumstances in which the gap between procurement and retail prices had steadily widened during the 1980s. Special wage and pension supplements and other subsidies served to cushion the cost to urban residents and thereby dampened its impact. Nevertheless, the state's willingness to sanction such price increases introduced an added element of flexibility into its pricing policy, which was likely to impinge on urban demand for grain and oilseed products. The subsequent decision to abandon the use of urban grain coupons was another watershed, although their re-introduction during the first half of 1995 raised questions about the sustainability of markets as a means of distributing staple foods to every section of the population.[44]

[40] See ZGWJNJ 1991, p. 32.

[41] Specifically, 10 kilograms of fertilizer for deliveries of wheat and maize; 15 kilograms for husked rice and soyabeans. See ZGWJNJ 1990, p. 44.

[42] Jihua gangyao, p. 139.

[43] "CCPCC 1991."

[44] The likelihood is that the reintroduction of the coupons was intended to address the inadequacy of food supplies to the most disadvantaged elements of the urban population. Chinese officials meanwhile denied that the reappearance of coupons presaged a partial return to central planning and interventionist methods of food distribution in urban areas.

Maintaining a dual-pricing framework for cereals demanded the creation of extra storage facilities in order to facilitate grain purchases by local granaries. One response to this need was the state's establishment, in the summer of 1990, of a system of "special grain reserves."[45] The impact of this initiative was considerable and by October, the new warehouses had already purchased almost 18 million tonnes of grain.[46] That the new system could not wholly obviate difficulties was, however, made clear in a warning by the Minister of Agriculture, Liu Zhongyi, that storage problems were likely to appear, as well as in appeals to *local* governments to establish their own reserve systems.[47]

The shortage of granary space has exacerbated other difficulties associated with monetary and fiscal constraints. One was the shortage of cash with which to pay farmers for their grain. During the second half of the 1980s, local authorities' use of "IOUs" or "blank slips" (*baitiaozi*) in order to circumvent having to pay cash was the origin of a problem which was eventually to lead to demonstrations and violent protests by peasants in many provinces.[48]

Meanwhile, however, the state's commitment to buy large amounts of grain continued to threaten its fiscal viability. The extent of this threat was ominously suggested in the clear change of emphasis reflected in the following statements dating, respectively, from autumn 1990 and spring 1991:

... All localities ... [should] ... procure unlimited quantities of grain at the protected price in order to satisfy the peasants' demand to sell their surplus grain ... [49]

... We may consider changing procurement under the special grain reserve system from unlimited purchase to fixed quantity purchase, starting this year [1991], the size of purchase being decided by the state. After fulfilling the state procurement target and the special reserve target [the latter at a minimum protected price], excess grain would be channelled into the market.[50]

---

[45] The State Council's decision to build additional warehouses in order to accommodate anticipated additional grain sales was announced by Tian Jiyun in a report to the 16th session of the Seventh NPC Standing Committee on 27 October 1990. See Ash, "QCD", in *The China Quarterly*, No. 125 (March, 1991), pp. 192 and 202. Note that the novelty of the State Council's 1990 decision lay in its proposal to establish the system of special grain reserves, rather than to increase physical storage capacity. As Nicholas Lardy has pointed out, authorization to add 20 million tonnes to the national grain storage capacity was, for example, given by the State Council in 1983 (personal communication).

[46] See Aubert, *Rural China*, p. 12.

[47] Ash, "QCD", *The China Quarterly*, No. 127 (September 1991), pp. 663–4.

[48] One source reported that in the first half of 1993, more than 170 outbreaks of peasant disturbances and rioting had occurred throughout China (Hong Kong, *South China Morning Post*, 27 June 1993). The most notorious case was that of Renshou county in Sichuan province (see *SWB*, FE/1714, B2/1). Resentment was also fuelled by the widespread imposition of illegal exactions (*tanpai*) in order to finance non-budgetary development projects, often unrelated to the needs of agriculture.

[49] Tian Jiyun, 27 October 1990, introducing the system of special grain reserves. Quoted in Ash, "QCD", *The China Quarterly*, No. 125 (March 1991), p. 192.

[50] Ash, "QCD", *The China Quarterly*, No. 127, p. 664.

The prospect of moving from "unlimited" to "fixed quantity" purchase within a mere six months highlights the real fiscal constraints which threatened the state's grain procurement operations. Until the looked-for realignment of wholesale and retail prices had been achieved, there was no guarantee that the budgetary problems of the past would not recur.

Consideration should also be given to the *technical* strategy for agricultural development in the 1990s. China's fundamental scarcity of land and limitations on further increases in multiple cropping made it clear that the main burden of accelerated growth would rest on higher yields and improvements in farm efficiency. This in turn required major increases in the supply of working and fixed capital (fertilizers, insecticides, plastic sheeting and machinery), as well as the popularization of advanced farming techniques.

China's record in these areas during the 1980s had been impressive;[51] Table 4 summarizes some of those achievements and also sets out input targets contained in the 8FYP.

The transformation of more than 2.7 million hectares of low-and medium-yielding land between 1988 and 1990 had already been the source of significant increases in the output of grain, cotton, oil seeds and sugar and it was clear that this process was intended to continue.[52] In addition, plans were announced to extend the sown areas of hybrid rice and hybrid maize to 16.7 and 18.7 million hectares by 1995. "Advanced cultivation techniques" would be popularized on a further 6.7 million hectares under rice, wheat and maize.[53]

The development of new hybrid strains and the increased provision of chemical fertilizers were likely to play a crucial role in determining future yield increases. Forecasting future trends in the application of fertilizers is always difficult, dependent as it is on the government's willingness to reallocate resources to both the domestic industry and to imports. In this respect, the future performance of agriculture is intimately connected with *industrial* policy. Nevertheless, empirical research had already demonstrated the importance of enlarged supplies of chemical fertilizers and new hybrids in stimulating yield increases during the 1980s.[54] There was no reason to suppose that future yield trends would not continue to be influenced by the availability of such inputs.

The targets summarized in Table 4 no doubt reflect a determination to extend the application of science and technology in order to raise agricul-

---

[51] For a careful analysis, see Bruce Stone, "Developments in agricultural technology", *The China Quarterly*, No. 116 (December 1988), pp. 767–822.

[52] *Jihua gangyao*, p. 126.

[53] *Ibid.*, p. 103.

[54] See Bruce Stone, "Developments in agricultural technology," pp. 790–818. Also Y. Y. Kueh, "Fertilizer supplies and foodgrain production in China, 1952–82", *Food Policy*, August 1984.

TABLE 4. *Agricultural Inputs and 8FYP Targets*

	Unit	1980	1990	1995 plan
Tractor ploughed area	Mill.ha.	40.99 (a)	48.26 (a)	56.7 (d)
Mechanized sown area	Mill.ha.	14.98 (b)	21.57 (c)	31.1 (d)
Mechanized harvested area	Mill.ha.	4.36 (b)	11.00 (c)	18.7 (d)
Mechanized irrigated area	Mill.ha.	25.32 (a)	27.15 (a)	28.00 (d)
Large/med tractors	Million	0.56 (a)	0.81 (a)	1.1 (d)
Small/hand tractors	Million	1.37 (a)	6.98 (a)	8.0 (d)
Combines	Thousand	27.05 (a)	38.72 (a)	70.0 (d)
Farm trucks	Million	0.14 (a)	0.62 (a)	1.0 (d)
Chemical fertilizer	M. tonnes (standard weight)			100.0 (e)

Note:
The figures for tractors, combines and farm trucks show year-end stocks of these items.
Sources:
(a) *TJZY 1991*, p. 63
(b) He Kang (General Editor), *Zhongguo nongye nianjian 1981 (Chinese Agricultural Yearbook 1981)*, hereafter *NYNJ 1981*, (Beijing: State Statistical Publishing House, 1982), p. 63.
(c) *TJNJ 1991*, p. 329.
(d) Frederick W. Crook, "China's Eighth Five Year Plan: goals and targets for the agricultural sector", p. 42.
(e) *Jihua gangyao*, p. 110.

tural yields. But their fulfilment was dependent on the provision of an appropriate framework for technological research, training and dissemination. In this respect, it was significant that the establishment of "agricultural technical training bases" at provincial and prefectural levels, as well as the formulation of agricultural scientific plans, also emerged as high priorities in development plans at the beginning of the 1990s.[55]

By way of conclusion, it will be useful to comment briefly on the extent to which some of these technical targets have in fact been fulfilled since the beginning of the 1990s. The findings are inconclusive. As of 1993, the effectively irrigated area was some 3 per cent higher than in 1990, while the total area subject to flooding had fallen by a similar proportion.[56] During the same period, however, the total area of water loss and soil erosion had risen markedly (by some 20 per cent) and so, albeit more marginally had that of saline-alkaline land.[57] Chemical fertilizer consumption meanwhile rose by 22 per cent, although it was reported that after adjustment for

[55] "CCPCC 1991", p. 5.
[56] *TJNJ 1994*, p. 336. Interestingly, the effectively irrigated area in 1993 (2.45 million hectares) was almost identical to the total area susceptible to flooding (2.44 million hectares)!
[57] *Ibid.*

inflation, real investment in this and other inputs actually declined in 1993. Financial constraints were also evident in reports that about one-sixth of all local-level rural technology centres had been closed because of budget cuts in 1993.[58]

Agricultural Production Targets for the 1990s

The 8FYP and 10YP outline followed the precedent of earlier plans in containing virtually no projections of changes in the arable, or sown, area sown under various crops. Specific targets were confined to levels of *total* production of major items for 1955 and, in some cases, 2000. For a few crops, projected five-year average levels of production were also made available.

Table 5 provides a summary of these production targets. It also shows total output in 1990 and average production during the 7FYP period (1986–90) in order to facilitate a comparison between recent performance and projected trends.

The average annual rates of growth implied by these figures for the Eighth and Ninth FYP periods are shown in Table 6. So, for purposes of comparison, are the average growth rates achieved during the 7FYP (1986–90).

The use of five-year averages eliminates distortions associated with anomalous base and/or end-year conditions and is the more useful basis for comparison.[59] Seen from this perspective and compared with the average rates of increase achieved between 1986 and 1990, the production targets for the 1990s are less modest than they would otherwise appear to be. Indeed, the estimates in Table 6(b) show some consistency between performance during the 7FYP and projections for the Eighth and Ninth plans.[60]

[58] US Central Intelligence Agency, *China's Economy in 1993 and 1994: The Search for a Soft Landing* (report prepared for submission to the Subcommittee on Technology and National Security of the US Congress, Joint Economic Committee) (22 July 1994).

[59] For example, both grain and cotton experienced a sharp fall in total output in 1985, but a sharp increase in 1990. In both cases, these changes were against the previous trends and they lend a spurious impression of growth. The case of oil crops is analogous, but different: total production rose sharply in 1985 and 1990, so that a growth estimate derived from these two years *understates* the "true" trend.

[60] It is not of course coincidental that targets for 1995 and 2000 were drawn up against the background of the slower growth of 1986–89, rather than that of the fine 1990 harvest. There may of course be political advantages too in formulating conservative plans: better by far to claim the over-fulfilment of low targets than have to admit the under-fulfilment of high ones! Notice that the 1990 bumper grain harvest owed most to the regional performance of the North and North-east. Together, they contributed two-thirds of the increase in national production during 1990 (half coming from the North-east – i.e. Liaoning, Jilin and Heilongjiang – alone) (*TJNJ 1990*, p. 367 and *TJNJ 1991*, p. 350). We shall return to this regional dimension later.

TABLE 5. *Plans for Agriculture in the 1990s*
(a) Total production of major agricultural products in 1990 and targets for 1995
and 2000

	1990 actual production	*1995 planned production*	*2000 planned production*
Food grains	446.24	455.00	500.00
Cotton	4.51	4.75	5.25
Oil seeds	16.13	18.00	
Sugar	72.15	75.00	
Pork	22.81	23.00	
All meats	25.14	30.00	
Aquatic products	12.37	14.50	

Sources:
  1990 data from *TJNJ 1991*, pp. 346–8, 357, 361 and 363.
  1995 and 2000 targets from *Jihua gangyao*, pp. 103–4.

(b) Average total production 1986–90 and planned average total production
1991–95 and 1996–2000

	Average total production 1986–90	*Average planned production 1991–95*	*Average planned production 1996–2000*
Food grains	408.47	447.00	478.00
Cotton	4.05	4.64	5.00
Oil seeds	14.46	17.26	
Sugar	61.22	73.72	

Sources:
  As Table 5(a).
Notes:
  All figures in Tables 5 (a) and (b) are shown in million tonnes.

Estimates of total agricultural output up to 1993 (and in some cases, preliminary figures for 1994) are available and make it possible to assess extent to which the 8FYP targets are being fulfilled. The quantitative basis of such an assessment is presented in Table 7.

There seems little reason to doubt the ability of most branches of agriculture to fulfil their 1995 targets. Indeed, targeted levels of production for oil seeds, meat and fish have been overfulfilled well in advance of that date. The estimates of average realized annual output of grain and cotton (1991–94) would also seem to lend themselves to an optimistic interpretation. But as the data for 1994 suggest, these averages conceal wide annual fluctuations, which undermines such a confident assessment.

TABLE 6. *Average Annual Rates of Growth of Total Production During the Seventh, Eighth and Ninth Five-Year Plans*

(a) Comparison of base and end years only

| | Average annual rate of increase (% p.a.): | | |
	1986–1990 actual	1991–1995 planned	1996–2000 planned
Food grains	3.3	0.4	1.9
Cotton	1.6	1.1	2.0
Oil seeds	0.4	2.2	
Sugar	3.6	0.8	
Pork	6.6	0.2	
All meats	7.7	3.6	
Fish	11.9	3.2	

(b) Comparison of average 5-year periods

| | Average rate of annual increase (% p.a.) | | |
	1981–85 – 1986–90 actual	1986–90 – 1991–95 planned	1991–95 – 1996–2000 planned
Food grains	1.9	1.8	1.3
Cotton	−1.3	2.8	1.5
Oil seeds	3.7	3.6	
Sugar	6.0	3.8	

Source:
  As Table 5.

The performance of grain gives special cause for concern. Since 1990 the total production of grain has displayed no clear upward trend.[61] The lack of direction highlights the uncertainty which is bound to characterize any projection of the grain sector's immediate growth prospects. It is worth recording too that the regional dimension of the recent grain performance is noteworthy in that just seven provinces have accounted for three-quarters of the increase in China's production between 1989 and 1993.[62]

The vagaries of agriculture's performance during the 1990s cannot simply be attributed to natural disasters and changing climatic conditions. Other factors were also at work. The differential performances of the various

[61] Indeed, on a year-to-year basis, the average rate of growth of total output between 1990 and 1994 was negative (−0.1% p.a.).
[62] The seven provinces are Liaoning, Jilin, Heilongjiang, Inner Mongolia, Hebei, Henan and Shandong. Collectively, they achieved an average rate of growth of 6.9% p.a. (1989–93).

TABLE 7. *Planned and Realized Agricultural Production During the Eighth Five-Year Plan (1991–95)*

	Average annual total output, 1991–94 realized	*Average annual total output 1991–95 planned*	*Total output 1994 realized*	*Total output 1995 planned*
Food grains	444.70	447.00	444.50	455.00
Cotton	4.54	4.64	4.25	5.25
Oil seeds	17.67	17.26	19.84*	18.00
Sugar	82.84**	73.72		
Pork			28.54*	23.00
All meats			36.70	30.00
Aquatic products			20.98	14.50

Sources:
  Planned data from Table 5.
  Estimates of realized output from *TJNJ 1994*, pp. 345–6, 352 and 354 (1991–93); *SWB*, FE/ 2245 S2/1, 7 March 1995 (1994 preliminary).
Notes:
  * Estimates for 1993 only.
  ** Average realized output for 1991–93 only.

sectors would appear to exemplify the difficulties which have continued to impede the sustained, and above all balanced agricultural growth which the planners have for so long sought. Unless they can be overcome, there is a danger that structural imbalances within the agricultural sector will become even more pronounced. Most serious of all is the situation of the grain sector, which still has to demonstrate its ability to meet the goals set for it in the national plans.

If a comparison of the five-year averages shown in Table 5 indicates consistency between recent performance and projected trends, there is an area of the plan in which such harmony appears to have been lacking. One of the basic macroeconomic goals is that by the turn of the century, living standards for the majority of the population should have reached a "comfortably well-off" (*xiaokang*) level[63] – a phrase which implies higher consumption of "meat, eggs, milk, fish, vegetables and fruit" for urban and rural residents.[64] Such targets seem to be at variance with the data in Tables 5 and 6, which indicate a significant planned reduction, during the 8FYP

[63] Tian Jiyun was specific about this: ". . . in the 1990s China's agriculture will be required to meet the demand of over 1.2 billion people at a comfortably well-off standard of living . . ." (addressing a national meeting on rural economic work, March 1991) (*SWB*, FE/1026, 21 March 1991).
[64] *Jihua gangyao*, pp. 83 and 146.

period, in the growth of meat and fish production – precisely the sectors whose performance, unlike that of grain, cotton and oil seeds, was *consistently* buoyant during the second half of the 1980s.

It may be that the cautious assessment of agriculture's sector's capabilities, current at the beginning of the 1990s, explains the apparent contradiction between grain production targets for the 1990s and the objective of securing significant improvements in living standards. Could it be that fears that slow growth of cereal production in the 1990s would generate a serious shortage of *feed* grain[65] led planners to lower their expectations of dietary improvements in the interests of more balanced agricultural development?[66]

The shift from a predominantly grain-based diet has already begun in China's urban sector. In more prosperous rural areas, the same process is under way. But in most parts of the Chinese countryside, direct consumption of grain has probably not yet reached saturation point and rising income is still associated with increased demand for grain for direct human consumption.[67] Continuing rises in per capita income will nevertheless compel a change in the pattern of food consumption and dictate a fundamental transformation of the structure of cereal production and use. Once the demand for "fine" grain (in China, rice, wheat and soya) has been met, a more far-reaching change will occur, as consumers seek to achieve a better diet by increasing their consumption of non-grain – especially animal-based – foods.

This latter shift has serious implications for the grain sector, which can only accommodate the evolving pattern of demand by supplying more grain for feed purposes. Given that about 3.5 kilograms of grain are needed in

[65] It may be that China already suffers a feed deficit, which it has accommodated by a combination of imports, running down reserves, cutting rations and using less than efficient grain-meat conversion ratios. See Claude Aubert, "Problems of agricultural diversification: some aspects of animal husbandry and grain utilization in China", in Eduard B. Vermeer (ed.), *From Peasant to Entrepreneur: Growth and Change in Rural China* (Pudoc: Wageningen, March 1992), pp. 105–28. Elsewhere, the same author has pointed out that consumption of grain fodder rose from 13 to 18 per cent of total production between 1978 and 1984 and reached 25 per cent (100 million tonnes) in 1988 (C. Aubert, "The agricultural crisis in China at the end of the 1980s" in Jorgen Delman, Clemens Stubbe Ostergaard and Flemming Christiansen (eds.), *Remaking Peasant China: Problems of Rural Development and Institutions at the Start of the 1990s* (Aarhus: Aarhus University Press, 1990), p. 25.

[66] It is worth recording that in July 1990, in an address to a conference on non-staple foodstuffs, Li Peng noted that ". . . with China's limited availability of arable land and low level of grain consumption per head, it would be impossible to raise the animal protein intake by a big margin . . ." (Ash, "QCD", *The China Quarterly*, No. 123 (December 1990), p. 767). Note too that every 1% increase in the animal protein content of human food consumption requires an extra 5 million tonnes of feed grain: see He Kang (principal editor), *Zhongguo liangshi fazhan zhanlue duice (Strategic Measures for the Development of Food Grains in China)*, hereafter *ZGLSFZZL*, (Beijing: Agricultural Publishing House, 1990), p. 31.

[67] See Kenneth R. Walker, "Forty Years on: Provincial Contrasts in China's Rural Economic Development", *The China Quarterly*, No. 119 (September 1989), p. 472.

order to produce 0.5 kilogram of meat,[68] the rapid development of animal husbandry requires an acceleration in the rate of increase of grain production in order to meet rising feed demand. Even allowing for an extension of pasturage on the grasslands of northern China, regional water and climatic constraints mean that plans to increase supplies of meat and dairy produce remain critically dependent upon the accelerated growth of cereal production.

The pressure which increasing demand for animal fodder has already placed upon the grain sector is illustrated in the finding that between 1978 and 1988, China's consumption of feed grain more than doubled, to reach 100 million tonnes (25 per cent of total production).[69] Such pressure is certain to have intensified during the present decade.[70] Realization that the grain sector may be unable to accommodate the change may, however, have delayed the planners' expectation of further qualitative improvements in diet for the majority.

Shortfalls could in theory be offset by imports. There are, however, several factors which militate against the adoption of such a strategy. One is the limited availability of foreign exchange. Another is the perception that dependence on outside supplies of an essential item, such as food, should be avoided. Infrastructural constraints, such as the shortage of port and transport facilities, are further limiting factors. China's trade orientation is in any case towards the import of more obviously developmental goods. Nor is there any guarantee that overseas supplies would be available on the requisite scale: international reserves are after all limited. All these

[68] This is a rough figure. Conversion ratios differ between individual meats and dairy produce so that the true ratio depends upon the structure of meat production. See Aubert, "Problems of agricultural diversification."

[69] Aubert, "The agricultural crisis in China at the end of the 1980s", p. 25.

[70] Remember too that demand for grain for *industrial* processing is also likely to increase dramatically in the coming years: see Ash, "Prospects for the Grain Sector: A Chinese Perspective", Wolfgang Klenner (ed.), *Trends of Economic Development in East Asia* (Berlin, Heidelberg, New York, London, Paris, Tokyo: Springer-Verlag, 1989) pp. 419–31. There exists a wide variety of estimates of grain requirements in the year 2000, ranging from 480 to 593 million tonnes! For some of the relevant evidence, see Chinese Academy of Agricultural Sciences (CAAS), Research Group for the Development of Food Grains and Economic Crops, "Woguo liangshi he jingji zuowu de fazhan" ("A study of the development of food grains and economic crops in China"), *Zhongguo nongcun fazhan zhanlue wenti* (*Strategic Issues Relating to China's Rural Development*), hereafter *CAAS, 1985*, (Beijing: Agricultural Scientific Publishing House, 1985), pp. 377–456; Gu Jingde, "2000 nian woguo nongcun fazhan de qige da qushi" ("Seven major trends in China's rural development to the year 2000"), reprinted in *Agricultural Economics*, No. 5 (1985), pp. 20–3; Guo Shiping, "2000 nian woguo heli shiwu jiegouliang de queding ji shengchan nengli de guji" ("Determining a rational food structure and estimating the production capacity of China in the year 2000"), *Nongye Xiandaihua Yanjiu* (*Research on Agricultural Modernization*), No. 3 (1985), pp. 23–6; Cong Anni *et al*, "Lengjing yuce nongye xingshi; shenzhong jueze zhanlue juece" ("A sober projection of the agricultural situation; a careful choice of strategic decisions"), *Caizheng Yanjiu* (*Financial Research*), No. 2 (1989), pp. 34–9; Ma Hong (chief editor), *2000 Nian de Zhongguo* (*China in the Year 2000*) (Beijing: China – Social Science Publishing House, 1989), pp. 206–29; Chen Liang Yu and Allan Buckwell, *Chinese Grain Economy and Policy* (Wallingford, Oxon: C.A.B. International, 1991).

considerations underline the priority requirement of maintaining the fundamental role of the grain sector in the domestic economy.[71]

Yet in the absence of any clear trend in total grain production during the 1990s, there seems to be no secure base for future growth to take total output to the targeted 500 million tonnes by the year 2000.[72] The most gloomy scenario to which such doubts have given rise is that painted by Lester R. Brown, who has predicted that excess demand for food could generate a domestic shortfall of 216 million tonnes (trade weight) of grain by 2030.[73] Such conditions seem unlikely to materialize. Nevertheless, Brown's projections are a salutary reminder that the absence of significant renewed growth could compel greater participation by China in world grain markets.

The Land Constraint and Projected Changes in Sown Area Distribution During the 1990s

A notable feature of China's agricultural development in recent years is that increases in output have been achieved against the background of a contraction of cultivated area. Official statistics show that between 1978 and 1990 the total arable area fell by almost 4 per cent (from 99.45 to 95.67 million hectares)[74] – an annual loss of 344,000 hectares. Since 1990, a further 572,000 hectares have disappeared out of cultivation.[75] Even allowing for a deceleration after the mid-1980s, these figures indicate a faster rate of contraction than had taken place before 1978. Despite the potential for land reclamation, it is unlikely that the net decline in cultivated area will be reversed.[76] The scarcity of land remains a fundamental constraint.

[71] Paradoxically, China has been an exporter of feed products. One Chinese source highlights the irrationality of such exports through the following example: in 1987, 4.3 million tonnes of animal feed were exported. Had these supplies been used domestically, they would have raised 12.28 million pigs. These would, in turn, have yielded 861,000 tonnes of pork, which, if exported, might have earned US $7.83 million *more than* the value of the original feed exports. Meanwhile, the 12.28 million pigs would have generated the equivalent of 890,000 tonnes of chemical fertilizer and so raised domestic grain production by an estimated 1.96 million tonnes. If the additional foreign exchange earned through the sale of the pork were allocated to the grain sector, several extra million tonnes of cereals could have been produced! See *ZGLSFZZL*, p. 35.

[72] Fulfilment of this target will require annual rises of 10 million tonnes of grain a year for the rest of the decade.

[73] Lester R. Brown, *International Herald Tribune*, 28–9 September 1994.

[74] The 1978 figure is from Kenneth R. Walker, "Trends in crop production, 1978–86", *The China Quarterly*, No. 116 (December 1988), Table 1, p. 595. The 1990 figure is given in *TJNJ 1991*, p. 314.

[75] Based on arable area data for 1993 in *TJNJ 1994*, p. 329.

[76] Most Chinese sources would appear to concede the likelihood of a continuing decline in arable area during the 1990s. See, for example, *CAAS, 1985*, pp. 394–5; and *2000 Nian de Zhongguo*, pp. 230–1. A recent source predicts a loss of 6.67 million hectares by the end of the century, but argues that this figure underestimates the true loss by some 50–100% because so much of the encroachment is likely to affect good-quality land. (See Wu Ziping *et al.*, "Bawu

A shrinking land base can be offset by higher multiple cropping.[77] Between 1978 and 1990 the total sown area fell from 150.1 to 148.36 million hectares; by 1993, it had fallen to 147.74 million hectares.[78] The decline was smaller than that of arable area, implying that an increase in the multiple cropping index (MCI) from 150.9 (1978) to 155.1 (1990) to 155.4 (1993) had compensated for, but not entirely offset, the loss of cultivated land.

It has been pointed out elsewhere that projections of arable area which indicate a continuing decline from the level of the 1980s have ". . . powerful implications for the multiple cropping index that would be needed to maintain a desirable total sown area [for China] . . .".[79] Throughout the 1980s the pressures for land encroachment were more powerful than the will to reverse the arable decline. If, as suggested earlier, the same pressures are maintained during the 1990s, improvements in land utilization will require the further extension of multiple cropping. The context in which this will have to take place is illustrated by Table 8, with the findings summarized in Table 9.

The data confirm that in the immediate post-1978 years, the decline in arable area was unrelieved by any offsetting increase in the MCI, so that the total sown area throughout China also contracted (the single, marginal exception was the North-east). Worst affected were the Central and Southern regions, although the loss of multiple cropped area was also serious in the North and South-west. Economic factors are likely to have been mainly responsible for the changes. It was widely accepted that higher costs associated with high MCIs had an adverse effect upon farm incomes and incentives. Accordingly, the search for profit maximization, which guided household operations under the production responsibility systems, dictated that the multiple cropped area should be reduced. This is what occurred.

By 1983 this contraction had attracted critical comment. One view suggested that an optimum MCI for China was between 156 and 158 – significantly higher than the previous peak and well above the then-current level (146). From this time dates a steady recovery in the multiple cropped area – a recovery in which every region, except the North-east, shared. By 1990, a new peak of around 155 had been attained. The fact that the 1993 level showed virtually no change suggests that the MCI may now be close to the putative "optimum".[80]

qijian he 2000 nian woguo nongye fazhan de chubu yuce" ("Initial projections of agricultural development during the 8FYP period and in the year 2000"), *Yuce (Projections)*, No. 1 (1991), p. 51. I am grateful to Dr. K. C. Yeh for bringing this article to my attention.

[77] Or by increased application of inputs, designed to raise yields per unit area.

[78] *TJNJ 1991*, p. 340 and *TJNJ 1994*, p. 342. Differences between sowing and harvesting seasons of crops make it possible to obtain more than one harvest a year from a single piece of land. Sown area differs from arable area by the extent to which such multiple cropping is practised.

[79] Walker, "Trends in crop production", p. 594.

[80] In its projections for the 1990s, *CAAS, 1985*, p. 395 had looked to the re-establishment of a MCI at the 1977 level of 155.

TABLE 8. *Arable, Sown and Multiple Cropped Area in China and its Regions: 1978, 1983 and 1990s*

	CHINA	NE	N	NW	C	S	SW
AA							
1978	99.49	16.33	29.82	13.50	21.10	7.15	11.54
1983	98.51	16.47	29.41	13.38	20.71	7.05	11.50
1990	95.67	16.23	28.46	12.83	20.15	6.78	11.21
1993	95.10	16.28	28.13	13.16	19.77	6.61	11.16
TSA							
1978	150.96	16.37	42.11	12.77	44.27	15.55	19.89
1983	144.02	16.42	40.63	12.37	42.36	13.35	18.89
1990	148.36	16.22	41.60	12.75	42.66	14.38	20.76
1993	147.74	16.33	41.41	12.95	41.28	14.15	21.62
MCI							
1978	151.7	100.2	141.2	94.6	209.9	217.5	172.4
1983	146.2	99.7	138.2	92.5	204.5	189.4	164.3
1990	155.1	99.9	146.4	98.8	212.1	211.8	185.0
1993	155.4	100.3	147.2	98.4	208.8	214.1	193.7
MCA							
1978	51.47	0.04	12.29	−0.73	23.17	8.4	8.35
1983	45.51	−0.05	11.22	−1.01	21.65	6.30	7.39
1990	52.69	−0.02	13.19	−0.15	22.55	7.59	9.54
1993	52.64	0.05	13.28	−0.21	21.51	7.54	10.52

Abbreviations:
  AA   Arable area
  TSA   Total sown area
  MCI   Multiple cropping index
  MCA   Multiple cropped area
Notes:
  (a) All figures in million hectares, except MCI, which is expressed in percentage terms
  (b) The regional breakdown used here follows *CAAS, 1985*, p. 425. The individual regions comprise the following provinces: *North-east*: Liaoning, Jilin, Heilongjiang; *North*: Shanxi, Hebei, Henan, Shandong, Shaanxi, Beijing, Tianjin; *North-west*: Inner Mongolia, Ningxia, Gansu, Qinghai, Xinjiang; *Centre*: Hunan, Hubei, Jiangxi, Jiansu, Anhui, Zhejiang, Shanghai; *South*: Fujian, Guangdong, Guangxi, Hainan; *South-west*: Sichuan, Guizhou, Yunnan, Tibet.
Sources:
  1978 and 1983: Walker, "Trends in crop production", pp. 622–3 and 628–9. 1990: *TJNJ 1991*, pp. 314 and 341. 1993: *TJNJ 1994*, pp. 329 and 342.

It is difficult to predict what further changes will take place between now and the end of the century. The stabilization of the cultivated area – especially evident in the 1990s – and the maintenance of a high multiple cropping index does generate a more hopeful picture than the perspective of the mid-1980s offered. This is a significant achievement and one that would have appeared unlikely only a few years ago.

But further increases in the MCI will not readily be achieved in the near

TABLE 9. *Changes in Arable, Sown and Multiple Cropped Area: 1978–1983 and 1983–1990*

	CHINA	NE	N	NW	C	S	SW
Change during 1978–1983:							
AA	−0.98	0.14	−0.41	−0.12	−0.39	−0.10	−0.04
TSA	−6.94	0.05	−1.48	−0.40	−1.91	−2.20	−1.00
MCA	−5.96	0.09	−1.07	−0.28	−1.52	−2.10	−0.96
1983–1990:							
AA	−2.84	−0.23	−1.00	−0.48	−0.60	−0.26	−0.28
TSA	4.34	−0.20	0.97	0.38	0.30	1.03	1.87
MCA	7.18	−0.02	1.97	0.86	0.90	1.29	2.15
1990–1993:							
AA	−0.57	0.05	−0.33	0.33	−0.38	−0.17	−0.05
TSA	−0.62	0.11	−0.19	0.20	−1.38	−0.23	0.86
MCA	−0.05	0.07	0.09	−0.06	−1.06	−0.05	0.90

Note:
  All figures in million hectares.
Source:
  As Table 8.

future. Natural conditions preclude any significant improvement in the North-east and North-west. In the South-west a sharp decline in the multiple cropped area during 1978–83 has been reversed and since 1983 more than 2 million hectares have been added. The result is that the current index is already higher than the maximum level thought feasible for this region.[81] Central and Southern China have traditionally contributed most to the multiple cropped area and their loss of 3.62 million hectares between 1978 and 1983 accounted for over 60 per cent of the national decline. By 1990 more than 2 million hectares had been recovered and the Centre's MCI had returned to its previous peak. It is unfortunate that this recovery was not maintained during the early 1990s, when both arable and sown area once more contracted. A significant rise in MCI conceals the reality that a parallel decline in arable and sown area has also taken place in the South since 1990. Rapid development and structural change make it unlikely that any significant departure from this pattern will occur in these regions in the future. Perhaps the firmest foundation for sown area expansion lies in the North, where climatic conditions are favourable and the returns from irrigation are high.[82]

Overall it is possible that China's total sown area will remain around 150 million hectares during the 1990s – close to the level of pre-1978 years. If an

[81] *CAAS, 1985*, p. 446.
[82] But the increase in the North's MCI from 138 (1983) to 147 (1993) already constituted an impressive achievement which will be hard to sustain.

TABLE 10: *The Changing Distribution of China's Sown Area: 1978, 1990 and 1992*

	Total sown area	Food grains	of which: Economic crops	Other
1978	150.10	120.59	14.44	15.08
	[100.00]	[80.34]	[9.62]	[10.05]
1990	148.36	113.47	21.42	13.48
	[100.00]	[76.48]	[14.44]	[9.09]
1992	149.01	110.56	24.28	14.17
	[100.00]	[74.20]	[16.29]	[9.51]

Sources:
Zhongguo nongcun jingji tongji daquan, p. 131; *TJNJ 1991* p. 341 and *TJNJ 1993*, p. 359.

accelerated decline in arable area were to re-assert itself and/or the multiple cropped area contract, the figure could fall to 145 million hectares by 1995 – and to little more than 140 million by the year 2000. But despite the loss of almost 1.3 million hectares in 1993, earlier progress in easing the land shortage through higher multiple cropping suggests that such estimates are still worst-case scenarios.[83]

The earlier reference to a "desirable sown area" suggests the need for a rational pattern of land use between various crop categories. Before 1978 China's agricultural development was driven by the imperative of grain self-sufficiency. By contrast, agricultural policy in the 1980s encouraged diversification, the previous overwhelming emphasis on grain giving way to a more rational and efficient structure of production, in part dictated by considerations of comparative advantage and geared towards market demand. Price rises after 1978 raised the profitability of all crops, but particularly enhanced the returns available from economic crops, such as cotton, sugar and tobacco. Admittedly, the stagnation of grain production after 1984 introduced a potential new constraint on further shifts in land use. Nevertheless, by the 1990s significant changes in land utilization had taken place, as shown in Table 10.

Here is evidence of striking structural change. Between 1978 and 1993, against the background of a tiny contraction in total sown area (less than 1 per cent), the grain sown area fell by some 10 million hectares (more than 6 per cent), whilst that of economic crops expanded by almost the same amount (a 68 per cent rise). In the meantime, the residual area declined by almost one million hectares.[84]

[83] Projections in *CAAS, 1985*, p. 409 indicate a sown area of 146.4–151.5 million hectares (1990), and 143.3–153.6 million hectares (2000).
[84] Under the "other" category, what Table 10 does not reveal is that between 1978 and 1990, there was a major expansion of the area sown to vegetables at the expense of green fertilizers (leys).

TABLE 11. *Estimating the Burden on Grain Yields During the 1990s*

	Average grain yield (tonnes per sown hectare)
1986–90	3.66
1991–93	4.00
1995 plan	4.14
2000 plan	4.55

Sources:
  1986–89 and 1991–93 averages from *TJNJ 1991*, p. 353; *TJNJ 1993*, p. 371 and SSB, *Zhongguo nongcun tongji nianjian 1994 (Chinese Rural Statistical Yearbook, 1994)* (Beijing, Statistical Publishing House, 1994), p. 183.
  1995 and 2000 estimates derived from total output targets shown in Table 5 and an assumed grain sown area of 110 million hectares.

It is of some interest to compare the changes with two CAAS projections for 1990.[85] These anticipated sown areas under grain and economic crops of, respectively, 112–114 million and 19.9–21.6 million hectares (vegetables, leys and other crops meanwhile occupying 14.5–15.9 million hectares). This distribution derived from a projected total sown area of 146.4–151.5 million hectares. The reality is that by 1990 the higher targets for cereals and cash crops had been fulfilled, but with total sown area falling almost exactly halfway between the projected levels, the residual area under vegetables, green fertilizers, etc. had failed to expand.

A Note on Grain Yields

The earlier analysis of likely arable and sown area trends strongly suggests that the burden of growth of grain production during the 1990s will rest, as it did throughout the 1980s, on rises in sown area yields. How heavy that burden will be is much more difficult to estimate, for it depends on changes in grain sown area and the choice of base year. The estimates in Table 11 attempt to quantify that burden by comparing realized yields in the late 1980s and early 1990s with projected planned levels needed to fulfil 8FYP and 10YP targets.

On the basis of the average yield recorded during the 7FYP period, fulfilment of the projected 1995 yield demanded an average increase of 96 kilograms per sown hectare per year during the 8FYP period. The reality is that during 1991–93, grain yields rose, on average, by 67 kilograms p.a. To put such figures into perspective, during 1978–84 increases of more than 300 kilograms per hectare were achieved in four out of six years. Subsequently, however, not until 1990 was the 1984 peak surpassed.

Attention has already been drawn to the disappointing performance of grain after 1990. But in one important respect, the experience of the early 1990s differs from that of the second half of the 1980s. During the earlier period, the stagnation of grain production reflected the failure of grain yields to rise.[86] By contrast, as Table 11 suggests, post-1990 yields displayed an upward trend, reaching a record level in 1993.[87] The clear inference is that in the 1990s, a contracting sown area has been the major constraint on grain production in China.

Concluding Remarks

The peculiar combination of factors – natural and technical, economic and institutional – which determines farm performance in any country makes the projection of future trends hazardous. As China has sought to fulfil its recent agricultural plans, it has faced fundamental institutional and economic dilemmas – caught, as it were, "... between the plan and the market."[88]

That the government recognizes these difficulties is not in question. Indeed, one of the intriguing features of developments in China in the 1990s has been the reappearance of a slogan, originally conceived in the early 1960s, to the effect that "agriculture is the foundation of the national economy". When this phrase was first used,[89] its rationale was self-evident. China was just emerging from an unprecedented famine, which had re-sulted in the "excess deaths" of some 30 million people, and the farm sector was in a state of total collapse. In these circumstances, a strategy which sought to prioritize the farm sector – above all, food grain production – made obvious sense.

Against the background of very different conditions in the 1990s, the slogan's continuing currency is more intriguing. In 1962 average per capita grain output was 238 kilograms; by 1993, it had reached 385 kilograms. In the early 1960s, the agricultural sector contributed almost half of China's NDP; some 30 years on, the figure was around 25 per cent. If growth was agriculture-led in the early 1980s, a decade later it was being driven by industry and foreign trade. By the first half of the 1990s, the familiar

---

[86] By 1989, the grain sown area was some 2.9 million hectares more than in 1985.

[87] In only one out of four years during 1990–93 did China's average grain yield decline.

[88] Jean C. Oi, *State and Peasant in Contemporary China: The Political Economy of Village Government* (Berkeley, Los Angeles, Oxford: University of California Press, 1989), p. 235.

[89] The strategy of "taking agriculture as the foundation [of] the economy" has its origins in the deliberations of the Ninth Plenum of the Eighth CCP Central Committee (January 1961).

structural consequences of modern economic growth had already mani-
fested themselves, with the role of primary activities declining in favour of
secondary and tertiary sector expansion.

This chapter has sought to highlight some of the factors which have
fuelled the concern voiced by senior government and Party officials in the
face of agriculture's problems in the first half of the 1990s.[90] No doubt much
of that concern reflects the potential social and political implications of such
difficulties. The speed of the government's response to problems associated
with the issue of "IOUs" to farmers and to reduce illegal exactions amongst
peasants is evidence enough of the seriousness with which it regarded the
threat which these practices posed to their authority.

There is also a regional dimension to China's agricultural problems. In
contrast to coastal regions, where the farm sector accounted for less than a
quarter of GDP, the average contribution of agriculture "proper"[91] in the
interior provinces remained close to 40 per cent in the early 1990s. And
whereas the farm sector's share of employment had fallen to 46 per
cent along the coast, the corresponding figure inland was still well over
60 per cent. The structure of coastal and interior *rural* economies had
also changed markedly, with agriculture accounting for only a quarter of
rural social-value output along the coast, compared with more than half
elsewhere.

The lagging performance of crop farming vis-a-vis other agricultural
pursuits was another significant factor. Following an almost universal contraction in the output share of the crop sector in the first half of the 1980s,
regional patterns diverged. In coastal China, there was a continuing decline,
which elsewhere more or less came to a halt. The outcome is that by 1993,
crop farming still accounted for almost two-thirds of agricultural output in
the interior, compared with some 55 per cent in coastal provinces. The
inference is that farmers in China's coastal regions had benefited from rises
in income which had increasingly derived from higher-return, non-cropping
farm activities.

Even without the benefit of hindsight, one ought not perhaps to be
surprised at the intractability of some of the problems confronting China's
agriculture and impeding sustained growth in the 1990s. The commitment
to preserve contractual arrangements with individual farm households has
been a consistent cornerstone of government policy. But the simultaneous

---

[90] There is no lack of evidence of such concern. Cf. Wan Li (1993), arguing that farm
problems had "... severely undermined the interests of the peasants and damaged relations
between them and the Party" and referring to the dangers of "... peasant revolt ... peasants
turning against the state ... agriculture [sliding] into chaos" (*SWB*, FE/1736). Witness Li
Peng's warning that rural conditions could become "even more explosive". And see too
references to Deng Xiaoping's reported fear that economic problems in the 1990s might come
from the farm sector and his belief that such a setback would take a long time to overcome (e.g.
in *RMRB*, 8 December 1994).

[91] That is, crop farming, forestry, animal husbandry, fishing and sidelines.

advocacy of two-tier management and the maintenance of dual-track pricing have hinted at a more ambiguous attitude by policy-makers towards agricultural development policy. Such tensions no doubt reflect ideological differences within the government. But to explain them in such terms is too simplistic. Rather, if we are to understand the obstacles to rapid and sustained agricultural growth during the 1990s, it is essential to appreciate the very real underlying *economic* issues that are at stake.

Ironically, the most fundamental of these is still that of grain.[92] Even allowing for accelerated agricultural growth, it is clear that the production and procurement of sufficient grain to meet consumption and other requirements will remain an absolute imperative in the foreseeable future. These issues seem destined to continue to dominate the formulation and implementation of agricultural development policy during the 1990s.[93]

The regional complexion of grain production deserves the final comment. In contrast to the experience of the first three decades of communist rule, the focus of output growth is shifting towards the northern half of the country.[94] By the early 1990s this reversal of the previous pattern was already under way, with significant implications for relative levels of per capita grain output in the various regions, as shown in Table 12.

In the early 1980s, when the CAAS investigations were undertaken, Northwest China lacked sufficient grain even to meet basic subsistence requirements, whilst the North had achieved no more than basic self-sufficiency.[95] By contrast, only the provinces of the Centre enjoyed a surplus which allowed significant diversion of grain to animal feed and other purposes.[96] The North-east, South and South-west fell somewhere between these positions.

The figures for the 1990s suggest some of the strengths and weaknesses of

---

[92] If agriculture is the "foundation of the national economy," orthodoxy requires us to add that "grain is the basis of that foundation".

[93] The same conclusion was reached by Kenneth Walker in 1989: see his "Forty years on", *The China Quarterly*, No. 119 (September 1989), p. 474.

[94] The contribution to the increase in total grain output of Centre, South and South-west between the First and Sixth FYP periods was 60%. That of the Northern regions of China was 40%. The CAAS projections anticipated a dramatic reversal of this pattern, the Northern provinces accounting for 52% of the expected rise in total grain production between 1982 and 2000, compared with only 48% from Central and Southern regions. See Ash, "Prospects for China's Grain Sector", p. 427.

[95] This statement follows Kenneth R. Walker in assuming that basic self-sufficiency may be defined in terms of levels of per capita grain output between 275 and 309 kilograms. See *Food Grain Procurement and Consumption in China* (Cambridge: Cambridge University Press, 1984), p. 3.

[96] An average per capita grain production of 400 kilograms or above is my benchmark in making this statement. This is a figure which has acquired almost talismanic status in China in recent years – although it is noticeable that 8FYP and 10YP targets imply levels that fall below it. See *ZGLSFZZL*, pp. 30–1. It is worth recording that an average per capita grain output of 400 kg. was achieved in the United States and developed European countries some 50–60 years ago. Current levels in these countries are typically in excess of 750 kg. – and over 1,500 kg. in Canada, Australia and the USA.

TABLE 12. *Per Capita Grain Output in China – A Regional Perspective*

Average per capita grain output (kg)

	1982	1990	1993	1990A plan	1990B plan	2000A plan	2000A plan
CHINA	348	390.3	385.2	375.5	388.3	418.1	440.2
NE	362	585.8	584.9	438.8	455.1	533.9	564.0
N	305	363.0	390.9	348.7	361.5	388.2	413.6
NW	269	383.7	337.3	292.4	324.4	347.2	391.0
C	419	429.1	401.7	421.8	433.4	442.3	460.5
S	337	301.2	276.0	340.1	341.2	371.4	399.7
SW	328	338.5	331.2	368.6	383.9	433.0	439.4

Sources:
  1982 estimates from *CAAS, 1985*, p. 433.
  Note that the 1982 was the base year for this part of the CAAS exercise. Hence its inclusion here.
  1990 figures from total population data in *TJNJ 1991*, p. 81; and total grain output in *TJNJ 1991*, p. 350. 1993 figures from total population data in *TJNJ 1990*, p. 60; and total grain output in *TJNJ 1994*, p. 345.
  1990A, 1990B, 2000A and 2000B are derived from the two sets of projections for total population and total grain output given in *CAAS, 1985*, pp. 379 and 433. In order to obtain the estimates for each region, I have simply assumed that the 1990 regional 1990 regional distribution of total population, as revealed in *TJNJ 1991*, p. 81, remains constant through the 1990s. This is of course unrealistic, although it is hoped that the crude approach will not do violence to the findings.

the grain sector's recent performance. Most spectacular is the extraordinarily high figure already attained by the North-east in 1990 and sustained through 1993.[97] Also impressive was the steady improvement in the position of North China, where a steady increase in per capita output took it into surplus by 1993. The performance of the North-west was more mixed: to have moved out of deficit into comfortable surplus by 1990 was a remarkable achievement, but such progress was not subsequently maintained. In any case, in stark contrast to such successes, marginal improvements registered during the 1980s in the South-west and, in particular, Central China were later reversed. Most disastrous of all, average per capita grain production in the South showed a sustained *decline* (by almost 20 per cent) between 1982 and 1993.

Comparison of realized output in 1990 with the CAAS targets for that year offers a further perspective to developments during the 1980s. It underlines the remarkable achievements of North-east and North-west

[97] In 1990 average per capita grain production in the North-east rose by 46% (from 400.1 kg). The point has already been made that the fine 1990 harvest owed most by far to the performance of this single region. The region remained a major source of national grain supplies in subsequent years.

China and the disappointing performances of the South and South-west.[98] The figures for Central and Northern regions are just about in line with the projected levels.

Looking ahead to 2000, it is telling that the CAAS figures reveal a determination that every region should achieve a level of per capita grain production compatible with the attainment of a "comfortably well-off" living standard. The 1990 estimates of realized output suggested that from the perspective of that year, the provinces of the North-east had already fulfilled that goal and that those of the North-west were well on the way to doing so. Conditions in the North were also apparently moving in a favourable direction. The real problem areas were the South and South-west, where recent trends had made the fulfilment of the 2000 targets less likely.

From the perspective of 1993, the situation was less hopeful. It is true that the North-east and North remained on course. But elsewhere the situation had deteriorated. Not only had conditions in the South and South-west worsened, but the sharp decline in per capita output in Central provinces between 1990 and 1993 had taken it back to a position even below that of 1982.

It is true that the validity of the original CAAS projections has become more questionable in the light of subsequent developments. The comparative perspective which they offer nevertheless remains interesting. First, through the contrasting performances of South and South-west, and North-east and North-west, they suggest the restraining and liberating forces which regional development is likely to play in the continuing search for the basic welfare goal articulated in economic and social development plans for the 1990s. Second, it highlights the gap that now exists between the 8FYP and 10YP targets and production levels needed to fulfil that same goal. Calculations suggest that in order to reach the national average per capita level of grain output originally cited by CAAS, total grain output in 2000 will need to rise to 544–572 million tonnes (9–14 per cent above the official target).[99] Such figures suggest why the optimism of the early 1980s has given way to caution and even pessimism. They are also perhaps a more reliable measure of the burden which rests upon agriculture during the 1990s, as the government continues to search for an appropriate balance between planning and marketization.

---

[98] For the former, overfulfilment of targets by 29.6–34.4% and 17.7–30.6%; for the latter, underfulfilment by 7.1–10.8% and 12.7–20.6%.

[99] These figures are obtained by multiplying the projected national average per capita estimates given in CAAS by a projected population of 1.3 billion in the year 2000.

China's Industrial Performance Since 1978

Robert Michael Field

In the late 1970s, Chinese industry was on the verge of collapse. Its high but erratic rate of growth since 1949 had been achieved by using ever-increasing amounts of labour and capital. Not only was industry operating inefficiently, but the output mix was inappropriate and inventories had accumulated to very high levels. However, the true state of affairs had been obscured by the political turmoil of the Cultural Revolution (1966–76) and the virtual disbanding of the State Statistical Bureau (SSB).

By 1978, the Party leadership understood the economic problems well enough to endorse a strategic shift in policy. In December, at the Third Plenum of the 11th Party Central Committee, they concluded that it was necessary to simplify economic administration, to shift power to local authorities and to grant managers of industrial enterprises broader decision-making authority in order to provide the conditions necessary for rapid economic growth.[1] In the next three or four years, they undertook a bewildering variety of experiments and reforms that began on an extremely small scale – primarily in Sichuan – and then spread rapidly throughout the country.[2] The reforms had an immediate and dramatic impact in the rural areas, where communes were disbanded, free markets were established, and township and village industry blossomed. Large-scale state-operated industry, however, remained inefficient and unresponsive to demand.

In 1983 and 1984 a new wave of reforms was launched, including a campaign to eliminate losses at state-operated enterprises, the substitution of income taxes for the remission of profits to the state, and a further expansion of the decision-making authority of enterprise managers. These reforms had some initial success, but in October 1984, at the Third Plenum of the 12th Party Congress, the leadership decided that the urban economy must be invigorated.[3] They characterized the major defects of the system as: the lack of clear distinction between the functions of governmental institutions and those of enterprises; the existence of administrative barriers that separated the various ministries and geographic regions; the overly tight control of enterprises by the state; the limited use of the market; and an

[1] "Communiqué of the Third Plenum of the 11th Central Committee of the Communist Party of China," adopted 22 December 1978, *Foreign Broadcast Information Service Daily Report–China* (FBIS), 26 December 1978, pp. E4–E13.

[2] For a discussion of some of the experiments and the results achieved during 1978–82, see Robert Michael Field, "Changes in Chinese industry since 1978," *The China Quarterly*, No. 100 (December 1984), pp. 745–56.

[3] "Communiqué of the Third Plenum of the 12th Central Committee of the Communist Party of China," FBIS, 22 October 1988, pp. K1–K9.

overemphasis on an egalitarian distribution of income. The major thrust of the decision – designed to ensure social stability, to raise output, to improve standards of living and to increase state revenue – was to make enterprises relatively independent economic entities responsible for their own profit and loss, and to link incomes with job performance.

Implementing this decision would have required a whole range of specific reforms, including the reform of planning, commodity pricing, economic management by state institutions, and the labour and wage systems – each a complex task in itself. But events overtook it almost immediately: a downturn in the economy, the struggle between moderates and conservatives, and Tiananmen and its aftermath. The problems faced today are still the same as in 1978 and 1984.

Classification of Industrial Activity

The definition of industry (mining, manufacturing and the generation of electric power) and the basic reporting unit (the enterprise) have remained the same since the 1950s. Enterprises are classified by the administrative level of ownership, by the particular type of ownership and by branch of industry. Because of the changes in the system of classification and the frequent failure to identify coverage explicitly, however, data for the value of output in the 1980s are confusing.

By level of ownership

The gross value of industrial output (GVIO) for 1988 is shown by level and type of ownership in Table 1. Since 1986, it has not always been clear to what level of ownership a particular figure refers. Until then, coverage was unambiguous because the output of enterprises at and below the village level was included in the gross value of agricultural output.[4] At that time, because of their extremely rapid growth, the value of their output was transferred to industry. Thus, what was simply referred to as total industrial output before 1986 should now be classified as excluding village and below. The situation was further complicated in 1987 by the introduction of the category township and above. This is not just another name for excluding village and below because there is at least one source in which the values for township and above and village and below did not add to the total. The classification city co-operative and individual has been inserted to make the difference explicit.

Finally, independent-accounting units are a subset of township and above

---

[4] The State Statistical Bureau (SSB) had added a total specifically identified as including village and below in its annual reports for internal use as early as 1981. Totals in other sources and detailed data in the annual reports, however, did not include village and below.

TABLE 1. Gross Value of Industrial Output, by Level and Type of Ownership, 1988

		Billion current yuan			
	Total	Excluding village and below	Township and above	City co-operative and individual	Village and below
Total	1,822.46	1,539.88	1,529.11	10.78	282.57
State	1,035.13	1,035.13	1,035.13	–	–
Central	250.38	250.38	250.38	–	–
Local	784.75	784.75	784.75	–	–
County	142.84	142.84	142.84	–	–
Local state, n.e.c.	641.91	641.91	641.91	–	–
Collective	658.75	448.38	444.45	3.93	210.37
County	68.29	68.29	68.29	–	–
Urban street	33.41	33.41	33.41	–	–
Township	184.67	184.67	184.67	–	–
Village	170.36	–	–	–	170.36
Co-operative	43.94	3.93	–	3.93	40.01
City co-operative (1986)	3.93	3.93	–	3.93	–
County town co-operative (1985)	40.01	–	–	–	40.01
Collective, n.e.c.	158.09	158.09	158.09	–	–
Individual	79.05	6.85	–	6.85	72.20
City individual (1980)	6.85	6.85	–	6.85	–
County town individual (1984)	72.20	–	–	–	72.20
Other	49.53	49.53	49.53	–	–
Joint state-collective (1980)	20.87	20.87	20.87	–	–
Joint state-individual (1982)	7.39	7.39	7.39	–	–
Joint collective-individual (1980)	2.29	2.29	2.29	–	–
Joint foreign (1980)	16.03	16.03	16.03	–	–
Overseas Chinese (1982)	1.36	1.36	1.36	–	–
Foreign owned (1983)	0.89	0.89	0.89	–	–
Other, n.e.c. (1980)	0.69	0.69	0.69	–	–

Note:
The figures in parentheses are the years in which the categories were first used.
Source:

that includes only those enterprises that must keep their own accounts for profit and loss. They constitute about 95 per cent of the total.

By type of ownership

Before 1980 there were only state and collectively operated enterprises.[5] But new types of ownership were included as they became important.[6] Individual enterprises in cities and three types of joint ownership were put on the list in 1980, sometimes lumped together as "other" (which included city individual until 1985, when individual was listed as a separate group). Still more categories were added to "other" in 1982–83, and county town individual in 1984. Finally, county town and city co-operative appeared in 1985 and 1986 respectively.

By branch of industry

In 1985, the SSB introduced a major revision of the branches of industry that had been in use more or less in the same form since the 1950s; at that time, the old system of 15 branches was replaced by 40 branches.[7] The new system (which corresponds at least roughly to the International Standard Industrial Code) is organized by stage of production. It starts with mining and extraction, runs through light industrial goods and the processing of raw materials, and ends with manufactures such as metal products, machinery and electronics. This system offers some theoretical advantages, but its adoption has given rise to a major discontinuity: the old data cannot easily be converted to the new system. However, the Statistical Bureau has converted the figures for output in current prices for 1980 and 1984[8] and continues to publish the series for the old branches of industry in 1980 constant prices.[9]

Branch of industry data, whether for new branches or old, can be given for any level or type of ownership, can be restricted to independent-

---

[5] The joint state–private and private enterprises that existed in the 1950s had all been abolished by 1958. See SSB, *Ten Great Years* (Beijing: Foreign Languages Press, 1960), p. 38.

[6] The year in parentheses shown in Table 1 after the various forms of ownership indicates when the form was first recognized as a separate category. Wherever possible, data for these new categories have been included for the earlier years.

[7] The complete list of branches and sub-branches introduced in 1985 is given in SSB, *Zhongguo dazhongxing gongye chiye* (*China's Large and Medium Scale Enterprises*) (Beijing: China Urban Economics Society Press, 1989), pp. 264–82. For the 15 branches (as revised in 1972) and a concordance, see SSB, Industrial and Transportation Statistics Department, *Zhongguo gongye jingji tongji nianjian, 1988* (*China Industrial Economics Statistical Yearbook, 1988*) (Beijing: China Statistics Press, 1989), pp. 373–9 and 280–398.

[8] SSB, *Industrial Economics Statistical Yearbook, 1991*, pp. 133–41. The yearbook contains data from 1990 for a variety of industrial statistics.

[9] Figures from 1988 are given in SSB, *Industrial Economics Statistical Yearbook, 1989*, pp. 58–9; those for 1989 and 1990 are only given as a per cent of total in SSB, *Industrial Economics Statistical Yearbook, 1991*, pp. 72–3.

accounting units, or may include all enterprises. For example, data exist for
state-operated independent-accounting enterprises, for all enterprises at
the township level and above and for village-operated enterprises.

Sources

All the figures in this paper, collected over the last five or six years, are
official data – or derived from official data[10] – that originated in the Industrial and Transportation Statistics Department of the SSB. Major published
sources are the industrial section of the SSB's *Zhongguo tongji nianjian*
(*China Statistical Yearbook*)[11] and the Industrial Statistics Department's
Zhongguo gongye jingji tongji nianjian (*China Industrial Economics Statistical Yearbook*).[12] The manner in which they are presented, however, is a
reclassification of the old data into the categories currently in use.[13] My
procedure was to prepare tables with the data collected and then to ask
Chinese colleagues to help correct errors and fill blanks.

Ironically, this very generous help caused a serious mistake in compiling
the data. There was no available data on village and below in 1980 constant
prices for the years since 1986, so I asked for and was given figures for
1987–89 that turned out to be the same as those reported in current
prices. I assumed this was the result of a deliberate decision not to use
constant prices. The Industrial Statistics Department had told me in 1987
that a price index to deflate the current prices data was being compiled,
so when after three years the constant price data was still the same
as current prices it appeared that the price index had not yet been
developed.[14]

Then, while calculating growth rates to use in the text, I discovered the
rates for total, collective and individual industry implicit in the collected

[10] With a few exceptions, they are derived by simple addition or subtraction. The exceptions
are estimates in 1980 constant prices for village industry, city co-operative, county town co-
operative, city individual and county town individual in 1987–89, and for total, collective and
individual in 1990. The estimates were derived from the corresponding figure for the previous
year and a reported index or percentage increase.

[11] Beijing: China Statistics Press, 1982 to 1991.

[12] Beijing: China Statistics Press, 1985 to 1991.

[13] I wish to thank the Industrial Statistics Department, the State Planning Commission, the
State Information Agency and the Chinese Academy of Social Sciences. They all helped to
correct my errors and to fill gaps in the data. The remaining errors are my responsibility.

[14] In 1987 I was working on the value of agricultural output and discovered that the current
and constant price data for village and below-village industry in 1985 were identical for every
province in China and that most provinces had never distinguished between current and
constant prices. See Robert Michael Field, "Trends in the value of agricultural output, 1978–
86," *The China Quarterly*, No. 116 (December 1988), pp. 556–91, especially Table 3. When
asked, the Industrial Statistics Department said that it could not accept the constant price data
submitted to it by the provincial statistical bureaus for village and below in 1985 but had not
yet had time to prepare its own figures.

data were not the same as the reported rates.[15] Instead of constant prices, the figures for village, city co-operative, county town co-operative, city individual and county town individual industry were in current prices. The figures for village industry had been submitted as constant prices, and for the other four categories recently published current price data[16] are the same as previously published constant price data.[17] No constant price data by type of ownership have been published since 1986.

To investigate this problem, I made estimates for the five categories from the figures for 1986 and the reported annual percentage increases and then recompiled Table A3. Because the table added correctly and the implicit growth rates for the total and collective were virtually the same as those that had been reported, I accepted the estimates. It appears that the figures for village and below had been given in error and that current price data for the other four categories are no longer doubling as constant prices.

Weaknesses in the Data for the Value of Industrial Output

The use of gross value

Industrial enterprises report the gross value of their output, not including intra-enterprise transfers. GVIO for the country as a whole is simply the sum of the reported output values.[18] Because there are no deductions for the costs of raw materials or semifinished inputs purchased from other enterprises or for capital depreciation, GVIO contains a substantial amount of double counting, which introduces a bias in the level of output and its rate of growth.

The double counting is affected by changes in the organization of industry independently of any actual change in the level of output. For example, the merger of enterprises at different stages of production would decrease the purchase of semi-finished inputs and thus reduce GVIO, and the evolution of new types of joint enterprises would increase purchases and thus increase GVIO. It is also affected by changes in the degree of vertical integration. Traditionally, Chinese enterprises are highly integrated. When performance was measured primarily by fulfilling physical output targets for specific commodities, the enterprises manufactured as many components as possible (irrespective of cost) so that they would not have to

[15] SSB, *Zhongguo tongji nianjian, 1990 (China Statistical Yearbook, 1990)* (Beijing: China Statistics Press, 1991), p. 395.

[16] SSB, *Statistical Yearbook, 1991*, p. 391.

[17] SSB, *Statistical Yearbook, 1985*, p. 315; *1986*, pp. 273 and 276; or *1987*, p. 257.

[18] The Industrial Statistics Department is well aware of the problems with GVIO. It is currently experimenting with collection of value added data directly from all enterprises in five cities. When the results of the experiment have been evaluated, it intends to implement the system nation-wide.

depend on other enterprises or the vagaries of the transport system. With the development of markets, and as products become more complex, specialization and the purchase of inputs are becoming more widespread, which will tend to increase the distortion in GVIO.

The factory reporting method

The Chinese have compiled GVIO data by the factory reporting method since the 1950s. Under this system, the entire output of each enterprise is assigned to a single branch of industry irrespective of the nature of the goods actually produced. For example, the value of spindles manufactured by a textile plant would be included under the textiles rather than machinery. The use of the method affects both the reported composition of output and the rate of growth shown by individual industries.

The data in Table 2 show the gross value of light and heavy industrial commodities and the value of output produced by enterprises classified as light and heavy industry in 1980 constant prices for the years 1981 and 1986. In 1981, under the factory reporting method, enterprises classified as light industry produced 3.96 billion *yuan* of heavy industrial commodities (or 1.5 per cent of their output), and enterprises classified as heavy industry pro-

TABLE 2. *Gross Value of Industrial Output, by Light and Heavy Industrial Commodities and by Light and Heavy Industrial Enterprises, 1981 and 1986*

| | Billion 1980 yuan | | |
	All industrial commodities	Light industrial commodities	Heavy industrial commodities
1981			
All industrial enterprises	517.77	270.56	247.21
Light industrial enterprises	266.29	262.33	3.96
Heavy industrial enterprises	251.48	8.23	243.25
1986			
All industrial enterprises	902.85	439.37	463.48
Light industrial enterprises	448.99	417.20	31.79
Heavy industrial enterprises	453.86	22.17	431.69
Index (1981 = 100)			
All industrial enterprises	174.37	162.39	187.48
Light industrial enterprises	168.61	159.04	802.75
Heavy industrial enterprises	180.48	269.38	177.47

Note:
   Excluding village and below.
Source:
   State Statistical Bureau.

duced 8.23 billion *yuan* of light industrial commodities (or 3.3 per cent of their output). By 1986, these percentages had risen to 7.1 and 4.9 respectively. Because of the compensating misclassification, the distortion in the reported rates of growth between 1981 and 1986 was not great: production at all light industrial enterprises and production of all light industrial commodities grew at nearly the same rate. However, the output of heavy industrial commodities produced in light industrial enterprises in 1986 was eight times that of 1981.

Three points should be made. First, the factory reporting method does not affect the value of industry as a whole, or its rate of growth, but rather distorts the structure of industry, as well as the rate of growth shown by individual branches or sub-branches. Secondly, the distortion has undoubtedly continued to worsen since 1986 because of the rate at which production has diversified. And thirdly, similar data for individual branches would be even more distorted because the likelihood of offsetting errors is less.

The use of current instead of constant prices

Current prices have been used instead of constant prices in two ways, both of which introduce an upward bias in the reported constant price data and the reported rate of growth when prices are rising.[19] First, collective, individual and other enterprises have tended to use at least some current prices when filling out forms that should be in constant prices. These enterprises have no practical use for constant prices, and many of them do not know what the constant prices of the commodities they produce should be. The widespread nature of the problem is suggested by the differences in the 1988 price indexes for enterprises at different levels and by different types of ownership, shown in Table 3. The indexes range from a low of 101.95 for overseas Chinese enterprises to a high of 142.70 for county level state-operated ones. In general, the price rise at state-operated enterprises (which averaged 33.2 per cent) has been two to three times that at any other type of enterprise – with the exception of joint foreign and wholly foreign-owned enterprises, at which prices rose 20.1 and 25.4 per cent respectively.

Differences in the commodity of output among enterprises of various types probably account for some of the disparity, but the price indexes by branch of industry in Table 4 (for independent-accounting units at township level and above) show even greater divergence between state-operated and all other enterprises than that in Table 3. The differences range from 64.7 percentage points (for logging) to –27.2 (for power generation). Of course, even more detailed price indexes by branch and type of ownership might show that the disparities are due to differences in the commodity com-

---

[19] The Chinese refer to the upward bias in constant price data as *shuifen*.

TABLE 3. Price Indexes for the Gross Value of Industrial Output, by Level and Type of Ownership, 1988

	Total	Output in 1980 constant yuan = 100			
		Excluding village and below	Township and above	City co-operative and individual	Village and below
Total	124.33	126.01	126.09	116.04	115.87
State	133.18	133.18	133.18	–	–
Central	131.31	131.31	131.31	–	–
Local	133.79	133.79	133.79	–	–
County	142.10	142.10	142.10	–	–
Local state, n.e.c.	132.07	132.07	132.07	–	–
Collective	114.74	113.36	113.34	116.08	117.81
County	116.83	116.83	116.83	–	–
Urban street	105.79	105.79	105.79	–	–
Township	111.98	111.98	111.98	–	–
Village	119.66	–	–	–	119.66
Co-operative	111.03	116.08	–	116.08	110.56
City co-operative	116.08	116.08	–	116.08	–
County town co-operative	110.56	–	115.21	–	110.56
Collective, n.e.c.	115.21	115.21	–	–	–
Individual	111.01	116.01	–	116.01	110.56
City individual	116.01	116.01	–	116.01	–
County town individual	110.56	–	–	–	110.56
Other	114.35	114.35	114.35	–	–
Joint state-collective	113.58	113.58	113.58	–	–
Joint state-individual	107.56	107.56	107.56	–	–
Joint collective-individual	110.56	110.56	110.56	–	–
Joint foreign	120.15	120.15	120.15	–	–
Overseas Chinese	101.95	101.95	101.95	–	–
Foreign owned	125.39	125.39	125.39	–	–
Other, n.e.c.	113.77	113.77	113.77	–	–

Note:
The indexes are calculated from data in current and in 1980 constant prices.
Sources:

TABLE 4. *Price Indexes for the Gross Value of Industrial Output for Independent Accounting Units at Township Level and Above, by 40 Branches of Industry, 1988*

| | Output in 1980 constant yuan = 100 | | |
	Total	State	Other
Total	125.99	132.97	113.23
of which:			
Light	119.78	127.26	109.74
Agricultural materials	127.00	136.33	112.66
Industrial materials	106.59	107.70	105.42
Heavy	132.10	137.46	118.44
Extraction	157.09	164.40	122.61
Raw materials	149.30	150.24	144.27
Manufacturers	117.44	120.97	111.57
of which:			
Large	130.18	131.06	111.07
Medium	130.22	132.20	117.10
Small	121.97	136.40	113.02
of which:			
Coal mining	143.19	147.90	124.90
Petroleum extraction	165.83	165.83	–
Ferrous metal mining	137.92	148.72	118.74
Non-ferrous metal mining	149.39	152.48	139.86
Non-metal mineral mining	121.47	138.86	112.49
Salt mining	115.50	112.61	131.71
Other mineral mining	114.29	100.00	120.00
Logging	253.08	255.22	190.51
Public water supply	131.51	132.70	119.05
Food manufacture	142.12	147.04	123.56
Beverage manufacture	150.40	159.96	128.04
Tobacco manufacture	151.49	151.97	132.55
Forage manufacture	128.88	131.18	121.21
Textile manufacture	117.15	120.10	112.95
Clothing	102.79	110.29	101.52
Leather and fur	127.71	157.70	116.50
Timber processing	148.12	173.75	129.38
Furniture manufacture	108.27	111.02	107.88
Paper making	138.23	157.60	114.82
Printing	119.93	126.74	109.54
Cultural and sports articles	110.29	119.00	105.41
Arts and crafts	107.68	122.89	106.09
Power generating	125.82	125.19	152.41
Petroleum processing	136.57	136.35	144.07
Coke and coal-gas	162.41	176.52	124.32
Chemical industry	138.49	144.57	119.58
Pharmaceutical products	107.29	108.14	103.67

TABLE 4. (Cont.)

| | Output in 1980 constant yuan = 100 | | |
	Total	State	Other
Chemical fibres	94.33	94.93	90.47
Rubber goods	106.47	108.22	102.94
Plastic goods	127.24	140.89	123.47
Building materials	145.62	159.37	133.67
Ferrous metal smelting	161.86	163.64	150.27
Non-ferrous metal smelting	149.27	153.43	134.50
Metal products	114.45	129.18	109.81
Machine building	114.72	119.13	106.07
Transportation equipment	116.59	115.96	118.28
Electrical equipment	113.60	123.15	106.09
Electronic equipment	87.93	89.60	84.48
Instruments and meters	101.59	104.27	97.27
Other	114.92	161.68	108.59

Note:
    The indexes are calculated from data in current and in 1980 constant prices.
Source:
    State Statistical Bureau.

position of output within the various types of enterprise,[20] but it seems unlikely.

Secondly, many enterprises appear to have used the initial current price of a new product as its constant price. New products can be narrowly defined as commodities on an official list or more broadly as commodities not previously produced. And they can be either genuinely new or falsely claimed to be new. (The motive in falsely claiming a product to be new, of course, is to avoid official price controls.) The official way to establish the 1980 constant prices of a new product is to deflate its initial current price by the ratio of the average current price to the average constant price for a basket of similar products, but this elaborate procedure does not appear to be followed frequently.

It has never been clear to western observers, or probably to most Chinese economists, how serious a problem the valuation of new products is.[21] The

[20] It would be very easy for the Statistical Bureau – or anyone else who had access to data cross-classified by branch of industry and form of ownership – to test this hypothesis.
[21] The 1985 industrial census collected but never tabulated information that would have thrown light on the extent of the upward bias, at least for the first half of the 1980s. Enterprises were required to fill out a form that listed each new commodity, the year it was first introduced, how much was produced in 1985 and the total value of its output in current prices. Tabulating the data by year first produced would have provided the information necessary to estimate 1985 price indexes for commodities first produced in 1981, 1982, etc.

TABLE 5. *Bias in the Gross Value of Industrial Output, 1985–87 and 1986–87*

	1985–87	1986–87
Ex-factory price index	112.0	107.9
Output indexes		
In current prices	142.2	123.4
In 1980 constant prices	131.1	117.7
In 1985 prices	126.9	114.4
Upward bias (in percentage points)		
State Information Centre	2.6	3.5
State Statistical Bureau	0.6	1.2
Estimated	4.2	3.3

Note:
The indexes are for all industry, including village and below.
Sources:
State Statistical Bureau and State Information Centre.

1985 industrial census collected data on 7,329 new products introduced between 1981 and 1985. It found that the output of these products in 1985 was worth 22,126 million *yuan*, or 12.45 per cent of the total output of the 365 key-point enterprises that produced them.[22] An article in *National New Products* reported the share of new products was 3.3 per cent in 1983, 6.1 per cent in 1986 and 6.9 per cent in 1987.[23] But these percentages may not represent the full extent of the problem: the census data undoubtedly, and the figures in the article probably, refer to commodities on the official list.

The State Information Centre and the SSB have both attempted to measure the size of the bias introduced by the use of current instead of constant prices over the period 1985–87 and in 1987 alone. Table 5 presents their estimates and my attempt at a similar calculation. The measure they use is the difference between the official output index (which is based on data reported by the provincial statistical bureaus) and an independently-estimated output index.[24] For comparison, I deflated the gross value of industrial output in current prices by the ex-factory price index although this may not in fact be an appropriate measure. Despite these uncertainties, the data in Table 5 suggest that the official index may be overstated by as

[22] SSB, *Industrial Economics Statistical Yearbook, 1988*, p. 44.
[23] Hou Junpu, "About the significance of establishing development funds for exploring new products for export," *Quanguo xinchanpin* (*National New Products*), No. 3 (1990), pp. 12–14.
[24] The difference (which is in percentage points) is not a good measure because the sum of separate estimates for two consecutive years is not the same as the estimate for the two years taken together. The figures for 1985–87 and 1987 alone in Table 5 imply that there was a downward bias in 1986, whereas my estimate for 1986 was an increase of 0.4 percentage points. If they had used the ratio of official to estimated output indexes as their measure of bias, the product of separate figures for any series of years would have equalled the figure for the period as a whole and the measure could be used to deflate both indexes and output values.

much as two or three index points a year, at least in the second half of the 1980s.

Conditions in the 1980s

Growth and structural change

GVIO in 1980 constant prices (shown in Figure 1 and Table A3) rose from 523 billion *yuan* in 1980 to 1,714 billion *yuan* in 1990, averaging 12.6 per cent per year. The year-to-year pattern of change, however, was erratic. The rate of growth soared from 4.3 per cent in 1981 to 21.7 per cent in 1985, dropped to 11.4 per cent in 1986 and then rose by leaps to 20.8 per cent in 1988, and finally sank to 8.5 per cent in 1989 and even further to 7.8 per cent in 1990. The reforms that fuelled these spurts of growth – especially the greater decision-making authority granted to local governments and individual enterprises – were intended to stimulate state-operated enterprises, but the output of collective industry in 1990 was five times that of 1980, whereas that of state-operated industry was only double. As a result, the share of state-operated industry declined steadily from 75.5 per cent in 1980 to 48.5 per cent in 1990 while that of collective industry rose from 24.0 per cent to 40.3 per cent.

The primary beneficiaries of the new policies were enterprises at the township level and below (that is, township, village, co-operative and indi-

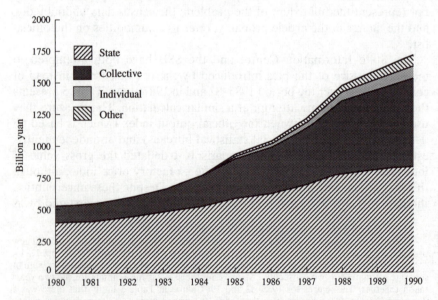

FIGURE 1. *Gross Value of Industrial Output in 1980 Constant Prices By Type of Ownership*

vidual industry).[25] They were the least regulated, and thus the freest to plan and market their own output. The output data in Table 6 contrast their behaviour with that of enterprises above the township level. Their output in 1990 was nearly ten times that of 1980, compared with 2.5 times for enterprises above the township level. Within collective industry, the output of township and village were each more than seven times that of 1980. The output of individual industry grew more than 1,000 times.

After an initial surge that raised their rate of growth to 41.8 per cent in 1984 and 53.7 per cent in 1985, their annual percentage increases drifted down to 14.1 per cent in 1990, but they were still from two to five times those of enterprises above the township level. Of course, the upward biases discussed in the previous section were most serious in these enterprises, but even if their true growth was only half the reported rate, the change in structure of ownership would still have been extremely rapid. This disparity in the rates of growth had a profound impact on the structure of industry: township and below rose from 10.5 per cent of the total in 1980 to 31.8 per cent in 1990.

The period was also characterized by a wide range in the rates of growth by branch of industry and a rapid change in the commodity composition of output. The average annual rates of growth for 1980–90 shown in Table 7 ranged from a low of 5.4 per cent for timber to 13.9 per cent for cultural goods. Growth was dominated by three branches of heavy industry (machinery, building materials, chemicals) and cultural goods. The lowest rates were shown by the branches producing energy and industrial materials.

The tabulation in Table 8, which compares the growth achieved in the 1980s with the long-term rate, makes it clear that the reforms undertaken since 1978 had a considerable impact on the structure of growth: Every branch in which output consists primarily of consumer goods grew faster than its historic rate, while most branches with a primary output of producer goods grew more slowly. Of the four exceptions, machinery has a large consumer goods component, and building materials and timber have been in chronic short supply.

Performance of enterprises

While the Chinese have achieved a high rate of growth, they have not yet been able to raise significantly the productivity of labour or the efficiency with which capital is used, particularly at state-operated enterprises.[26] The

---

[25] This is my grouping of the official categories of ownership.

[26] Capital is the sum of the net value of fixed assets at year end (at original purchase price) and the average value of working capital (in current prices). For a discussion of the upward bias in the data for the value of fixed assets and an estimate for state-operated independent-accounting industrial enterprises, see K. Chen, G. Jefferson, T. Rawski, H. C. Wang and Y. K. Zheng, "New estimates of fixed investment and capital stock for Chinese state industry," *The China Quarterly*, No. 114 (June 1988), pp. 243–66.

Table 6. *Gross Value of Industrial Output Above Township Level and at Township and Below, 1980–90*

	1980	1981	1982	1983	1984	1985	1986	1987	1988	1989	1990
Billion yuan											
Total	523.09	545.55	588.21	654.06	760.63	925.53	1,030.95	1,213.46	1,465.87	1,590.99	1,714.45
Above township	467.93	485.26	521.97	574.36	647.64	751.91	802.75	908.74	1,047.81	1,112.82	1,169.01
Township and below	55.16	60.29	66.24	79.70	112.99	173.62	228.21	304.72	418.06	478.17	545.45
Percentage shares											
Total	100.00	100.00	100.00	100.00	100.00	100.00	100.00	100.00	100.00	100.00	100.00
Above township	89.46	88.95	88.74	87.81	85.15	81.24	77.86	74.89	71.48	69.95	68.19
Township and below	10.54	11.05	11.26	12.19	14.85	18.76	22.14	25.11	28.52	30.05	31.81
Indexes											
Total	100.00	104.29	112.45	125.04	145.41	176.94	197.09	231.98	280.23	304.15	327.76
Above township	100.00	103.70	111.55	122.75	138.41	160.69	171.55	194.21	223.92	237.82	249.83
Township and below	100.00	109.30	120.08	144.49	204.84	314.77	413.73	552.44	757.93	866.90	988.87
Annual percentage changes											
Total	—	4.29	7.82	11.19	16.29	21.68	11.39	17.70	20.80	8.54	7.76
Above township	—	3.70	7.57	10.04	12.76	16.10	6.76	13.20	15.30	6.20	5.05
Township and below	—	9.30	9.86	20.33	41.77	53.66	31.44	33.53	37.20	14.38	14.07

Note:
  Above township consists of state, county collective, urban street collective, and other; township and below consists of township, village, co-operative and individual.
Source:
  Table A3.

TABLE 7. *Percentage Shares in and Indexes of the Gross Value of Industrial Output in 1980 Constant Prices, by 15 Branches of Industry, 1980 and 1990*

	Percentage shares		Average annual rates of growth	
	1980	1990	1980–90	1957–78
Total	100.0	100.0	10.7	8.8
of which:				
Metallurgy	9.5	7.3	7.8	9.2
Electricity	3.8	3.0	8.1	13.2
Coal and coke	3.2	2.1	6.1	7.4
Petroleum	5.8	3.8	6.1	18.8
Chemicals	11.4	12.7	11.9	15.0
Machinery	22.5	28.9	13.5	13.1
Building materials	3.9	4.3	11.7	9.9
Timber	2.1	1.3	5.4	2.3
Food	12.3	10.5	9.0	4.7
Textiles	14.6	14.0	10.3	6.4
Clothing	2.6	2.8	11.5	n.a.
Leather	1.0	1.2	12.3	n.a.
Cultural goods	2.3	3.0	13.9	n.a.
Paper	1.4	1.3	9.9	5.9
Other	3.4	3.8	12.1	n.a.

Note:
   The rate of growth for 1957–78 for clothing, leather, cultural goods and other combined was 8.5 per cent.
Sources:
   Robert Michael Field, "China: the changing structure of industry," in Congress of the United States, Joint Economic Committee, *China's Economy Looks Toward the Year 2000* (Washington, D.C.: U.S. Government Printing Office, 1986), pp. 529–30; Table A6.

TABLE 8.

	Below historic rate of growth	Above historic rate of growth
Consumer goods	–	Food
		Textiles
		Clothing
		Leather
		Cultural goods
		Other
Producer goods	Metallurgy	Machinery
	Electricity	Building materials
	Coal and coke	Timber
	Petroleum	Paper
	Chemicals	

TABLE 9. *Productivity of Independent-Accounting Industrial Enterprises, 1985–90*

	Gross value of industrial output (billion 1980 yuan)	Capital (billion yuan)	Average number of workers and employees (million)	Gross value per 100 yuan of capital (1980 yuan)	Gross value per worker and employee (thousand 1980 yuan)	Capital per worker and employee (thousand yuan)
Total						
1985	794.0	697.2	64.2	113.9	12.4	10.9
1986	863.5	814.9	68.5	106.0	12.6	11.9
1987	990.7	949.0	71.0	104.4	14.0	13.4
1988	1,157.8	1,114.9	73.1	103.9	15.8	15.2
1989	1,229.5	1,355.3	74.2	90.7	16.6	18.3
1990	1,302.4	1,595.3	74.8	81.6	17.4	21.3
State						
1985	565.7	563.8	37.5	100.3	15.1	15.0
1986	600.5	649.6	38.9	92.4	15.5	16.7
1987	668.7	745.7	40.1	89.7	16.7	18.6
1988	748.0	860.3	41.4	86.9	18.1	20.8
1989	775.7	1,031.8	42.3	75.2	18.3	24.4
1990	800.4	1,208.9	42.9	66.2	18.6	28.2
Collective						
1985	217.5	126.1	26.5	172.5	8.2	4.8
1986	249.3	156.5	29.0	159.3	8.6	5.4
1987	299.2	189.3	30.0	158.1	10.0	6.3
1988	372.7	231.9	30.6	160.7	12.2	7.6
1989	400.5	283.8	30.4	141.1	13.2	9.3
1990	429.5	328.0	30.1	131.0	14.3	10.9
Other						
1985	10.8	7.2	0.5	150.2	22.8	15.1
1986	13.6	8.8	0.6	153.5	22.0	14.3
1987	22.8	14.0	0.9	163.0	26.2	16.1
1988	37.0	22.6	1.1	164.1	32.9	20.0
1989	53.2	39.8	1.5	133.9	36.5	27.3
1990	72.5	58.5	1.7	123.9	41.5	33.5

Sources:

SSB, *Statistical Yearbook, 1989*, pp. 268 and 275.
SSB, *Statistical Yearbook, 1990*, pp. 417 and 423.
SSB, *Statistical Yearbook, 1991*, pp. 397 and 403.

data in Table 9 show that the 64 per cent increase in output at independent-accounting enterprises between 1985 and 1990 required more than twice as much capital but only 16.6 per cent more labour. Thus, the gross value of output per 100 *yuan* of capital fell 28.3 per cent while the gross value per worker and employee rose 40.7 per cent. This was accomplished by a doubling of capital per worker and employee during the five-year period.

The data in the table show the contrast between the level and growth of productivity at state-operated and collective enterprises. In 1985, each worker and employee at a state-operated enterprise used three times as much capital as his counterpart at a collective enterprise but produced only 60 per cent as much output per 100 *yuan* of capital. Productivity was 1.8 times that at collective enterprises. Between 1985 and 1990, collective enterprises acquired capital and increased output faster than state-operated enterprises; the growth of labour was about the same. By 1990, gross value per 100 *yuan* of capital at state-operated enterprises had fallen to half that at collective enterprises, while gross value per worker and employee was only 30 per cent higher. Output, capital and labour at other enterprises all grew extremely rapidly, but by 1990 they accounted for only 5.6 per cent, 3.7 per cent and 2.3 per cent of the total, respectively. Their gross value per 100 *yuan* of capital declined only 17.5 per cent between 1985 and 1990, while gross value per worker and employee increased 82.2 per cent.

In the light of the biases in GVIO discussed in the previous section, it is clear that the growth of gross value per worker and employee is overstated at collective enterprises and may be overstated at state-operated enterprises. The bias in the gross value of output per 100 *yuan* of capital, however, is uncertain. Because gross value and capital are both subject to an upward bias, the bias (if any) in their ratio depends on their relative magnitudes. The change in gross value per 100 *yuan* of capital may be approximately correct.

In the early 1980s, the Chinese launched a drive to eliminate losses at state-operated enterprises. Nationally, one enterprise in four had been losing money since 1978, and their total losses exceeded 4 billion *yuan* annually,[27] the equivalent of 6 to 8 per cent of their total profit. The drive included public criticism in the newspapers, closing or reorganizing some enterprises and the unprecedented step of firing a few enterprise managers. In the first nine months of 1983, the number of state-operated enterprises operating at a loss was halved and losses were 40 per cent below the corresponding period of 1983,[28] and in the first nine months of 1984, losses were reduced a further 20.5 per cent.[29]

[27] "Communiqué of the State Statistical Bureau of the People's Republic of China on fulfilment of China's National Economic Plan," 1978, 1979, 1980, 1981 and 1982.

[28] *Zhongguo jingji ribao* (*China Economic Daily*), No. 4 (1983), p. 27.

[29] BBC, *Summary of World Broadcasts*, FE/W1316/A1, 5 December 1984.

The drive, however, had little long-term effect. The data in Table 10 show that losses at state-operated enterprises in 1986 were 14.6 per cent above the level of 1982, although the number of unprofitable enterprises had declined by 37.1 per cent. Total losses increased a further 12.0 per cent in

TABLE 10. *Profit and Loss at Independent-Accounting Industrial Enterprises, 1982 and 1986–90*

| | Billion yuan | | | | |
	Gross profit	*Loss*	*Net profit*	*Loss as a percentage of gross profit*	*Percentage of enterprises suffering loss*
Total					
1982	68.4	5.6	62.8	8.2	14.8
1986	95.0	7.2	87.8	7.6	13.2
1987	109.0	8.5	100.5	7.8	14.4
1988	129.6	10.7	119.0	8.2	11.7
1989	123.4	23.4	100.0	19.0	15.9
1990	101.3	45.4	56.0	44.8	21.1
State					
1982	56.9	4.8	52.2	8.4	20.8
1986	74.4	5.4	69.0	7.3	13.1
1987	84.8	6.1	78.7	7.2	13.0
1988	97.4	8.2	89.2	8.4	10.9
1989	92.3	18.0	74.3	19.5	16.0
1990	73.7	34.9	38.8	47.3	27.6
Collective					
1982	11.0	0.8	10.2	7.3	13.5
1986	19.1	1.6	17.5	8.5	13.2
1987	21.7	2.2	19.5	10.1	14.7
1988	28.3	2.2	26.1	7.8	11.7
1989	26.5	4.6	21.9	17.3	15.7
1990	22.2	8.4	13.7	38.1	19.4
Other					
1982	0.5	ngl	0.5	ngl	11.9
1986	1.5	0.2	1.3	11.8	15.8
1987	2.5	0.2	2.3	6.9	15.5
1988	3.9	0.3	3.7	6.8	17.2
1989	4.6	0.8	3.8	17.3	26.7
1990	5.5	2.1	3.5	37.3	32.6

Note:
    Components may not add to totals because of rounding.
Sources:
    SSB, *Industrial Economics Statistical Yearbook, 1991*, pp. 97 and 124. State Statistical Bureau.

1987 and 34.2 per cent in 1988, while the number of enterprises losing money continued to decline. There was an abrupt break in 1989, when losses more than doubled. They then increased a further 93.6 per cent in 1990. The number of unprofitable enterprises increased by 46.9 per cent in 1989 and 71.8 per cent in 1990. By 1990, losses at state-operated enterprises were more than seven times those of 1982, and the number of associated enterprises had increased more than a third. The share of gross profit offset by losses rose from 8.4 per cent in 1982 to 19.5 per cent in 1989 and an astonishing 47.3 per cent in 1990.

Moreover, state-operated enterprises were not the only ones to lose money, although they accounted for 76.9 per cent of all losses. Losses at collective enterprises rose more than ten times between 1982 and 1990. While they had offset only 7.3 per cent of gross profit in 1982, this rose to 38.1 per cent by 1990. Losses at other enterprises, negligible in 1982, were 37.3 per cent in 1990. Thus it is clear that in spite of serious efforts to reverse the trend, enterprises were steadily and increasingly losing money during the 1980s.

A second major development in the early 1980s was the substitution of an income tax for the remission of profit by state-operated enterprises. Referred to as "a major step to restructure China's economic system" by the minister of finance, Wang Bingqian, the tax required large-scale enterprises to pay 55 per cent of their net income to the state.[30] Because of the irrational price structure, the tax was to be implemented in two phases, with the second to be delayed until after price reform. In the first phase, which went into effect in 1983, enterprises also had to pay an "adjustment" tax (that is, a share of after-tax profit) to replace the profit formerly remitted to the state. Otherwise, many enterprises would have had windfall gains in retained profits, and state revenue would have fallen sharply.

A disadvantage of the arrangement under the first phase was that the adjustment tax had to be negotiated between individual enterprises and the various ministries and industrial bureaus, which meant the enterprises still had a bureaucratic relationship with the state that may have enabled some of them to extract extra advantages or allowed the state to interfere in their management. For this reason, the State Council decided to start a gradual shift to the second phase in late 1984 even though prices still remained irrational. Under this it was planned that enterprises would still pay the 55 per cent income tax and, in addition, pay a product tax that was to be the same nationally for each commodity.

Taxes paid by independent-accounting enterprises (shown in Table 11) have nearly doubled since 1985, with taxes paid by collective enterprises rising slightly faster than those by state-operated enterprises. The government has made considerable progress in switching to taxes from the old

[30] FBIS, 30 March 1983, p. K10. Smaller enterprises paid according to a progressive eight-level scale.

TABLE 11. *Profit and Taxes at Independent-Accounting Industrial Enterprises, 1985–90*

	Billion yuan					
	Net profit and taxes	Net profit	Profit retained	Profit submitted	Taxes	Profit submitted and taxes
Total						
1985	165.7	92.9	25.3	67.6	72.7	140.3
1986	166.5	87.8	28.9	58.9	78.8	137.6
1987	189.3	100.5	34.4	66.1	88.8	155.0
1988	228.9	119.0	43.0	76.0	109.9	185.9
1989	227.5	100.0	40.6	59.4	127.5	187.0
1990	194.6	56.0	31.1	24.9	138.6	163.5
State						
1985	132.6	71.8	n.a.	n.a.	60.9	n.a.
1986	134.1	69.0	22.8	46.2	65.1	111.3
1987	151.4	78.7	26.5	52.2	72.7	124.9
1988	177.5	89.2	32.4	56.8	88.3	145.1
1989	177.3	74.3	30.9	43.4	103.0	146.4
1990	150.3	38.8	22.4	16.4	111.5	127.9
Collective						
1985	31.0	19.8	n.a.	n.a.	11.2	n.a.
1986	30.3	17.5	5.8	11.7	12.9	24.5
1987	34.4	19.5	7.2	12.3	15.0	27.3
1988	45.8	26.1	9.6	16.6	19.7	36.3
1989	43.8	21.9	8.4	13.5	21.9	35.4
1990	37.7	13.7	6.9	6.8	23.9	30.7
Other						
1985	2.0	1.4	n.a.	n.a.	0.7	n.a.
1986	2.1	1.3	0.3	1.1	0.7	1.8
1987	3.5	2.3	0.7	1.7	1.2	2.8
1988	5.6	3.7	1.1	2.6	1.9	4.5
1989	6.4	3.8	1.3	2.6	2.6	5.2
1990	6.6	3.5	1.7	1.7	3.2	4.9

Note:
   Retained profit in 1985 is the sum of retained profit in large, medium and small enterprises. Retained profit in small enterprises is estimated on the assumption that the share of retained profit in net profit was the same as in 1986.
Source:
   SSB, *Industrial Economics Statistical Yearbook, 1991*, pp. 124 and 133.

system of collecting a share of profit. The amount of profit submitted to the state budget in 1990 was only a third of what it had been in 1985.

Government revenue received from these enterprises increased sharply in 1988 and 1989, but ended the decade only 16 per cent higher than it had

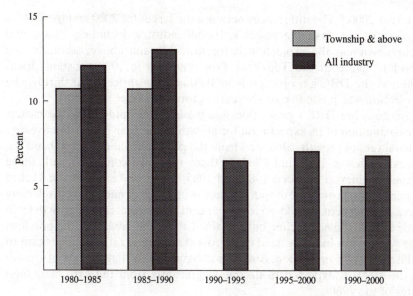

FIGURE 2. *Growth of Gross Value of Industrial Output*

been in 1985. During the period, its receipts drifted down from 18 per cent of final sales to less than 10 per cent. State-operated enterprises, which were responsible for a little more than 70 per cent of final sales, accounted for about 80 per cent of all profit and taxes paid. Profit retained by the enterprises followed the same pattern, although it rose faster in 1988–89 and dropped less in 1990, ending the decade 22.8 per cent above the level of 1985. Retained profit declined from 3.2 per cent of final sales in 1985 to only 1.9 per cent in 1990.

Outlook for the 1990s

The Eighth Five-Year Plan (1991–95) calls for the gross value of industrial output, including village and below, to be 3,270 billion 1990 constant *yuan* in 1995, and the Ten-Year Programme (1991–2000) set a target of about 4,600 billion *yuan* for the year 2000.[31] The average annual rates of growth are planned to be 6.5 per cent for 1990–95 and 7.1 per cent for 1995–2000, and 6.8 per cent for the entire ten years. Figure 2 compares these rates with the actual rates for the Sixth and Seventh Five-Year Plans and the 5.0 per cent[32] implicit in the Development Research Centre's (DRC) projection for

[31] *Renmin ribao* (*People's Daily*), 14 April 1991.
[32] The rate is derived from the projected total for 2000 in *2000 nian de Zhongguo* (*China in the Year 2000*) (Beijing: China Social Science Press, 1989), p. 578 and the actual figures for 1980 and 1990 in Table A3.

the year 2000.[33] The differences between the target for 2000 and the DRC's projection are, first, the target is for all industry, including village and below, whereas the projection is for township and above; secondly, the absolute figure in the Ten-Year Programme is in 1990 constant prices whereas the DRC's projection is in 1980 constant prices; and thirdly, the projection was made five or six years before the target was set.

Because the DRC's projection was made in the mid-1980s, the closest approximation of its expectation for growth to the year 2000 is the average annual rate of growth calculated from the projected value for 2000 and the actual values in 1980 and 1985. If these rates are compared with those actually achieved between 1980 and 1985, it can be seen that the Centre expected the growth of output at the township level and above to decline from 10.7 per cent in 1980–85 to 6.9 per cent. The actual rate of growth from 1985 to 1990 did not decline but remained about the same as in the previous five years. Thus industry need only grow at an annual rate of 5.0 per cent to fulfil the DRC's projection. Both sets of figures show that the rate of growth in the 1990s is expected to decline significantly from the extremely high rates of the 1980s.

Taken together, the official target and the projection suggest that the Chinese expect village, co-operative and individual enterprises to continue to grow more rapidly than enterprises at the township level and above. In the 1980s, they grew much more quickly than state-operated industry or the rest of collective industry, but can this continue? I believe that the rate of growth is bound to decline. It was high because these enterprises filled a niche. The new freedom given by the reforms in the early 1980s meant they could produce goods quickly in response to the pent-up demand for consumer goods in both urban and rural areas and to the new demand for producer goods in rural areas. At the same time, they provided needed employment for the millions of rural workers no longer required on the farm. However, as this niche is filled, village enterprises will find themselves competing directly both with old-line enterprises and with other village enterprises. They have reached a considerable size and have probably satisfied most of the demand for the types of products they are most successful at producing, so that it will become much more difficult to start new enterprises. Village industry, however, continues to play an important role.

The only guide we have for the structure of industry anticipated for the year 2000 is found in the DRC's projections by branch of industry. Table 12 presents these projections together with the actual figures for 1980, 1985 and 1990, and the percentage shares and average annual rates of growth implied by the figures. The rates for 1985–2000 are the best approximations

[33] The DRC undertook a massive study, *China in the Year 2000*, in the mid-1980s. Its findings were published in 15 volumes between 1987 and 1989, and summarized in English in Wang Huijiong and Li Boxi, *China Towards the Year 2000* (Beijing: New World Press, 1989).

TABLE 12. *Gross Value of Industrial Output at Township Level and Above in 1980 Constant Prices, by 15 Branches of Industry, 1980, 1985, 1990 and 2000*

	Billion yuan				Percentage shares				Average annual rates of growth				
	1980	1985	1990	2000	1980	1985	1990	2000	1980–85	1985–90	1980–2000	1985–2000	1990–2000
Total	496.53	826.11	1,374.70	22,375.7	100.0	100.0	100.0	100.0	10.7	13.6	7.8	6.9	4.5
of which:													
Metallurgy	47.34	66.40	100.35	1,679.9	9.5	8.0	7.3	7.5	7.0	10.9	6.5	6.4	4.8
Electricity	18.91	27.27	41.24	878.0	3.8	3.3	3.0	3.9	7.6	10.9	8.0	8.1	7.1
Coal and coke	15.98	20.85	28.87	513.3	3.2	2.5	2.1	2.3	5.5	8.5	6.0	6.2	5.4
Petroleum	29.01	37.26	52.24	904.4	5.8	4.5	3.8	4.0	5.1	8.8	5.8	6.1	5.1
Chemicals	56.55	92.67	174.59	2,877.3	11.4	11.2	12.7	12.9	10.4	17.2	8.5	7.8	4.6
Machinery	111.82	223.51	397.29	5,794.0	22.5	27.1	28.9	25.9	14.9	15.5	8.6	6.6	3.5
Building materials	19.58	35.06	59.11	1,107.0	3.9	4.2	4.3	4.9	12.4	13.9	9.0	8.0	5.9
Timber	10.59	13.31	17.87	380.0	2.1	1.6	1.3	1.7	4.7	7.6	6.6	7.2	7.1
Food	61.22	95.17	144.34	2,769.1	12.3	11.5	10.5	12.4	9.2	11.0	7.8	7.4	6.1
Textiles	72.51	127.32	192.46	2,744.1	14.6	15.4	14.0	12.3	11.9	10.9	6.9	5.3	3.3
Clothing and leather	18.09	27.58	54.99	1,007.9	3.6	3.3	4.0	4.5	8.8	18.8	9.0	9.0	5.7
Cultural goods and paper	18.18	32.08	59.11	927.8	3.7	3.9	4.3	4.1	12.0	16.5	8.5	7.3	4.2
Other	16.74	27.61	52.24	792.9	3.4	3.3	3.8	3.5	10.5	17.3	8.1	7.3	3.9

Sources:

Development Research Centre, *2000 nian de Zhongguo (China in the Year 2000)* (Beijing: China Social Science Press, 1989), p. 578. Table A6.

of the DRC's expectations. Comparing them with the actual growth for 1980–85 suggests that the DRC had anticipated that: the growth of the timber industry (the only branch for which they expected a moderate rise in the rate of growth) would increase 2.5 percentage points; metallurgy (–0.6 percentage points), electricity (0.5), coal and coke (0.7), petroleum (0.9) and clothing and leather (0.2) would remain about the same; and chemicals (–2.5), machinery (–8.3), building materials (–4.4), textiles (–6.7) and cultural goods and paper (–5.0) would all decline substantially.

Between 1985 and 1990 the growth shown by half the branches (metallurgy, electricity, coal and coke, petroleum, timber and food) was about what the DRC had expected, but the rest (chemicals, machinery building materials, textiles, clothing and leather and cultural goods and paper) all declined far less, or rose far more, than the DRC had expected. The pattern of growth implied for the 1990s by the projections and actual growth during 1990 seems reasonable, although demand for chemicals, machinery, building materials, clothing and cultural goods may be stronger than the DRC had anticipated.

Although China ended the 1980s with a downturn in the economy, a struggle between moderates and conservatives, and Tiananmen, it began the 1990s with a new surge of growth. After a lull of two years, GVIO rose 14.2 per cent in 1991, with the same pattern of growth by type of ownership as in the 1980s: collective and individual enterprises increased 18 per cent and 24 per cent respectively, but state-operated enterprises only 8 per cent. Because Chinese industry has been faced with low productivity and declining profit over the last five years, however, it seems likely that the rate of growth over the rest of the decade will decline. Nevertheless, the targets for 1995 and 2000 should be met.

Despite this growth, serious problems remain to be solved. The litany sounds remarkably similar to that of the early 1980s: losses, taxes, subsidies, budget deficits, the irrational price structure, and so on. There are, however, signs of change. Wang Bingqian announced at the National People's Congress in March 1994 that both central and local budgets will be split into separate operating and capital budgets (which will allow better control of investment), and the top income tax bracket for enterprises will be reduced from 55 to 33 per cent (which will help raise profits). In addition, other changes have been announced: more than 1,000 enterprises have been closed or merged; energy prices have been raised; unprofitable enterprises will have authority to set their own wages; and Shenzhen will be enlarged six-fold. It still remains to be seen, however, whether fundamental economic reform will be resumed.

In 1978, the Party leadership set out to simplify economic administration, to shift power to local authorities and to grant managers of industrial enterprises broad decision-making authority, but they have failed to separate government and management and failed to make enterprises truly responsible for profit and loss. Prices have been changed and many are free to fluctuate according to supply and demand, but so far the leadership has been unwilling to abandon a system of administered prices because changes in the price level affects government revenue, the distribution of profits and the urban cost of living – all of which set off political and bureaucratic struggles. A final question is whether economic reform is possible without some political reform?

Appendix Tables

TABLE A1. *Gross Value of Industrial Output in Current Prices, by Level and Type of Ownership, 1978–90*

100 million yuan

	1978	1979	1980	1981	1982	1983	1984	1985	1986	1987	1988	1989	1990
Total	4,237.00	4,681.30	5,154.26	5,399.78	5,811.22	6,460.44	7,617.30	9,716.47	11,194.26	13,812.99	18,224.58	22,017.06	23,924.36
Excluding village and below	4,067.10	4,483.30	4,896.70	5,120.02	5,506.26	6,087.56	7,042.20	8,755.65	9,849.13	11,909.37	15,398.84	18,485.15	19,862.80
Township and above	4,067.10	4,483.30	4,895.89	5,118.12	5,502.86	6,080.06	7,027.39	8,722.26	9,799.44	11,828.79	15,291.09	18,345.42	19,701.03
City co-operative and individual	–	–	0.81	1.90	3.40	7.50	14.81	33.39	49.69	80.58	107.75	139.73	161.77
Village and below	169.90	198.00	257.56	279.76	304.96	372.88	575.10	960.82	1,345.13	1,903.62	2,825.74	3,531.91	4,061.55
State	3,289.18	3,673.60	3,915.60	4,037.10	4,326.00	4,739.40	5,262.70	6,302.12	6,971.12	8,250.09	10,351.28	12,342.91	13,063.75
Central	n.a.	n.a.	n.a.	n.a.	n.a.	n.a.	n.a.	n.a.	1,773.71	2,097.46	2,503.81	3,025.52	3,446.42
Local	n.a.	n.a.	n.a.	n.a.	n.a.	n.a.	n.a.	n.a.	5,197.40	6,152.63	7,847.47	9,317.39	9,617.33
County	n.a.	n.a.	n.a.	n.a.	n.a.	n.a.	n.a.	n.a.	942.85	1,132.22	1,428.35	1,672.86	n.a.
Local state, n.e.c.	n.a.	n.a.	n.a.	n.a.	n.a.	n.a.	n.a.	n.a.	4,254.55	5,020.41	6,419.12	7,644.53	n.a.
Collective	947.82	1,007.70	1,213.36	1,329.38	1,442.42	1,663.14	2,263.09	3,117.19	3,751.54	4,781.74	6,587.49	7,858.05	8,522.73
of which:													
Excluding village and below	777.92	809.70	955.80	1,049.62	1,137.46	1,290.26	1,687.99	2,302.73	2,685.82	3,330.24	4,483.76	5,294.10	5,644.24
Township and above	777.92	809.70	955.80	1,049.62	1,137.46	1,290.26	1,687.99	2,302.73	2,665.26	3,299.93	4,444.49	5,244.07	5,589.71
City co-operative	–	–	–	–	–	–	–	–	20.56	30.31	39.27	50.03	54.53
Village and below	169.90	198.00	257.56	279.76	304.96	372.88	575.10	814.46	1,065.72	1,451.50	2,103.73	2,563.95	2,878.49

of which:

	C1	C2	C3	C4	C5	C6	C7	C8	C9	C10	C11	C12	C13
County	–	–	–	–	–	–	–	–	527.29	555.02	682.88	n.a.	857.55
Urban street	–	–	–	–	–	–	–	–	244.27	255.31	334.05	n.a.	442.04
Township	210.50	234.20	282.80	316.30	348.00	407.70	513.30	760.55	981.08	1,284.19	1,846.69	2,193.84	2,441.41
Village	166.90	198.00	257.56	279.76	304.96	372.88	575.10	662.71	838.49	1,165.35	1,703.62	2,117.68	2,394.02
Co-operative	–	–	–	–	–	–	–	151.75	247.79	316.46	439.38	496.30	539.00
City co-operative	–	–	–	–	–	–	–	–	20.56	30.31	39.27	50.03	54.53
County town co-operative	–	–	–	–	–	–	–	151.75	227.23	286.15	400.11	446.27	484.47
Collective, n.e.c.	–	–	–	–	–	–	–	–	912.62	1,205.41	1,580.87	n.a.	1,848.71
Individual	–	–	0.81	1.90	3.40	7.50	14.81	179.75	308.54	502.39	790.49	1,057.66	1,290.30
City individual	–	–	0.81	1.90	3.40	7.50	14.81	33.39	29.13	50.27	68.48	89.70	107.24
County town individual	–	–	–	–	–	–	–	146.36	279.41	452.12	722.01	967.96	1,183.06
Other	–	–	24.49	31.40	39.40	50.40	76.70	117.41	163.06	278.77	495.32	758.44	1,047.57
Joint state-collective	–	–	24.00	29.70	36.80	44.70	57.70	77.45	98.40	140.30	208.73	283.08	286.41
Joint state-individual	–	–	–	–	0.60	0.50	4.50	7.93	15.80	33.75	73.94	130.81	208.86
Joint collective-individual	–	–	0.04	0.10	–	–	0.20	1.63	3.90	9.71	22.92	52.37	93.30
Joint foreign	–	–	0.39	0.70	1.10	3.00	9.20	21.69	34.45	75.19	160.33	247.62	386.72
Overseas Chinese	–	–	–	–	0.50	0.50	0.20	2.84	3.01	5.35	13.57	19.88	33.46
Foreign owned	–	–	–	–	–	0.70	3.40	2.60	4.18	5.47	8.89	16.04	28.77
Other, n.e.c.	–	–	0.02	0.90	0.40	1.00	1.50	3.26	3.31	9.01	6.94	8.64	10.05

Note:

This table is my retrospective classification of the gross value of industrial output by type of ownership into the categories used in 1990. As a result, totals and subtotals may not be the same as those originally reported.

TABLE A2. *Gross Value of Industrial Output in 1970 Constant Prices, by Level and Type of Ownership, 1978–81*

	100 million yuan			
	1978	1979	1980	1981
Total	4,400.81	4,788.68	5,232.63	5,457.33
Excluding village and below	4,230.75	4,590.70	4,992.43	5,198.83
Township and above	4,230.75	4,590.70	4,991.62	5,196.96
City co-operative and individual	–	–	0.81	1.87
Village and below	170.06	197.98	240.20	258.50
State	3,416.39	3,719.84	3,928.38	4,027.68
Central	288.36	390.88	451.49	532.42
Local	3,128.03	3,328.96	3,476.89	3,495.26
County	497.56	472.67	502.35	516.10
Local state, n.e.c.	2,630.47	2,856.29	2,974.54	2,979.16
Collective	984.42	1,068.84	1,274.60	1,389.77
of which:				
Excluding village and below	814.36	870.86	1,034.40	1,131.27
Township and above	814.36	870.86	1,034.40	1,131.27
City co-operative	–	–	–	–
Village and below	170.06	197.98	240.20	258.50
of which:				
County	174.48	178.89	207.23	217.00
Urban street	81.61	78.68	94.30	106.71
Township	211.91	233.68	280.45	309.76
Village	170.06	197.98	240.20	258.50
Co-operative	–	–	–	–
City co-operative	–	–	–	–
County town co-operative	–	–	–	–
Collective, n.e.c.	346.36	379.61	452.42	497.80
Individual	–	–	0.81	1.87
City individual	–	–	0.81	1.87
County town individual	–	–	–	–
Other	–	–	28.84	38.01
Joint state-collective	–	–	28.43	36.49
Joint state-individual	–	–	–	–
Joint collective-individual	–	–	0.05	0.13
Joint foreign	–	–	0.34	0.62
Overseas Chinese	–	–	–	–
Foreign owned	–	–	–	–
Other, n.e.c.	–	–	0.02	0.77

Note:

This table is my retrospective classification of the gross value of industrial output by type of ownership into the categories used in 1990. As a result, totals and subtotals may not be the same as those originally reported.

TABLE A3. *Gross Value of Industrial Output in 1980 Constant Prices, by Level and Type of Ownership, 1980–90*

100 million yuan

	1980	1981	1982	1983	1984	1985	1986	1987	1988	1989	1990
Total	5,230.87	5,455.48	5,882.11	6,540.60	7,606.30	9,255.33	10,309.54	12,134.60	14,658.71	15,909.90	17,144.51
Excluding village and below	4,972.72	5,177.67	5,577.45	6,164.41	7,029.85	8,294.51	9,028.46	10,381.30	12,220.00	13,057.72	n.a.
Township and above	4,971.91	5,175.79	5,574.01	6,156.87	7,015.04	8,261.12	8,978.77	10,307.15	12,127.14	12,944.94	13,747.03
City co-operative and individual	0.81	1.88	3.44	7.54	14.81	33.39	49.69	74.15	92.86	112.78	n.a.
Village and below	258.14	277.81	304.66	376.19	576.45	960.82	1,281.08	1,753.30	2,438.71	2,852.18	n.a.
State	3,951.72	4,054.37	4,340.30	4,747.78	5,171.17	5,840.20	6,201.35	6,901.96	7,772.42	8,072.74	8,311.48
Central	465.74	549.23	646.55	831.32	1,159.84	1,422.39	1,530.41	1,712.43	1,906.79	2,049.59	2,178.76
Local	3,485.98	3,505.14	3,693.75	3,916.46	4,011.33	4,417.81	4,670.94	5,189.53	5865.62	6,023.15	6,132.74
County	532.46	547.03	584.53	676.33	598.58	794.48	817.91	913.45	1,005.14	1,023.78	n.a.
Local state, n.e.c.	2,953.52	2,958.11	3,109.22	3,240.13	3,412.75	3,623.33	3,853.03	4,276.08	4,860.48	4,999.37	n.a.
Collective	1,254.08	1,367.08	1,497.47	1,730.42	2,334.23	3,115.25	3,638.48	4,481.39	5,741.02	6,337.68	6,909.34
of which:											
Excluding village and below	995.94	1,089.27	1,192.81	1,354.23	1,757.78	2,300.79	2,636.81	3,164.92	3,955.37	4,294.64	n.a.
Township and above	995.94	1,089.27	1,192.81	1,354.23	1,757.78	2,300.79	2,616.25	3,137.03	3,921.54	4,254.11	4,574.38
City co-operative		—	—	—	—	—	20.56	27.89	33.83	40.53	n.a.
Village and below	258.14	277.81	304.66	376.19	576.45	814.46	1,001.67	1,316.47	1,785.65	2,043.04	n.a.
of which:											
County	201.85	211.37	228.58	246.09	371.39	494.53	516.81	518.81	584.49	619.68	643.79
Urban street	93.62	105.94	116.44	135.90	172.24	206.45	229.02	254.09	315.77	366.58	395.84
Township	292.63	323.21	354.26	413.26	538.61	741.99	951.28	1,219.74	1,649.06	1,816.75	2,056.98
Village	258.14	277.81	304.66	376.19	576.45	662.71	774.44	1,040.00	1,423.75	1,678.61	n.a.

TABLE A3. (Cont.)

100 million yuan

	1980	1981	1982	1983	1984	1985	1986	1987	1988	1989	1990
Co-operative	–	–	–	–	–	151.75	247.79	304.36	395.73	404.96	n.a.
City co-operative	–	–	–	–	–	–	20.56	27.89	33.83	40.53	n.a.
County town co-operative	–	–	–	–	–	151.75	227.23	276.47	361.90	364.43	n.a.
Collective, n.e.c.	407.84	448.75	493.53	558.98	675.54	857.82	919.14	1,144.39	1,372.22	1,451.10	1,477.77
Individual	0.81	1.88	3.44	7.54	14.81	179.75	308.54	483.09	712.09	881.39	1,067.46
City individual	0.81	1.88	3.44	7.54	14.81	33.39	29.13	46.26	59.03	72.25	n.a.
County town individual	–	–	–	–	–	146.36	279.41	436.83	653.06	809.14	n.a.
Other	24.24	32.15	40.90	54.86	86.09	120.13	161.20	268.17	433.18	618.09	861.16
Joint state-collective	23.79	30.54	38.24	47.69	63.70	79.01	96.16	135.81	183.77	225.37	229.97
Joint state-individual	–	–	0.70	0.48	4.68	8.27	18.02	35.53	68.74	107.64	180.51
Joint collective-individual	0.05	0.13	0.03	0.03	0.16	1.56	3.97	9.44	20.73	46.39	81.76
Joint foreign	0.38	0.69	1.01	3.90	12.27	21.13	31.44	65.84	133.44	199.67	306.64
Overseas Chinese	–	–	0.50	0.50	0.22	2.82	3.26	6.99	13.31	19.17	29.42
Foreign owned	–	–	–	0.68	3.41	4.13	5.07	6.10	7.09	13.13	24.48
Other, n.e.c	0.02	0.79	0.42	1.58	1.65	3.21	3.28	8.46	6.10	6.72	8.38

Notes:
1. This table is my retrospective classification of the gross value of industrial output by type of ownership into the categories used in 1990. As a result, totals and subtotals may not be the same as those originally reported.
2. The figures for 1980 in 1980 constant prices are estimated from the figures in 1970 constant prices and price indexes derived from output in 1981 in 1970 and 1980 constant prices.
3. Because the estimates for 1980 are deflated by type of ownership, the total for township and above differs slightly from the total in Table A6 (which was deflated by branch of industry).

TABLE A4. *Gross Value of Industrial Output at Township Level and Above in Current Prices, by 15 Branches of Industry, 1985–88*

| | 100 million yuan | | | |
	1985	1986	1987	1988
Total	8,722.25	9,799.41	11,828.79	15,291.08
of which:				
Light	4,059.57	4,508.40	5,477.35	7,260.11
Heavy	4,662.64	5,291.01	6,351.44	8,030.97
of which:				
Metallurgy	788.91	961.54	1,129.46	1,391.37
Ferrous metals	554.55	678.88	793.21	961.40
Non-ferrous metals	234.36	282.66	336.25	429.97
Electricity	292.91	313.23	370.89	452.94
Coal and coke	242.40	260.04	284.60	352.43
Petroleum	471.14	529.39	633.76	700.72
Chemicals	934.99	1,057.79	1,345.69	1,855.10
Light	n.a.	411.62	516.76	728.22
Heavy	n.a.	646.17	828.93	1,126.88
Machinery	2,267.25	2,419.96	2,991.16	3,962.86
Light	n.a.	613.76	775.37	1,080.88
Heavy	n.a.	1,806.20	2,215.79	2,881.98
Building materials	425.51	527.02	602.08	773.12
Timber	166.36	187.83	240.88	298.04
Light	n.a.	69.20	70.61	88.55
Heavy	n.a.	118.63	170.27	209.49
Food	1,083.31	1,225.36	1,457.52	1,923.83
Textiles	1,169.04	1,300.10	1,540.48	1,952.18
Clothing	183.89	194.37	235.90	299.12
Leather	85.33	102.03	122.52	155.25
Cultural goods	213.21	235.15	294.83	376.00
Paper	115.92	135.25	172.88	239.43
Other	282.08	350.35	406.14	558.69
Light	n.a.	221.56	290.48	416.65
Heavy	n.a.	128.79	115.66	142.04

TABLE A5. *Gross Value of Industrial Output at Township Level and Above in 1970 Constant Prices, by 15 Branches of Industry, 1978–81*

| | 100 million yuan | | | | 80 yuan |
	1978	1979	1980	1981	1981
Total	4,230.75	4,590.70	4,991.62	5,196.96	5,175.79
of which:					
Light	1,805.71	1,979.55	n.a.	n.a.	n.a.
Heavy	2,425.04	2,611.15	n.a.	n.a.	n.a.
of which:					
Metallurgy	368.91	410.27	430.27	415.40	456.59
Ferrous metals	256.21	287.02	298.89	280.86	313.78
Non-ferrous metals	112.70	123.25	131.38	134.54	142.81
Electricity	161.42	176.72	188.39	194.09	194.86
Coal and coke	126.66	128.18	124.01	122.05	157.26
Petroleum	233.29	249.57	252.31	245.37	282.13
Chemicals	524.98	561.84	622.30	651.28	591.43
Light	179.20	185.41	221.18	250.06	223.32
Heavy	345.78	376.43	401.12	401.22	368.11
Machinery	1,155.46	1,244.84	1,273.62	1,226.17	1,079.95
Light	217.37	239.33	289.96	338.45	312.19
Heavy	938.09	1,005.51	983.66	887.72	767.76
Building materials	153.91	167.32	181.53	180.87	195.07
Timber	77.41	84.75	86.65	86.16	104.90
Light	27.83	29.49	35.25	36.73	40.03
Heavy	49.58	55.26	51.40	49.43	64.87
Food	471.71	518.72	567.96	640.23	690.12
Textiles	529.09	593.06	735.46	868.25	856.02
Clothing	90.79	100.97	134.70	153.43	147.24
Leather	33.92	37.84	50.92	57.79	58.58
Cultural goods	83.09	96.49	112.06	121.48	121.76
Paper	53.84	60.30	64.14	64.02	69.40
Other	166.27	159.83	167.30	170.37	170.48
Light	118.87	117.94	n.a.	n.a.	n.a.
Heavy	47.40	41.89	n.a.	n.a.	n.a.

TABLE A6. Gross Value of Industrial Output at Township Level and Above in 1980 Constant Prices, by 15 Branches of Industry, 1980–90

	1980	1981	1982	1983	1984	1985	1986	1987	1988	1989	1990
						100 million yuan					
Total	4,965.27	5,175.79	5,574.01	6,156.87	7,015.04	8,261.12	8,978.77	10,307.15	12,127.14	12,944.94	13,747.03
of which:											
Light	n.a.	n.a.	n.a.	n.a.	n.a.	4,085.52	4,405.13	5,070.34	6,033.61	n.a.	n.a.
Heavy	n.a.	n.a.	n.a.	n.a.	n.a.	4,175.60	4,573.64	5,236.81	6,093.53	n.a.	n.a.
of which:											
Metallurgy	473.38	456.59	485.23	523.68	579.36	664.04	749.93	822.36	885.39	944.98	1,003.53
Ferrous metals	333.92	313.78	337.28	364.78	400.92	444.32	506.16	554.48	597.13	n.a.	n.a.
Non-ferrous metals	139.46	142.81	147.95	158.90	178.44	219.72	243.77	267.88	288.26	n.a.	n.a.
Electricity	189.14	194.86	207.07	220.23	235.58	272.73	292.19	322.79	356.06	388.35	412.41
Coal and coke	159.79	157.26	166.30	178.33	194.72	208.45	215.55	224.76	241.47	271.84	288.69
Petroleum	290.11	282.13	287.98	310.09	334.11	372.64	405.21	434.67	472.66	504.85	522.39
Chemicals	565.55	591.43	659.01	741.14	830.32	926.74	1,039.50	1,217.05	1,468.83	1,579.28	1,745.87
Light	197.53	223.32	246.90	273.44	217.35	375.09	435.49	511.96	635.91	n.a.	n.a.
Heavy	368.02	368.11	412.11	467.70	512.97	551.65	604.01	705.09	832.92	n.a.	n.a.
Machinery	1,118.20	1,079.95	1,225.06	1,440.48	1,757.10	2,235.14	2,372.44	2,887.10	3,508.91	3,844.65	3,972.89
Light	267.46	312.19	342.96	386.24	465.91	586.48	655.29	807.27	1,047.38	n.a.	n.a.
Heavy	850.74	767.76	882.10	1,054.24	1,291.19	1,648.66	1,717.15	2,079.83	2,461.53	n.a.	n.a.

Table A6. (Cont.)

100 million yuan

	1980	1981	1982	1983	1984	1985	1986	1987	1988	1989	1990
Building materials	195.78	195.07	222.58	245.44	287.27	350.61	408.19	459.57	533.42	569.58	591.12
Timber	105.87	104.90	112.25	116.06	126.81	133.13	142.74	157.50	177.14	181.23	178.71
Light	38.42	40.03	43.93	46.95	52.59	52.17	63.81	64.50	77.80	n.a.	n.a.
Heavy	67.46	64.87	68.32	69.11	74.22	80.96	78.93	93.00	99.34	n.a.	n.a.
Food	612.22	690.12	755.52	794.25	865.84	951.65	1,032.55	1,147.79	1,324.13	1,372.16	1,443.44
Textiles	725.10	856.02	866.85	956.04	1,082.94	1,273.18	1,351.31	1,512.87	1,700.85	1,799.35	1,924.58
Clothing	129.27	147.24	141.94	153.46	178.67	199.29	209.33	242.83	290.57	336.57	384.92
Leather	51.62	58.58	55.67	57.01	62.21	76.54	89.60	104.34	122.16	129.45	164.96
Cultural goods	112.32	121.76	129.37	134.14	151.92	213.16	227.24	276.99	332.26	375.40	412.41
Paper	69.53	69.40	73.96	81.41	92.22	107.68	120.31	138.21	160.57	168.28	178.71
Other	167.41	170.48	185.22	205.11	235.97	276.14	322.68	358.32	552.72	478.96	522.39
Light	n.a.	n.a.	n.a.	n.a.	n.a.	250.28	220.20	263.58	341.98	n.a.	n.a.
Heavy	n.a.	n.a.	n.a.	n.a.	n.a.	25.86	102.48	94.74	210.74	n.a.	n.a.

Notes:

1. The figures for 1980 in 1980 constant prices are estimated from the figures in 1970 constant prices and price indexes derived from output in 1981 in 1970 and 1980 constant prices.

2. Because the estimates for 1980 are deflated by branch of industry, the total differs slightly from the total for township and above in Table A3 (which was deflated by type of ownership).

A Note on Chinese Industry in the First Half of the Eighth Five-Year Plan

Chinese industry began the 1990s with a new surge of growth. The gross value of industrial output (GVIO) rose 14.5 per cent in 1991,[34] and then skyrocketed 26.7 per cent in 1992. The pattern of growth by type of ownership in 1991 was the same as in the late 1980s: collective and individual enterprises increased 18 per cent and 24 per cent, respectively, but state-operated enterprises only 8 per cent.

The policy of austerity introduced after the sharp burst of inflation in 1988 brought prices under control almost at once. The price rise, which had been 11.3 per cent in 1989, dropped to only 0.8 per cent in 1990; and the increases were only 3.1 per cent in 1991 and 2.8 per cent in 1992. Figure 1 shows that here too the pattern of change by type of ownership – that is, the relatively high price increases in state-operated enterprises and relatively low increases (or small declines) in collective, individual and other industry – was the same as in the late 1980s.[35]

Figure 2 shows that China had already overfulfilled the Eighth Five-Year Plan (1991–95) target for the value of industrial output by the end of 1992. The rate of growth will certainly fall from its current high level, but China will easily achieve the 3.6 per cent average annual rate of growth now required to reach the goal for the year 2000. The efficiency with which industry operates, however, will be much more important than fulfilling the goal.

Through 1992, industry grew more rapidly than planned and inflation was kept under control; but as austerity ended, the economy began to overheat once again. During the spring of 1993, the money supply increased,[36] inflation resumed,[37] retail sales surged,[38] and a third of all state-operated enterprises were operating at a loss. But does Beijing have the ability to stop inflation without the disruption, without the unemployment, and without the build-up of unwanted inventories that had occurred in 1989–90?

In a bold move, Zhu Rongji was appointed governor of the People's Bank of China (the central bank) on 2 July with the mission of controlling inflation and restoring people's confidence.[39] In May/June 1991, a World Bank mission concluded

---

[34] See Table 13. Detailed data on industry in 1991 and 1992 are not yet available. The 1993 *Zhongguo tongji zhaiyao* (China Statistical Abstract) has some data on industry in 1992; however, it is too early to expect great detail. In contrast, the detail for 1991 is overdue. The 1992 *Zhongguo tongji nianjian* (China Statistical Yearbook) includes the usual section on industry through 1991, but the best data will be in the 1992 *Zhongguo gongye jingji tongji nianjian* (China Industrial Economics Statistical Yearbook), which has not yet appeared. It is normally available soon after the turn of the year. Note that the preliminary figure of 14.2 per cent that I cited in my article has been revised.

[35] The pattern also suggests that the distortion introduced by the use of current rather than constant prices at many collective, individual and other enterprises has not been corrected.

[36] The money supply rose 40 per cent during the first five months of the year.

[37] In June, prices of consumer goods in large cities were 21.6 per cent higher than they had been in June 1992.

[38] Retail sales in May reached a record level of 109.4 billion yuan, and the 27 percent increase over May 1992 was the biggest increase since 1988–89.

[39] He was already and continues to be the Vice Premier in charge of day-to-day economic affairs.

TABLE 13. *Gross Value of Industrial Output, by Type of Ownership, 1989–92*

| | 100 million yuan | | | |
	1989	1990	1991	1992
Current *yuan*				
Total	22,017.06	23,924.36	28,248.01	36,802.00
State	12,342.91	13,063.75	14,954.58	17,820.00
Collective	7,858.05	8,522.73	10,084.75	14,070.00
Individual	1,057.66	1,290.30	1,609.10	2,484.00
Other	758.44	1,047.57	1,599.58	2,428.00
1980 constant *yuan*				
Total	15,909.90	17,144.51	19,633.89	24,875.14
State	8,072.74	8,311.48	9,027.93	n/a
Collective	6,337.68	6,909.34	8,145.42	n/a
Individual	881.39	1,067.46	1,323.65	n/a
Other	618.09	861.16	1,292.69	n/a

Sources:
    State Statistical Bureau, *Zhongguo tongji nianjian, 1992* (Beijing: China Statistics Press, 1992), pp. 406–7.
    State Statistical Bureau, *Zhongguo tongji zhaiyao, 1993* (Beijing: China Statistics Press, 1993), p. 10.
    See also Table A1 and Table A3.

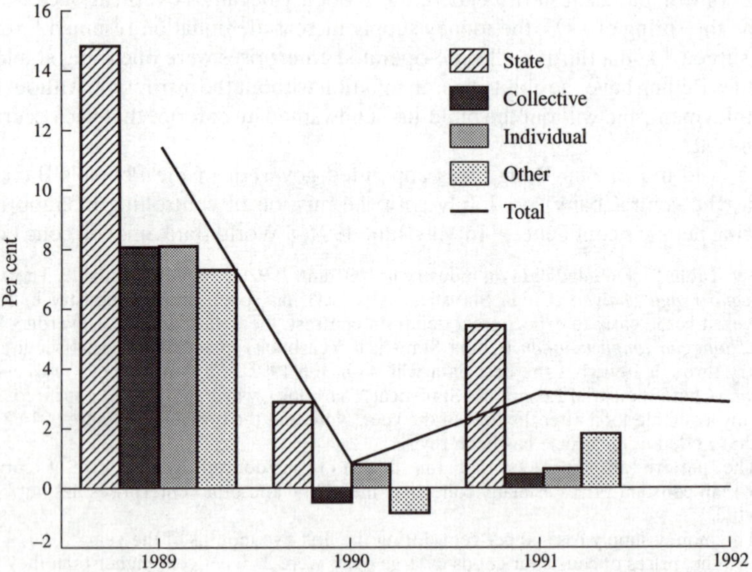

FIGURE 1. *Change in Industrial Prices, By Type of Ownership*

Note:
    Derived from the gross value of industrial output in current and 1980 constant prices in the table in this note.

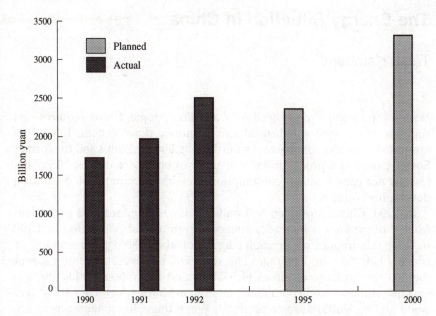

FIGURE 2. *Gross Value of Industrial Output in 1980 Constant Prices*

Note:
  Planned output in 1990 constant prices is converted to 1980 consant prices by the ratio of 1990 to 1980 prices that prevailed in 1990.
Sources:
  [CQ 131] p. 598 and the table in this note.

that in the Eighth Five-Year Plan (1991–95) China has begun to move away from mechanical targeting and to place more emphasis on the macroeconomic framework.[40] This framework, however, is still incomplete, and a considerable amount of decision-making power has already been delegated to provinces, local authorities, and even to enterprises and individuals. And with the rapid growth of market forces, the central government may no longer be able to control things such as provincial and local bank loans and investment. It remains to be seen if the reforms of the last five years have put the tools necessary to regain control of the economy in Vice Premier Zhu's hands.

[40] The World Bank, *China: Reform and the Role of the Plan in the 1990s* (Washington, D.C.: The World Bank, 1992).

The Energy Situation in China

Tatsu Kambara

With a total population of well over a billion people, China requires vast supplies of energy for industrial and economic development. Indeed, in absolute terms, the country ranks third to the United States and the former Soviet Union as a producer and consumer of energy resources. Nevertheless, its per capita energy consumption remains extremely low even for a developing country.

In 1990, China consumed 980 million tonnes standard coal equivalent (SCE)[1] of primary commercial energy. Given a total population of 1,140 million, this implies a per capita figure of about 860 kg per annum, or roughly half the world average. This does not, however, take into account the fact that in large countries like China and India, households also use vast quantities of non-commercial energy, much of which consists of fuel wood and agricultural waste products. When these 200 million tonnes are included, total consumption climbs to over 1,200 million tonnes SCE,[2] which is the equivalent of about one tonne SCE per person per annum.

Nevertheless, it is still true that the ratio of GNP to unit energy consumption is far lower in China than in other developing countries. To state the same point differently, China's energy intensity (the amount of energy consumed relative to GNP) is very high. It follows that there is much room for improvement and development in China's energy situation.

Taken as a whole, China falls into the "developing country" category. But the vast size of the country means that there are many regions already well on the way towards industrial and economic development. Differences in the pace of industrialization have widened regional gaps in economic development, leaving some areas in intermediate positions. No doubt it is entirely predictable that as a socialist, industrial nation, China has, in general, been able to achieve a certain level of development. What is important for present purposes is that differences in regional economic levels have resulted in wide gaps in energy consumption. This has been exacerbated by China's long-term policy of self-reliance. While there are marked regional differences between supplies of, and demand for, energy, lack of transport facilities and other factors have prevented the country from reaching its goal of energy self-sufficiency. This does not merely reflect supply and demand conditions in specific regions: it is not simply a question of linking the north, which produces large amounts of energy, with the south, which

---

[1] In China, standard coal is deemed to be 7,000 Kcal/kg.

[2] According to Wang Qing Yi (ed.), *Energy in China* (Beijing, 1988), p. 50, non-commercial energy consumption was 228,400 thousand tonnes SCE in 1984.

consumes large quantities. Rather, it is a nation-wide problem. It has been a basic principle of official Chinese policy that the country cannot depend on external sources for its industrial energy requirements. Admittedly, this view is gradually losing ground as the economy is opened up and the normal rules of economic activity take over. Indeed, China today is a net exporter of energy – perhaps an apparent exporter, since it has achieved this status by intentionally depressing indigenous energy demand.

In socialist command economies, energy resource management tends to be handled directly by the central government. In recent years China has, however, adopted policies which give local communities and corporations greater authority over production volumes, processing, supplies, and prices. The aim of these policies, which have undoubtedly had a positive effect on the economy, has been to promote the smooth circulation of energy resources. But the gains have been insufficient, and since the principle of competition is not given free rein, there are still significant distortions in energy supplies.

At the root of such problems is the low level of energy prices, which has become a serious impediment to economic development. Low energy prices force the giant national energy companies (coal, petroleum, electricity) into deficit, which must then be made up for with large borrowings and government subsidies. Furthermore, low prices render the principle of price elasticity impotent where large industrial consumers are concerned, so that little if any progress is made towards conservation.

Energy and transport have long been considered the two main obstacles to Chinese economic development. This article examines to what extent economic stagnation has been caused by shortfalls in energy supplies and what can be done to alleviate the situation in the future.

In recent years, the focus of China's industrial structure has moved away from heavy industry in favour of light industry, services, and transport. Although it is difficult to derive a statistical picture of these sectors, an attempt is made here to comment on their current energy consumption and future prospects.

There are two other factors which demand investigation before any conclusions can be reached: energy quality and environmental protection. Energy quality influences energy efficiency, while environmental problems must be considered in the context of long-term energy planning.

This article therefore investigates these considerations, which will form the basis for the creation and implementation of a rational, integrated energy policy.

Economic Growth and Energy Consumption: The Macro Picture
Economic growth and energy consumption

Of all the statistics published in China, the one that most readily reflects economic growth and is closest to the capitalist idea of GNP is "national income." The figure is found by subtracting from what capitalist countries would call "national income" tertiary industrial sectors other than commerce and transport. In Chinese terms, this represents the net production of the five "material production sectors" (manufacturing and mining; agriculture, livestock and forestry; construction; transport and telecommunications; and commerce and restaurants). Intermediate goods are not included in national income, which facilitates comparison with capitalist GNPs. The *Statistical Yearbook of China*, 1992 gives real and index figures for national income from 1952 to 1990.[3]

The increase in China's national income has been tremendous. Thanks partly to improvements in statistical techniques during the 1980s, the figure soared from 368,800 million *yuan* in 1980 to 1,442,900 million *yuan* in 1990. An index using an inflation coefficient to adjust these nominal figures shows real growth of 2.3 times during this period.

Growth was particularly rapid during the early 1980s (the Sixth Five-Year Plan), when real national income rose 1.6 times; during the late 1980s (the Seventh Five-Year Plan), the overall increase was 1.4 times. Average annual growth rates were almost 10 per cent (9.98 per cent) during the early 1980s, and 7.56 per cent during the latter half. Growth for the decade as a whole was 8.76 per cent. In short, rapid economic growth was achieved during this period. The magnitude of these gains can be seen more clearly when compared with the record of the 1970s. Statistics for the earlier decade are admittedly not quite so credible, but during the Fourth Five-Year Plan (1971–75), real national income growth was 5.48 per cent per annum, rising to 6.06 per cent during the Fifth Five-Year Plan (1976–80) (see Table 1).

Economic expansion caused energy demand to increase, which in turn resulted in rises in absolute consumption each year. Primary energy consumption increased from 602,750 thousand tonnes SCE in 1980 to 766,820 thousand tonnes (1985) and reached 987,030 thousand tonnes SCE in 1990.[4] The average growth rate rose from 4.93 per cent in the early 1980s to 5.18 per cent in the latter half of the decade. The conclusion is that the rates of growth of economic expansion and energy consumption moved in opposite directions during the 1980s.

Primary energy consumption grew on average by 5.06 per cent over the 1980s (see Table 1). Meanwhile, at an average of 6.06 per cent per annum, energy production growth outpaced that of consumption during the first half of the decade, though it fell below consumption growth during the last five years, at only 3.97 per cent. The overall rate of increase of production during the 1980s averaged 5.01 per cent per annum.

In absolute terms, China produced 637,350 thousand tonnes SCE in 1980, rising to 855,460 thousand in 1985 and 1,039,220 thousand in 1990. A

[3] *Statistical Yearbook of China* (1992 ed.), pp. 32–3.
[4] *Energy Statistics Yearbook of China* (1991 ed.), p. 5.

TABLE 1. *Economic Growth (National Income) and Energy Demand and Supply in China*

	Economic growth (national income) (%/year)	Primary energy production increase (%/year)	Primary energy consumption increase (%/year)	Energy elasticity of gross national income (average per year)
1971–75 (4FYP)	5.48	9.49	9.17	1.67
1976–80 (5FYP)	6.06	5.51	5.82	0.96
1981–85 (6FYP)	9.98	6.06	4.93	0.49
1986–90 (7FYP)	7.56	3.97	5.18	0.69
1981–90	8.76	5.01	5.06	0.58

Sources:
  Statistical Yearbook of China, 1992, pp. 32 and 33, and *Energy Statistics Yearbook of China*, 1989, p. 7 and 1991, p. 5.

comparison of these figures with those of consumption indicates that the gains in China's energy resource production went to meet demand in both expanding domestic markets and export markets. It may appear that there is still some leeway in the balance between primary energy supplies and demand, but export volumes are, in fact, declining each year. In any case, geopolitical and strategic considerations have been more important determinants of China's energy exports than have economic factors.

A clear macroeconomic view of the relationship between energy consumption and economic growth may be obtained by calculating the gross income elasticity of primary energy consumption. The elasticity value was as low as 0.49 in the early 1980s, but rose to 0.69 in the latter half, so generating a figure of 0.58 for the entire decade (see Table 1). Energy consumption was therefore more efficient in the first half of the 1980s than in the second half. There are doubts about the validity of statistics for earlier periods, but they show a large elasticity value of 1.67 for 1971–75, falling to 0.96 for 1976–80. These figures highlight Chinese efforts in the 1980s to achieve greater energy efficiency for economic growth. As shown later, the gross income elasticity of primary energy consumption is an important factor in predicting future energy demand.

Table 2 gives an overview of the intensity of China's primary energy consumption during the 1980s. Statistics for this period reflect a significant improvement in quality. Calculations of primary energy consumption intensity for the 1960s and 1970s are, by contrast, wholly unreliable, thanks to gross inaccuracies in statistical data. Primary energy intensity shows how much primary energy was consumed per unit of economic results; changes in this measure over time indicate the extent to which a country's energy

TABLE 2. *Energy Intensity in China*

	National income (real term index) (1)	Primary energy consumption (million tonnes SCE) (2)	Energy intensity (2)/(1)	Energy saving rate (%)
1980	516.3	602.75	116.74	4.04
1981	541.5	594.47	109.78	6.96
1982	585.8	620.67	105.95	3.83
1983	644.2	660.40	102.52	3.43
1984	731.9	709.04	96.88	5.64
1985	830.6	766.82	92.32	4.56
1986	894.5	808.50	90.39	1.93
1987	985.7	866.32	87.89	2.50
1988	1,097.2	929.97	84.76	3.13
1989	1,137.2	969.34	85.24	−0.48
1990	1,195.5	987.03	82.56	2.68

Average of 1981–85: 4.88
Target of 1981–85: 4.7
Average of 1986–90: 1.95
Target of 1986–90: 3.0

Sources:
   Statistical Yearbook of China, 1992, p. 33, and *Energy Statistics Yearbook of China*, 1989, p. 150 and 1991, p. 5.

consumption is becoming more, or less, efficient. The proxy for economic results is an index of national income that takes 1952 as 100. The calculations show primary energy intensity to have risen to 116.74 in 1980, but subsequently to have fallen to 92.32 (1985) and 82.56 (1990). The only year-on-year rise in energy intensity occurred in 1989, when more primary energy was required to produce the same volume of national income.

Such declines in energy intensity are astounding. To describe them as expressing China's *nominal* rate of energy conservation would be to ignore the fact that these figures are precisely the ones that are normally used in discussions of Chinese energy conservation rates. They suggest a rate of 4.88 per cent between 1981 and 1985 (higher than the target of 4.7 per cent), but only 1.95 per cent for 1986–1990, when the target was 3 per cent. It should be emphasized, however, that this is merely the nominal energy conservation rate: a true estimate would require more adjustments. Even so, these figures do indicate the rough magnitude of the gains that have been made.

To follow this examination of the relationship between economic growth and energy consumption, the next section looks at statistical measures of

TABLE 3. *Industry-Specific National Income in China (billion yuan)*

	1980	1985	1990
National income (nominal)	368.8 (100%)	702.0 (100%)	1,438.4 (100%)
Agriculture	132.6 (36.0%)	249.2 (35.5%)	500.0 (34.8%)
Manufacturing Industry	180.4 (48.9%)	316.3 (45.1%)	661.0 (45.9%)
Construction	18.5 (5.0%)	40.9 (5.8%)	83.9 (5.8%)
Transport	12.6 (3.4%)	25.9 (3.7%)	78.7 (5.5%)
Commerce etc.	24.7 (6.7%)	69.7 (9.9%)	114.8 (7.9%)
National income (1980 price)	368.8	593.3	854.0 (8.76%)*
Agriculture	132.6	199.8	244.0 (6.29%)
Manufacturing Industry	180.4	293.6	477.8 (10.23%)
Construction	18.5	32.0	42.3 (8.62%)
Transport	12.6	22.1	35.2 (13.63%)
Commerce etc.	24.7	46.0	54.8 (8.29%)

Average increase rate of 1981–85: 9.98%
Average increase rate of 1986–90: 7.56%

Notes:
   * increase rate of industry-specific national income from 1981 to 1990.
Source:
   Statistical Yearbook of China, 1992, pp. 32 and 33.

the extent to which industrial development has been impeded by shortfalls in China's energy supplies. Chinese sources provide yearly estimates of shortfalls in various energy sources, although questions remain about the basis of their compilation.[5] Furthermore, economic activities continue notwithstanding energy shortfalls and it is therefore useful to investigate whether, and to what extent, the decline in energy-intensity has made up for the deficiencies and enabled growth to be maintained in China.

Industry-specific energy consumption trends

Table 3 shows the percentage contribution to China's national income of various industries in the key years of 1980, 1985 and 1990. Table 4 shows industry-by-industry primary energy consumption for the same years: it includes consumption figures not only for material production sectors (the equivalent of national income), but also for non-material production sectors and the household sector.

The two tables indicate that although there was some change in the

[5] In *Energy of China*, No. 3 (1991), p. 5, the energy shortfall is estimated at 3% a year during the Seventh Five-Year Plan period.

TABLE 4. *Change of Industry-Specific Primary Energy Consumption in China (million tonnes SCE)*

	1980	1985	1990
Primary energy consumption			
Total	602.75 (100%)	766.82 (100%)	987.03 (100%)
Material production sectors (= national income)			
Agriculture	34.71 (5.8%)	40.45 (5.3%)	48.52 (4.9%)
Manufacturing Industry	410.10 (68.0%)	510.68 (66.6%)	675.78 (68.5%)
Construction	9.56 (1.6%)	13.02 (1.7%)	12.13 (1.2%)
Transport	29.02 (4.8%)	37.13 (4.8%)	45.41 (4.6%)
Commerce etc.	5.18 (0.9%)	7.66 (1.0%)	12.47 (1.3%)
Non-material production sectors	18.35 (3.0%)	24.70 (3.2%)	34.73 (3.5%)
Household sector	95.83 (15.9%)	133.18 (17.4%)	157.99 (16.0%)

Average increase rate of 1981–85: 4.93%
Average increase rate of 1986–90: 5.18%

Source:
Energy Statistics Yearbook of China, 1989, p. 156 and 1991, p. 143.

relative proportions of national income accounted for by different sectors during the decade, this was not large. For example, in 1980 agriculture contributed 36 per cent of the national income; in 1990 the corresponding figure was 34.8 per cent – only a slight decline. Manufacturing also fell slightly from 48.9 per cent in 1980 to 45.9 per cent in 1990. The gains were made by the construction, transport and commercial sectors, which respectively accounted for 5 per cent, 3.4 per cent and 6.7 per cent of the national income in 1980, but 5.8 per cent, 5.5 per cent and 9.9 per cent ten years later.

The real implications of these figures are shown at the bottom of Table 3 and indicate the actual rate of increase of national income. They are derived on the basis of an indexed version of 1980 prices. What emerges is that during the first five years of the decade, real national income rose by 60.9 per cent compared with a rise of only 43.9 per cent during the subsequent five years.

In sectoral terms, national income generated by manufacturing rose by a steady 10.23 per cent per year during the period, but that of agriculture increased by only 6.29 per cent. The relative importance of construction, transport, and commerce is smaller, although it is worth recording that all of them still experienced two or three-fold growth over the ten-year period. This contrasts with industry-specific primary energy consumption. Between

1980 and 1990, consumption for the agricultural sector rose from 34,710 to 48,520 thousand tonnes SCE in absolute terms, although this sector's percentage of total consumption declined from 5.8 to 4.9 per cent. Similarly, manufacturing increased from 410,100 to 675,780 thousand tonnes SCE, but maintained its share virtually unchanged (68 to 68.5 per cent). Transport rose from 29,020 thousand to 45,410 thousand tonnes SCE, and its share also remained virtually unchanged: 4.8 per cent at the beginning of the period compared with 4.6 per cent at the end.

Where primary energy consumption saw its largest increase was in non-material production sectors and households, which respectively rose from 18,350 thousand (3 per cent) and 95,830 thousand tonnes SCE (15.9 per cent) in 1980 to 34,730 thousand (3.5 per cent) and 157,990 thousand tonnes (16 per cent) in 1990. China's non-material production sectors combine with the commercial sector to constitute what in the west would be called the "service sector." The general trend, therefore, was for the share of primary energy consumption accounted for by the agriculture, manufacturing, construction and transport sectors to decline (though they remained the dominant sectors in absolute terms), and that of service and household sectors to rise.

Table 5 compares growth rates of sector-specific national income and

TABLE 5. *Industry-Specific National Income and Primary Energy Consumption (%)*

	Average increase rate of 1981–85	Average increase rate of 1986–90	Average increase rate of 1981–90
National income (actual)	9.98	7.56	8.76
Agriculture	8.54	4.08	6.29
Manufacture	10.23	10.23	10.23
Construction	11.58	5.74	8.62
Transport	11.89	9.76	13.63
Commerce etc.	13.24	3.56	8.29
Primary Energy Consumption	4.93	5.18	5.06
Agriculture	3.1	3.7	3.41
Manufacture	4.5	5.8	5.12
Construction	6.4	−1.4	2.41
Transport	5.1	4.0	4.58
Commerce etc.	8.1	9.7	9.18
Non-material production sectors	6.1	7.1	6.59
Household section	6.8	3.5	5.13

Source:
   Statistical Yearbook of China, 1992, pp. 32 and 33, and *Energy Statistics Yearbook of China*, 1989, p. 156 and 1991, p. 143.

primary energy consumption. It reveals that manufacturing (the weightiest sector) experienced a high 10.23 per cent average annual growth rate during the 1980s (the rate was the same for both the first and second halves), while over the same period its growth in primary energy consumption rose by only 4.5 per cent in the first half and a slightly steeper 5.8 per cent in the second. This is the main reason why aggregate primary energy consumption grew more sharply in the second half of the decade than in the earlier 1980s.

In the first half of the 1980s agriculture grew at an annual rate of 8.54 per cent, slowing to 4.08 per cent in the latter half, and generating a decade-long growth rate of 6.29 per cent per annum. By contrast, its primary energy consumption increased by only 3.1 per cent during the earlier period, but then accelerated to 3.7 per cent. Most of this can be accounted for by an increase in fuel energy consumption: China introduced more irrigation pumps, agricultural machinery and agricultural and fishing vehicles in the last five years of the decade.

Though transport experienced the highest growth rate (13.6 per cent) of any sector, its primary energy consumption grew by only about half – 4.6 per cent. The reasons for this paradoxical result are probably first, that consumption of motor car fuels (petrol, diesel oil) increased despite strict rationing, and secondly, that mass-transit facilities (railways, shipping and airlines) become more energy efficient.

A look at the changes in relative size of the heavy and light industrial sectors illustrates the strategic changes in the structural composition of Chinese industry. Chinese policy has traditionally emphasized heavy industry, but economic liberalization measures were associated with increasing emphasis on light industries. On the basis of official statistics, 1980-indexed real figures show heavy industry and light industry to have been roughly equal in 1985. But by 1990, the 1980 situation in favour of heavy industry had been reversed and light industry had become the larger sector, albeit by a small margin (see Table 6). By the same token, although primary energy consumption continues to be far larger for heavy industry, light industry's share has been growing. In 1980, heavy industry accounted for 82.6 per cent of all the primary energy consumed by the manufacturing sector, compared with only 17.4 per cent for light industry. By 1985, the corresponding figures were to 80.1 per cent and 19.9 per cent; and by 1990, 79.7 per cent and 20.3 per cent.

Annual primary energy consumption growth rates highlight this change even more clearly. The growth rate for heavy industry was 3.84 per cent per annum during the first half of the decade and 5.65 per cent during the second. For light industry, however, the figures were 7.35 and 6.2 per cent. (The rates for the entire manufacturing sector were 4.48 and 5.76 per cent.)

The conclusion to be drawn from this analysis is that much of the energy conservation achieved by China during this period derived from changes in the industrial structure. It is virtually impossible to calculate the precise

TABLE 6. *Industrial Gross Value and Primary Energy Consumption of Heavy and Light Industries in China*

| | *(unit: billion yuan, million tonnes SCE)* | | |
	1980	*1985*	*1990*
Industrial gross value (Nominal)	515.4 (100%)	971.6 (100%)	2,392.4 (100%)
Heavy industry	272.4 (52.9%)	514.1 (52.9%)	1,211.1 (50.6%)
Light industry	243.0 (47.1%)	457.5 (47.1%)	1,181.3 (49.4%)
Industrial gross value (actual, 1980 price)	515.4 (100%)	907.1 (100%)*	1,688.9 (100%)*
Heavy industry	272.4 (52.9%)	452.3 (49.7%)	804.2 (47.6%)
Light industry	243.0 (47.1%)	457.6 (50.3%)	886.0 (52.4%)
Primary energy consumption	410.10 (100%)	510.68 (100%)	675.78 (100%)
Heavy industry	338.86 (82.6%)	409.12 (80.1%)	538.59 (79.7%)
Light industry	71.24 (17.4%)	101.56 (19.9%)	137.19 (20.3%)
Average increase rates of primary energy consumption	*1981–85*	*1986–90*	
Industry sector total	4.48%	5.76%	
Heavy industry	3.84%	5.65%	
Light industry	7.35%	6.20%	

Note:
Total marked* do not coincide with the sum of their parts because the index of heavy and light industries and the total industry index are not comparable.
Source:
Statistical Yearbook of China, 1992, pp. 54 and 55, and *Energy Statistics Yearbook of China*, 1989, p. 156 and 1991, p. 143.

contribution to aggregate energy conservation, but the best estimates put the figure at about 70 per cent.[6]

Regional breakdown of energy supplies and demand

This section looks briefly at regional differences in the supply and demand balance for primary energy. Neither regional energy production nor consumption changed significantly during the 1980s, and the discussion is therefore limited to 1990 statistical data. Regional divisions follow those in the *Statistical Yearbook of China*, which divides all the country's cities, provinces and autonomous regions into six districts: North, North-east, East, Central South, South-west, and North-west.

Aggregate primary energy resource production reached 1,039,220 thou-

---

[6] Estimated by the Energy Research Institute, Beijing.

TABLE 7. *Regional Primary Energy Supply and Consumption, Economic Growth and Energy Intensity in China (1990)*

	North	North-east	East	Central South	South-west	North-west	Total
	(United: million tonnes SCE, billion yuan)						
Primary energy production	303.1	216.8	160.0	144.3	109.2	87.2	1,039.2
−export + import primary energy supply (net)	–	–	–	–	–	–	993.6
Primary energy consumption	180.4	166.6	240.4	185.2	104.4	76.9	987.0
% nation-wide	18.9%	17.5%	25.2%	19.4%	10.9%	8.1%	100%
Economic growth (national income)	185.4	169.6	488.8	354.5	154.4	81.2	1,442.9
% nation-wide	12.9%	11.8%	34.1%	24.7%	10.8%	5.7%	100%
Energy intensity	0.97	0.98	0.49	0.52	0.68	0.95	0.67

Sources:
Statistical Yearbook of China, 1991, p. 36, and *Energy Statistics Yearbook of China*, 1991, pp. 93, 170 and 206.

sand tonnes SCE during 1990. After subtracting exports and adding imports, China's indigenous supply was 993,600 thousand tonnes SCE. Regionally, the North has traditionally been a major coal producer and it generated 303,100 thousand tonnes SCE; the North-east and East are rich in petroleum and they too had large production volumes respectively of 216,800 and 160,000 thousand tonnes SCE. They were followed by the Central South, South-west, and North-west in that order. As Table 7 shows, the top-ranked North produced three times more energy resources than the bottom-ranked North-west.

China's exports mainly consist of oil from the Daqing oil field in Heilongjiang province (North-east); and coal from Shanxi province and Inner Mongolia Autonomous Region in the North. Exports have been subtracted from regional totals. Imports consist of crude oil and petroleum products destined for the East and Central South; and coal (from Australia) for the East. These have been added to regional totals.

In 1990, China's leading regional *consumer* of primary energy was the East, with 240,400 thousand tonnes SCE, followed by the Central South (185,200 thousand tonnes SCE), and the North (180,400 thousand tonnes SCE). The North-east was also a relatively large consumer, using 166,600 thousand tonnes SCE. The South-west and North-west were, by contrast, much less significant. Notice that statistics are not available for Hainan Island and Tibet, so that the total is less than 987,030 thousand tonnes SCE.

Table 7 summarizes regional supplies of, and demand for, primary energy. It emerges that the North-east, South-west and North-west have been able to achieve local balance and even demonstrate a small surplus. As of 1990, the North showed a large supply surplus, whereas the East and the Central South suffered deficits. These latter two regions have had to secure their energy resources through inputs from other regions or overseas.

A comparison of regional energy consumption and economic activity generates unexceptional conclusions. First, China's most important economic region is the East, which in 1990 produced 488,800 million *yuan* of national income, or 34.1 per cent of the total. Yet this region was responsible for only 25.2 per cent of national primary energy consumption (its energy intensity only 0.49). Next in importance in terms of national income was the Central South, which produced 354,500 million *yuan* or 24.7 per cent of the total. It accounted for only 19.4 per cent of total primary energy consumption and had an energy intensity value of 0.52. Then came the North, the North-east and the South-west, with energy intensities of 0.97, 0.98 and 0.68 respectively. At the bottom was the North-west, which produced only 81,200 million *yuan* of national income, but consumed 76,900 thousand tonnes SCE of primary energy to achieve an intensity value of 0.95.

These figures highlight the efficiency with which the East has been able to use energy in pursuit of its economic activities. An important factor is that much of the region's manufacturing income comes from light industry, which in recent years has also contributed much to its growth. The same may be said of the Central South. In the North, North-east and North-west, however, heavy industry accounts for a large percentage of manufacturing, and energy intensity values are consequently higher.

Changing pattern of energy sources of supply and demand

The mainstay of China's energy structure has for many years been coal, a situation which continues to this day and is unlikely to change in the near future. During the 1980s the coal component in the energy structure actually rose: in 1980 coal accounted for 69.5 per cent of primary energy production but by 1990 it had gained another 3.7 percentage points to reach 74.2 per cent. During the same period, petroleum's share declined from 23.7 to 19 per cent; and that of natural gas from 3 to 2 per cent. By contrast, hydroelectricity's contribution rose from 3.8 to 4.8 per cent. These changes are attributable to large increases in coal production during the decade, side by side with more modest gains for petroleum and natural gas. Meanwhile, the coal component of primary energy consumption rose 4 percentage points from 72.2 to 76.2 per cent, while the petroleum component declined from 20.7 to 16.6 per cent and that of natural gas also fell from 3.1 to 2.1 per cent. The hydroelectricity component again increased – from 4 to 5.1 per cent.

In 1990, China produced 1,080 million tonnes of raw coal compared with only 620 million in 1980. This represented a 5.7 per cent annual growth rate for the decade. During the same period, petroleum (crude oil) production increased from 105.95 million to 138.31 million tonnes – an average annual growth rate of 2.7 per cent. Natural gas production increased from 14,200 million to 15,300 million cubic metres, implying an annual growth rate of only 0.7 per cent. Hydroelectricity generation, however, more than doubled – from 58.2 TWh to 126.4 TWh – to give an annual growth of 7.9 per cent. Total electricity output, including secondary energy produced at thermo-electric plants, also doubled, rising from 300.6 TWh in 1980 to 621.2 TWh in 1990 (an annual growth of 7.5 per cent).

The growth rate for coal production did, however, fall from 7 per cent in the early 1980s to 4.4 per cent in the latter five years. During the first half of the decade, China encouraged the development of local non-state-operated coal mines, but thereafter cut back on such expansion. Overall, the growth rate for the 1980s exhibited no change from the 5.7 per cent annual growth rate recorded during the 1970s. By contrast, petroleum growth rates fell sharply from the levels of 20 per cent per annum achieved while the Daqing and Shengli fields were developed in the 1960s and 1970s. Meanwhile, hydroelectricity growth accelerated during the 1980s, from 6.4 per cent at the beginning of the decade to 8.6 per cent at the end.

Consumption growth rates for various primary energy sources more or less mirror production growth rates: coal consumption grew by 5.6 per cent, petroleum 2.8 per cent, natural gas 0.8 per cent and hydroelectricity 7.9 per cent (see Table 8). It is, however, worth noting that oil consumption grew faster than oil production. This can be attributed to the sharp increase (China's strict rationing system notwithstanding) in liquid fuel consumption in the transport and agricultural sectors – a factor which also contributed to the decline in China's oil exports. Consumption of petroleum products has been converted to a crude oil basis in order to determine primary energy consumption. For both oil and coal, consumption is defined as export/import-adjusted supplies (production minus exports plus imports) minus conversion and transport losses.

Primary energy consumption figures provide a useful means of comparing the consumption of different fuels, but final energy consumption figures are required before one can discover what kind of fuel is being used by which industrial sectors. Table 9 contains summary figures by sector and fuel calculated from data in the *Energy Statistics Yearbook of China, 1991*, relating primarily to the 1990 energy balance sheet. This table takes into account energy conversion (processing to produce petroleum and coal derivatives, and power generated at thermoelectric plants), subtracts energy losses, and is stock-adjusted. Some of these energy sources, however, are used as raw materials for petroleum and coal derivatives and industrial gas

TABLE 8. *Primary Energy Production and Consumption in China (million tonnes SCE)*

	1980	1985	1990	Average increase rate, 1981–90
Production				
Coal (raw)	442.97 (69.5%)	623.07 (72.8%)	771.36 (74.2%)	5.7%
Crude oil	151.36 (23.7%)	178.43 (20.9%)	197.58 (19.0%)	2.7%
Natural gas	18.98 (3.0%)	17.20 (2.0%)	20.35 (2.0%)	0.7%
Hydroelectricity	24.04 (3.8%)	36.76 (4.3%)	51.48 (4.8%)	7.9%
Total	637.35 (100%)	855.46 (100%)	1,039.22 (100%)	5.01%
Consumption				
Coal	435.18 (72.2%)	581.25 (75.8%)	752.02 (76.2%)	5.6%
Crude oil	124.77 (20.7%)	131.13 (17.1%)	164.14 (16.6%)	2.8%
Natural gas	18.69 (3.1%)	16.87 (2.2%)	20.23 (2.1%)	0.8%
Hydroelectricity	24.11 (4.0%)	37.57 (4.9%)	51.60 (5.1%)	7.9%
Total	602.75 (100%)	766.82 (100%)	987.03 (100%)	5.06%

Source:
Energy Statistics Yearbook of China, 1991, pp. 81 and 135.

TABLE 9. *Final Energy Consumption in China (1990) (million tonnes SCE)*

	Raw coal and coal products	Crude oil and petroleum products	Natural gas	Electricity	Heated water	Total
Manufacture	328.32	75.02	14.43	870.97	17.48	616.22 (67.4%)
Construction	3.11	4.77	1.41	2.65	0.03	11.97 (1.3%)
Agriculture	15.47	15.08	0	17.40	0	47.95 (5.2%)
Transport	15.11	23.98	0.07	4.32	0.02	43.5 (4.8%)
Commerce etc.	21.30	12.27	0.16	11.36	0.47	45.56 (5.0%)
Household	118.69	4.57	2.47	19.60	3.05	148.38 (16.2%)
Total	502.05 (54.9%)	135.68 (14.9%)	18.54 (2.0%)	236.29 (25.9%)	21.05 (2.3%)	913.61 (100%)

Source:
Energy Statistics Yearbook of China, 1991, pp. 230–31 (Energy Balance Sheet, 1990).

TABLE 10. *Final Energy Consumption in China, various shares in the 1980s (%)*

		Raw coal and coal products	Crude oil and petroleum products	Natural gas	Electricity	Heated water
Manufacture and	1980	54.4	14.5	4.7	24.2	2.2
construction	1985	55.7	13.1	3.3	25.7	2.2
	1990	52.8	12.7	2.5	29.2	2.9
Agriculture	1980	32.8	34.9	0	32.3	0
	1985	40.0	27.7	0	32.3	0
	1990	32.3	31.4	0	36.3	0
Transport	1980	49.7	46.4	–	3.9	–
	1985	46.0	46.8	–	7.2	–
	1990	34.8	55.2	–	9.9	–
Commerce etc.	1980	48.7	32.9	0.3	15.3	2.8
	1985	53.3	24.9	0.2	20.7	0.8
	1990	46.7	26.9	0.3	24.9	1.0
Household	1980	91.0	2.3	0.3	4.7	1.7
	1985	88.2	2.8	0.4	7.1	1.5
	1990	79.9	3.1	1.7	13.2	2.1
Total	1980	58.6	16.1	3.3	20.1	1.9
	1985	60.0	14.3	2.3	21.6	1.8
	1990	54.9	14.9	2.0	25.9	2.3

Source:
Energy Statistics Yearbook of China, 1989, p. 156 and 1991, p. 143.

rather than as fuels,[7] and this is ignored in the final energy consumption calculations. The table yields the following shares of total final energy consumption throughout China in 1990: manufacturing 67.4 per cent, construction 1.3 per cent, agriculture 5.2 per cent, transport 4.8 per cent, commerce 5 per cent and households 16.2 per cent. This, it will be noted, is roughly the same distribution as was observable for primary energy consumption.

Coal converted to electricity at thermoelectric plants and petroleum processed at refineries are included in the primary energy consumption of the manufacturing sector. This gives the sector higher consumption than its actual energy requirements, but since the manufacturing sector is also the largest consumer of these secondary energy sources, sector-by-sector shares do not show any significant variation between primary and final energy consumption. The breakdown of final energy consumption by fuels is as follows: coal 54.9 per cent, petroleum 14.9 per cent, natural gas

[7] Wang Qing Yi, *Energy in China,* p. 47 (Tables 2–13) calculates that 49,446 thousand tonnes SCE were used in this way during 1985, but leaves it in the total.

2 per cent, electric power 25.9 per cent and miscellaneous (heated water) 2.3 per cent.

It is true that Chinese statistics are not always based on rigorous criteria. For example, data which should be included under transport may end up under manufacturing or agriculture; nor is the distinction between heavy and light industry unambiguous. Certain caveats must therefore be kept in mind in an analysis of sector-specific economic and energy data. Even so, the final energy statistics do make clear which sector is using how much of what kind of fuel. Table 10 summarizes this information.

The estimates in Table 10 illustrate absolute and percentage changes over time through a comparison of the years 1980, 1985 and 1990. Note that the decline in the increase of the production rate of petroleum and natural gas means that fuel's share of consumption in individual sectors in most cases did not change and actually fell slightly in a few cases. Consumption of coal, which is clearly the dominant source of energy for all sectors, contracted quite sharply in the transport and household sectors, where electricity and oil expanded. Electricity will probably continue to take up coal's share in the future.

Critical Issues in the Supply–Demand Balance and the Outlook for the Future

Unequal distribution of resources

With its large surface area and continental shelf, China has vast reserves of natural resources. Geological estimates indicate the existence of enormous ultimate reserves of energy resources, although these are not all proved to be recoverable. There is now a trickle of data available for recoverable resources, although the figures are still small.

However it is known that in 1991 China's proved and provable reserves of coal, its largest energy resource, were calculated at 966,700 million tonnes, some 30 per cent of which (290,000 million tonnes) are recoverable.[8] Petroleum reserves stood at 12,500 million tonnes proved and provable, 2,200 million tonnes recoverable; the corresponding figures for natural gas were 800,000 million cubic metres and approximately 240,000 million cubic metres. Developable hydropower capacity was estimated to be 380 GW, of which 35 GW has already been developed.

Coal is found virtually everywhere in China, though the major deposits are in the North, North-east, and North-west. Together, these three regions contain about 84% of the total. Bituminous coal accounts for 75 per cent of the country's proved and provable reserves (30 per cent of this is coking coal), anthracite 12 per cent and lignite 13 per cent. In the North, Shanxi and Inner Mongolia are known for their large coal mines. In general,

---

[8] *Energy in China 1992* (Beijing: Ministry of Energy), p. 8

only about 7 per cent of China's coal is suitable for open-cast mining, and some 70 per cent of this is lignite. Nevertheless, China's reserve/production ratio of over 200 years means that the country can depend on coal to supply the major portion of its energy requirements well into the future.

There are, however, problems of distribution: most coal is mined at locations far from where it is consumed. Coal from Guizhou also suffers from quality problems. Its high sulphur content makes it an environmentally-unsafe fuel, although it remains one of the region's principal energy sources.

Statistics show a clear decline in China's proved and recoverable petroleum reserves – from 2,323 million tonnes at the end of 1985 to 2,199 million tonnes at the end of 1990.[9] This has reduced the reserve/production ratio from 18.6 to 15.9 years. Crude oil production is meanwhile on the increase and new deposits are being discovered, although these are not enough to replace what has been lost through production. Between 1986 and 1990, for example, China produced 682 million tonnes of petroleum; yet its proved and recoverable reserves were 124 million tonnes less at the end of 1990 than they had been at the end of 1985 because discoveries of newly-exploitable oil had averaged only 111.6 million tonnes a year. A further contributory factor was that only a small part of the additional proved and recoverable reserves was located in new areas. Rather, they were the result of the further exploitation of undeveloped reserves in existing oil fields or the use of secondary and tertiary recovery technology in order to improve recovery rates in already-developed sites. Like coal, oil is unevenly distributed in China, in favour of the North-east, East, and North-west.

There are two kinds of natural gas reserves: independent supplies and reserves which are associated with oil fields. Independent fields are the larger of the two. China's development of this energy source is limited, the largest regional producer of natural gas being Sichuan province, whose 6,620 million cubic metres account for 43 per cent of the total 15,300 million. Many other regions have still failed to develop their reserves because, unlike Sichuan, they lack both the production and consumption infrastructure. Use and production of LPG from gas associated with oil fields has, nevertheless, grown in recent years. China now has proved recoverable natural gas reserves of 240,000 million cubic metres. This is equivalent to 16 years of production at current rates, which during the last decade have held more or less steady at 12,000–15,000 million cubic metres per annum. The failure to increase more rapidly is due to the absence of the required infrastructure: production facilities, transport pipelines and urban gas supply systems are all lacking. Nevertheless, China's natural gas resources are

[9] From *Energy of China*, No. 2 and No. 3 (1991) p. 6 and p. 7.

estimated to be large and more will to doubt be confirmed and developed in the future. The most promising fields are in the Ordos Basin, the Caidam Basin, and the Yinggehai Basin off Hainan Island.

China has developed 9 per cent (35 GW) of its hydroelectric capacity (380 GW). Even with the 20 GW of new capacity under construction, the country will have developed only 15 per cent of its potential, leaving 85 per cent untapped. Almost 70 per cent of the latent capacity is located in the South-west – much of it (70 GW) in the form of smaller projects (under 12,000 KW each), which are easier to develop than large, costly complexes. If this capacity were tapped, it could provide electricity requirements across several regions – hence the government's encouragement of hydroelectric construction. As of 1989, China had 63,000 small-scale hydroelectric plants producing a total of 11.8 GW of power. Larger plants are also under construction, the main projects being along the upper and middle reaches of the Huanghe (Yellow) River, and along the Changjiang (Yangzi), Hongshui and Lancang rivers. At the beginning of 1992, the National People's Congress also gave the go-ahead for a massive 17.68 GW project at the Sanxia (Three Gorges) Dam.

Large gains have been made in the production of thermoelectricity, which is a secondary form of energy. Output rose from 310 TWh in 1985 to 494.5 TWh in 1990. This sharp growth (10 per cent per annum) is expected to continue and China's goal is to produce 1,200 TWh a year and 240 GW of generation-capacity by the year 2000 (three-quarters of which will be dependent on the thermoelectric plants). All the new thermoelectric plants will burn coal, the government having totally banned new oil-fuelled sites. Unfortunately, China is near the limit of its capacity to transport coal and the construction of new railways requires long lead times. As a result, it has been necessary to locate larger thermoelectric plants adjacent to areas of coal production: Shanxi, Inner Mongolia, Shaanxi, Ningxia, Henan, Anhui, Shandong and Guizhou.

China completed its first nuclear power plant – the Qingshan facility in Hai Yan prefecture, Zhejiang province (near Shanghai) – in December 1991. Phase I is scheduled to produce 1.7 TWh a year; phase II will add two more reactors of 600 MW each. The Daiya Bay facility (two reactors, 900 MW) in Guangdong Province will produce 3,300 MW by 2000. Other projects are meanwhile being formulated to fulfil an ultimate goal of 6,000 MW in nuclear capacity.

The general inference of the foregoing analysis is that whilst China possesses more than adequate energy resources, in terms of current production and latent capacity, it nevertheless suffers from the uneven distribution of these resources over its enormous territory. The North and North-east are rich in coal and oil respectively and the South-west has hydro-power. But the coastal regions, where most major cities and industrial areas are located, are compelled to rely on outside and frequently distant sources of energy

TABLE 11. *Geographical Distribution of Energy Resources in China (1990 end)*
(billion tonnes SCE)

	North	North-east	East	Central South	South-west	North-west	Total
Coal	414.3	20.2	42.3	23.1	69.2	77.9	647.0 (67%)
	(64.0%)	(3.1%)	(6.5%)	(3.7%)	(10.7%)	(12.0%)	(100%)
Oil and natural	2.7	9.2	3.4	0.5	0.5	2.7	19.0 (2%)
gas	(14.4%)	(48.3%)	(18.2%)	(2.5%)	(2.5%)	(14.0%)	(100%)
Hydroelectricity	5.3	5.3	13.0	28.0	206.5	36.9	295.0 (31%)
	(1.8%)	(1.8%)	(4.4%)	(9.5%)	(70.0%)	(12.5%)	(100%)
Total	422.3	34.7	58.7	51.6	276.2	117.5	961.0
	(43.9%)	(3.6%)	(6.1%)	(5.4%)	(28.7%)	(12.2%)	(100%)

Notes:
   Raw coal: 901.5 billion tonnes of proved and provable reserves is calculated to 647 billion tonnes SCE. Crude oil: 12.5 billion tonnes of proved and provable reserves is calculated to 17.8 billion tonnes SCE. Natural gas: 800 billion cubic metres of proved and provable reserves is calculated to 1 billion tonnes SCE. Hydroelectricity: 340 GW of potential power is calculated to 295 billion tonnes SCE.
Source:
   Energy in China 1990 (Beijing: Ministry of Energy), various pages.

supplies. Shanghai, for example, has to import all its coal, oil and electricity (hydro and nuclear) from elsewhere (see Table 11).

Furthermore, most major fuel deposits are located in remote areas and are therefore costly to transport. It is even reported that coal lies piled up in Shanxi for lack of a means of hauling it out. What is more, the situation is likely to become even worse. There is insufficient water to provide either a slurry pipe or facilities for coal washing, which would help rationalize transport. It may be that the high cost of bringing in water supplies explains why only 17 per cent of China's coal is washed at all.

In order to combat such deficiencies, the decision has been taken to build thermoelectric plants at the quarries themselves and to distribute electricity by means of high-voltage lines. But even this does not provide a total solution: there are power plants and factory boilers scattered throughout the country which still need their own coal. Similarly, if hydroelectricity is developed in the South-west, it will still require massive power line construction so that it can be distributed to where it is needed. The same applies to oil developed in the Tarim Basin in the North-west, where over $5,000 million will be required to build the pipeline needed to carry supplies 3,000 km to consumers in the East.

All these problems derive from the uneven distribution of energy resources. The upshot is that China's economically-developable energy reserves are not, after all, so impressively large.

Rising costs, limited funds

In 1981, China invested some 14,124 million *yuan* in its energy industry. By 1990, this figure had risen to 84,674 million *yuan*. Total investment during

TABLE 12. *Capital Investment in Energy Industries in China (billion yuan) (state companies)*

	1981	1985	1990
Energy industries (total)	14.124	36.641	84.674
Capital construction	9.464	20.529	55.827
Replacement	4.660	5.592	12.511
Miscellaneous	–	10.520	14.051
Coal mining industry	3.606	8.716	16.446
Capital construction	2.315	5.511	9.882
Replacement	1.291	2.425	4.751
Miscellaneous	–	0.780	0.980
Oil and gas development industry	4.686	13.029	23.113
Capital construction	2.314	2.707	7.556
Replacement	2.372	0.915	1.973
Miscellaneous	–	9.407	13.071
Electricity industry	4.755	12.621	37.223
Capital construction	4.014	10.945	33.455
Replacement	0.741	1.380	3.194
Miscellaneous	–	0.296	
Petroleum refining industry	0.718	1.203	4.547
Capital construction	0.481	0.610	2.510
Replacement	0.237	0.576	1.733
Miscellaneous	–	0.017	–

Source:
Energy Statistics Yearbook of China, 1991, pp. 23, 24, 25 and 26.

the first half of the 1980s was 117,100 million *yuan*, which rose almost threefold to 318,400 million *yuan* in the second half. China divides its capital investments into three categories: capital construction, replacement and miscellaneous. Capital construction commands the lion's share of the budget, absorbing 271,900 million *yuan* (63 per cent) over the decade. The "miscellaneous" investment category was first used in 1982 and has mainly assisted the oil sector. Included in this budget are loans from overseas. Most investment in the energy industry is undertaken by national state-run companies, though some investment by local companies is included in the 1989 statistics. This accounted for 1.4 per cent of the 1988 total and much of it is thought to have come from urban collectives in the coal mining industry (see Table 12).[10]

Most investment was allocated to the electric power industry, which received 37,223 million *yuan*, or 44 per cent of the total of 84,674 million

[10] Investment in urban-collective-owned mines is estimated at 7,272 million *yuan* for 1989 in *Coal Industry Yearbook of China* (1990 ed.), p. 20.

yuan in 1990. Next largest was petroleum and natural gas development, with 23,113 million *yuan* or 27 per cent, followed by coal mining with 16,446 million *yuan* (19 per cent), oil refining at 4,547 million *yuan* (5 per cent), and miscellaneous others at 2,100 million *yuan* (4 per cent). Investment concentration in electric power dates from the mid-1980s and peaked in 1986. Earlier in the decade, investment was divided more or less equally between coal, petroleum and electric power.

Energy is a capital-intensive industry. On its own, it embodies over 25 per cent of all fixed assets of the manufacturing sector. No other industrial branch even approaches it in this respect. In terms of production volume, however, it only accounts for 10 per cent of total industrial output – an indication of the unequal balance between investment and production. The main reason for this imbalance lies in the extremely low level of both raw and final product prices. It is this that constrains the development of the energy industry. The consequent dependence on outside investment (either government funding or loans) naturally inhibits expansion.[11] The situation is exacerbated by China's policy of maintaining low energy prices for fear that price increases would lead to inflation. This is not an easy problem to solve.

Nevertheless, China is making an all-out effort to promote the development of the energy industry, as its concentration of investments there attests. Funding sources include the national coffers, domestic loans, foreign capital and internally-generated funds. Domestic finance is still the coal industry's largest source of funds; but since 1988 foreign capital has emerged as the main financier of petroleum and natural gas development.

Other funding sources include the "Coal Replacement for Oil Fund," and the "Energy Transportation State Concentrative Construction Fund," the latter established in 1982. Both are financed from a 10 per cent (15 per cent since 1984) tax levied on companies' off-budget monetary income. Petroleum companies are required to deliver the first 100 million tonnes they produce to the state at a fixed price, but thereafter may sell their output at international rates (in Chinese terminology, "negotiated prices"). Some of this extra income is also directed to these funds. In recent times, the funds have increasingly been used for investment in the electric power industry.

But production has not kept pace with rising investment in the energy sector for the simple reason that it is now more costly to produce energy resources. A higher level of investment is needed each year in order to maintain existing output unchanged. This was particularly evident in the late 1980s: raw material prices rose, working conditions deteriorated, management was inefficient and standards were raised. As a result, investment in the coal industry grew at an annual rate of 9.12 per cent in the latter half of the 1980s – but in the meantime, the investment requirement per tonne

---

[11] See *Energy of China*, No. 3 (1991) p. 5.

of coal output rose from 127.5 (1985) to 180.8 *yuan* (1990). Likewise, in the electric power industry production costs per kilowatt rose by an average of 11.4 per cent per annum, from 1,746 *yuan* per kilowatt in 1985 to 3,000 *yuan* in 1990. Investment needs for the expansion of crude oil's production capacity increased, on average, by 18.9 per cent per annum, from 470 million *yuan*/one million tonnes in 1985 to 940 million *yuan*/one million tonnes in 1990. Exploration costs entailed in uncovering new oil reserves also rose by an average of 24.8 per cent. It cost 560 million *yuan* to discover 100 million tonnes in 1986, but by 1989 the corresponding figure was 1,360 million *yuan*.[12]

Such estimates of cost cannot be calculated directly from publicly available data, but those data do show unequivocally that costs have been rising. Table 13 provides a comparison of costs for the coal, petroleum and electric power industries during 1986–90. It divides "additional production capacity" by newly-productive capital construction investments. The energy industry operates under long construction lead times and it may be misleading to compare capacity and investments in any given year. A year may, for instance, witness few investments but may still experience a significant jump in capacity thanks to the completion of a construction project undertaken over several years. This would inevitable skew the data. Nevertheless, Table 13 demonstrates clearly that costs have risen significantly, especially in the oil industry. There is little disputing that new capacity gained per unit of investment has declined.

A consequence of rising investments unaccompanied by a corresponding rise in production or capacity has been to undermine corporate profitability in the energy industry. All the national companies suffer large deficits, which can only be covered by borrowing and government subsidies. Since they cannot file for bankruptcy, production cannot be halted.

China is now seeking to phase out low energy prices, which are the major source of such difficulties. Oil prices have already risen quite sharply and coal prices can be expected to do the same. Corporate efforts alone, however, will not solve the problem, and the fragile financial position of energy companies will probably continue to constrain future new investment.

Long-term energy plans: The Eighth Five-Year Plan and plans for the year 2000

Under the Eighth Five-Year Plan, the guiding principle in managing the Chinese economy is that growth should be "balanced, sustainable and stable." In pursuit of this goal China seeks to loosen government control and regulation in the interests of market-orientated reforms. It has also

---

[12] See *Energy of China*, No. 3 (1991) p. 7, and Ma Hong and Song ShangQing (eds.), *Economic Situation and Prospect of China 1990–91* (Beijing), p. 61.

TABLE 13. *Additional Production Capacity Constructed and Productivity Capital Construction Investment in Energy Industries in China*

	Additional production capacity constructed (1)	Newly-productive capital construction invested (billion yuan) (2)	(1)/(2)
Coal industry	(unit: million tonnes)		
1986	21.05	4.07	5.17
1987	21.06	3.83	5.50
1988	33.02	4.99	6.62
1989	28.45	5.48	5.19
1990	23.36	5.33	4.38
Oil and gas development industry	(unit: million tonnes)		
1986	15.485*	1.88	8.24
1987	16.400	3.07	5.34
1988	15.810	4.31	3.67
1989	16.500	6.18	2.67
1990	13.244	6.23	2.13
Electricity industry	(unit: million KW)		
1986	6.638	9.41**	0.71
1987	8.744	14.15	0.62
1988	11.170	16.78	0.66
1989	10.609	17.90	0.59
1990	9.156	21.54	0.43

Note:
(1)/(2) = additional production capacity constructed in each energy industry unit per billion *yuan* investment.
* Oil industry only.
** includes the investment of heating water constructions.
Source:
Energy Statistics Yearbook of China, 1989, pp. 32, 33, 50, 51, 52 and 56, and 1991, pp. 49, 50, 51, and 56.

targeted 6 per cent annual GNP growth, a level thought to be neither too high nor too low.

In the current and subsequent Five-Year Plans, coal production targets are 1,230 million tonnes (1995); and 1,400 million tonnes (2000), compared with 1,080 million tonnes in 1990. The target for oil production is 145 million tonnes in 1995, compared with 138 million tonnes in 1990. Generation of electricity is intended to rise from 621.2 TWh in 1990 to 820 TWh in

1995 and 1,113 TWh in 2000. Of course these are only targets and subject to revision over the course of the plans. At one point, the petroleum production targets were set at 150 million tonnes (1995) and 200 million tonnes (2000), but these have been revised downwards to the more achievable level of 145 million tonnes for 1995. No target at all is now available for 2000. Caution is clearly counselled in predicting future levels of coal and electricity production.

The last section showed how uneven distribution of resources, burgeoning investment and rising costs have come to constrain China's energy supplies. There are other contributing factors. China has been, and remains, slow in its development of new energy exploitation and use of technologies; nor is the government particularly enthusiastic about technology imports. Meanwhile, the growing size of energy companies has combined with highly centralized control to add to the difficulties of making the industry more competitive. But the socialist system is not entirely counter-productive. Large-scale industries like energy cannot develop without government protection and aid. This is especially true in less-industrialized countries. China's system makes it comparatively easy to implement such policies, and one can conceive of an appropriate mix of policy and strategy that will facilitate the fulfilment of its energy supply targets.

China does not have an overarching energy policy, but it does have policies and strategies for each of its energy sectors. Through these policies it hopes to overcome chronic shortfalls and meet the economic growth targets outlined in the Eighth Five-Year Plan.

In the coal sector, China will seek to accelerate the construction of new state-owned coal mines; build more coal-burning power plants in regions such as Shanxi, Shaanxi and Inner Mongolia; and promote reforms in local and urban-collective-operated mines. During the 1980s, the government tried to encourage production by allowing free development of non-nationalized mines on a regional basis. The excessive development which followed has thrown the industry into disarray and appropriate remedial and rationalization measures are now needed. The construction of large state-run mines and adjacent power stations is expensive, but the current Five-Year Plan is unclear about the likely level of future investment. Past experience suggests, however, that investment will be concentrated in specific areas.

The strategy for the petroleum industry is to "stabilize the East and develop the West." The government will promote steady, sustainable production at existing oil fields in the East and undertake new exploration and development in Western locations like Tarim. It is also intended to step up offshore development.

Policy in the electric power industry calls for parallel development of thermoelectric and hydroelectric plants and the construction of nuclear plants where appropriate. Priority is given to hydroelectricity, since it is clearly the superior choice. China also plans to push cogeneration and will, of course, build new thermoelectric plants adjacent to resources. Another focus will be the expansion of China's power transmission capability.

Before determining whether energy supplies will meet demand, however, we must consider how rapidly demand is forecast to grow. The Eighth Five-Year Plan targets an economic growth rate of 6 per cent per annum. However, the economic growth elasticity of primary energy consumption is expected to be a low 0.4, which implies an annual growth of 2.4 per cent for energy consumption. This suggests a level of primary energy demand of approximately 1,104 million tonnes SCE in 1995, rising to 1,240 million tonnes SCE in 2000 (Table 14).

Production growth for the coal industry is targeted at about 2.4 per cent per annum during the first half of the 1990s, rising to 2.6 per cent in the second half. The petroleum growth rate target is as low as 1 per cent per annum during the first half of the decade (it remains unannounced for the second half, but will probably be about the same); by contrast, electric power growth targets are 5.7 per cent and 6.3 per cent respectively. This implies a total energy production of 1,182 million tonnes SCE in 1995 and 1,349 million tonnes SCE by 2000. On this basis, targeted supplies will meet targeted demand.

But is the elasticity value of 0.4 too low? If the figure were 0.6, it would translate into a 3.6 per cent annual increase in primary energy consumption, which would reach 1,170 million tonnes SCE in 1995 and approximately 1,400 million tonnes SCE in 2000. This would indicate a 12 million tonne surplus in 1995, but a 51 million tonne shortfall at the end of the century. China's economic planners insist that they will achieve their 0.4 elasticity target through conservation measures – this despite the fact (see above) that conservation rates *declined* from 4.88 per cent in the early 1980s to 1.95 per cent in the latter half of the decade.

Conservation gains will therefore be the key factor in balancing supplies against demand in the 1990s. Chinese experts predict a conservation rate of 2.34 per cent in 2000, which would save some 32,940 thousand tonnes SCE. Between 1989 and 2000, they expect that 341,230 thousand tonnes SCE will be conserved.[13] If China were to achieve annual conservation gains of 2 per cent, then on the basis of primary energy consumption of 987,030 thousand tonnes SCE in 1990, it would achieve a saving of 22,000 thousand tonnes SCE in 1995 – that is, a total of about 100,000 thousand tonnes SCE conserved during the first five years of the decade. Conservation in 2000 would reach 25,000 thousand tonnes SCE, indicating a total saving of 120,000 thousand tonnes SCE in the latter half. But if gains of these magnitudes are to be made, extra investment in new technology and greater changes in the industrial structure will both be required.

Nevertheless, assuming that China can meet its conservation goals and

---

[13] Analysed by the Energy Research Institute, Beijing.

TABLE 14. *Primary Energy Supply and Consumption Target in 1995 and 2000 in China*

	1990 (actual)	1995 (target)	2000 (target)
Production			
Raw coal	1.08 billion tonnes (0.77 billion tonnes SCE)	1.23 billion tonnes (0.88 billion tonnes SCE) Average increase rate, 1991–95, 2.4%	1.4 billion tonnes (1.0 billion tonnes SCE) Average increase rate, 1996–2000, 2.6%
Crude oil	138 million tonnes (197 million tonnes SCE)	145 million tonnes (207 million tonnes SCE) Average increase rate, 1991–95, 1.0%	152 million tonnes (217 million tonnes SCE) Average increase rate, 1996–2000, 1.0%
Natural gas	15.3 billion m^3 (20 million tonnes SCE)	20.0 billion m^3 (27 million tonnes SCE)	30.0 billion m^3 (40 million tonnes SCE)
Electricity (including thermo-electricity)	621.2 billion KWh (253 million tonnes SCE)	820 billion KWh (334 million tonnes SCE)	1,113 billion KWh (453 million tonnes SCE)
Hydro and nuclear electricity	126.7 billion KWh (52 million tonnes SCE)	167 billion KWh (68 million tonnes SCE) Average increase rate of electricity, 1991–95, 5.7%	227 billion KWh (92 million tonnes SCE) Average increase rate of electricity, 1996–2000, 6.3%
Primary Energy Total	1.039 billion tonnes SCE	1.182 billion tonnes SCE Average increase rate, 2.56%	1.349 billion tonnes SCE Average increase rate, 2.73%
Consumption			
Primary Energy Total	980 million tonnes SCE	Target (energy elasticity, 0.4, increase rate, 2.4%) 1.104 billion tonnes SCE Forecast (energy elasticity, 0.6, increase rate, 3.6%) 1.170 billion tonnes SCE	1.240 billion tonnes SCE 1.400 billion tonnes SCE

that production volumes increase on schedule, it should be possible to maintain a balance between supplies and demand.

Tentative forecasts of the econometric analysis and alternatives

Economic data can be used to make fairly accurate forecasts of the long-term balance between energy supplies and demand. Unfortunately, it is almost impossible to forecast energy supplies themselves. To do so would require a detailed study of energy resources, development and production: even then, one could only hope to make a "macroeconomic hunch."[14] This article, therefore, only discusses general trends. It must also be borne in mind that production is not the same as supply. Transport losses, net trading differences and inventory corrections must also be taken into consideration.[15]

As far as coal is concerned, it has already been shown that most of the gain in production during the 1980s came from regional, non-national mines. The output of nationalized mines grew very little. But output growth from regional mines is almost certain to be limited during the 1990s. Chaotic development has already depleted resources, cost lives and damaged the environment. Chinese planners intend to tighten the regulation of this sector in future. Meanwhile, a number of large-scale national mine projects are reaching completion and will contribute to production. This will allow nationalized mines to regain part of their earlier share and put them back in the lead of the coal industry. Raw coal production was only slightly higher in 1991 than the 1,080 million tonnes achieved in 1990, but by 1995 will reach 1,200 million tonnes, and by 2000, 1,300 million. This is still, however, significantly lower than targeted levels (see Table 15).

Petroleum (crude oil) production also showed only a minor increase between 1990 and 1991, from 138,300 to 139,500 thousand tonnes. Nevertheless, it will probably succeed in reaching its 1995 target of 145,000 thousand tonnes. Plans for 2000 remain undecided, but a level of 160,000 thousand tonnes seems likely. This will derive more from the redevelopment of existing fields than from the development of the Tarim Basin. Technological advances, especially enhanced oil recovery and horizontal drilling in producing wells, will provide the impetus here. Such improvements can be expected to improve recovery rates and production volumes in fields such as Daqing and Shengli, which have vast quantities of oil in place.

[14] Each oil field or coal mine should be carefully examined in respect to its past production history and projected future output volume, taking into consideration geological reserves and production facilities under construction or completed. The sum of these individual production estimates will provide an estimate of total production for each source of energy. Making such calculations is a daunting task, but available data and other information make the exercise feasible.

[15] Net supply of energy through the limited Chinese transport and distribution system can be said to reflect a real supply volume.

TABLE 15. *Primary Energy Demand and Supply Forecast in 1995 and in 2000 in China*

	1991 (actual)	1995 (forecast)	2000 (forecast)
Production			
Raw coal	1.09 billion tonnes (778 million tonnes SCE)	1.2 billion tonnes (857 million tonnes SCE)	1.3 billion tonnes (928 million tonnes SCE)
Crude oil	139.5 million tonnes (199 million tonnes SCE)	145 million tonnes (207 million tonnes SCE)	160 million tonnes (228 million tonnes SCE)
Natural gas	15.2 billion m^3 (20 million tonnes SCE)	20.0 billion m^3 (27 million tonnes SCE)	30.0 billion m^3 (40 million tonnes SCE)
Electricity (including thermoelectricity)	675 billion KWh (275 million tonnes SCE)	950 billion KWh (387 million tonnes SCE)	1,200 billion KWh (489 million tonnes SCE)
Hydro and nuclear electricity	123.5 billion KWh (52 million tonnes SCE)	240 billion KWh (98 million tonnes SCE)	300 billion KWh (122 million tonnes SCE)
Primary energy total	1.047 billion tonnes SCE	1.189 billion tonnes SCE Average increase rate, 1991–95, 2.7%	1.318 billion tonnes SCE Average increase rate, 1996–2000, 2.08%
Consumption			
Primary energy total			
Target (energy elasticity, 0.4 and increase rate, 2.4%)		1.104 billion tonnes SCE	1.240 billion tonnes SCE
Difference between production and consumption		85 million tonnes SCE	78 million tonnes SCE
Forecast (energy elasticity, 0.6 and increase rate, 3.6%)		1.170 billion tonnes SCE	1.400 billion tonnes SCE
Difference between production and consumption		19 million tonnes SCE	−82 million tonnes SCE

China currently produces about 15,000 million cubic metres of natural gas a year, which is to be raised to 20,000 million cubic metres in 1995 and 30,000 million in 2000. Natural gas production could increase even further if China were prepared to invest sufficient money in it.

Most investment is, however, earmarked for the electric power industry, where new thermoelectric and hydroelectric plants will be built and power lines enhanced. Output of 675 TWh in 1991[16] will rise to 950 TWh in 1995, which is 140 TWh higher than the target of 810 TWh. Output in 2000 should reach 1,200 TWh, which is 100 TWh above the target of 1,100 TWh. Thermoelectric plants will provide 75 per cent of the projected volume, hydroelectric and nuclear plants 25 per cent. Production of primary energy hydro-power and nuclear power will grow to about 240 TWh in 1995, 300 TWh in 2000.

These estimates of primary energy production translate into 1,189 million tonnes SCE in 1995 and 1,318 million tonnes SCE in 2000. Given an energy elasticity of 0.6, this implies a 19 million tonne surplus in 1995 (demand forecast at 1,170 million tonnes SCE) but an 82 million tonne *shortfall* in 2000 (demand forecast at 1,400 million tonnes SCE). If, on the other hand, elasticity is indeed 0.4, China will have more than enough energy to meet demand in both years.

But is such optimism justified? This forecast assumes primary energy production growth of 2.7 per cent per annum in 1995, dropping to 2.08 per cent between 1996 and 2000. This is a modest projection. Primary energy production totalled 1,047 million tonnes SCE in 1991,[17] which was only slightly above the 1990 level of 1,039 million tonnes SCE – but 1991 was a year of adjustment in energy supplies. In recent years, China has tended to be conservative in all its economic forecasts and the 1992 target is only 1,057 million tonnes SCE.[18]

The conclusion can be drawn that low growth rates will allow China to keep energy supplies and demand balanced during the 1990s, but not to the extent of eliminating the country's shortfall. The best guess is that the deficit will continue and will remain a constraint on economic growth. There is always a gap between forecasts and reality, and China's energy shortfalls appear to be chronic. In any case, economic growth breeds new energy demand: there is no reason to believe these two will cease to feed off one another in the near future.

Conclusion

This overview of China's energy situation suggests that supplies of energy and demand for energy will grow in a balanced fashion that will keep pace

---

[16] Official statistic of national economic and social development in 1991. JETRO, Tokyo, *Chugoku keizai* (*Chinese Economy*), No. 315 (March 1992), p. 65.
[17] *Ibid.*   [18] *Energy of China*, No. 1 (1992), p. 5.

with economic development. But while the balance may be maintained, China will still suffer a chronic shortfall in energy supplies. Supplies are insufficient to meet the demand from new industries and new economic activities; both energy demand and economic development feed off each other in a cycle of growth.

But while there are many constraints on energy supplies, there are also ways of ameliorating and removing bottlenecks. China is already starting to overcome problems, such as the uneven distribution of resources, through a combination of increased investment and technological advances. Conservation will also be an important focus of activity in the future. What is, however, lacking is an integrated energy plan that links these programmes.

Energy policies can be divided into short-term strategies and long-term guidelines. Short-term strategies embrace the implementation of whatever steps are available at the time, and China has a good record in this respect. One area that demands more effort is the rationalization of the organizations and systems which dominate the energy industry. Some progress has already been made, such as the creation of divisions out of the gigantic national energy companies – a policy which should be continued. Many of the construction and transport divisions in the Daqing Petroleum Bureau have already become independent units, and Sinochem's foreign sales are now being handled by a separate company. Even so, China will have to ensure that these companies function under the principle of competition.

But the most important task is to reform energy prices. In the oil industry, 40 per cent of the well-head prices are already made at "negotiated prices," near international levels.[19] More is needed in this direction, and the 30 per cent of coal prices that are fixed low by the government should also be reformed. China must find ways of eliminating the waste generated by low energy prices, and establishing a price structure which makes further waste prohibitive. Coal-burning consumers will probably eventually switch to electricity, which will be supplied as final energy; the rationalization of electric power prices is therefore an urgent task. In any case, current partially-liberalized prices actually cause more confusion than anything else.

China must also reform its regulatory systems. Projects that meet the conditions outlined in the country's energy policies should be given immediate approval. The elimination of complex approval procedures and unnecessary double checks would go a long way to promoting worthwhile energy projects.

The Eighth and Ninth Five-Year Plans provide long-term energy guidelines. They should not, however, simply constitute plans for the 1990s; they should also represent the foundation for the 21st century. Any discussion of

---

[19] Information made available by the Energy Research Institute, Beijing.

China's long-term energy prospects must keep several basic points in mind. First, the country does possess sufficient energy resources for its needs. Secondly, it also has sufficient human resources to develop and exploit these energy resources. Thirdly, if it were to undertake long-term planning and forecasting, it could attract the financing it needs from both internal and external sources. Finally, its energy production remains relatively insulated from international trends. These considerations, as well as a healthy respect for the environment, should form the basis of a long-term integrated energy policy. If such a policy were to be implemented in a balanced fashion by both central and local authorities and with proper degrees of liberalization and adjustment, it would be almost certain to succeed. The launch of large projects, such as the Sanxia Dam, should be seen for what they are: some of the most massive projects undertaken this century, not mere political battles. Like the Tarim oil field development, greater efforts should be made to attract foreign funding.

Even more important than protection of the environment is the creation of a system which guarantees that the development of unevenly-distributed energy resources will bring future returns for local regions. Without such guarantees, it will be impossible to attract the necessary human resources. Larger-scale energy projects should also command a national consensus. Promised returns and similar methods should be used to stave off recurrences of the recent "Daqing petroleum struggle." In any case, the main point to be made is the need for long-term planning that will sustain the balance between energy supplies and consumption.

Postscript

The rapid economic growth of the 1980s has continued into the 1990s and ensured that increases in energy consumption have also been maintained, as shown in Table A.

The energy elasticity of national income averaged 0.45 during these years.[20]

Meanwhile, the early 1990s have witnessed a change in the relationship between the demand and supply of primary energy (see Table B).

The energy shortage in China, which emerged in 1992, was made up from coal stocks at mining sites. It was augmented by a net trade outflow of 22 million tonnes (SCE).

The shortage of energy supplies is likely to continue into the foreseeable future – certainly during the last three years of the (Eighth) Five-Year Plan. The unexpected shortfall in energy production of the early 1990s will exacerbate the supply situation to a degree unanticipated in the original version of this article. The outcome will be accelerated energy imports, not only of crude oil and petroleum products, but also of coal. Thus, thermal power stations destined for construction in China's coastal regions will be entirely fired by imported coal; and coastal oil refineries will be fed by imported crude oil from the Middle East and elsewhere.

Nevertheless, in making long-run forecasts of energy demand and supply, it still seems reasonable to assume that sufficient energy reserves exist in China. By extension, as long as appropriate production and transportation facilities can be developed, energy supplies can be improved. In the oil sector, efforts are called for to intensify exploration, whereas improved transportation and the reform of the distribution system are priorities for the coal sector.[21] The construction of large-scale hydroelectric power plants, already under way, as well as the completion of thermal power stations in coal-mining areas and the creation of a high-voltage electricity transmission line, will also help fulfil electricity consumption needs.

China will no doubt seek to establish a coherent pattern of indigenous production in order to meet its energy requirements. The likely outcome is that coastal industrial regions will remain energy importers, whilst the North, North-east, West and South-west gradually move towards self-sufficiency and the generation of an export surplus. The expansion of oil and coal production in the interior of the country will place a premium on the development of transport facilities (railways and pipelines). But these are long-term objectives and with a rapid increase in energy demand, the persistence of supply shortages will necessitate continued reliance on imports for some years (at least until the end of the century) to come. By the year 2000, China can be expected to be importing 50 million tonnes of oil (crude and petroleum products)[22] and some 20 million tonnes of coal.

[20] The elasticity value in each individual year was as follows: 1990, 0.35; 1991, 0.66; 1992, 0.34.

[21] Notice that the extent of China's coal reserves has recently been re-evaluated. The Fifteenth World Energy Congress (1992) estimated recoverable coal reserves to be 114.5 billion tonnes – about one-eighth of the previously-published figure (see Table 11). However, this would still imply availability of adequate supplies for 100 years – sufficient, that is, to meet long-term requirements.

[22] Equivalent to about one million barrels of oil per day.

TABLE A. *Annual Increases in National Income and Primary Energy Consumption,*
1990–92

| | *% increase over previous year* | |
	National income	*Primary energy consumption (SCE)*
1990	5.1	1.8
1991	7.7	5.1
1992	14.4	4.9

TABLE B. *Primary Energy Production and Consumption*

| | *Production and consumption of primary energy (SCE) (million tonnes)* | | |
	Production	*Consumption*	*Balance*
1990	1039.22	987.03	+52.19
1991	1048.44	1037.83	+10.61
1992	1072.56	1089.00	−16.44

TABLE C. *The Figures in Table C Summarize Trade Flows During 1992.*

| | *Energy and energy-related trade flows, 1992 (million tonnes)* | | |
	Exports	*Imports*	*Balance*
Coal	19.70	1.23	+18.47 [13.2 SCE]
Crude oil	21.51	11.36	+10.15 [14.5 SCE]
Petroleum products	5.39	7.84	−2.45 [−3.5 SCE]

Note:
   In addition, China imported about 5 billion kwh (some 2 million tonnes
SCE) of electricity from Hong Kong. China's net energy exports therefore
totalled some 22 million tonnes.

   Whether and to what extent China's energy shortage will constrain its rate of
economic growth will depend on the nature of its economic policies (especially
foreign trade policies). If domestic shortfalls are made up through imports, growth
need not be hindered. The current wisdom in China seems to be that against the
background of present world energy and oil supplies, the government should not
hesitate to maintain its partial dependence on foreign supplies.[23]

[23] *Energy of China*, various issues.

Foreign Investment and Economic Change in China

Y. Y. Kueh

China
P21
P27
P33
F24
O19

The Chinese Policy Perspective

Foreign direct investment (FDI) in China is the most dramatic manifestation of China's open-door policy. Together with continuous import and export expansion, FDI has increasingly exposed the Chinese economy to the western world during the past decade. There are, however, several differences between FDI and foreign trade in terms of their implications for the domestic economy. The most obvious is that FDI directly helps to relieve domestic capital supply bottlenecks and to promote employment and economic growth. By contrast, increased capital formation through imports of machinery and equipment must be financed by extra export earnings.

Within the Chinese economic context, even more important is the fact that FDI may increase interactions between the planned domestic economy and the outside world. For example, to the extent that FDI seeks to promote import substitution (that is, to substitute for direct imports in production for the domestic market), the primacy of central planning may have to give way to accommodation of foreign interests. A further practical question is how to provide for the conversion of FDI-led *Renminbi* earnings into foreign currency without eroding the system of foreign exchange control, an integral part of the economic rationale of any Soviet-style system of economic control. This is the background against which foreign exchange swapping (or regulatory) centres were increasingly established in Chinese cities in order to facilitate limited exchange of *RMB* for foreign currency among FDI ventures and chosen local enterprises, which held excessive volumes of *RMB* or foreign currency.

Such complications need not arise in circumstances in which a country's economic relations are confined to foreign trade alone. Where – as in China – imports and exports are subject to centralized control, the planned domestic economy can be largely insulated from outside interference. The central planners' main concern is that increased reliance on imports to balance critical domestic supply deficits may leave central planning increasingly vulnerable to outside supplies. Any associated relaxation of import policy may eventually threaten the very *raison d'être* of the Soviet-style strategy of creating an independent, self-sufficient industrial system.

It is, however, impossible to speculate when increased dependence on imports will push the Chinese economy across the threshold of planning instability and undermine its search for long-term industrial independence. Thus it is difficult to judge whether the Chinese government's increased "openness" during the past decade in terms of foreign trade expansion means that it has already effectively abandoned the import substitution strategy (replacing imports with domestic production without FDI) in favour of an outwardly-orientated strategy of import liberalization which seeks to "link the domestic economy to the world economy in order to foster industrialization."[1] In fact, despite vigorous efforts to expand trade and court foreign capital and technology, the current Chinese strategy continues to retain many of the former Soviet policy elements: key industrial products are still largely subject to centralized distribution; their prices are officially controlled in order to ensure financial compliance with the planners' physical allocative priorities; pervasive wage, income and consumption controls, commensurate with the required high accumulation rate (currently 34 per cent of national income), remain in place to guarantee investment maximization; and state investment allocation is still strongly skewed towards the preferential growth sector of heavy industry.[2]

A corollary of this conventional Stalinist strategy is that imports are bound to be selective in order to protect central planning against outside interference. The basic elements of the established import-substitution policy have therefore remained intact, its essential hallmarks being reflected in the government's policy towards FDI. For example, foreign investors are generally expected to furnish their own machinery, equipment and – where possible – raw materials, to be combined with cheap Chinese labour to generate an output destined for export, rather than the domestic market. In other words, FDI ventures are expected to seek to balance their own foreign exchange requirements and help generate extra hard foreign currency to finance the desired import programmes.

This FDI strategy, which the former Party Secretary-General, Zhao Ziyang, referred to as "[placing] two heads outside" (*liangtou zaiwai*), that is, relying on the outside world for both input supplies and market outlet, is very different from the policy of most industrializing Asian countries, which solicit manufacturing foreign direct investment for import substitution. The essential feature of the Chinese approach is that it has simultaneously moved away from "import substitution" to "export-orientated" foreign investment, whilst retaining the basic elements of an inwardly-orientated industrialization strategy, the antithesis of opening up the vast domestic market to foreign competition. Stated in these terms, China's FDI strategy has taken the Stalinist rationale to its ultimate conclusion. By using FDI to

[1] Nicholas R. Lardy, *Foreign Trade and Economic Reform in China, 1978–1990* (Cambridge: Cambridge University Press, 1992), p. 5. See also pp. 1–15 for a more detailed discussion of the different foreign trade regimes in relation to the emerging Chinese situation.

[2] See *Zhongguo tongji nianjian* (*Chinese Statistical Yearbook 1991*) (hereinafter *ZGTJNJ* 1991), p. 40 for the accumulation ratio, and p. 150 for investment fund allocation among the major economic sectors.

bring in new "hardware" and "disembodied technology" (industrial blue-prints and managerial-technical know-how), the strategy has also enhanced the conventional Stalinist urge to borrow advanced technology from the west through regular import channels.[3]

Nevertheless, from the outset China apparently found it necessary to accommodate foreign interests by allowing technologically selected joint ventures to target the domestic market. Moreover, the urge to court foreign capital also prompted the Chinese authorities increasingly to compromise their established import-substitution policy, by opening up areas of hitherto strictly-controlled domestic goods and service markets to foreign direct investment.[4] The potential consequences of such opening up are quite different from those resulting from controlled relaxation of import restrictions. In addition to possible implications for foreign exchange control (see above), central planners may be compelled increasingly to accommodate requirements made by FDI ventures for domestic inputs and make price readjustments in order to make the return from privileged domestic sales conform to international levels. Those familiar with Soviet economics will know that this is inherently subversive to the entire system of central planning. Against the background of intensified American pressure on China to liberalize imports and the country's own greater readiness to accommodate GATT's requirements for membership admission,[5] the 1990s may well see the Chinese economy's integration with the western system of free trade and investment flows accelerate.

This is the background against which this study seeks to consider the impact of FDI during the coming years. The focus is primarily on the coastal provinces, which have absorbed the largest share of FDI and which are most directly exposed to western influences. In addition to FDI, considera-tion is given to indirect foreign investment – foreign capital essentially borrowed through government channels for investment projects. This latter category is similar to FDI to the extent that conditions are normally set

[3] For an elaboration on the implications of the Stalinist legacy on economic reforms in foreign trade and Chinese industry at large, see Y. Y. Kueh, "Growth imperatives, economic recentralization, and China's open-door policy" in *Australian Journal of Chinese Affairs*, No. 24 (July 1990), pp. 93–119; and "The Maoist legacy and China's new industrialization strategy," *The China Quarterly*, No. 119 (September 1989), pp. 441–4.

[4] Good examples of FDI ventures being allowed wholly or partly to target output for domestic sales include Schindler Elevators (Switzerland), Pilkington Glass (England), Bell Telephone (Belgium), and Volkswagen Santana (Germany). For an earlier survey of repre-sentative joint ventures in China see Samuel P. S. Ho and Ralph Huenemann, *China's Open-Door Policy: The Quest for Foreign Technology and Capital* (Vancouver: University of British Columbia Press, 1984). The Trade Development Council of Hong Kong has recently become highly optimistic that the vast Chinese market is poised to open up to its wide variety of consumer goods; see *South China Morning Post* (hereafter *SCMP*), 20 March 1992 (Business Post, p. 5), and *Ta-kung pao* (Hong Kong)(hereafter *TKP*), 17 June 1992, p. 15.

[5] The American government successfully negotiated with the Chinese an agreement on 16 January 1992 relating to protection of intellectual property rights, and moved swiftly after-wards to press for the lifting of essential import barriers by October 1992, under Section 301 of the American Trade Act.

TABLE 1. Major Indicators of the Economically Opened Coastal (Econocoas) Areas in China, 1987 (value in billion yuan in current prices)

	No. of xian (1)	Land million km² (2)	Population (millions) (3)	GDP (4)	Local budget Revenue (5)	Local budget Expenditure (6)	GVIO (7)	Industrial capital (k) stock (8)	Industrial employee (millions) (9)	Relative share of Population in Land area (2)/(3) (10)	GDP (4)/(3) (11)	Industrial employment in GVIO (7)/(9) (12)	K stock (8)/(9) (13)
4 SEZs	15	0.013	9.749	15.655	2.868	3.001	16.684	6.141	1.587	–	–	–	–
% share of													
Shenzhen	2	12.84	5.70	32.50	30.51	23.22	33.23	22.96	18.30	2.251	5.698	1.816	1.254
Zhuhai	2	16.90	4.53	10.02	9.46	9.58	7.81	14.63	3.09	3.729	2.211	2.531	4.737
Shantou	9	70.26	89.77	44.82	43.19	55.45	39.90	35.90	69.30	0.783	0.499	0.576	0.518
Xiamen	2	n.a.	n.a.	12.66	16.84	11.76	19.06	26.52	9.31	n.a.	n.a.	2.046	2.847
15 OCCs	91	0.134	87.926	183.668	37.688	16.176	272.074	118.734	19.775	–	–	–	–
% share of													
Dalian	4	9.23	5.59	6.38	5.87	7.84	6.78	10.46	5.26	1.653	1.141	1.288	1.989
Tianjin	6	8.41	9.46	11.98	14.82	19.26	13.42	19.35	11.63	0.888	1.266	1.154	1.663
Qingdao	7	8.58	13.11	9.31	5.09	5.56	8.71	n.a.	10.41	0.654	0.710	0.837	n.a.
Shanghai	11	4.71	14.21	29.70	44.86	33.29	36.01	44.51	23.22	0.332	2.090	1.551	1.917
Guangzhou	5	5.55	6.43	9.40	9.06	9.35	8.61	8.96	5.47	0.864	1.462	1.573	1.638
11 OCPs	286	0.42	210.70	369.88	60.81	30.50	545.22	283.63	39.70	–	–	–	–
% share of													
Liaoning	24	12.56	10.08	12.73	12.55	14.43	14.06	21.26	12.31	1.246	1.263	1.142	1.727
Hebei	15	4.06	3.40	2.63	1.07	1.97	2.06	3.83	3.05	1.194	0.774	0.675	1.256
Tianjin	6	2.71	3.95	5.95	9.19	10.23	6.70	8.10	5.79	0.686	1.506	1.157	1.399
Shandong	32	12.53	12.69	10.43	6.27	7.77	8.78	8.71	10.54	0.987	0.822	0.833	0.826

Jiangsu	49	13.94	19.58	18.85	15.00	11.48	20.04	16.88	22.80	0.712	0.963	0.879	0.740
Shanghai	11	1.52	5.93	14.75	27.81	17.67	17.97	18.63	11.57	0.256	2.487	1.553	1.610
Zhejiang	37	10.72	12.31	11.26	10.00	7.54	12.83	7.86	14.98	0.871	0.915	0.856	0.525
Fujian	33	10.48	8.85	4.46	3.24	6.33	3.23	4.89	2.58	1.184	0.504	0.661	0.528
Guangdong	52	18.90	18.08	17.44	13.78	19.05	13.35	10.81	12.78	1.045	0.965	1.045	0.846
Hainan	19	8.13	2.92	1.51	0.49	2.20	0.40	0.80	0.67	2.784	0.517	0.597	1.194
Guangxi	8	4.47	2.22	n.a.	0.60	1.31	0.59	0.55	0.62	2.014	n.a.	0.952	0.887
PRC Total	–	9.50	1080.73	1105.42	234.66	242.69	1381.29	915.82	118.69	–	–	–	–
& share of													
SEZs	–	0.13	0.90	1.42	1.22	1.24	1.21	0.67	1.34	0.148	1.570	0.903	0.502
OCCs	–	1.40	8.14	16.62	16.06	6.67	19.70	12.96	16.66	0.172	2.042	1.182	0.778
OCPs	–	4.38	19.50	33.46	25.91	12.57	39.47	30.97	33.45	0.224	1.716	1.180	0.926

Notes:

SEZs   Special Economic Zones
OCCs   Opened coastal cities (The original list covers 14 cities, but Weihai in Shandong province was later added to give a total of 15. For the complete list see Table 7.)
OCPs   Opened coastal provinces
GDP   Gross domestic product
GVIO   Gross value of industrial output

Figures for industrial capital stock covers industrial enterprises with independent accounting (*duli hesuan gongye qiye*) only, and refer to original acquisition prices of year-end fixed assets. The 11 OCPs presumably comprise a total of 288 opened municipalities and *xians*, but the figures given for the individual OCPs add up to only 286.

Sources:

State Statistical Bureau (SSB). *Yanhai jingji kaifangqu jingji yanjiu he tongji ziliao* (*Economic Research and Statistical Materials for the Economically Opened Coastal Areas*) (Beijing: Zhongguo tongji chubanshe, 1989), hereafter *KFQTJZL*. The data were generated from a comprehensive survey undertaken by the SSB in 1988 following the official declaration early that year to open the entire coastal region for foreign investment and trade.

down by creditors in order to guarantee an accountable return on investment. It may, however, differ from FDI in terms of capital efficiency in that
any misuse of funds may be covered by the borrowing governmental
authority.

The first section discusses the economic importance of the "economically
opened coastal (*econocoas*) areas"[6] and suggests the reasons for their
choice as recipients of foreign investment. The article then examines overall
quantitative trends in foreign investment and its distribution amongst
econocoas areas and economic sectors, before analysing the contribution of
foreign investment to overall capital formation and considering its impact
on output and income growth. The available statistical evidence is used to
investigate the foreign trade performance of foreign-funded enterprises,
with particular reference to the central problem of foreign exchange balance requirements. The final substantive section looks at future trends in
foreign investment and highlights the major policy issues of the 1990s.
Although the scope of the subject matter means that the discussion is
frequently brief, every effort has been made to provide a rounded and
integrated overview of China's foreign investment strategy.

The Econocoas Areas

Table 1 sets out the major economic indicators of *econocoas* areas in 1987,
when the Chinese strategy of seeking foreign capital was already firmly in
place. The opened municipalities and counties in the 11 "opened coastal
provinces" (OCPs) clearly constitute a considerable concentration of national wealth. With a population of only 19.5 per cent of the national total,

---

[6] Reference is to the summary terms "Yanhai jingji kaifanqu" as used by the State Statistical
Bureau for its 1988 survey (see notes and sources to Table 1). The *econocoas* areas cover, in
the order that they were declared open for foreign investment (and as in Table 1): (1) the four
Special Economic Zones (SEZs) set up in 1979/1980 in Guangdong and Fujian provinces, (2)
the 14 opened coastal cities (OCCs), from Dalian in Liaoning province in the North to Beihai
in Guangxi province in the South, made available in 1984, and (3) the opened coastal provinces
(OCPs), from Liaoning to Guangxi and Hainan provinces, comprising a total of 288 *xian*
(counties), which were all covered by a single government decree for opening up in early 1988.
Between 1984 and 1988 smaller pockets of coastal areas (notably the Pearl River Delta, the
Yangzi River Delta, and the Liaoning peninsula) were similarly opened, and earlier both
Guangdong and Fujian were given special privileges to shape their own external economic
relations. Likewise, Hainan Island was converted into an independent province in 1988 and
made a Special Economic Zone at the same time. Both the centrally-controlled municipalities
of Tianjin and Shanghai were included in the list of the 14 OCCs, but they also form part of the
11 OCPs, with all their subordinated municipals and *xians*. For simplicity, this study merely
distinguishes between the three major categories of area, i.e. SEZs, OCCs and OCPs, ignoring,
for example, distinctions within the major opened cities between the city proper and the
districts designated as economic-technological development areas (*jingji jishu kaifaqu*). However, while initially the different areas represented different schemes of tax and money
incentive, the distinction has become increasingly blurred over the years amidst increased
Chinese efforts to court foreign capital.

they accounted for almost 40 per cent of national gross value of industrial output (GVIO), 33.45 per cent of gross domestic product and 25.91 per cent of all local budget revenue. Even more remarkably, these areas absorbed a tiny fraction – 4.38 per cent – of China's land area.

It is interesting that the capital–labour ratio for all the *econocoas* areas was, at best, comparable with the national average. (Note that Table 1 shows their combined relative share of industrial employee in capital stock to have been 0.93.) This may reflect an underlying abundance of labour. But it also highlights the fact that these wealthy regions' capacity for capital stock expansion has been squeezed by continuous fiscal extraction by the central authorities. Thus, the percentage share of the 11 OCPs in the national accumulated local budget expenditure (12.57 per cent) was only half the size of their comparable revenue share (25.91 per cent) in 1987. This clearly points to large-scale fiscal transfers from the OCPs to provinces in the interior – and perhaps to non-opened areas within the OCPs themselves. From this point of view, China's strategy of seeking foreign capital may be interpreted as a means of assisting in the industrialization of the Chinese hinterland by diverting the major proportion of hard foreign currency returns earned in the coastal region towards the less inhabited interior provinces. If correct, this would imply a continuation of foreign exchange control and centralized regional allocation – and might pose a limit to any fully-fledged relegation of decision-making powers to local authorities in the management of foreign investment.

Considerable variations exist within *econocoas* areas. Shanghai remains the single most important contributor to budgetary revenue, following years of "extortion" by the central planners. Various per capita indicators show that the municipality is still the most advanced regional entity, in the context of both OCPs and OCCs ("opened coastal cities"). A minor exception is the measure of per worker capital endowment, in which respect Shanghai trailed marginally behind China's heavy-industrial base of Liaoning province (see Table 1). The differentiation amongst the 15 OCCs, implied by the above-average per capita performance indicators for the five listed major municipalities (except Qingdao) is equally revealing. Undoubtedly the entire *econocoas* complex represents a mix of highly diverse economic entities, ranging from mere rural-town settings to well-known cosmopolitan conglomerates.[7] The only characteristic shared by all 288 *econocoas* localities is their situation on or near the coastline. One may justifiably ask how such varied localities were chosen to join the enlarged group of opened areas early in 1988.

In theory, possible policy considerations ranged from the advantages of surplus labour, raw material supplies, easy transport facilities and existing conglomerate economies to the simple desire to balance regional disparities

---

[7] The disparity can indeed be easily confirmed if one probes into the detailed *xian* data for the 11 OCPs as given in *KFQTJZL* (cited under Table 1).

in income and living standards. In practice, the 1988 decision seems to have been conditioned by euphoria prompted by foreign investors' renewed confidence in South China and their increased interest in the OCCs in 1987–88, following the notorious setbacks of 1986.[8] No doubt it also reflected the belief that China too could emulate the successful export-led growth strategy of the "four little dragons," after the launch of Zhao Ziyang's theory of "great international circulation" in the declaration that the entire coastal strip would be opened up to foreign investment.[9]

This is not the place to examine Zhao's calculus and his perception of the world market potential to be derived from the new strategy. What is apparent is that with a total population (211 million) three times larger than that of the four little dragons, and with some 288 municipalities and *xian* (counties) opening up simultaneously, it was impossible for central or provincial authorities to concentrate domestic investment into selected areas in order to create the infrastructure necessary to attract foreign capital. The result is that many, perhaps most, of the 288 *xian* and cities have never been visited by potential investors since their designation as possible foreign capital recipients.

From this perspective, the much-publicized Pudong project in Shanghai emerges as a strategic initiative. A considerable volume of capital resources has already been committed for basic construction and the area promises to become even more "special" than any of the other five special economic zones (SEZs) and the 13 economic-technological development districts, in terms of tax concessions, tariff treatment and other preferential measures for foreign-funded enterprises.[10]

Deng Xiaoping's tour of South China from January to February 1992 and his associated call to take still bolder steps to open up China to the west have created even greater euphoria than that which existed during 1988.

---

[8] FDI pledged declined sharply from US$5,931 million in 1985 to US$2,834 million in 1986, and the growth rate of FDI realized was also reduced substantially in 1986. See *ZGTJNJ* 1991, p. 629. Nicholas Lardy, in his *China's Entry into the World Economy* (Lanham: University Press of America, 1987) attributed the decline to the Chinese "requirement that each joint-venture project be self sufficient in terms of foreign exchange" (p. 36) and rising office rental and labour costs (pp. 36–7). The World Bank's *China: External Trade and Capital* (Washington, D.C.: The World Bank, 1988) has similar explanations (pp. 256–7). But these problems have always been encountered by foreign investors, and cannot fully explain the abrupt downturn in 1986.

[9] Essentially, Zhao's theory is that by requesting FDI ventures to "[place] two heads outside" (see Introduction), China could follow the path of South Korea, Taiwan, Hong Kong and Singapore in order to benefit from the international investment and commodity flows and generate extra foreign earnings for domestic finances, without exposing the centralized industrial core to the outside world.

[10] For the Eighth Five-Year Plan (1991–95), the Shanghai government planned to inject 20 billion *yuan* into Pudong, at an estimated total of 50 billion *yuan* needed for infrastructure investment. See *TKP*, 24 March 1992, p. 3. The 40% share is equal to Shanghai's total fixed asset investment for 1991. For a comprehensive report on the Pudong project against the background of Greater Shanghai, see CERD Consultants Ltd., *Shanghai-Pudong baogao (Report)*, Hong Kong, September 1991.

The consequent nation-wide scramble for foreign capital seems to indicate that virtually anyone can enter the race, even without the official endorsement of central or provincial authorities. This is contrary to the selective approach adopted in 1988, although preferential policy provisions for targeted localities, such as the SEZs and Pudong, remain the prerogative of the central government. It is true too that in line with comprehensive opening up, a number of cities along the Russian border in Heilongjiang and Xinjiang, as well as others along the Vietnamese border in Yunnan and Guangxi, have also recently been declared open for foreign investment and trade.[11]

Overall Trends in Foreign Investment

Differentiation between various categories of foreign capital will facilitate the discussion which follows. The first distinction is between foreign direct investment (FDI) and indirect investment financed by foreign borrowing or loans made by foreign governments, the World Bank, Asian Development Bank and major western private banks or bank syndicates. A second is between foreign capital taken up separately by provincial and central authorities, including the Ministries of Finance, Foreign Economic Relations and Trade, Energy and – notably – the Bank of China. The final distinction is between foreign investment or capital borrowing pledged and that actually taken up, or realized, by the investors or borrowers.

The first and third distinctions are probably familiar. But the second has a special significance in any analysis of the *econocoas* areas. This is because capital loans raised by ministries may also be applied to major projects undertaken by provincial authorities, whilst centrally-sponsored FDI projects necessarily have a provincial home base. Unfortunately, no estimates are available of the regional allocation of such central funds to make possible a more comprehensive investigation of the impact of foreign investment. Note too that most of the subsequent analysis focuses on realized foreign investment, rather than what has been contractually pledged (but not necessarily implemented).

The data contained in Table 2 provide measures of China's absorption (realized) of foreign capital between 1979 and 1991. They suggest a number of important findings. First, the provincial absorption of FDI has been consistently higher than that of the various central ministries. Indeed, the share of the provinces has increased in both absolute and relative terms, at the expense of the ministries. This trend reflects the delegation of decision-making powers relating to foreign investment accommodation down to the provincial level.

---

[11] *TKP*, 18 June 1992, p. 2.

TABLE 2. *Chinese Intake of Foreign Capital, 1979–91 (million US$)*
(a) Realized loans and FDI by provincial and ministerial borrowers (percentage shares in brackets)

| | Loans | | FDI | | Total | | |
	Provincial (1)	Ministerial (2)	Provincial (3)	Ministerial (4)	Provincial (1) + (3) (5)	Ministerial (2) + (4) (6)	PRC Total (5) + (6) (7)
1979–84 average	—	—	476.50 (69.70)	207.16 (30.30)	—	—	—
1983	—	—	—	—	—	—	1,980.64
1984	—	—	—	—	—	—	2,704.52
1985	281.09 (11.22)	2,224.87 (88.78)	1,318.04 (67.38)	638.11 (32.62)	1,599.13 (35.84)	2,862.98 (64.16)	4,462.11 (100.00)
1986	1,033.66 (20.61)	3,980.91 (79.39)	1,741.65 (77.62)	502.08 (22.38)	2,775.31 (38.24)	4,482.99 (61.76)	7,258.30 (100.00)
1987	1,428.42 (24.61)	4,376.53 (75.39)	1,782.73 (67.36)	863.88 (32.64)	3,211.15 (37.99)	5,240.41 (62.01)	8,451.56 (100.00)
1988	2,460.20 (37.93)	4,026.53 (62.07)	3,149.69 (84.22)	589.93 (15.78)	5,609.89 (54.86)	4,616.46 (45.14)	10,226.38 (100.00)
1989	2,410.88 (38.35)	3,874.82 (61.65)	3,437.37 (91.09)	336.12 (8.91)	5,848.21 (58.14)	4,210.94 (41.86)	10,059.15 (100.00)
1990	2,057.63 (31.49)	4,476.89 (68.51)	3,436.15 (91.51)	318.79 (8.49)	5,493.78 (53.39)	4,795.61 (46.61)	10,289.39 (100.00)
1991	—	—	—	—	—	—	11,137.98

(b) Realized FDI by types of joint ventures (JV) (percentage shares in brackets)

	FDI total	Equity JV	Contractual JV	Joint exploration	Wholly-foreign owned ventures	Compensation trade	Others
1979–81 average	373.56 (100.00)	21.77 (5.83)	117.77 (31.53)	106.04 (28.39)	0.33 (0.09)	94.08 (25.18)	33.57 (8.99)
1982	649.27 (100.00)	34.29 (5.28)	177.77 (27.38)	178.52 (27.50)	39.31 (6.05)	122.40 (18.85)	96.98 (14.94)
1983	915.96 (100.00)	73.57 (8.03)	227.38 (24.82)	291.50 (31.82)	42.76 (4.67)	197.28 (21.54)	83.47 (9.11)
1984	1,418.85 (100.00)	254.73 (17.95)	465.02 (32.77)	522.92 (36.86)	14.94 (1.05)	98.45 (6.94)	62.79 (4.43)
1985	1,956.15 (100.00)	579.88 (29.64)	585.04 (29.91)	480.61 (24.57)	12.95 (0.66)	168.59 (8.62)	129.08 (6.60)
1986	2,243.73 (100.00)	804.47 (35.85)	793.79 (35.38)	260.33 (11.60)	16.30 (0.73)	181.10 (8.07)	187.74 (8.37)
1987	2,646.61 (100.00)	1,485.82 (56.14)	619.96 (23.42)	183.20 (6.92)	24.55 (0.93)	222.26 (8.40)	110.82 (4.19)
1988	3,739.66 (100.00)	1,975.40 (52.82)	779.93 (20.86)	212.19 (5.67)	226.16 (6.05)	316.59 (8.47)	229.39 (6.13)
1989	3,773.45 (100.00)	2,037.16 (53.99)	751.79 (19.92)	232.20 (6.15)	371.42 (9.84)	261.29 (6.92)	119.19 (3.16)
1990	3,754.87 (100.00)	1,886.07 (50.23)	673.56 (17.94)	244.31 (6.51)	683.17 (18.19)	158.74 (4.23)	109.02 (2.90)
1991	4,370.00	—	—	—	—	—	—

Notes:
   See text and notes to Appendix Tables A1 and A2 for definitions of foreign loans and FDI, and the distinction between provincial and ministerial borrowings. A detailed explanation of the different types of foreign-funded ventures and their possible behavioural implications is given in Y. Y. Kueh and Christopher Howe, "China's international trade: policy and organizational change and their place in the 'Economic Readjustment'," *The China Quarterly*, No. 100 (December 1984), pp. 834–35. The residual category of "others" in section (b) of the table represents the settlement value of equipment provided by foreign partners for purpose of "processing/assembling" (*jiagong zhuangpei*), and that of equipment leased (*guoji zulin*). "Compensation trade" is valued similarly.

Sources:
   Appendix Tables A1 and A2; and *ZGTJNJ* and *JMNJ*, various issues.

Secondly, similar changes favouring the provinces occurred in the absorption of foreign loans, even though during 1985–90 the ministries consistently enjoyed a substantially higher share of borrowing. It should of course be borne in mind that the ministries are representative of the state and are therefore likely to have better access to foreign governmental loans.

Thirdly, if FDI and foreign borrowing are taken together, it is clear that China's provinces (whose share rose from 36 to 53 per cent between 1985 and 1990) have gained significantly at the expense of the ministries (64 and 47 per cent, respectively). Even so, the central government, as represented by the ministries, has continued to exert important leverage in the allocation of foreign loans, with the amount under its control in 1990 (US$4,477 million) far exceeding that within the purview of the provinces (US$2,058 million).

Fourthly, within the total FDI intake, equity joint ventures have gained – at an accelerating pace – at the expense of contractual joint ventures to become the most important form of foreign joint venture in China. This development underlines the increasing confidence felt by foreign partners seeking to make long-term commitments, in the wake of improvements in China's legal framework and investment environment.[12]

Finally, the dramatic increases in FDI in the form of wholly foreign-owned ventures particularly reflect added confidence by foreign investors, as does the declining importance of compensation trade. Trial-and-error adjustments have probably allowed many arrangements in this latter category to be upgraded over the years to become equity or contractual joint ventures.

In short, the changes observed in Table 1 point in the direction of irreversible decentralization of the decision-making powers of both FDI and foreign loans to local authorities, and to the increased exposure of the Chinese economy to foreign capital.

Other aspects of the changes also indicate increased penetration by foreign capital. Figure 1, for example, shows that in the second half of the 1980s, as recipients of foreign capital for fixed asset investment, urban-collective enterprises have gained in importance at the expense of the state-ownership sector. Further, while the bulk of foreign capital has been allocated to new capital construction during the same period, the investment share of existing state industrial enterprises for purposes of "technical innovation and transformation" (i.e. overhaul) of old machinery and equipment has steadily increased.

Table 3 shows that for China as a whole, realized FDI stock grew on

---

[12] This is quite different from earlier observations when most of the FDI went to contractual joint ventures as a safeguard against possible investment risks. See Y. Y. Kueh and Christopher Howe, "China's international trade: policy and organizational change and their place in the 'Economic Readjustment'," *The China Quarterly*, No. 100, (December 1984), pp. 813–48.

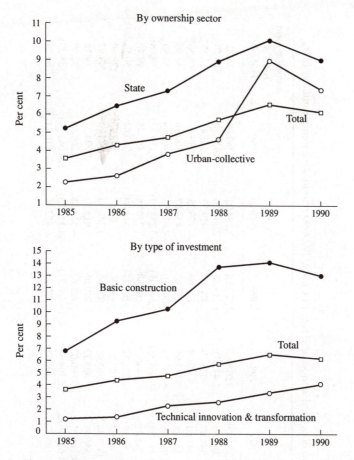

FIGURE 1. *Share of Foreign Capital in Fixed Assets Investment in China, 1985–90 (%)*

Notes:
   The figures refer to the percentage share in total investment in the respective ownership sectors, or types of investment, as against the shares by the state budget, domestic bank loans, and enterprises' self-raised funds.
Sources:
   ZGTJNJ 1991, pp. 144, 145, 150, 175 and 194.

average by 29.67 per cent per annum during 1985–90 (33.52 per cent, if FDI sponsored by central authorities is excluded).

   Notice that the choice of 1985 as base year in this instance reflects the fact that the national experiment with FDI was by this time firmly established. In any case, such growth rates attest to a very impressive performance, even with allowance for inflationary adjustments for the U.S. dollar. The corresponding growth rate for FDI and capital borrowing combined is

TABLE 3. *Growth of Foreign Direct Investment in the Econocoas Areas in China, 1979–90 (cumulative total in million US$)*

	1979–84	1985	1986	1987	1988	1989	1990	Annual growth rate (%) 1985–90
SEZs	895.87	1,230.64	1,711.43	2,078.89	2,520.86	3,134.05	3,789.68	25.23
Shenzhen	589.05	782.45	1,163.18	1,443.31	1,743.30	2,045.76	2,435.70	25.50
Zhuhai	246.24	299.69	344.87	378.69	426.09	479.37	548.47	12.85
Shantou	9.41	24.05	45.00	80.98	127.60	175.25	299.11	65.56
Xiamen	51.17	124.45	158.38	175.91	223.87	433.67	506.40	32.40
OCCs	472.59	747.71	1,082.06	1,559.73	2,097.10	2,823.53	3,465.69	35.90
	(472.59)	(774.24)	(1,148.38)	(1,665.45)	(2,346.31)	(3,254.93)	(4,116.32)	(39.68)
Dalian	–	14.32	44.81	94.71	169.59	250.16	451.45	99.40
Tianjin	12.87	45.38	88.19	221.32	282.47	313.89	350.82	50.54
Qingdao	–	2.30	13.03	27.03	39.36	97.37	143.25	128.49
Shanghai	123.00	230.54	379.44	593.45	826.62	1,248.74	1,425.93	43.97
Guangzhou	336.72	455.17	556.59	623.22	779.06	913.37	1,094.24	19.18
OCPs	2,120.18	3,050.12	4,161.07	5,290.07	7,221.62	9,555.15	12,266.59	32.09
	(2,256.05)	(3,326.04)	(4,628.70)	(6,104.84)	(8,330.71)	(11,117.78)	(14,043.34)	(33.39)
Liaoning	33.11	57.69	105.87	196.71	327.26	453.40	710.71	65.24

Hebei	4.95	13.19	24.46	34.80	53.90	97.63	142.10	60.87
Shandong	16.42	50.62	115.64	180.51	292.06	455.39	641.09	66.16
Jiangsu	–	33.47	67.23	153.58	279.09	406.22	540.19	74.41
Zhejiang	33.62	60.25	85.02	121.32	165.11	219.07	268.21	34.80
Fujian	69.83	188.43	250.93	306.28	451.75	799.78	1,119.67	42.82
Guangdong	1,862.27	2,491.77	3,275.39	4,006.18	5,218.44	6,541.68	8,123.99	26.66
Hainan	19.11	43.10	75.69	84.80	207.25	302.22	405.24	56.55
Guangxi	80.87	111.60	160.84	205.89	226.76	279.76	315.39	23.09
Beijing	350.00	438.82	588.53	694.32	1,197.50	1,517.66	1,796.61	32.57
Province total	2,859.02	4,177.06	5,918.71	7,701.44	10,851.17	14,288.50	17,724.65	33.52
PRC total	4,102.00	6,071.00	8,315.00	10,962.00	14,701.00	18,475.00	22,230.00	29.64

Notes:

Figures in brackets for OCCs and OCPs refer respectively to the sum total for all the 15 OCCs and the 11 OCPs (including Tianjin and Shanghai). The PRC total covers FDI sponsored by the various central branch ministries (including notably offshore oil exploration), in addition to the provincial total.

The figures are all book values gross of depreciations. Figures for some areas are incomplete for 1979–84, and the total for the 15 OCCs for the same period is assumed to be the same as that for the five selected cities listed here. This means the estimated growth rate for SEZs, OCCs and OCPs does not match exactly that for their constituent areas. Where the 1979–84 total is an underestimate, especially in the case of the 15 OCCs total, the estimated growth rates for 1985–90 are clearly biased upwards. The same is true for the provincial total to the extent that the cumulative total for 1979–84 may be an underestimate (see notes to Appendix Table A1). Similarly, the growth rates for those areas with incomplete figures for 1979–84 (especially Shantou, Dalian, Qingdao, Hebei, Shandong and Jiangsu) should be interpreted with care.

Source:

Appendix Table A1.

somewhat lower (26 per cent per annum), but still constitutes a remarkable achievement.[13]

The national FDI rate of growth is overwhelmingly dominated by the performance of the 11 OCPs, which have absorbed the lion's share of the national total. For Guangdong and the four SEZs (but not Fujian) taken together, the performance does not, however, appear to be so impressive. This reflects the fact that by the mid-1980s, these pioneer *econocoas* areas had already enjoyed several years' experience of foreign capital absorption and were well-established destinations for overseas investors; it also suggests the rapid proliferation of FDI ventures into spheres outside these areas.

The data in Table 3 do indeed show that almost all the later-established OCPs and OCCs experienced much higher rates of growth of FDI (see in particular Liaoning, Hebei, Shandong, Shanghai, Jiangsu and Hainan). The outcome (see Figure 2) is that after the mid-1980s, there was a definite trend towards the equalization of relative FDI shares between such pioneer *econocoas* areas as Shenzhen, and advanced municipalities such as Shanghai and Beijing whose developed economic base initially made them the most obvious destinations for foreign capital.

Following a brief slowing during 1989–90, FDI in China rapidly regained its momentum and in 1991 total realized FDI, sponsored by both provincial and central authorities, reached US$4,370 million (*cf.* the low point of US$3,755 in 1990, shown in Table 2). If current (1992) exhortations to open up China even more are sustained, the 1990s may well witness a continuing upsurge in FDI.

Regional and Industrial Distribution

In terms of FDI stock accumulated since 1979, the U.S. dollar figures presented in Table 3 generate the following regional percentage shares in the national FDI total (FDI sponsored by the central ministries is excluded):

	1979–84	1985	1986	1987	1988	1989	1990
11 OCPs	79	80	78	79	77	78	79
of which:							
Guangdong	66	60	55	52	49	46	46
3 SEZs of							
Guangdong	29	26	26	25	22	19	18
Shenzhen	21	19	20	19	16	14	14

These figures highlight the importance of the 11 OCPs, but also show the special role of Guangdong and its three SEZs as recipients of FDI. It is true

[13] The figure can be obtained from Appendix Table A2.

FIGURE 2. *Share of Beijing and the Econocoas Areas in Foreign Investment in China, 1985–90 (%)*

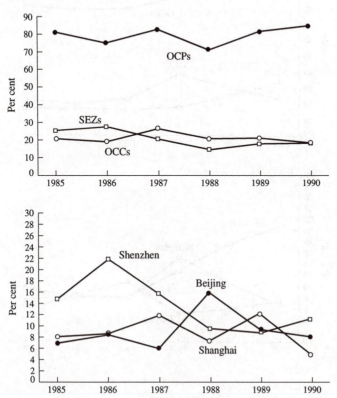

that the percentage share for Guangdong during 1979–84 may contain an upward bias,[14] but there is no doubt that the provincial share has declined steadily since the mid-1980s. The same applies to the three SEZs. Thus, to reiterate a point made earlier, the absorption by new *econocoas* areas of any net annual addition to FDI stock has increased at the expense of the pioneer localities.

Even so, Guangdong and its SEZs still account for the largest share of accumulated FDI stock. It is worth emphasizing that the FDI stock estimates are all expressed in terms of original acquisition prices. If adjustments could be made to deflate figures for later years, the shares of Guangdong and Shenzhen would be well in excess of the 46 and 14 per cent shown in the table. The importance of Shenzhen is highlighted by the fact

[14] See notes to Table 3 and Appendix Table A1.

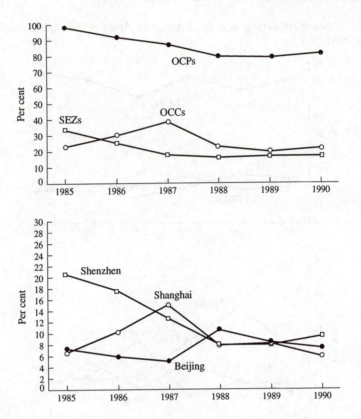

Notes:
  SEZs   Special Economic Zones
  OCCs   Opened coastal cities (see Tables 1 and 7)
  OCPs   Opened coastal provinces (see Table 1)
  The figures for OCCs cover only Dalian, Tianjin, Qingdao, Shanghai and Guangzhou and those for OCPs include both Tianjin and Shanghai. All the figures exclude capital borrowing and FDI sponsored by various central branch ministries, such as, amongst others, investment in offshore oil exploration.
Sources:
  Appendix Tables A1 and A2

that in almost all the years under investigation, its FDI intake was no less than that of any single province or municipality, including Shanghai and Beijing.[15] The comparison with nearby Guangzhou (Guangdong's provincial capital, only 60 miles north of Shenzhen) is even more telling. The SEZ's receipt of FDI, whether calculated in terms of net annual additions or accumulated total, has consistently been twice as high as that of Guangzhou. It is, however, clear that Shenzhen's prosperity derives over-

[15] This is revealed in Appendix Table A1.

whelmingly from its propinquity to Hong Kong – which raises the question of whether its example can ever be emulated by other new FDI frontiers within China.

The regional distribution of FDI also reveals that the relative share of the 11 OCPs in the national stock total has remained constant (around 80 per cent) during 1979–90. If adjustments were made for inflationary pressures, this figure would have been even higher by the late 1980s. This suggests that the observed regional redistribution of FDI reflects a shift from the south along the coast to new northern frontiers, rather than from coastal to interior provinces. Such a development has occurred in spite of inland provinces' desire to share in foreign investors' increased enthusiasm for investment in China.

Thus, locational benefits appear to be a prime consideration for foreign investors contemplating participation in any FDI venture in China. In the fierce scramble to secure foreign capital, many municipalities have sought to by-pass central regulations by offering potential overseas investors additional benefits such as concessions on land rentals, labour charges and other local levies, both legal and illegal. Such preferential treatment often outweighs the advantage which the status of being an SEZ confers over other areas designated for foreign investment. Shenzhen has, for example, increasingly felt the competitive edge of other regions and recently appealed to the central authorities to be permitted to extend the boundaries of the SEZ to include neighbouring Baoan county.

If *indirect* foreign investment is included in the calculations, it is interesting that total combined volume absorbed by the 11 OCPs declined from 98 to 83 per cent between 1985 and 1990. The corresponding decline for Guangdong province alone is from 58 to 42 per cent.[16] The inference is that whilst the 11 OCPs dominated the intake of both direct and indirect foreign investment flows, the interior provinces have increasingly gained from them as beneficiaries of capital borrowing from overseas. To the extent that such funds are channelled through the central government, this suggests that the powerful centralized fiscal redistribution mechanism amongst the various provinces must also have been at work in the allocation of foreign capital.

Accelerated increases in foreign investment and changes in its regional allocation have also been accompanied by significant changes in its industrial distribution. Table 4 shows its absorption by the major economic sectors. It is clear that foreign investment has been heavily skewed towards

---

[16] The figures for the intervening years 1986–89 for the 11 OCPs and Guangdong are respectively 94, 91, 86 and 84, and 54, 47, 46 and 44%. These figures refer to the changes in the cumulative total, but they are not exactly comparable to those given in Table 3, because for the base years 1979–84, the categories FDI and foreign borrowings have different missing figures. See Appendix Tables A1 and A2.

industry and services, whereas agriculture has received a minimal share (especially of FDI). There has, however, been a pronounced shift from services to industry since 1985 in terms of realized FDI – a trend which holds good for all *econocoas* areas. This development no doubt reflects investors' improved confidence in China as an investment outlet. It is worth recalling that the initial concentration of FDI in tourist industries (hotel and catering services) was explained by the relative ease with which such investment could be recouped, as these areas catered exclusively for overseas visitors in possession of hard foreign currencies.

Most of the *econocoas* areas (especially Fujian and Guangdong provinces) which absorbed a significant proportion of FDI in manufacturing in both 1985 and 1990 were apparently those which had ready access to world markets – particularly through investors from Hong Kong – and were therefore in a better position to balance foreign exchange requirements. By contrast, in spite of its political and cultural importance, Beijing has remained an insignificant destination of foreign investment. The overwhelming proportion of its FDI (90 and 83 per cent in 1985 and 1990 respectively) was in the service sector and dominated by hotel business and the construction of residential blocks for sale to foreign investors (again, especially from Hong Kong).

But notwithstanding the marked shift in favour of manufacturing, at the beginning of the 1990s the service sector continues to be a substantial recipient of foreign capital. This is particularly the case with "late-comers," such as Shanghai, Hainan and even Guangxi. If the current frenzy with which Hong Kong capital is being poured into real estate in South China is any indication,[17] the 1990s may well witness a further rise in the service sector's share of foreign investment.

The accelerated increases in FDI, together with the shift from services towards manufacturing since the mid-1980s, also point to increased industrial dispersal. It is difficult to be both comprehensive and precise, but given that most foreign partners in joint ventures are investors from Hong Kong, there is little doubt that these have mainly involved labour-intensive manufacturing activities driven by soaring local land rentals and labour costs across the border to the Pearl River Delta and other congenial sites in China.[18] The nature of the exercise dictates that the output is destined, exclusively or overwhelmingly, for re-export through Hong Kong. This is of

---

[17] Because of exorbitant property prices in Hong Kong in 1991/1992 many real estate developers from Hong Kong have recently turned to Guangdong province across the border, aimed both at commuting Hong Kong residents and foreign investors in China. Hong Kong newspapers contain advertisements for sales of such properties almost on a daily basis, although it is difficult to estimate the possible volume of FDI made by this.

[18] This is confirmed by a recent comprehensive survey conducted by the Federation of Hong Kong Industries, entitled *Hong Kong's Industrial Investment in the Pearl River Delta*, Hong Kong, 1992.

TABLE 4. *Distribution of Foreign Investment by Economic Sectors in the Econocoas Areas in China, 1985 and 1990 (%)*

	Total (US$ million)		Agriculture		Industry		Services		Real estate	
	1985	1990	1985	1990	1985	1990	1985	1990	1985	1990
SEZs										
Shenzhen	206.63(d)(f)	349.20(d)	0.18	–	53.54	80.33	46.27	19.67	7.98	15.97
Zhuhai	110.54(d)(f)	62.19(d)	0.20	1.30	24.39	88.78	75.41	9.92	3.36	7.80
Shantou	7.87(d)(f)	61.25(d)	1.27	0.56	41.80	79.27	56.93	20.18	–	12.33
Xiamen	181.62(d)(e)	–	–	–	39.50	–	60.50	–	11.71	–
OCCs										
Dalian	55.84(d)	–	21.49	–	32.16	–	46.35	–	–	–
Tianjin	–	83.15(d) (351.50)(d)(e)	–	0.39 (0.27)	–	78.81 (65.72)	–	20.79 (32.21)	–	–
Qingdao	n.a.	n.a.	–	–	–	–	–	–	–	–
Shanghai	362.82(d)(e) (296.87)(b)(f)	422.12(c)(f)	–	2.13	64.40 (16.85)	58.57	35.60 (83.15)	41.41	10.43 (80.84)	38.93
Guangzhou	102.16(d)	180.87(d)	4.20	0.21	29.14	77.25	66.66	22.54	45.04	6.79
OCPs										
Liaoning	163.53(b)	467.03(b)	0.75	0.71	15.31	82.65	83.94	17.10	81.67	0.46
Hebei	n.a.	n.a.	–	–	–	–	–	–	–	–
Shandong	n.a.	n.a.	–	–	–	–	–	–	–	–
Jiangsu	n.a.	n.a.	–	–	–	–	–	–	–	–
Zhejiang	n.a.	n.a.	–	–	–	–	–	–	–	–
Fujian	376.81(b)	1,161.83(b)	3.25	1.49	45.73	77.65	51.02	18.55	0.77	17.84
Guangdong	515.29(d) (919.10)(c)	1,459.84(d) (2,023.47)(c)	4.46 (2.68)	0.91* (1.87)	49.18 (66.20)	86.36 (77.58)	46.36 (31.12)	12.74 (20.54)	31.62 (22.37)	6.28 (4.53)

TABLE 4. (Cont.)

	Total (US$ million)		Agriculture		Industry		Services		Real estate	
	1985	1990	1985	1990	1985	1990	1985	1990	1985	1990
Hainan	26.43(c)	189.82(c) (100.55)(d)	12.64	2.99 (5.65)	33.11	22.39 (36.64)	54.26	74.62 (57.71)	32.12	21.04 (39.72)
Guangxi	37.00(d)(f)	30.25(d)	–	2.94	3.78	75.07	96.22	21.98	96.22	20.93
Beijing	591.93(d)(e)	276.96(d)	–	–	9.70	16.74	89.50	83.26	76.01	64.64
PRC total	(9,867.42)(a)	6,596.11(b) (12,085.69)(a)	(4.18)	1.85 (7.68)	(36.39)	87.19 (65.20)	(59.44)	10.97 (27.11)	(23.01)	6.86 (3.98)

Notes:
(a) pledged total of FDI and capital borrowing
(b) pledged FDI only
(c) realized total of FDI and capital borrowing
(d) realized total of FDI
(e) cumulative total
(f) 1984 or 1986 figures, as 1985 figure is not available

The standard *JMNJ* classification of branch distribution of foreign investment includes (1) agriculture, forestry, animal husbandry and fishery, (2) industry, (3) construction industry, (4) transport and telecommunication, (5) commerce and catering services, (6) real estate and public utilities, (7) health, sport and social welfare, (8) education, culture and arts, (9) scientific research and integrated technical services, (10) financial and insurance business, and (11) others. There are considerable variations among the provincial and municipal classifications. For our summarized categories, agriculture covers branch (1), industry (2) and (3), and service sector all the remaining branches. The "real estate" sector refers to branch (6) and its percentage figures are shared in the national total.

Considerable discrepancy exists between some of the figures shown here and in Appendix Tables A1 and A2. Some can be explained by the fact that FDI in this table does not include compensation trade investment, international leasing, etc., which are covered in Table A1. Other possible factors include differences in geographic coverage (such as whether the SEZs refer to the zone proper or the greater municipality), and sources and timing of reporting. The main problem is that the standard national yearbooks which are to be preferred to the comparable provincial sources do not give breakdowns by economic sector for the different provincial FDI and capital borrowings. As a result, the table relies on the latter sources which very often give different base figures. Nevertheless the discrepancies are not substantial, except for Dalian (US$55.84 million for 1985) and Tianjin (US$83.15 million for 1990). These figures are much larger than those shown in Table A1 (respectively US$14.32 million and US$36.93 million), and cannot easily be explained. Curiously, the Tianjin figure is given in the original provincial source alongside a cumulative figure for 1979–90 which is virtually identical to the one which may be obtained from Table A1 for the same period.

Sources:
As Appendix Table A1.

course consistent with China's strategy of using foreign investment for export purposes.

There have been some FDI projects which were designed and approved by Chinese authorities in line with the policy of import substitution.[19] But these have been the exceptions, not the rule. The more important point is that the relevant FDI ventures, whether export-orientated or import-substitution undertakings, have for the most part involved products at the very end of the relevant product cycle.[20] In other words, they have been internationally well-known products, embodying appropriate technological standards. Bearing in mind the predominant Hong Kong share in FDI ventures, many can probably be described as "sunset" industries in terms of their marketability and technological level.

Contribution to Capital Formation

There are various ways in which the impact of foreign investment upon the recipient country's economy can be assessed. The most direct measure is its contribution to capital formation and thereby to output and income growth. Technology transfer is another important potential benefit, although it is difficult to quantify, especially in terms of "disembodied" technology. Likewise it is virtually impossible to verify the competitive impact of import-substituting foreign investment on domestic production and marketing efficiency. The ensuing analysis therefore focuses on the more readily measurable variables.

Estimating the likely contribution of foreign investment to capital formation in China is bedeviled by the need to convert foreign capital into *RMB* equivalent, so that a comparison can be made with the total domestic investment outlay. In the absence of an exchange rate which reflects purchasing-power-parity, any attempt to make the conversion on the basis of the official Chinese exchange rate is potentially hazardous. This is not only because of erratic exchange rate adjustments made by the Chinese authorities during the past decade, but also because no realignment of the administered exchange rate can fully take into account distortions in China's price system which tend to favour industrial, rather than agricultural, products. The data tend to favour industrial, rather than agricultural, products. The data in Table 5, showing the relative share of foreign investment in total fixed asset formation in China during 1985–90, should be considered with these caveats in mind.

[19] See n. 4, above.
[20] See Jean-Francois Hennart, *A Theory of Multinational Enterprise* (Ann Arbor: The University of Michigan Press, 1982), pp. 19–20, for an elaboration of the product cycle model initially developed by Raymond Vernon in 1966, to explain the expansion of FDI by American overseas multinationals.

TABLE 5. Relative Contribution of Foreign Investments to Total Fixed Assets Investment in the Econocoas Areas in China, 1985–90 (%)

	FDI only				FDI and capital borrowing			
	1985	1988	1990	1985–90	1985	1988	1990	1985–90
SEZs	16.01	15.56	33.72	23.66	25.79	32.72	49.30	38.66
Shenzhen	18.37	25.53	34.68	30.53	31.27	37.82	46.11	43.42
Zhuhai	16.14	14.26	34.56	19.43	27.49	65.47	54.16	46.68
Shantou	4.76	4.66	49.21	11.45	10.77	10.35	62.99	22.37
Xiamen	18.31	14.44	19.76	22.83	21.49	49.40	47.03	40.37
OCCs	3.08	3.93	6.61	4.84	4.10	9.46	12.23	9.85
Dalian	1.91	7.15	33.44	10.12	1.98	20.38	65.49	24.84
Tianjin	1.42	2.56	1.99	2.63	3.03	14.41	5.32	10.21
Qingdao	0.63	1.75	7.69	4.66	5.18	5.66	12.61	10.35
Shanghai	2.65	3.28	3.72	4.17	2.68	6.20	6.75	6.80
Guangzhou	7.95	6.41	9.53	7.01	10.43	10.50	15.72	11.27
OCPs	2.90	3.76	6.77	4.30	4.33	7.16	10.12	7.17
	(2.66)	(3.10)	(2.96)	(3.50)	(3.89)	(7.03)	(9.14)	(6.94)
Liaoning	0.52	1.81	4.72	2.10	0.88	4.06	13.33	5.33
Hebei	0.21	0.30	1.17	0.52	0.27	0.44	2.56	1.00
Shandong	0.52	1.12	2.65	1.41	0.94	1.43	3.28	1.92
Jiangsu	0.65	1.24	1.77	1.20	1.00	1.54	3.27	1.82
Zhejiang	0.74	0.71	0.91	0.80	1.72	2.11	2.36	2.14
Fujian	6.32	5.88	14.06	8.60	9.11	11.88	18.77	12.85
Guangdong	9.99	13.57	18.56	14.14	14.59	27.32	23.65	23.17
Hainan	6.64	21.45	12.54	11.94	7.32	22.38	14.24	12.67
Guangxi	2.14	1.00	2.48	2.33	3.13	3.20	4.36	3.83
Beijing	2.75	11.49	6.98	6.64	3.60	13.33	11.93	8.73
PRC total	2.26	3.09	4.03	3.11	5.14	8.44	11.04	8.72

Notes:
FDI and capital borrowing in US$ are converted into RMB (based on official annual average of exchange rate) to be related to the total fixed assets investment figures (all undeflated) for the years concerned. The OCPs total (in parentheses) covers all the 11 OCPs, including Tianjin and Shanghai.
Sources:

The high shares shown for 1990 are likely to reflect the effect of the major *RMB* depreciation (by 22 per cent) against the U.S. dollar in December 1989. By contrast, the estimated shares for 1988 probably understate the contribution of foreign investment to domestic capital formation: the *RMB* exchange rate had, after all, not been readjusted since the 17 per cent devaluation of summer 1986. In other words, the high inflation rate experienced in 1988 (by 18.5 per cent over 1987) reinforced the already-overvalued *RMB* – especially *vis-à-vis* the prices of industrial goods – and led to an understatement of the potential foreign capital shares in this year.

Given that the December 1989 *RMB* devaluation may not have been sufficiently "realistic,"[21] the average contribution of foreign investment to capital formation during 1985–90, as shown in Table 5, may well be understated. Nevertheless, with an estimated share close to 9 per cent for FDI and capital borrowing combined for 1985–90, or 11 per cent for 1990 alone, foreign investment can hardly be discarded as being of only marginal significance![22]

Of course, complementary domestic investment (especially for infrastructural purposes, such as the provision of electricity, transport, telecommunications, etc.) is needed in order to realize the potential of FDI. Chinese estimates suggest that for each dollar of foreign capital received, an average of 3 *RMB* must be spent.[23] (This does not include the Chinese capital contribution to Sino-foreign joint ventures.) Application of this 3:1 ratio to total foreign investment indicates that the shares of foreign and related investment in total fixed assets were 16 per cent (the average for 1985–90) and 18 per cent in 1990 alone.[24] These are of course substantial contributions – all the more so, if estimated combined foreign and related investment as a proportion of fixed capital formation in the state-ownership

[21] A United States government report maintains, however, that after adjusting for China–U.S. inflation differentials, the *RMB* exchange rate against the U.S. dollar has depreciated in real terms since 1989, although "from 1984 through 1988, nominal devaluation of the *yuan* against the dollar was not sufficient to offset the impact of rising prices in China," resulting in a real appreciation of *RMB*. See U.S. Information Services, EPF413, 16 May 1991, p. 40. The discrepancy evidently depends on what inflation rates are used for the estimates.

[22] The foreign capital shares as estimated in Table 5 are not exactly comparable to those shown in Figure 1. It is not known how the lower *ZGTJNJ* 1991 figures (for Figure 1) are calculated, especially with respect to the possible U.S. dollar conversion rate used. But the slightly higher shares obtained here (for Table 5) may be partly because these figures relate the whole of any FDI to the fixed assets investment base, although part of the FDI may not have constituted such investment.

[23] Wu Zhenkun and Song Zihe (eds.), *Duiwai kaifang jingji fazhan zhanlu bijiao yanjiu* (*A Comparative Study of the Development Strategies of Opening up the Economy*) (Beijing: Zhonggong zhongyang dangxiao chubanshe, 1991), p. 45. The estimate seems to cover both FDI and foreign borrowing.

[24] The estimated average 1985–90 share was obtained by applying the same ratio separately to each of the years concerned. This therefore ignores the possible implications of changes in the *RMB*'s exchange rate.

sector alone is considered, this being the pillar of the national economy and the single most important destination for foreign investment.[25]

A more important point to be made in this context is that the foreign investment share has increased across virtually all the *econocoas* areas during the years under investigation, although the regional distribution in 1990 remained highly unequal (see Table 5). Not surprisingly, given their economic *raison d'être*, it is the SEZs that enjoyed the highest foreign investment shares in total fixed asset creation: 24 per cent of FDI, or 39 per cent of FDI and capital borrowing combined, during 1985–90. Nevertheless, the difference in the relative contribution of foreign investment to capital formation between pioneer OCPs (for example, Guangdong and Fujian) and other OCPs, or even OCCs, has remained quite striking. The contrast between Guangzhou and Shanghai – both large, cosmopolitan centres – is particularly noteworthy. Despite an accelerated FDI absorption after 1988 (see Table 3), the foreign contribution to fixed asset investment in Shanghai was only 6.75 per cent in 1990, compared with 15.72 per cent in Guangzhou (Table 5). This suggests the potential that may be available for a late-comer, such as Shanghai, in terms of attracting foreign capital – not least, with Pudong now developing rapidly.

An increased share of foreign capital implies that the rate of increase of foreign capital absorption is outstripping that of domestic fixed investment. The relationship is illustrated in Table 6, which presents real rates of growth of foreign investment (with and without capital borrowing) and total fixed capital formation (with and without investment in the non-state-ownership sector). The growth of foreign capital intake during 1985–90 is seen to have been consistently many times higher than the rate of domestic capital formation in all the *econocoas* areas, including Beijing.

Several other points emerge from the table. First, in some areas, notably, Zhuhai, Xiamen, Dalian and possibly Tianjin, high rates of expansion of foreign investment contrast sharply with low rates of growth of total fixed asset creation. This may indicate that foreign funds were increasingly sought as a substitute for local resources. It should be noted that these are areas which exhibited relatively large foreign investment shares during 1985–90 (see Table 5).

Secondly, there are, however, areas which have enjoyed high foreign investment growth rates as well as rapid growth of overall fixed capital formation. These include Shenzhen and Guangzhou, the two mature OCPs (Fujian and Guangdong) and, though to a lesser extent, Shanghai. It may be that in these areas initial foreign-induced capital growth subsequently helped promote local investment.

Thirdly, almost all the new *econocoas* frontiers have exhibited exception-

[25] The shares would be 24.44% for 1985–90 combined and 27.40% for 1990, based on fixed assets investment of the state sector alone.

TABLE 6. *Average Annual Rates of Growth of Investment (I), Industrial Output (GVIO) and Income (Y) in the Econocoas Areas in China, 1985–90 (%)*

	I(a)	I(b)	FI(a)	FI(b)	GVIO	Y(a)	Y(b)
SEZs	6.57	8.29	25.14	20.92	32.68	14.62	15.19
Shenzhen	12.14	11.44	32.29	20.58	44.51	20.75	18.73
Zhuhai	−1.24	−1.74	17.31	23.92	45.92	18.88	18.28
Shantou	9.80	18.94	84.58	52.94	16.31	9.46	12.85
Xiamen	0.15	7.79	63.19	35.18	27.26	15.22	15.45
OCCs	9.12	8.68	27.57	44.68	6.76	3.46	5.03
	(18.06)		(46.62)	(38.32)	(33.27)		
Dalian	4.30	4.22	98.92	185.82	9.61	8.33	9.98
Tianjin	2.27	2.46	46.91	55.16	5.69	2.50	3.88
Qingdao	16.71	17.76	155.74	61.99	14.81	7.91	7.26
Shanghai	11.90	10.77	26.20	47.66	4.40	1.06	1.68
Guangzhou	12.61	13.67	27.66	39.32	12.13	8.54	12.88
OCPs	10.90	12.04	33.33	33.77	12.23	7.84	8.83
	(10.44)	(11.38)	(30.52)	(33.10)	(10.61)	(6.95)	(7.90)
Liaoning	11.66	10.02	84.25	99.64	5.79	5.25	7.00
Hebei	8.95	7.27	54.15	90.79	8.60	7.31	7.93
Shandong	10.47	8.70	52.08	42.43	14.50	7.74	8.41
Jiangsu	9.03	17.15	51.59	70.09	13.15	6.63	6.70
Zhejiang	11.52	17.19	22.24	56.57	12.51	6.89	7.56
Fujian	9.92	12.23	48.35	31.59	15.91	10.65	11.56
Guangdong	13.67	13.59	30.37	28.44	17.55	11.24	13.62
Hainan	18.56	26.43	208.06	218.84	10.75	8.69	9.03
Guangxi	9.27	7.27	30.50	20.31	9.49	9.18	8.94
Beijing	14.19	13.45	68.54	51.59	7.69	5.77	–
PRC total	8.69	8.63	30.05	38.51	9.49	7.53	7.89

Notes:
I(a) and I(b): Total fixed assets investments in the state ownership sector (a) and for the country as a whole, including collective and private-individual investment (b), in real terms
FI(a) and FI(b): Total foreign direct investment (FDI) (FI(a)) and FDI plus foreign capital borrowing (FI(b)) in *RMB* and in real terms
GVIO: Gross value of industrial output in constant 1980 prices
Y(a): National income (net material product) in comparable prices
Y(b): GDP/GNP in comparable prices
See notes to Appendix Table A3 for the conversion of I(a), I(b), FI(a) and FI(b) from nominal to real terms. Figures in parenthesis cover all the 15 OCCs and 11 OCPs, including Tianjin and Shanghai.
Sources:
Appendix Tables A1 to A7.

ally high rates of growth of foreign investment. The list includes the OCCs shown in Table 6 (Guangzhou excepted), as well as such OCPs as Liaoning, Hebei, Shangdong, Jiangsu, Zhejiang and Hainan. The rapid growth was in most cases accompanied by a remarkable implied expansion of domestic capital, compared with the average for China as a whole. The inference is that the substantial complementary domestic investment in infrastructural and other facilities needed to realize the potential available from overseas capital supplies has been forthcoming.

The general picture which emerges of the relationships between foreign investment and domestic outlays cannot be regarded as conclusive. Other factors are, after all, at work. For example, apart from regional policy differences, significant variations in the scale and gestation periods of capital formation from overseas are bound to have affected the nature and pace of foreign investment. The speed of *domestic* investment, especially in major provinces, may also have been triggered by forces other han foreign investment and have generated a momentum of its own. Nevertheless, against the background of the nation-wide campaign to emulate the successful coastal pioneers in attracting foreign capital, the rest of the 1990s may well witness the emergence of coastal provinces, such as Shandong, Jiangsu and Zhejiang (Shanghai too, with its Pudong development project) as important contenders with Guangdong and Fujian for the attention of overseas investors.

To conclude this discussion of the contribution of foreign investment to domestic capital formation, attention may be drawn to the changing relationship between direct and indirect foreign investment. Table 6 shows that the rate of growth of total foreign investment (including capital borrowing) for China as a whole during 1985–90 was higher than that of the OCPs (35.51 per cent, as against 33.10 per cent), whereas the OCPs' rate of growth of overall fixed investment was higher than the national figure (11.38 and 8.63 per cent, respectively). The difference in the rate of growth of FDI on its own (30.05 per cent for China, 30.52 per cent for the OCPs) was, however, not nearly so pronounced. These figures suggest once more that central government borrowing has been increasingly – and with some effect – directed to non-OCP areas in order to arrest deteriorating regional imbalances in the receipt of foreign capital. This development reflects the well-established system of centralized redistribution of fiscal resources between regions (see above).

The Impact on Output and Income Growth

Lack of industry-specific investment and output data make it difficult to make a precise estimate of the impact of foreign investment upon output and income growth in the *econocoas* areas of China. From the highly aggregative figures in Table 6, however, some assessment can be made.

First, the shift of FDI from services to the industrial sector, observed after 1985, should *a priori* have been accompanied by accelerated industrial expansion, as measured by the expansion of gross value of industrial output (GVIO). This is indeed the case in all SEZs, except perhaps Shantou (see below). For the SEZs as a whole, the rate of growth of GVIO during 1985–90 – averaging 33 per cent per annum – is extremely high. This is so no matter whether the basis for comparison is China (9.49 per cent) or such

TABLE 7. *Income (Y) Multiplier of Investment (I) in the Econocoas Areas in China, 1985–1990*

	DY(a) (1)	DY(b) (2)	100 million yuan DTI (3)	DFI (4)	DFI/DTI (5)	Multiplier (1)/(3) (6)	(2)/(3) (7)
SEZs	61.16	87.57	204.95	78.51	0.38	0.30	0.43
Shezhen	27.47	33.43	100.44	43.95	0.44	0.27	0.33
Zhuhai	7.64	9.49	26.15	11.74	0.45	0.29	0.36
Shantou	15.80	30.66	45.12	9.96	0.22	0.35	0.68
Xiamen	10.24	13.98	33.23	12.86	0.39	0.31	0.42
OCCs	101.27	203.80	1,038.28	101.49	0.10	0.10	0.20
Dalian	23.29	36.87	81.79	19.82	0.24	0.28	0.45
Tianjin	13.54	28.64	211.80	21.40	0.10	0.06	0.14
Qingdao	21.81	27.22	53.72	5.51	0.10	0.41	0.51
Shanghai	14.69	31.27	512.70	34.63	0.07	0.03	0.06
Guangzhou	27.95	79.80	178.27	20.14	0.11	0.16	0.45
OCPs	975.06	1,461.78	4,022.82	283.40	0.07	0.24	0.36
	(1,003.29)	(1,521.69)	(4,966.74)	(339.43)	(0.07)	(0.20)	(0.31)
Liaoning	84.57	151.04	574.81	29.87	0.05	0.15	0.26
Hebei	99.89	143.55	462.35	4.46	0.01	0.22	0.31
Shandong	171.68	243.68	767.54	14.54	0.02	0.22	0.32
Jiangsu	150.57	198.91	769.52	13.83	0.02	0.20	0.26
Zhejiang	98.46	139.47	488.91	10.27	0.02	0.20	0.29
Fujian	74.26	107.89	211.18	26.63	0.13	0.35	0.51
Guangdong	225.09	382.98	748.50	170.77	0.23	0.30	0.51
Hainan	12.56	18.31	55.06	6.79	0.12	0.23	0.33
Guangxi	57.99	75.95	164.36	6.26	0.04	0.35	0.46
Beijing	42.94	–	368.57	30.89	0.08	0.12	–
PRC total	2,126.29	3,096.53	9,769.20	406.89	0.04	0.22	0.32

Notes:
DY(a) and DY(b): absolute changes (in real terms) in National Income (Net Material Product) (a) and GDP/GNP (b) between 1985 and 1990.
DTI and DFI: cumulative total (in real terms) of total fixed assets investments for the country as a whole including collective and private individual investments (DTI) and FDI plus capital borrowings (DFI) between 1985 and 1990.
Figures in parenthesis cover all the 11 OCPs (including Tianjin and Shanghai).
Sources:
Appendix Tables A2, A3, A6 and A7.

new *econocoas* frontiers as Tianjin (5.69 per cent), Shanghai (4.4 per cent), Liaoning (5.74 per cent), or even Shandong (14.5 per cent), Jiangsu (13.15 per cent) and Zhejiang (12.51 per cent).

Secondly, it is noticeable that the lower GVIO growth rates in the new frontier provinces and the country as a whole (the latter dominated by OCPs) have been associated with high growth rates of foreign investment, compared with those of the SEZs, Guangdong and Fujian. This is readily explained, for unlike the SEZs, provincial output and investment have remained dominated by established sources (see the figures in absolute *yuan* in Table 7). In this respect, Shantou, which includes many counties in addition to the area of the SEZ proper, is closer to these provinces – or, more precisely, to such municipalities as Guangzhou and Qingdao – than to the other three geographically more concentrated SEZs.

Thirdly, the short gestation period associated with accelerated additions to the foreign capital stock in the new *econocoas* areas during 1985–90 made it impossible, in many cases, to translate investment into output. But this factor is unlikely to have contributed significantly to the lower rates of growth of GVIO, given the marginal contribution of foreign capital to overall investment in these areas (see column 5 in Table 7). By contrast, the higher GVIO rates of growth in the SEZs, and in Guangdong and Fujian, appear to reflect enhanced flows of output from sustained joint-venture investment undertaken in these pioneer *econocoas* regions since the early 1980s. Notice that these areas exhibit a significantly higher marginal foreign capital contribution during 1985–90, compared with other *econocoas* regions. By extension, extrapolating from the experience of the more mature *econocoas* areas and given the accelerated expansion of foreign capital absorption since the mid-1980s, it seems likely that industrial growth in other coastal provinces will come increasingly to deviate from the expansionary trend in foreign investment during the 1990s.

Regional differences in income growth rates relative to those of foreign investment (see Table 6) are generally consistent with the observed differences in terms of GVIO. This is the case, no matter whether the narrow measure (net material product), or the broad measure (gross domestic product (GDP) or gross national product (GNP)) is used.[26] There are, however, two minor qualifications to this general finding.

First, for the SEZs, the gap between the average annual rate of growth of GVIO during 1985–90 (32.7 per cent) and that of national income (14.6 per cent for Y(a) in Table 6) is wider than for the country taken as a whole (9.5 and 7.5 per cent). This probably reflects the predominance of processing industries, which have relatively low value-added contributions, in areas with heavy concentrations of foreign investment. The same point can be made of Guangdong and Fujian provinces, although not to the same extent as in the SEZs. In any case, the argument should not be pressed too far, for in the case of some major OCPs (notably, Shandong, Jiangsu and – especially – Shanghai) the gap between GVIO and national income growth rates (Y(a) in Table 6) turns out to be even wider than for Guangdong and Fujian. Clearly, the structure of domestic industry varies from province to province.

Secondly, using the GNP/GDP measure, the gap between GVIO and income growth rates narrowed significantly during 1985–90 in a number of *econocoas* areas, including Tianjin, Shanghai and Guangzhou. This was not, however, the case in Shenzhen, where the gap apparently grew wider. The explanation may be that tourism led to a more rapid expansion of the

---

[26] The Chinese GNP/GDP measures as adopted since the mid-1980s are still not exactly comparable to the familiar western counterparts because of incomplete coverage of the service sector, but the discrepancy has been very much narrowed from the conventional measure of "net material product" (*guomin shouru*) which excludes a large part of the tertiary sector.

tertiary sector in the three municipalities, whilst Shenzhen's expansion was based on what Hong Kong government statistics regard as "outward processing" industrial activities.

Changes in productivity are another important aspect of the economic impact of foreign investment. For want of appropriately disaggregated industrial investment and net output data, we are again compelled to use the aggregate income measures shown in Table 7.[27] The observed income multiplier of investment shows the income response per unit of investment outlay. But the estimated "incremental capital-output ratio" cannot without qualification be accepted as a measure of the marginal efficiency of capital.

Take, for example, the SEZs, which consistently exhibit an income multiplier which is greater than the national average, no matter which national income measure is used; or Guangdong and Fujian (even Guangxi), whose multipliers are higher than those of virtually all other *econocoas* regions. Quite apart from the assumed greater efficiency in capital utilization by foreign joint ventures, a number of factors could explain the differences in the value of the multiplier.

One may be that most foreign investment-based projects in the SEZs and the two pioneer provinces have been short-run income-maximizing undertakings. For example, the many thousands of joint ventures (including simple outward processing arrangements) set up in the Pearl River Delta by Hong Kong manufacturers in recent years have almost overnight generated accelerated income and employment opportunities in Guangdong province. Another factor is the erratic nature of the *RMB* devaluation in 1986 and, more especially, 1989. *Ceteris paribus*, to the extent that a large part of joint venture production is exported (see the next section), such devaluations, which help loss-making exporters cover their costs and transform them into profit-making concerns in *RMB* terms, have had the effect of boosting income. What cannot, however, be known is the relative strength of these factors and the possible efficiency implications of foreign involvement to raising the value of the income multiplier.

But by way of contrast, the other major OCPs, which have exhibited significantly lower income multipliers and enjoyed lower foreign capital shares than Guangdong and Fujian (let alone the SEZs), appear to have been characterized by the conventional Stalinist industrial structure and an investment policy favouring heavy industry or projects with long gestation periods. This pattern has inevitably been reflected in lower income multipliers in areas, such as Shanghai, Tianjin and Beijing, (see Table 7), which constitute the backbone of the Stalinist development strategy.

Thus the impact of foreign investment can be seen not only in terms of the disparity in income-generating capacity which it has created, but also of

[27] Related value-added data are rarely available, with the notable exception of Shenzhen: see *Shenzhenshi guomin jingji tongji ziliao 1989* (*National Economic-Statistical Material for Shenzhen Municipality*) (hereafter *SZGMJJTJZL* 1989).

the increasing spatial bifurcation of China's industrial structure which has resulted from the government's selective approach to it. It remains to be seen whether the massive effort currently under way to attract foreign investment to other major OCPs will eventually help bring the industrial structure in line with what the competitive international market for foreign capital would dictate – but without compromising China's search for a mix of industrial output appropriate to its modernization goals.

Foreign Trade and Export Performance

The Chinese government's goal of maximizing foreign exchange earnings is to finance its priority import programme. Accordingly, the most important criterion for judging the performance of FDI projects in China is the ability of the foreign-funded enterprises to balance their foreign exchange requirements. It will be useful to preface the analysis of such enterprises' currency balances by considering export production.

Table 8 sets out available industrial output and export data for *sanzi* ("three foreign-funded": equity and contractual joint ventures and wholly foreign-owned firms) enterprises in the *econocoas* areas for 1987–91. The figures are expressed as a proportion of total and exported GVIO.

Two major points emerge from the data. First, in virtually all cases, *sanzi* enterprises' share of both output and export increased steadily throughout the period. With the single exception of Shenzhen during 1987–89, for which actual export share data are available, the estimates are based on the assumption that all output from these enterprises was exported. This is of course to overstate the case. But even allowing for domestic sales under the general rule that more than 70 per cent of the output of *sanzi* enterprises should be exported, estimated share of exports for *econocoas* areas remains consistently higher than their share of output.[28] Moreover, a cross-sectional comparison reveals that regions with a higher export share generally also enjoyed a higher output share. These findings imply that most *sanzi* enterprises have targeted their output towards world markets and that China's export-orientated foreign investment strategy has been implemented fairly consistently across the various regions.

What also emerges from Table 8 is that *sanzi* enterprises' shares in output and export vary greatly between regions, though in a manner which is

---

[28] See *TKP*, 16 March 1982 for the 70% rule. Nevertheless, it appears that many Sino-foreign joint ventures cannot meet this requirement for export. The average for Shenzhen is 65% in 1987–88 (in 1980 prices) and 58% for 1988 (in current prices), but 73.4% for 1989 (current prices): see *SZGMJJTJZL* 1989, pp. 44, 50, 68, 74, 76 and 120. The last percentage should not however be taken as an accurate measure, because it is obtained by relating total *sanzi* export to GVIO of those *sanzi* enterprises with "independent accounting" only. But as virtually all *sanzi* GVIO is produced by enterprises operating as independent economic entities the discrepancy should be minimal.

TABLE 8. *Relative Contribution of Sanzi Enterprises to Total and Exported GVIO in the Econocoas Areas in China, 1987–91 (%)*

	Total GVIO					Exported GVIO				
	1987	1988	1989	1990	1991	1987	1988	1989	1990	1991
SEZs	–	–	52.11	50.03	54.99	–	–	111.22	105.79	109.37
Shenzhen	(61.45)* / (63.68)	(63.25)* / (61.16)	59.04 / (59.04)	68.35 / (66.29)	68.19	(75.97)	(74.36)*	(70.61)	–	113.93
Zhuhai	–	(73.19)	(45.17)* / 31.60	34.16	47.46	–	(73.19)	102.08 / 139.59	112.23 / 105.72	100.24
Shantou	–	–	(30.45)*	22.50	33.31	–	–	–	61.20	83.25
Xiamen	(30.20)	(43.20)	48.30 / (48.54)	45.74 / (56.37)	53.79	–	–	132.81	170.05	131.16
OCCs	2.02	3.52	3.59	3.26	8.68	18.08	19.60	29.76	35.01	53.30
Dalian	–	–	–	2.78	5.00	–	–	–	15.38	21.10
Qinhuangdao	3.39	5.58	5.08	4.15	7.20	–	–	–	41.62	58.89
Tianjin	(1.39)	(2.31)	(3.39)	4.17 / (3.49)	4.07	–	–	–	40.71	37.77
Yantai	–	0.37	0.30	0.72	17.61	–	2.85	2.04	4.71	18.06
Weihai	–	–	–	1.61	1.82	–	–	–	11.31	10.39
Qingdao	–	–	0.82	1.12	2.53	–	–	5.01	6.73	14.87
Lianyungang	0.58	0.58	2.05	3.24	4.18	8.78	8.28	20.89	37.08	43.59
Nantong	–	1.56	–	4.22	–	–	10.78	–	22.73	–
Shanghai	1.17	2.19	3.50	–	–	–	15.44	24.99	–	–
Ningbo	0.28	0.79	2.40	4.07	6.32	–	–	–	33.52	43.43

TABLE 8. (Cont.)

	Total GVIO					Exported GVIO				
	1987	1988	1989	1990	1991	1987	1988	1989	1990	1991
Wenzhou	0.01	0.14	0.25	0.98	–	–	–	1.99	8.30	–
Fuzhou	18.22	24.50	26.71	27.30	36.62	–	–	–	115.74	127.49
Guangzhou	3.28	7.52	12.23	15.53	20.96	18.53	36.66	63.75	78.82	94.44
Zhangjiang	–	–	3.93	4.93	4.76	–	–	28.88	54.54	51.01
Beihai	1.41	3.32	4.33	6.62	5.17	–	20.37	24.95	33.08	29.05
OCPs										
Liaoning	–	–	(0.27)	(0.79)	–	–	–	–	–	–
Shandong	–	–	(0.14)*	(0.40)*	–	–	–	–	–	–
Fujian	(9.67)*	(13.96)*	(15.55)*	(21.44)*	–	–	–	–	–	–
	(12.43)	(18.79)	(21.38)	(28.48)						
Hainan	–	6.51	10.03	8.60	14.28	–	127.98	222.07	–	192.41
Beijing	–	–	(4.81)	(6.05)*	–	–	–	–	–	–
				(7.59)						
Total (OCCs + SEZs)	2.02	3.52	9.37	11.51	16.71	18.08	19.60	51.37	58.39	75.04

Notes:

The GVIO figures cover the greater municipality, not just the city districts or the SEZs proper. They exclude, however, *cunban* (village operated) GVIO, as far as it can be determined. The original absolute figures are in current prices for all the figures with an asterisk and the unbracketed figures for 1990, and in 1980 *RMB yuan* for the rest. The unbracketed figures of *sanzi* share in exported GVIO are derived by assuming that all output from *sanzi* enterprises is exported. However, virtually all the SEZs' shares for 1988–91 exceed 100% which implies that parts of the *sanzi* output were in fact sold to the domestic market. The figures given in parenthesis show therefore the more accurate *sanzi* export shares. None of the figures includes output from "processing activities" which are still quite substantial for the SEZs. The total represents the weighted average of the unbracketed figures for OCCs, SEZs (including Hainan) only, not the national average.

Sources:

Appendix Table A1 for all figures in parenthesis; all the others are from *China's Latest Economic Statistics (CLES)*, Part 2, February 1989, pp. 51–5 (for 1987 to 1988); February 1990, pp. 44–7 (for 1989); February 1991, pp. 13–16 (for 1990); and February 1992, pp. 24–7 (for 1991).

consistent with regional differences in average and marginal foreign investment shares in overall fixed capital formation (see the analysis of Tables 5
and 7, above). For example, in 1991 such enterprises contributed 55 per cent
of GVIO, but 76 per cent of exports, in the four SEZs. The corresponding
figures for Guangzhou were 21 and 66 per cent. In the same year, the
average shares of GVIO and exports accounted for by *sanzi* enterprises
in OCCs were only 9 and 37 per cent respectively. Admittedly, Shanghai
is excluded from these last calculations. But the predominant industrial
and trade role of the municipality in China ensured that the implied
export share (18 per cent) of its *sanzi* enterprises was already by no means
negligible.[29]

At the beginning of the 1990s, *sanzi* enterprises in the SEZs and OCCs
taken together probably accounted for about 17 per cent of total GVIO
generated in these areas and contributed more than half of exported GVIO.
Even more remarkable is the fact that this has been achieved within a
decade. More questionable is whether the expansion of exports during the
1980s and into the 1990s could have been sustained without the participation of these enterprises. It is, however, clear enough that foreign joint
ventures not only brought China scarce capital, much-needed technology
and managerial know-how, but also – and more importantly – provided it
with the marketing skills needed for integration in international markets.
Furthermore, the competitive pressures which came in the wake of such
international involvement encouraged domestic export producers and trading firms to improve the efficiency of their operations.

A proper assessment of the trade performance of foreign-funded enterprises requires an examination of their foreign currency balances of exports
and imports. Table 9 presents comprehensive data showing the shares of
sanzi enterprises in total exports and imports of the *econocoas* areas between 1988 and 1991, based on U.S. dollar accounts.

Notice that the export data here differ from those in Table 8 not only in
terms of currency base, but also of coverage. That is, the figures in Table 9
embrace all exports (not only industrial output) from *sanzi* enterprises.
They include exports of agricultural products, services and real estate sales,
as well as any items which the enterprises may have been permitted to
procure from domestic sources for export purposes to help balance foreign
exchange requirements.[30]

[29] One of the representative FDI ventures in Shanghai is the Yaohua-Pilkington Glass
Corporation which had a total sales volume of 270 million *yuan*, including 160 million *yuan* (i.e.
59%) in 1991 for export sales: see *TKP*, 22 May 1992, p. 4, and *Zhongguo duiwai maoyi*
(*China's Foreign Trade*), No. 3 (1992), p. 18 for a more comprehensive survey of the joint
venture.

[30] As a means to mitigate the strict requirements for foreign exchange balance, a number of
new policy provisions were given in 1986, including "Guanyu waishang touzi qiye goumai
guonei chanpin chukou jiejue waihui shouzhi pingheng de banfa" ("Measures concerning the
purchases of domestic products by foreign-funded enterprises for export for balancing foreign
exchange requirements), 20 January 1990.

TABLE 9. *Percentage Share of Sanzi Enterprises in Total Export and Import in the Econocoas Areas in China, 1988–91*

	Export				Import			
	1988	*1989*	*1990*	*1991*	*1988*	*1989*	*1990*	*1991*
SEZs	22.47	33.31	40.50	45.80	28.91	33.33	54.01	52.74
Shenzhen	26.38	36.99	43.96	50.52	30.67	33.00	51.66	57.24
Zhuhai	15.36	32.53	41.75	44.73	25.85	38.39	90.87	48.52
Shantou	11.66	18.49	23.63	28.38	14.89	2.18	26.57	31.51
Xiamen	18.36	28.02	37.37	41.70	42.83	42.95	56.73	58.50
OCCs	3.11	7.86	11.51	18.87	19.06	26.34	35.53	42.74
	(5.99)	(8.05)	(11.71)	(18.78)	(20.00)	(26.51)	(36.70)	(50.35)
Dalian	6.73	18.70	24.10	40.43	60.77	36.77	50.23	61.64
Tianjin	2.29	3.94	6.00	10.41	13.17	20.91	28.65	33.71
Qingdao	1.39	5.23	7.54	13.07	29.58	37.63	30.83	37.41
Shanghai	1.71	4.65	6.38	10.82	15.81	22.93	29.74	43.87
Guangzhou	7.92	17.61	24.44	33.76	18.64	33.86	46.23	55.26
OCPs	7.61	12.99	17.19	21.97	19.76	25.69	38.35	37.12
	(6.56)	(11.60)	(15.57)	(20.43)	(19.05)	(25.13)	(37.13)	(37.58)
Liaoning	0.99	2.97	4.24	9.26	24.32	17.67	28.89	37.90
Hebei	0.25	0.65	1.25	3.42	37.57	25.79	42.56	33.86
Shandong	0.60	2.34	3.62	6.00	9.72	17.27	25.69	33.89
Jiangsu	2.03	4.37	6.43	12.06	12.25	18.81	36.38	44.53
Zhejiang	2.52	3.73	6.11	9.02	9.52	13.07	19.32	25.24
Fujian	16.97	27.17	36.85	40.95	43.23	47.82	60.59	63.23
Guangdong	12.48	19.56	24.77	29.41	18.56	26.10	38.14	34.82
Hainan	2.10	7.55	7.10	8.48	12.79	17.64	34.89	29.05
Guangxi	1.64	3.40	4.82	7.50	14.72	21.66	26.29	24.50
Beijing	2.68	4.88	7.64	11.47	51.58	65.57	52.87	52.44
Provincial total	5.51	9.62	13.32	17.59	26.05	30.06	36.07	35.61
PRC total	5.15	9.23	12.58	16.76	14.34	19.65	23.56	26.55

Notes:
    Figures in brackets are sum totals for all the 15 OCCs and 11 OCPs including Tianjin and Shanghai. There is a striking discrepancy in the *sanzi* share in imports between the provincial and PRC totals, compared with the very marginal difference in the *sanzi* share in exports. The implied percentage shares of total PRC import conducted at the central level for the four years amounted to 46.2 (1988), 42.3 (1989), 34.7 (1990) and 29.9 (1991), and that for export only 6.5, 4.2, 5.5 and 4.7 respectively. These figures may understate the real magnitude of centralized control, because in many instances both exports and imports as undertaken by the "provincial-level trading firms" (which make up the shown provincial total) are still subject to various non-tariff restrictions, including export/import licensing, quotas and foreign exchange allocation. Nevertheless, the discrepancy shows that despite the trade decentralization drive imports have remained subject to much greater central control than exports. The situation is thus basically the same as that in the mid-1980s (*cf.* Y.Y. Kuch, "Economic decentralization and foreign trade expansion in Chian," in J.C.H. Chai and C.K. Leung (eds.), *China's Economic Reforms* (Hong Kong: University of Hong Kong, 1987), pp. 462–6), although the degree of central control over import has tended to decline in recent years.
Sources:
    Appendix Tables A8 and A9.

The export data in Table 9 reveal that the *sanzi* shares in total *econocoas* exports increased steadily during 1988–91. The shares for individual regions are found to vary in a manner that is generally consistent with estimates of *sanzi* enterprises' shares in total and exported GVIO, and foreign shares in capital formation. For China as a whole, the *sanzi* share in total exports rose from little more than 5 per cent in 1988 to about 17 per cent in 1991. There is, however, significant variation between different regions: from a high of 46 per cent for the SEZs to 41 per cent (Fujian), 29 per cent (Guangdong) and a low of 11 per cent in both Shanghai and Beijing.

Sanzi exports are, in fact, strongly skewed towards Guangdong, which accounted for 66 per cent of the national total (Shenzhen alone contributed almost 40 per cent of the provincial total in 1991).[31] In absolute U.S. dollar terms, *sanzi* exports in Shenzhen, or Guangdong province, were consistently significantly higher than those of Shanghai or any other *econocoas* area (OCC or OCP). In 1991, for example, the values were US$29.24 million (Shenzhen) and $79.24 million (Guangdong), compared with US$6.59 million for Shanghai, or US$26.52 million for all 15 OCCs (including Guangzhou).[32] But the data in Table 9 reveal that regional skewing of *sanzi* export earnings has narrowed over time in favour of the non-pioneer *econocoas* regions.[33] This is entirely consistent with the earlier observation that foreign investment in these regions has grown more rapidly than in the earlier-established areas. The same trends are indeed also reflected in *sanzi* import shares – machinery, equipment and essential raw materials purchased by foreign partners in joint ventures – relative to those of exports (Table 9). Thus, the ratio of *sanzi* export to import share for the SEZs (52.74:45.80 per cent = 1.15) is much smaller than that of the 15 OCCs (50.35:18.78 per cent = 2.68), or of the 11 OCPs (37.58:20.43 per cent = 1.84). Notice that the OCP figures are dominated by Guangdong and its SEZs.

The implications of the regional variations in import and export shares are clear. If the new *econocoas* frontiers can effectively emulate the success stories of the SEZs, Guangdong or Fujian, assuming that the current scale of imports is translated into exports in accordance with the export-orientated foreign investment strategy, the *sanzi* share in national exports may be expected to increase to around 30 per cent by the middle of the 1990s. Making precise forecasts of such exports is very difficult. But assuming that most *sanzi* enterprises are cautious in their attitude to expected returns on investment and/or have access to established marketing and distribution networks overseas, there is no reason why the new *econocoas* frontiers should not expand their *sanzi* export shares in future. Nor need this be at the expense of the shares already achieved by such regions as Guangdong (30 per cent) and Fujian (41 per cent). Except for Jiangsu province, the *sanzi* export share of all other new OCPs is, after all, no more than 10 per cent.

The most striking finding to emerge from Table 10, which shows the trade balance of *sanzi* enterprises, is that throughout 1988–91 virtually no *econocoas* area succeeded in balancing its foreign exchange requirements.[34]

---

[31] See Appendix Table A8.   [32] *Ibid.*

[33] This can be shown by relating for example the given share of the SEZs to that of Shanghai. The ratio declines over the years.

[34] For details about the various components of *sanzi* enterprises' foreign exchange expenditure and receipts see Huang Xunpin, "Shilun Zhongwai heyin qiye de waihui pinheng wenti," in *Guangdong shehui kexue (Guangdong Social Sciences)*, No. 2 (1987), pp. 85–8.

It is likely that a number of factors were involved. But the essential explanation is probably to be found in the euphoric confidence which foreign interests have demonstrated in the Chinese investment market. In the new *econocoas* areas, the underlying gestation periods required to translate overseas investment into output and exports would explain the trade imbalances. What is interesting is that the same dynamism appears to have characterized *sanzi* investment in the established *econocoas* regions: the SEZs, Guangdong and Fujian provinces have all continued to exhibit substantial negative *sanzi* trade balances during 1988–91.[35]

The foreign exchange balances of *sanzi* enterprises vary between different industrial destinations of foreign investment. Lack of data makes it difficult to quantify such differences. Nevertheless, foreign exchange surpluses have generally characterized *sanzi* investment in hotels and recreational services, as well as in primary sector activities, especially the extraction of mineral ores, coal and oil for sale in world markets. This suggests that the imbalances suffered by manufacturing and processing enterprises are significantly greater than the net balance estimates in Table 10 suggest. Of course, it is the latter two categories which have attracted most of the accelerated increase in FDI since the mid-1980s (see Table 4). It is impossible to say whether all this indicates excessive optimism by foreign investors or the existence of a real competitive edge for *sanzi* products in western export markets.

Table 10 also shows, however, that during 1988–91 the deficits (exports minus imports) of *sanzi* enterprises tended to decline as a proportion of their own exports. Even more remarkable is the fact that for the SEZs, Guangdong and Fujian provinces, the shares were lower than in the other *econocoas* areas. This suggests that as investment generates increased volumes of output and exports, most *sanzi* enterprises in all *econocoas* areas (new and established) can hope to meet the requirements for foreign exchange balance in the years to come.

Finally, there is the redemption of borrowed foreign capital. The issue involved here is similar to that which affects *sanzi* enterprises, except that the redemption of loans undertaken by government depends, so it is argued, on the overall level of the relevant country's export earnings. The outstanding net balance of China's foreign debt was recently said to be "more than US$60 billion," with debt service obligations (amortization plus interest payments) reaching a peak of US$7–8 billion per year during 1992–95.[36] This gives an estimated debt service ratio of 9.7 to 10.8 per cent based

[35] Other factors accounting for the continued imbalances may include illicit sales of imported *sanzi* machinery and equipment to domestic buyers, "over-invoicing" of import bills, and depressed export quotations for tax evasion purposes. This seems to be a real and widespread practice among the *sanzi* enterprises, but it is impossible to estimate to what extent it accounts for the estimated *sanzi* deficit.

[36] These are the figures given by Li Guixian at a press interview during the 25th Annual Meeting of Asian Development Bank, held in Hong Kong; see *TKP*, 6 May 1992, p. 2.

TABLE 10. Trade Balance (Export minus import) of Sales Enterprises of the ... in Export

	(100 million US$)				As share of export (%)			
	1988	1989	1990	1991	1988	1989	1990	1991
SEZs	-4.01	0.74	-7.63	-6.07	-32.47	3.33	-23.73	-14.11
Shenzhen	-1.88	2.63	-1.70	-3.18	-19.46	15.81	-7.41	-10.88
Zhuhai	-1.11	-0.93	-4.82	-0.98	-130.59	-44.29	-137.32	-19.25
Shantou	-0.18	-0.14	-0.12	-0.57	-20.22	-9.15	-5.29	-16.76
Xiamen	-0.84	-0.82	-0.99	-1.34	-88.42	-41.62	-28.78	-25.28
OCCs	-9.23	-12.72	-11.55	-12.97	-340.59	-173.53	-93.83	-55.76
	(-7.64)	(-13.26)	(-12.28)	(-14.88)	(-137.91)	(-158.61)	(-86.05)	(-56.11)
Dalian	-1.87	-0.39	-0.61	-0.82	-623.33	-36.79	-35.47	-19.11
Tianjin	-0.71	-1.39	-1.04	-1.20	-182.05	-207.46	-97.20	-65.93
Qingdao	-0.30	-0.69	-0.36	-0.44	-1,000.00	-460.00	-128.57	-69.84
Shanghai	-4.23	-7.43	-6.90	-7.00	-503.57	-318.88	-197.14	-106.22
Guangzhou	-2.11	-2.83	-2.65	-3.51	-181.90	-90.71	-46.01	-35.35
OCPs	-20.57	-18.06	-28.96	-20.51	-91.59	-40.43	-40.49	-18.97
	(-25.51)	(-26.88)	(-36.89)	(-28.67)	(-107.68)	(-56.59)	(-48.48)	(-24.59)
Liaoning	-2.21	-0.91	-1.10	-1.23	-566.67	-71.09	-49.55	-23.61
Hebei	-1.36	-0.91	-1.32	-0.59	-3,400.00	-758.33	-550.00	-85.51
Shandong	-0.68	-1.12	-0.98	-1.39	-400.00	-157.75	-79.03	-61.78
Jiangsu	-0.77	-1.34	-2.45	-4.22	-157.14	-120.12	-129.63	-102.18
Zhejiang	-0.09	-0.13	0.21	0.25	-23.68	-18.57	15.67	9.54
Fujian	-3.71	-2.61	-2.43	-3.55	-154.17	-52.52	-26.91	-27.54
Guangdong	-10.95	-9.69	-19.57	-8.05	-59.38	-27.43	-35.71	-10.16
Hainan	-0.37	-0.87	-1.14	-1.57	-616.67	-348.00	-300.00	-296.23
Guangxi	-0.42	-0.46	-0.20	-0.16	-466.67	-209.09	-51.28	-27.59
Beijing	-4.72	-5.89	-4.44	-5.37	-1,815.38	-1,178.00	-516.28	-358.00
Provincial total	-54.76	-67.71	-47.55	-38.82	-223.69	-139.69	-60.86	-32.21
PPC total	-77.50	-66.00	87.40	81.19	–	–	–	–

Notes:
Figures in brackets refer respectively to the sum total of all 15 OCCs and 11 OCPs including Tianjin and Shanghai.
Sources:
Appendix Tables A8 and A9.

on total Chinese exports of US$719.10 million in 1991.[37] This is considerably
less than the 12–15 per cent, conventionally regarded as the critical debt
service ratio – "critical" in the sense that it threatens to "crowd out" a
country's import capacity to promote economic growth.[38]

Even when the 1991 *sanzi* deficit of US$38.82 million (see Table 10) has
been deducted from total export earnings, China's current debt service
ratio will remain below this critical level. In any case, its current foreign
exchange reserves (some US$43 billion as of December 1991) constitutes a
substantial hedge against unexpected eventualities. In short, for the foreseeable future, China's balance of payments vis-à-vis foreign debt servicing
looks healthier than the *sanzi* balances might suggest.

Trends and Policy Dilemmas in the 1990s

Any attempt to forecast trends in foreign direct investment in China during
the rest of the 1990s must confront two, closely related issues. The first
concerns the availability of foreign capital; the second, the likely rate of
return on investment in China relative to that available elsewhere. Both
issues should be viewed against the international perspective of global
economic interdependence or the economic evolution of the Asia-Pacific
Region. The collapse of the Soviet bloc may, for example, precipitate a
reallocation of international capital away from China. By contrast, political
upheaval in South-east Asia may cause a reassessment of regional investment risks which favours China. As for established *sanzi* enterprises, plans
for further capital injections are likely to be conditioned by the annual
decision whether to renew China's Most Favoured Nation (MFN) status,
given that a substantial proportion of *sanzi* products are exported to the
United States. Similarly, a positive outcome to the ongoing negotiations
on China's re-admission to GATT will almost certainly help boost foreign
investors' confidence in China.

Above all, the domestic political situation will remain a critical determi-
nant of outside perceptions of China's credit-worthiness and thereby the
scale of FDI there. This is evident from the impact of the Tiananmen
Square incident. The frenzy with which Hong Kong compatriots and overseas investors responded early in 1992 to Deng Xiaoping's call for an
accelerated opening-up of the Chinese economy is another case in point. By
the middle of 1992 many of the *econocoas* areas were already recording
dramatic rises in both the number of contracts for joint-venture projects

[37] Li Guixian (*ibid.*) gives a debt service ratio of 8%. *TKP*, 24 April 1992 cited a MOFERT
source to give a net foreign debt balance of US$52.58 billion, with a debt service ratio of 8.5%
up to the end of June 1991.

[38] See World Bank, *China's External Trade and Capital* (Washington D.C.: The World
Bank, 1988), p. 28.

which had been signed, and the level of foreign capital that had been pledged and realized.[39] Subsequent support for Deng's policy from "conservative" Chinese leaders and the military had the further effect of boosting the Hong Kong stock market index (the single most important indicator of investors' confidence in China) to an unprecedented degree. The increase in the Hang Seng Index from around 3,500 to 6,000 between March and early June 1992 could hardly have been predicted, not least against the background of a world-wide recession.[40]

The unpredictability of the internal and external factors which impinge upon foreign investment in China may explain the absence of any quantitative targets for such investment or capital borrowing in either the Ten-Year Economic Programme (1991–2000) or the Eighth Five-Year Plan (1991–95). Even so, the role of Hong Kong as a source of FDI during the second half of the 1980s (see Table 11) may provide valuable clues for future developments.

Between 1984 and 1990, in only one year did Hong Kong's share in China's total realized FDI fall below 50 per cent – and during 1987–89 the figure was closer to two-thirds. More remarkable still, virtually all the *econocoas* areas shared in the pre-eminent role of Hong Kong.[41] Second in importance was Japan. Its share of the overall FDI intake has, however, never been substantial (in 1989 and 1990, it reached 11 and 13 per cent); nor has that of the United States, which ranks third, closely behind Japan.[42]

Perhaps the most important lesson of Hong Kong's involvement in investment on the Chinese mainland is for Taiwan. Admittedly, Taiwan does not have Hong Kong's benefit of a rail link with China. But the distance across the Taiwan Strait to Fujian is hardly any longer than that between Hong Kong and Guangzhou. Taiwanese capital has made rapid inroads on to the mainland during recent years, although because of strict bans on direct commercial, navigational and postal links with the PRC, such progress has only been possible through cumbersome connections in third countries (above all, Hong Kong). The *Chinese Statistical Yearbook* still

[39] This has been prominently reported in the Hong Kong press. See for example *TKP*, 6 June 1992 about the FDI intake in Shenzhen (p. 18), Fujian (p. 4); and *TKP*, 28 May 1992 about Shanghai. *Cf.* also *SCMP* (Hong Kong), 3 April 1992 (Business Post, p. 2) for a similar report.

[40] Moreover the frenetic buying even extended to the "B shares" issued by Chinese enterprises; see *SCMP*, 7 June 1992 (Money Post, p. 6). These stock shares are backed by strong foreign exchange earnings and can only be bought with foreign currency, in contrast to the "A shares" which cater to domestic Chinese subscribers. Note that the Hong Kong Stock Exchange is still pondering whether the major Chinese companies with B shares could be allowed to be publicly listed in Hong Kong without complying with the strict local legal and accounting requirements for listing.

[41] An increased share seems to have been taken by mainland Chinese interests based in Hong Kong, but it appears unlikely that such ventures will overrule the importance of genuine Hong Kong investors. For a comprehensive study of Hong Kong's involvement in China see Y. W. Sung, *The China–Hong Kong Connection: the Key to China's Open Door Policy* (Cambridge: Cambridge University Press, 1991).

[42] See *ZGTJNJ* 1991, p. 630 for the country-wise distribution of FDI in China.

does not contain a separate entry for Taiwan, but quasi-official accounting now (1992) shows Taiwan to be the fourth largest investor in China.[43]

Looking ahead, political détente between Taiwan and the Chinese mainland is likely soon to be reflected in the establishment of direct links. This would pave the way for the further massive transfer of Taiwanese capital, on a scale similar to the expansion of Hong Kong manufacturing investment in China during the last decade.

In assessing the potential impact of expanded Taiwanese involvement, several factors need to be kept in mind. The first is that Taiwan has for some years enjoyed the highest level of foreign exchange reserves in the world (about US$80 billion, as of December 1991).[44] This provides both the wherewithal and opportunity to seek investment outlets overseas. Secondly, with a population (around 20 million) slightly more than three times that of Hong Kong (5.8 million), and a per capita income that is comparable (US$9,000, compared with US$12,000), Taiwan's foreign trade intensity approaches that of the British Crown Colony. Excluding re-exports, Taiwan's exports in 1991 totalled US$76 billion (*cf.* US$29 billion for Hong Kong; and US$72 billion for the PRC).[45] Given that both the export structure and income level of both regions of "Greater China" are comparable, Taiwan appears to be poised to emulate Hong Kong in relocating its labour-intensive export production to the mainland prior to technological upgrading.[46]

Hong Kong's exports may provide an approximate measure of the potential investment flow from Taiwan. The 1991 estimate of Hong Kong's total exports (US$29 billion), as noted above, took no account of re-exports – essentially involving China – which in the same year totalled US$69 billion, a sum that would have seemed inconceivable before the adoption of the open-door strategy.[47] Most of the exports were output from *sanzi* enterprises, funded by Hong Kong investors.[48] If the Hong Kong re-export ratio

---

[43] See for example *Wen hui pao* (Hong Kong), 5 June 1992, p. 2; and *TKP*, 13 February 1992, p. 23. A number of Chinese provincial statistical yearbooks do have a separate entry for Taiwanese FDI in recent years. *TKP* (*ibid.*) reports that Guangdong had the largest FDI intake from Taiwan in 1991, with 410 new Taiwanese enterprises with a pledge of investment of US$490 million. Fujian ranked second, with 329 enterprises and US$400 million. The same sources show that compared with 1990, pledged Taiwanese investment increased by 190% in Hainan, 50% in Shanghai, 34% in Liaoning, 30% in Beijing and 60% in Nanjing.

[44] See C. J. Lee, "An analysis of the international factors that influence the development of small and medium enterprises: the case of Taiwan," paper presented at the conference on "Global Interdependence and Asia-Pacific Co-operation," Hong Kong, 8–10 June 1992.

[45] GATT statistics as cited in *SCMP*, 30 March 1992 (Business Post, p. 2).

[46] Compared with Hong Kong, Taiwan certainly has a stronger industrial base and demand for technological upgrading of its industrial structure.

[47] See n. 45, above.

[48] The export of *sanzi* enterprises through Hong Kong has indeed become so substantial that in the last couple of years it has been the focal point of a China–U.S. trade dispute, with the Chinese arguing that its trade surplus with the U.S. should essentially be accounted for by "outward processing" from Hong Kong for which the Chinese partners earn only a minimal share of processing fees.

TABLE 11. *Share of Hong Kong in Total Foreign Investment in the Econocoas Areas in China, 1984–90 (%)*

	1984	1985	1986	1987	1988	1989	1990
SEZs							
Shenzhen	–	82.74 (d)	91.15 (d)	82.89 (d) (63.37)(c)	87.21 (d) (63.47)(c)	78.35 (d) (61.28)(c)	50.11 (d) (46.45)(c)
Zhuhai	–	100.00 (d) (71.69)(b)	100.00 (d) (82.84)(b)	79.38 (d)	98.63 (d)	97.25 (d) (51.22)(c)	84.82 (d) (67.94)(c)
Shantou	–	89.20 (d)	81.63 (d)	87.65 (d)	87.69 (d)	90.38 (d) (91.87)(c)	78.06 (d) 80.22 (c)
Xiamen	–	80.16 (d)	–	–	64.24 (b)(e)	64.61 (d)	61.98 (d)
OCCs							
Dalian	–	35.66 (d)	20.12 (d)	30.70 (d)	11.97 (d)	–	25.03 (d)
Tianjin	–	–	–	46.83 (b)	–	49.28 (b) (44.22)(b)(e)	(42.44)(d)(e)
Qingdao	–	–	–	–	–	–	–
Shanghai	–	–	10.95 (b)	64.41 (b) (27.16)(b)(e)	–	40.63 (c) (26.03)(c)(e)	–
Guangzhou	–	87.97 (b)	67.77 (b)	–	47.24 (b)	77.55 (d) (43.68)(c)	69.43 (d)
OCPs							
Liaoning	–	59.22 (b)	48.32 (b)	34.58 (b)	57.66 (b)	28.25 (b)	68.21 (b) (52.28)(b)(e)
Hebei	–	–	–	–	67.85 (c)	49.83 (c)	75.94 (d)
Shandong	–	–	–	–	69.02 (c)	70.87 (c)	53.79 (d)
Jiangsu	–	–	–	–	–	–	–

TABLE 11. (Cont.)

	1984	1985	1986	1987	1988	1989	1990
Zhejiang	–	–	–	19.30 (a)	51.10 (a)	45.60 (a)	52.99 (b) (51.51)(b)(e)
Fujian	–	– (80.16)(d)	35.72 (c)	24.87 (c)	61.43 (c) (61.89)(d)	52.22 (c) (59.39)(d) (68.78)(d)(e)	65.70 (c) (55.48)(d) (43.84)(c)(e) (57.50)(d)(e)
Guangdong	–	87.40 (d) (92.01)(c) (94.06)(a)	92.50 (d) (76.53)(c)	84.63 (d) (72.86)(c)	91.02 (d) (63.04)(c)	82.38 (d) (64.39)(c) (69.81)(a)	69.77 (d) (64.18)(c) (77.71)(a)
Hainan	75.00 (c)	77.56 (c)	64.74 (c)	100.00 (c) (100.00)(d)	82.18 (c) (77.87)(d)	89.53 (c)	49.11 (c) (70.48)(d)
Guangxi	–	100.00 (d)	100.00 (d)	99.89 (d)	97.13 (d)	94.41 (d)	87.73 (d)
Beijing	–	–	42.38 (b)	33.16 (b)	69.56 (b) (41.84)(d)	31.33 (b) (50.49)(d)	29.94 (b) (40.79)(d)
PRC total	52.69 (d) (27.87)(c)	48.86 (d) (22.78)(c)	59.22 (d) (21.67)(c)	68.35 (d) (24.74)(c)	64.93 (d) (30.40)(c)	62.06 (d) (28.96)(c)	56.42 (d) (23.63)(c)

Notes:
(a) pledged total of FDI and capital borrowing
(b) pledged FDI only
(c) realized total of FDI and capital borrowing
(d) realized total of FDI
(e) cumulative total

All the figures cover Macao where statistics are available. Except for Shenzhen, Zhuhai and Shantou, the figures for all the cities refer to the greater municipality rather than the city district or the SEZ (in the case of Xiamen) proper. However, for 1987 and 1988 for which the related figures are available for both the entire municipality and the SEZs proper, the Hong Kong shares for the three SEZs in Guangdong province show only very marginal differences between the two series. The PRC total for FDI covers the residual category "other investment from foreign investors." This is also widely listed as "commodity credits" to include investments made by way of compensation trade, international leasing and outward processing.

The main problems encountered are similar to those as explained in Table 6, as the country breakdowns for foreign investment are very often given alongside the classification by economic sectors.

Sources:
As Appendix Table A1: PRC totals are from *ZGTJNJ* and *JMNJ* (various issues).

(US\$69/\$29 billion) were applied to Taiwan's domestic export base (US\$76 billion), the present level of *sanzi* exports and investment in China deriving from the activities of Hong Kong investors might be doubled. Although crude, this estimate is an indication of the possible direction and magnitude of changes which could be triggered by the normalization of relations across the Taiwan Strait.

South Korea has also shown keen interest in investing in China (especially in Shandong province). The expected normalization of diplomatic relations is therefore another factor which may further contribute to the current "investment fever" in China.[49]

In the end, however, it is Japan which is likely to hold the key to any major breakthrough in foreign investment. It is a curious fact that Japanese involvement in China has been marginal, mainly confining itself to governmental loans.[50] Its FDI contribution (US\$1.93 billion during 1988–90) was, for example, little more than that extended to Indonesia between 1983 and 1987 (US\$1.65 billion).[51] Indonesia has in fact been the largest Asian recipient of Japanese FDI and virtually the only country to enjoy a trade surplus vis-à-vis Japan. It is difficult to know why Indonesia should have been preferred to China by the Japanese. No less strange is the fact that it was German and French companies (Volkswagen and Peugeot), rather than Toyota, Mazda, Nissan or Honda – all of which have made massive inroads into American and West European markets – which struck the first motor car investment agreements to produce for the Chinese market. What is more, the Volkswagen (Santana) deal was based on China's agreement to obtain the necessary foreign exchange by diverting funds which had originally been earmarked to facilitate car imports from Japan.

What explains this lack of interest in direct investment in China?[52] It may be that Japan perceives its share as already having been represented by Hong Kong and Taiwan investors, whose manufacturing investment in China has, after all, been based on the use of Japanese machinery and equipment and semi-manufactured materials for "outward processing." Nor is such a "trade-for-investment" substitution as cumbersome as it ap-

[49] Note that South Korea's export (virtually the same as China) ranks with Taiwan as the world's thirteenth (or fourteenth) largest exporter; see n. 45, above.

[50] *ZGTJNJ* 1991, p. 630 shows that for 1989 and 1990 Chinese foreign borrowings from Japan amounted to US\$2,595 and 2,500 million respectively, compared with US\$1,027 and 1,011 million from the second-largest lender, the World Bank.

[51] *Cf. ZGTJNJ* 1990, p. 654, *ZGTJNJ* 1991, p. 630 and Christopher Howe, "China, Japan and economic interdependence in the Asia Pacific region," in *The China Quarterly*, No. 124 (December 1991), pp. 662–93.

[52] Christopher Howe, "China, Japan and economic interdependence," attributes the Japanese disinterest partly to the cancellation by the Chinese of the Long-term Trade Agreement in the early 1980s and the souring of Sino-Japanese relations that followed. "Political frictions in the mid 1980s and the failure of the Chinese to satisfy Japanese demands for a stable and non-discriminatory investment environment have [also] led in recent years to an investment 'strike' by Japanese companies and a major mismatch of intentions and expectations" (p. 683).

pears. Nevertheless, Japan would undoubtedly benefit from increased accessibility to the Chinese domestic market. In this respect, it is significant that against the background of pressures from GATT and an increase in the American trade deficit with China in recent years, major service sectors (such as retail commerce, banking, transport and communications) now seem poised to receive direct foreign investment.[53] The lifting of all import regulatory taxes, beginning in April 1992,[54] can also be expected to help boost the inflow of import-substituting FDI, as overseas investors take advantage of the de-control of imports and foreign exchange. Japanese investors are in a stronger position than any of the major western countries to meet Chinese demand for industrial import-substitutes, except perhaps for nuclear, aircraft, satellite communications and advanced defence technologies.

Pudong seems to be a particular focus of China's renewed open-door policy. It was apparently Chen Yun himself (the arch-conservative opponent of Deng's strategy) who coined the term "new zone" (xinqu) to apply to this project, to distinguish it from other, well-established "special zones" (tequ). In contrast to the SEZs, which have been dominated by small-scale, labour-intensive and export-orientated manufacturing investment from Hong Kong, Pudong is expected to attract large-scale foreign investment, embodying the most advanced western technology. The new zone has also been described as a "dragon head" (longtou), designed to effect major economic changes throughout the Yangzi River Basin.

It is not clear in what degree of detail the Pudong strategy has been formulated. But given that another Hong Kong is simply not available to assist in creating a second Shenzhen, the core of the project would appear to be one of massive import substitution, designed to ensure that there is no premature collapse to damage public morale. It is also difficult to predict how quickly China's domestic market will be opened to FDI in coming years. What can be said is that any significant move in this direction will have major implications. These do not merely derive from subjecting domestic large and medium-scale industrial enterprises (the prime focus of central planning) to competitive international pressures. They also arise from potential shifts in the industrial structure and its regional complexion, consequent upon any decontrol of the direction and allocation of FDI in China – shifts which might reflect a fundamental realignment of industrialization strategy.

[53] Yaohan, a Hong Kong-based multinational of Japanese origin has recently completed a major deal to open in Shanghai the largest department store in China. This was closely followed by plans for Sun Hung Kai, a giant multi-purpose holding company from Hong Kong, to develop the largest commercial complex in Beijing, just to the east of the Forbidden City.
[54] See TKP, 3 March 1992, p. 2. The regulatory import taxes are primarily for marking up prices of imported producer foods to levels comparable to that produced domestically. The measure is designed partly to protect domestic industries from outside competition, and partly to balance the discrepancy between internal and external prices caused by the distorted Chinese price system.

It is beyond the scope of this study to speculate on whether such a policy shift would be politically acceptable. Certainly, associated economic changes – to wages, incomes, consumption, commodity prices and (not least) foreign exchange rate policy – might prove to be unpalatable. If this were so, the 1990s might well witness a gradualist approach, characteristic of Dengist pragmatism, of controlled economic integration with the west. Adverse political developments might delay this process. But given the strength of current commitment to reform and opening up – and against the background of the collapse of the Soviet bloc – it is unlikely that any new political leadership could wholly reverse it.

Concluding Remarks

This investigation has shown that following a decade of experimentation foreign direct investment has become a well-established and important part of Chinese economic activity. The strategy of seeking to maximize foreign exchange earnings through export-orientated foreign investment has meant that Sino-foreign joint ventures have been largely isolated from the core of the centrally-planned domestic economy. But there are two respects in which this "alienated" FDI sector has come to assume critical importance. First, it has become a major earner of foreign exchange. Secondly, it has become the bridgehead for the introduction of foreign capital into import-substitution investment in China.

The Chinese leadership is undoubtedly aware that there are limits to the expansion of foreign investment that is exclusively export-orientated. This is not simply because of western countries' limited capacity to absorb associated products. Rather, it reflects the fact that the accumulation of any substantial trade surplus, such as China presently enjoys with western countries, invites political pressures from those countries for a reciprocal opening-up of the domestic market. That said, Chinese authorities do appear to be willing gradually to expose protected domestic industries to competitive international pressures, even if it is difficult to predict how rapidly such controlled relaxation will proceed.

The official position is well summed up in the following extract from a recent textbook compiled by the Central Party School:

... In utilizing foreign capital, [we] should implement a strategy of combining import substitution and export promotion. First of all, [we] should make use of foreign capital in order to import advanced technology. As a reward, [we] should open up parts of the domestic market to products for which our country has hitherto relied on imports. The implementation of this strategy will have a positive effect on raising our country's economic capability and technological level, as well as realizing [the goal of] industrialization and building up an independent and integrated industrial system.[55]

[55] Wu Zhenkun and Song Zihe, *Development Strategies of Opening up the Economy*, pp. 45–6.

If this reads as a cautious statement (perhaps in order to pacify disgruntled hardliners), its rhetoric is certainly very different from that of the Cultural Revolution, when the same goal of industrialization was based exclusively on the principle of "self-reliance." Furthermore, the debt of foreign capital involvement in China is now such that, with or without Deng Xiaoping, the policy of the last decade is most unlikely to be reversed. Against the background of the collapse of the Soviet Union, one could even, in part, interpret the ongoing campaign to accelerate economic opening up as a political act. Hence the underlying political theme of repudiating the "leftists." From this point of view, the possibility of a political backlash seems remote.

Looking ahead, much will hinge on the pace of domestic economic reforms. More specifically, any significant shift in policy towards a genuine import-substitution foreign investment regime will necessarily require the de-regulation of large and medium-scale industrial enterprises. This is because these enterprises constitute the focus of centralized planning and are the locus of modern industrialization in China. Significant decontrol of this sector would encourage integration of the Chinese economy with the west and thereby facilitate the looked-for transfer of advanced technology via direct foreign investment.

This is again an area in which predictions are hazardous. It is, however, interesting that an increasing number of large and medium-scale enterprises, notably in Shanghai, have recently been accorded the kind of managerial flexibility hitherto extended to Sino-foreign joint ventures. In seeking the "invigoration" of this industrial core, policy emphasis has shifted markedly from the "contractual responsibility system" to "pushing [such enterprises] towards the market" (*tuixiang shichang*). Even more significant, the Central Committee's Document No. 4 (June 1992) may presage the regulation of the State Planning Commission – traditionally, the symbol of Soviet-style centralized planning and control in China – to a mere policy centre.[56] If this were to happen, its role would become one of macro-economic regulation, rather than of operational involvement in setting physical input and output targets and balancing material-technical supplies in state industries.

The changes that have taken place (and are still doing so) in China point to an alternative strategy to the "big bang" of the Soviet Union and Soviet bloc countries. Whatever the outcome may be, a host of western investors has already eagerly sought to cash in on the opportunity presented by the "whirlwind" unleashed early in 1992 by Deng Xiaoping.

---

[56] The document has not yet been publicly made available, but *TKP*, 15 June 1992, p. 2 disclosed considerable details.

Appendix

TABLE A1. *Foreign Direct Investment (FDI) in the Economically Opened Coastal (Econocoas) Areas in China, 1979–91 (million US$)*

	1979	1980	1981	1982	1983	1984	1985	1986	1987	1988	1989	1990	1991
SEZs						385.75	334.77	480.79	367.46	441.97	613.19	655.63	721.78
Shenzhen	15.37	32.64	112.82	73.79	143.93	210.50	193.40	380.73	280.13	299.99	302.46	389.94	398.75
Zhuhai	4.15	15.75	13.67	56.33	29.39	126.94	53.45	45.18	33.82	47.40	53.28	69.10	134.33
Shantou					1.54	7.87	14.64	20.95	35.98	46.62	47.65	123.86	56.14
Xiamen			[1979–83] 10.73			40.44	73.28	33.93	17.53	47.96	209.80	72.73	132.56
OCCs							275.12	334.35	477.67	537.37	726.43	642.16	797.27
							(301.65)	(374.14)	(517.07)	(680.86)	(908.62)	(861.39)	(1,087.90)
Dalian							14.32	30.49	49.90	74.88	80.57	201.29	261.11
Tianjin			[1979–84] 12.87				32.51	42.81	133.13	61.15	31.42	36.93	93.88
Qingdao							2.30	10.73	14.00	12.33	58.01	45.88	46.47
Shanghai			[1980–83] 87.00			36.00	107.54	148.90	214.01	233.17	422.12	177.19	164.20
Guangzhou	9.84	30.13	35.31	52.68	52.89	155.87	118.45	101.42	66.63	155.84	134.31	180.87	231.61
OCPs							929.94	1,110.95	1,129.00	1,931.55	2,333.53	2,711.44	—
							(1,069.99)	(1,302.66)	(1,476.14)	(2,225.87)	(2,787.07)	(2,925.56)	
Liaoning	1.13	4.57	0.80	4.67	7.20	14.74	24.58	48.18	90.84	130.55	126.14	257.31	—
Hebei						4.95	8.24	11.27	10.34	19.10	43.73	44.47	—
Shandong						16.42	34.20	65.02	64.87	111.55	163.33	185.70	—
Jiangsu			[1979–82] 33.62				33.47	33.76	86.35	125.51	127.13	133.97	—
Zhejiang							26.63	24.77	36.30	43.79	53.96	49.14	—
Fujian	0.83	3.63	1.50	1.21	14.38	48.28	118.60	62.50	55.35	145.47	348.03	319.89	—
Guangdong	91.43	208.29	262.57	271.29	397.23	631.46	629.50	783.62	730.79	1,212.26	1,323.24	1,582.31	1,823.00

TABLE A1. (Cont.)

	1979	1980	1981	1982	1983	1984	1985	1986	1987	1988	1989	1990	1991
Hainan	–	0.10	1.09	0.83	2.38	14.71	23.99	32.59	9.11	122.45	94.97	103.02	106.76
Guangxi	–	[1979–84] 80.87					30.73	49.24	45.05	20.87	53.00	35.63	–
Beijing	–		[1980–84] 350.00				88.82	149.71	105.79	503.18	320.16	278.95	–
Provincial total			[1979–84] 2,859.02				1,318.04	1,741.65	1,782.73	3,149.73	3,437.33	3,436.15	–
PRC total	[1979–81] 1,118.00			649.00	916.00	1,419.00	1,959.00	2,244.00	2,647.00	3,739.00	3,774.00	3,755.00	4,370.00

Notes:

Foreign direct investment as defined here covers FDI proper plus investment made by way of compensation trade, international leasing and other types of "commodity credits" (*chanpin xindai*). With the exception of the PRC total, the figures do not include FDI sponsored by the various central branch ministries, which include notably the National Offshore Petroleum Corporation, MOFERT and CITIC. It seems quite likely that a major proportion of these centrally-sponsored FDI are also allocated to the *econocoas* areas. However, they amounted to a rather small total of US$336.12 million for 1989 and US$318.72 million for 1990, for example, as compared with the provincial total of US$5,848.21 and 5,493.78 million respectively. The PRC total covers nevertheless both the provincial and central FDI.

Figures in parenthesis for OCCs (opened coastal cities) and OCPs (opened coastal provinces) are sum totals for all the 15 OCCs and 11 OCPs (including Tianjin and Shanghai) respectively. The SEZs figures cover not only the SEZ proper, but the *xian* as well. The same goes for Tianjin and Shanghai, and other OCCs. The OCP figures for Guangdong and Fujian include their SEZs' shares, and that of Guangzhou (in the case of Guangdong), and those for Liaoning and Shandong cover respectively Dalian and Qingdao as well. The provincial total for 1979–84 is estimated from the incomplete figures for the 11 OCPs for the same period by assuming that OCP total makes up 78.91% of the national provincial total. The assumed percentage is derived as the average for 1985–90. The result is clearly an underestimate, because most of the 1979–84 figures are missing for Hebei, Shandong and Jiangsu. Nevertheless the bias is probably not great, as the three provinces seem to have hardly any FDI in this period. No entry means either that FDI is nil or that figures are not available.

All the figures are in US$. Where *RMB* figures are used in this study they are obtained by applying the official annual average of exchange rates for the conversion; where deflated *RMB* figures are used, they are derived by applying the official capital accumulation deflator as explained in Table A3.

Sources:

Various standard Chinese statistical and economic yearbooks from central and provincial levels, including *Zhongguo tongji nianjian (Chinese Statistical Yearbook)* (hereafter *ZGTJNJ*), *Zhongguo duiwai jingji maoyi nianjian (Chinese Foreign Economic Relations and Trade Yearbook)* (hereafter *JMNJ*) and *Zhongguo jingji nianjian (Chinese Economic Yearbook)* (hereafter *JJNJ*), and similar provincial, municipal and SEZ yearbooks or special compendia. Figures for Shanghai and Beijing for 1980–84 are from Ulrich Hiemenz, "Foreign direct investment and capital formation in China since 1979," in Dieter Cassel and Gunter Heiduk (eds.), *China's Contemporary Economic Reforms as a Development Strategy* (Baden-Baden: Nomos Verlagsgesellschaft, 1990), p. 86. Where figures conflict, the central and latest Statistic Information Consultancy Service Centre (edited by *Zhongguo tongji xinxibao*) and distributed by CERD Consultants Ltd., Hong Kong (part 2) (February 1992), pp. 24–7. I am grateful to Dr Thomas Chan, managing director of CERD for making the information available.

TABLE A2. *Foreign Capital Borrowing and FDI in the Econocoas Areas in China (million US$)*

	1979	1980	1981	1982	1983	1984	1985	1986	1987	1988	1989	1990	1991
SEZs													
Shenzhen	15.37	32.64	112.82	73.79	143.93	230.13	329.25	489.33	404.49	444.29	458.09	518.57	579.88
Zhuhai	4.15	15.75	13.67	56.33	29.39	126.94	91.04	75.68	69.63	217.62	169.47	108.28	168.79
Shantou					7.04	16.10	33.14	76.93	63.18	103.64	157.41	158.53	264.78
Xiamen	[1979–83] 10.73					44.64	86.00	70.76	53.22	164.09	238.22	173.07	182.85
OCCs							367.16	840.71	1,247.70	1,292.91	1,163.87	1,187.38	2,200.99
							(458.86)	(928.91)	(1,355.14)	(3,648.54)	(2,336.46)	(1,538.87)	(2,658.48)
Dalian						–	14.86	43.61	270.11	213.46	193.63	394.17	417.05
Tianjin			[1979–84] 19.81				69.21	281.41	361.79	344.01	167.76	98.56	476.29
Qingdao			[1980–83] 87.00				18.99	51.53	43.65	39.78	101.72	75.19	78.95
Shanghai						178.75	108.79	285.84	485.68	440.47	466.49	321.04	851.28
Guangzhou	9.84	30.13	35.31	52.68	52.89	181.84	155.31	178.32	86.47	255.19	234.27	298.42	377.42
OCPs							1,389.12	1,981.85	1,951.85	3,678.89	3,971.87	4,052.90	–
							(1,567.12)	(2,548.55)	(2,799.32)	(4,463.37)	(4,606.12)	(4,472.50)	
Liaoning	1.13	4.57	0.80	7.50	7.20	15.23	41.92	64.49	174.70	292.47	388.14	727.39	–
Hebei						5.46	10.50	19.01	10.34	28.51	92.91	97.80	–
Shandong						16.42	62.31	116.79	102.19	142.31	208.33	230.42	–
Jiangsu							51.11	45.57	143.08	156.70	161.16	247.69	–
Zhejiang	[1979–82] 33.62						61.73	29.52	106.94	130.57	165.46	127.77	–
Fujian	42.34	9.18	4.51	2.63	47.93	61.68	171.09	165.51	142.44	293.95	387.92	426.84	–
Guangdong	91.43	214.00	288.00	281.00	407.00	644.00	919.00	1,428.00	1,217.00	2,440.00	2,390.27	2,015.41	2,571.66
Hainan		0.28	1.09	0.83	4.38	17.84	26.43	32.59	9.11	127.71	94.97	116.98	176.06
Guangxi	[1979–84] 80.87						44.93	79.82	46.05	66.67	82.71	62.60	–
Beijing		[1980–84] 350.00					116.28	162.82	161.74	583.89	477.04	392.02	–
Provincial total	[1979–84] 2,859.02						1,599.13	2,775.31	3,211.15	5,609.93	5,848.21	5,493.78	–
PRC total	[1979–81] 10,024.66			2,432.34	1,980.64	2,704.52	4,462.11	7,258.30	8,451.56	10,226.39	10,059.15	10,289.35	11,137.98

Notes:

None of the figures except for the PRC total includes FDI and capital borrowing (indirect investment) sponsored by the various central branch ministries including, notably, borrowing by the Bank of China. It is not known how capital borrowing by the central authorities may have been allocated to the various provinces, although the amounts concerned (US$3,874.82 million in 1989 and 4,476.89 million in 1990) greatly exceed the comparable provincial totals of US$2,410.88 million and 2,057.63 million respectively. The PRC total covers however both the provincial and central shares.

Figures in parenthesis for the OCCs and OCPs are the sum totals respectively for all the 15 OCCs and 11 OCPs (including Tianjin and Shanghai). For other similar definitions and method of conversion into *RMB* value, see notes to Table A1. Where the figures are the same as those given in Table A1, it implies that capital borrowing is either nil or relevant statistics are not available.

Sources:

As Table A1, except for the 1991 figures which are from *TKP*, 17 March 1992 for Guangdong; *CLES* (part 2) (February 1992), pp. 24–7 for the other *econocoas* areas; and *TKP*, 21 April 1992, p. 2 for the PRC total (obtained by subtracting the sum total of the annual figures for 1979–90 from the given cumulative total of US$79,627 million for 1979–91.

Table A3. *Total Fixed Assets Investments in the Econocoas Areas in China (100 million yuan in current prices)*

	1979	1980	1981	1982	1983	1984	1985	1986	1987	1988	1989	1990	1991
SEZs													
Shenzhen	0.50	1.25	2.70	6.33	9.11	15.56	30.84	21.84	28.52	43.62	51.75	53.66	70.40
Zhuhai	0.36	0.58	1.15	2.30	2.17	4.78	9.70	8.53	9.65	12.34	9.09	9.54	–
Shantou	1.90	–	–	–	2.93	3.32	9.01	11.07	22.32	37.18	12.53	12.01	–
Xiamen	1.07	1.28	1.78	2.43	2.83	5.61	11.72	9.89	10.65	12.33	12.73	17.56	–
OCCs					156.23	191.45	262.06	303.84	366.34	507.51	477.26	463.34	–
Dalian	–	–	–	–	8.56	12.01	22.00	29.60	37.60	38.89	28.25	28.72	–
Tianjin	24.77	23.92	27.60	35.06	41.58	48.66	66.94	72.04	77.75	88.65	85.27	88.48	–
Qingdao	3.50	4.75	3.96	5.30	4.94	6.49	10.74	15.05	17.45	26.11	26.22	28.46	–
Shanghai	–	–	–	71.33	76.01	92.51	118.76	141.16	185.28	263.64	244.19	227.09	–
Guangzhou	7.26	9.96	13.44	16.92	25.14	31.78	43.62	45.99	48.26	90.22	93.33	90.59	–
OCPs	–			475.41	494.27	680.57	940.54	1,167.77	1,510.16	1,907.25	1,780.15	1,911.52	–
				(580.80)	(637.16)	(855.22)	(1,178.89)	(1,448.97)	(1,852.14)	(2,358.15)	(2,205.36)	(2,334.87)	
Liaoning	–	–	–	69.44	72.94	96.17	139.02	177.71	218.98	267.26	251.03	260.36	
Hebei	–	–	–	73.45	63.87	86.32	113.11	134.03	178.46	239.34	214.29	182.12	
Shandong	61.35	69.97	79.60	85.00	94.09	139.27	193.42	223.07	297.76	369.82	336.64	334.79	
Jiangsu	–	–	–	75.41	104.41	129.12	149.97	236.27	316.68	377.15	324.60	361.10	
Zhejiang	–	–	–	41.71	43.98	64.89	105.44	130.18	185.47	230.18	212.72	257.90	
Fujian	10.80	12.99	18.11	23.71	26.27	34.43	54.99	60.01	78.09	91.87	87.88	108.54	
Guangdong	28.29	38.29	60.40	84.73	88.71	130.37	184.59	206.50	234.72	331.63	352.99	406.71	
Hainan	–	–	–	3.24	3.21	5.31	10.58	12.77	14.54	21.19	28.99	39.21	
Guangxi	9.61	12.56	10.98	17.72	22.09	28.17	42.07	55.23	64.41	77.42	66.76	68.57	
Beijing	–	–	–	38.52	50.68	68.83	94.52	105.17	140.15	162.60	146.24	190.81	
PRC total	–	910.85	961.01	1,230.40	1,430.06	1,832.87	2,543.19	3,019.62	3,640.86	4,496.54	4,137.73	4,449.29	5,276.82

Notes:

The figures cover the most comprehensive measure of fixed assets investments comprising "basic construction," investment in "technical innovation and transformation" and others, as undertaken in both the state and collective ownership sectors, as well as by private individuals. Both "productive" and "non-productive" investments are included. All the figures are in current prices, and the official sources do not provide any investment price index. Where deflated figures are used in this study, they are all derived from the capital accumulation index which may be estimated by resorting to the available official deflators for national income (*guomin shouru*) and its consumption component. (We assumed constant weights based on the 1952 consumption and accumulation shares, and ignore the discrepancy between the production and expenditure sides of national income as the overall index is available only for the former series.) I am grateful to K.C. Yeh for suggesting this method of deflating. For the problems involved with adjusting for inflation in this respect, and for an alternative approach of deflating see G.H. Jefferson, "China's iron and steel industry," *Journal of Development Economics*, No. 33 (1990), pp. 330, 336–7, and 352–3.

The OCP totals in parenthesis include the shares of Tianjin and Shanghai which form part of the OCPs. A number of figures (Shantou 1983; Dalian 1983–84; Hainan 1982–83; Guangzhou 1981–82 and Guangxi 1981) are derived from the growth rates of investment in the state sector (see Table A4).

Sources:

ZGTJNJ (various issues) supplemented by similar provincial, municipal and SEZ volumes; and *Zhongguo guding zichan touzi tongji ziliao* (*Chinese Fixed Assets Investment Statistical Materials*), 1980–85 and 1986–87, various pages. The 1991 figure for Shenzhen is from *TKP*, 17 March 1992 (which appears to cover the SEZ proper only), and the 1991 PRC total from premier Li Peng's government work report delivered at the National People's Congress on 20 March 1992.

TABLE A4. *Fixed Assets Investments by the State Ownership Sectors in the Economic-coastal Areas in China (100 million yuan in current prices)*

	1979	1980	1981	1982	1983	1984	1985	1986	1987	1988	1989	1990	1991
SEZs	-	-	-	-	15.74	28.46	53.74	46.25	50.41	75.28	76.80	81.73	110.89
Shenzhen	0.50	1.25	2.70	6.33	8.86	16.37	29.19	21.19	22.68	35.37	45.40	52.49	70.02
Zhuhai	0.13	0.34	0.58	1.25	1.49	3.73	8.65	7.47	8.23	10.22	9.09	9.15	15.16
Shantou	-	-	-	-	2.93	3.32	7.06	9.19	10.40	20.98	12.53	10.03	14.00
Xiamen	1.06	1.17	1.38	2.11	2.46	5.04	8.84	8.40	9.10	8.71	9.78	10.06	11.71
OCCs	-	-	-	117.98	129.01	156.04	215.93 (257.80)	263.35 (611.70)	308.63 (385.20)	398.82 (497.30)	377.39 (460.84)	391.44	452.55 (572.98)
Dalian	-	-	-	6.74	7.69	10.79	19.76	27.50	32.40	36.54	29.03	27.24	40.97
Tianjin	-	-	25.28	30.04	33.81	38.56	55.08	61.03	62.28	71.07	68.40	72.18	106.44
Qingdao	3.27	4.21	3.21	4.32	4.39	5.68	9.24	12.70	15.10	22.22	23.05	23.62	31.46
Shanghai	-	-	44.26	61.62	65.08	75.80	95.91	119.00	154.45	198.68	178.81	192.23	195.77
Guangzhou	6.86	8.98	12.12	15.26	18.04	25.21	35.94	43.12	44.40	70.31	78.10	76.17	77.91
OCPs	-	-	218.63 (288.17)	277.20 (368.86)	303.70 (402.59)	392.06 (506.42)	591.21 (742.20)	708.51 (888.54)	862.08 (1,078.81)	1,089.11 (1,358.86)	969.10 (1,216.31)	1,125.27 (1,389.68)	1,259.14 (1,561.35)
Liaoning	-	46.10	47.94	54.41	56.18	72.76	107.05	137.42	172.13	210.65	201.30	215.44	235.76
Hebei	-	-	30.98	39.25	42.38	48.65	62.59	73.89	86.36	111.34	101.25	110.98	122.87
Shandong	31.62	35.83	30.35	43.06	46.74	66.21	100.42	121.95	155.64	192.20	162.30	184.59	215.06
Jiangsu	-	-	27.55	34.78	45.48	51.59	77.10	93.81	125.07	151.31	119.14	129.78	153.13
Zhejiang	13.06	15.99	15.82	20.74	21.29	27.28	39.46	49.45	59.44	69.73	68.60	78.58	83.13
Fujian	10.51	12.61	12.81	15.12	16.92	21.07	36.99	40.04	48.89	53.69	50.29	64.69	68.84
Guangdong	20.06	25.72	38.99	51.77	55.92	80.65	131.11	148.58	162.27	232.26	201.54	269.46	289.79
Hainan	3.22	3.47	3.58	4.53	4.49	7.42	12.46	12.99	11.45	14.99	23.26	30.59	41.74
Guangxi	9.81	12.18	10.61	13.54	14.30	16.43	24.03	30.38	40.83	52.94	41.42	41.16	48.82
Beijing	-	-	32.21	32.94	39.94	53.31	72.87	87.65	115.83	133.24	116.30	152.03	140.09
PRC total	699.36	745.90	667.51	845.31	851.96	1,185.18	1,680.51	1,978.50	2,297.99	2,762.76	2,535.48	2,918.64	3,558.15

Notes:

See notes to Table A3 for explanation and method of deflating. The OCC and OCP figures in brackets cover all the 15 OCCs and the 11 OCPs (including Tianjin and Shanghai) respectively. The 1991 figures should be regarded as preliminary statistics. The same source (as noted below) also provides figures for percentage increases over 1990, but most of the figures differ from what can be estimated from the absolute data given here, except the PRC total for which no inconsistency is detected.

Sources:

As Table A3, except for the 1991 figures which are from CLES, part 2 (January 1992), p. 37, and (February 1992), pp. 24–7.

TABLE A5. *Gross Value of Industrial Output (GVIO) in the Econocoas Areas in China (100 million yuan in 1980 prices)*

	1979	1980	1981	1982	1983	1984	1985	1986	1987	1988	1989	1990
SEZs	–	–	–	–	42.98	63.24	86.18	103.90	153.20	225.73	270.75	346.89
Shenzhen	0.61	0.84	2.43	3.62	7.20	18.15	27.04	35.70	57.60	88.81	116.46	167.55
Zhuhai	0.61	0.75	0.93	1.05	2.84	4.98	5.94	6.80	13.00	25.41	30.20	33.11
Shantou	17.57	21.79	–	–	20.92	25.02	40.14	48.89	68.00	94.28	68.61	74.95
Xiamen	8.05	9.43	10.39	11.32	12.02	15.09	21.85	24.69	32.86	48.16	55.49	71.28
OCCs	–	–	–	1,097.56	1,188.43	1,306.07	1,485.33	1,570.15	1,709.13	1,913.37	1,993.68	2,054.97
(OCC total)							(1,847.45)	(1,986.30)	(2,185.80)	(2,505.30)	(2,694.59)	(7,766.95)
Dalian	–	–	76.44	77.17	84.29	91.85	106.46	116.70	129.50	148.25	162.43	167.98
Tianjin	–	–	199.49	211.86	229.25	251.49	285.80	300.40	325.63	362.56	373.61	375.75
Qingdao	–	–	–	67.28	77.63	85.00	99.37	111.10	129.00	160.01	176.84	197.35
Shanghai	–	–	608.70	636.70	678.55	744.37	832.27	873.55	923.50	996.77	1,021.84	1,030.73
Guangzhou	–	91.23	99.10	104.55	118.71	133.36	161.43	168.40	201.50	245.78	258.96	283.16
OCPs	–	–	2,112.74	2,263.83	2,517.95	2,936.09	3,585.36	3,994.55	4,748.72	5,456.28	5,855.02	6,360.47
(OCP total)			(2,920.93)	(3,112.39)	(3,425.75)	(3,931.95)	(4,703.43)	(5,168.50)	(5,997.85)	(6,815.61)	(7,250.47)	(7,766.95)
Liaoning	–	–	451.36	476.31	516.69	577.66	664.39	709.80	782.20	845.96	876.99	878.01
Hebei	–	–	217.65	229.94	252.61	290.25	333.46	358.95	409.92	452.21	483.19	502.47
Shandong	–	–	343.62	367.58	405.55	456.24	539.98	591.25	699.45	858.75	971.92	1,056.77
Jiangsu	–	–	465.69	503.21	569.62	680.13	863.53	983.26	1,192.69	1,391.27	1,450.47	1,590.88
Zhejiang	–	–	213.67	230.70	268.15	333.85	443.95	515.17	613.57	717.60	746.42	794.60
Fujian	–	–	81.81	87.63	95.83	115.76	140.79	156.01	189.24	233.56	260.90	293.09
Guangdong	–	–	250.36	272.18	306.01	366.90	461.01	527.03	681.98	761.95	858.72	1,027.16
Hainan	–	–	6.97	7.52	8.60	11.11	14.57	15.49	19.24	24.06	25.23	23.54
Guangxi	–	–	81.61	88.76	94.89	104.19	123.68	137.59	160.43	170.92	181.18	193.95
Beijing	–	–	216.61	228.69	250.64	281.72	314.67	322.03	357.45	406.81	432.01	454.10
PRC total	–	–	5,177.67	5,577.45	6,166.54	7,029.85	8,294.51	9,028.46	10,364.67	11,577.85	12,294.56	13,023.73

Notes:

All the figures exclude *cunban* (village operated) industries. The figure for Shantou for 1979 is assumed the same as for 1978, and for 1990 it is derived by applying its national income growth rate for 1990/89 (see Table A6). The OCC and OCP total (in brackets) cover respectively all the 15 OCCs and 11 OCPs (including Tianjin and Shanghai). The PRC total refers to output from enterprises with "independent accounting" (*duli hesuan*) only. This may or may not be comparable to the other given figures. However, the possible discrepancy should be negligible, as these figures include most enterprises above the village level.

Sources:

As Table A3.

TABLE A6. *National Income (Net Material Product) in the Econocoas Areas in China, 1979–90 (100 million yuan in current prices)*

	1979	1980	1981	1982	1983	1984	1985	1986	1987	1988	1989	1990	1991
SEZs	26.86	–	–	–	50.30	68.30	95.45	98.92	130.74	196.31	215.34	262.48	329.21
Shenzhen	1.60	2.21	4.20	6.77	10.75	20.22	26.37	27.29	36.26	56.85	72.16	94.26	–
Zhuhai	1.91	2.32	2.99	3.55	4.80	5.95	8.52	8.75	11.79	18.87	22.18	27.92	–
Shantou	18.51	–	–	–	26.59	31.80	45.54	46.77	62.86	91.90	89.45	97.72	–
Xiamen	4.84	5.86	6.66	7.65	8.16	10.33	15.02	16.11	19.83	28.69	31.55	42.58	–
OCCs	–	–	–	–	593.41	666.55	812.32	872.26	959.73	1,223.40	1,298.89	1,372.02	–
Dalian	–	42.60	42.00	42.80	47.00	56.40	69.79	85.18	100.88	128.10	140.17	147.87	–
Tianjin	84.63	93.10	96.00	101.03	108.37	121.68	150.91	165.95	185.66	221.09	234.41	244.05	–
Qingdao	37.32	41.60	41.28	42.69	50.77	59.92	68.77	76.89	91.66	120.32	132.30	143.36	–
Shanghai	–	–	–	–	311.03	341.20	409.73	425.08	473.61	565.34	586.84	617.22	–
Guangzhou	–	–	–	–	76.24	87.35	113.12	119.16	107.92	188.55	205.17	219.52	–
OCPs	–	–	–	–	2,075.85	2,478.52	3,082.19	3,463.57	4,183.86	5,292.05	5,979.55	6,420.48	–
					(2,495.25)	(2,941.40)	(3,642.83)	(4,054.60)	(4,843.13)	(6,078.48)	(6,800.80)	(7,281.75)	
Liaoning	219.50	249.60	249.40	261.60	298.00	354.15	425.72	481.43	566.39	694.48	770.95	783.79	–
Hebei	175.24	188.36	189.47	211.35	238.61	282.01	340.87	375.70	448.77	558.32	631.37	693.73	–
Shandong	220.02	252.17	298.38	332.35	379.33	447.86	552.29	595.84	735.62	915.26	1,055.98	1,144.22	–
Jiangsu	–	–	–	–	390.54	466.31	578.46	663.90	789.19	969.22	1,055.52	1,138.31	–
Zhejiang	139.67	158.34	179.06	204.88	220.18	276.70	365.79	422.10	508.35	638.69	698.41	726.49	–
Fujian	62.91	72.87	89.79	98.54	105.76	128.70	164.79	183.61	226.22	307.59	359.83	388.77	–
Guangdong	180.39	217.61	250.81	285.47	303.26	366.27	467.27	525.53	656.25	894.57	1,034.91	1,132.21	1,279.40
Hainan	13.81	15.17	18.44	23.22	24.94	31.11	35.71	39.42	45.52	62.09	72.30	76.98	–
Guangxi	72.06	81.92	95.30	111.51	115.23	125.41	151.29	176.04	207.55	251.83	300.28	335.98	–
Beijing	–	–	–	–	–	157.30	194.50	206.00	236.20	307.70	336.80	366.95	–
PRC total	3,350.00	3,688.00	3,941.00	4,258.00	4,736.00	5,652.00	7,020.00	7,859.00	9,313.00	11,738.00	13,125.00	14,429.00	16,477.92

Notes:
Figures in parenthesis cover Tianjin and Shanghai which are both part of the 11 OCPs. Where deflated figures are used in this study, they are all obtained by applying the official national income deflator, although for quite a number of the *econocoas* areas, local deflators are also available. We ignore therefore the possible regional variations in inflation rates. The 1983 figures for Shantou, Shanghai and Jiangsu are derived from the GVIO growth rates (see Table A5).

Sources:
As Table A3, except for the 1991 PRC total which is from *TKP*, 21 March 1992, and the 1991 Shenzhen and Guangdong figures which are derived from reported percentage increases as in *TKP*, 17 March 1992.

TABLE A7. Gross Domestic (National) Product in the Econocoas areas in China, 1979–90 (100 million yuan in current prices)

	1979	1980	1981	1982	1983	1984	1985	1986	1987	1988	1989	1990	1991
SEZs	33.12	–	–	–	–	80.44	115.01	121.24	160.96	239.92	269.60	320.33	–
Shenzhen	1.96	2.70	4.96	8.26	13.12	23.42	33.25	35.50	47.48	73.75	97.81	107.20	–
Zhuhai	2.99	3.75	3.98	4.73	5.61	7.38	10.31	11.10	15.55	25.07	32.31	31.67	–
Shantou	22.85	–	–	–	–	37.35	53.49	54.93	73.83	105.61	101.55	130.88	–
Xiamen	5.32	6.40	7.41	8.67	9.44	12.29	17.96	19.71	24.10	35.49	37.93	50.58	–
OCCs	–	–	–	–	–	787.19	949.80	1,029.39	1,181.84	1,464.46	1,588.66	1,711.42	–
Dalian	–	–	–	–	–	68.00	79.30	96.30	114.05	151.24	165.44	178.60	
Tianjin	93.00	103.52	107.96	114.10	123.40	147.47	175.71	194.67	220.00	259.64	283.34	300.31	
Quingdao	43.45	48.30	49.40	51.77	61.71	70.95	84.25	94.48	112.60	142.56	155.47	168.24	
Shanghai	–	–	–	–	–	404.74	486.18	504.39	561.98	670.83	696.54	744.67	
Guangzhou	43.09	57.55	–	–	–	96.03	124.36	139.55	173.21	240.19	287.87	319.60	
OCPs	–	–	–	–	–	2,926.53	3,575.77	4,052.24	4,869.57	6,223.28	7,032.84	7,687.33	–
						(3,478.74)	(4,237.66)	(4,751.30)	(5,651.55)	(7,153.75)	(8,012.72)	(8,732.31)	
Liaoning	223.20	266.20	285.80	301.90	347.20	415.60	489.60	567.60	663.70	839.30	922.10	964.89	
Hebei	183.06	–	–	–	–	328.24	396.75	437.29	522.34	654.23	748.99	819.95	
Shandong	255.00	294.40	337.90	379.10	428.30	543.60	631.30	689.90	822.30	1,050.79	1,175.07	1,332.13	
Jiangsu	–	–	–	–	–	544.63	675.62	775.41	921.74	1,132.01	1,232.80	1,314.39	
Zhejiang	157.64	179.68	203.26	230.57	251.26	314.21	413.84	479.79	575.45	721.73	792.32	836.81	
Fujian	73.67	85.91	103.60	114.49	123.06	149.98	190.80	210.65	258.90	351.52	413.58	459.48	
GNP	(73.86)	(86.37)	(104.29)	(114.97)	(123.57)	(151.08)	(191.97)	(212.12)	(260.36)	(354.09)	(416.65)	(465.84)	
Guangdong	207.07	245.71	284.21	331.27	357.43	441.81	553.05	637.75	807.70	1,098.61	1,311.67	1,471.84	1,670.54
Hainan	–	–	–	–	–	38.19	43.84	48.39	55.88	74.76	86.87	95.01	–
Guangxi	84.59	97.33	113.46	129.15	134.60	150.27	180.97	205.46	241.56	300.33	349.44	392.83	–
Beijing	–	–	–	–	–	–	–	–	–	410.20	455.80	500.72	–
PRC total	3,998.10	4,470.00	4,473.00	5,193.00	5,809.00	6,902.00	8,557.60	9,696.30	11,301.00	14,018.20	15,916.30	17,686.10	18,924.13

Notes:

The figures refer generally to GDP, except for the PRC total and the 11 OCPs (including Tianjin and Shanghai) for 1988 to 1990, and for Zhuhai, Dalian and Qingdao. Figures in parenthesis for the OCPs total for 1989 and 1990 refer to the sum total of all the 11 OCPs. For a number of areas (Shantou 1984–86; Dalian 1987; Shanghai 1984–86; Guangzhou 1984; Hebei 1984, 1986–87; Jiangsu 1984; and Hainan 1984–86) the figures are derived from the growth rates of national income as shown in Table A6. Where deflated figures are used in this study, they are all obtained by applying the national GNP deflator, although for quite a number of the *econocoas* areas, the official provincial or municipal deflators are also available. We therefore ignore the possible variations in inflation rates.

Sources:

As Table A3, except for the 1991 PRC total which is from *TKP*, 21 March 1992, and the Guangdong figure which is derived from reported percentage increase in *TKP*, 17 March 1992.

TABLE A8. *Total Export and the* Sanzi *Share in the* Econocoas *areas in China, 1988–91 (100 million US$)*

	Total				Sanzi share			
	1988	1989	1990	1991	1988	1989	1990	1991
SEZs	54.99	66.75	79.37	93.95	12.35	22.24	32.15	43.03
Shenzhen	36.64	44.96	52.16	57.88	9.66	16.63	22.93	29.24
Zhuhai	5.56	6.46	8.41	11.38	0.85	2.10	3.51	5.09
Shantou	7.63	8.29	9.61	11.98	0.89	1.53	2.27	3.40
Xiamen	5.16	7.05	9.20	12.71	0.95	1.97	3.44	5.30
OCCs	87.05	93.29	106.94	123.26	2.71	7.33	12.31	23.26
	(92.43)	(103.86)	(121.82)	(141.22)	(5.54)	(8.36)	(14.27)	(26.52)
Dalian	4.48	5.68	7.12	10.61	0.30	1.06	1.72	4.29
Tianjin	17.09	16.92	17.78	17.49	0.39	0.67	1.07	1.82
Qingdao	2.09	2.84	3.68	4.82	0.03	0.15	0.28	0.63
Shanghai	48.80	50.15	54.83	60.93	0.84	2.33	3.50	6.59
Guangzhou	14.59	17.70	23.55	29.41	1.16	3.12	5.76	9.93
OCPs	295.31	343.98	416.16	492.15	22.46	44.67	71.53	108.14
	(361.21)	(411.05)	(488.76)	(570.57)	(23.69)	(47.67)	(76.09)	(116.59)
Liaoning	40.00	43.16	52.49	56.25	0.39	1.28	2.22	5.21
Hebei	17.05	17.99	19.01	20.19	0.04	0.12	0.24	0.69
Shandong	29.11	30.26	34.16	37.51	0.17	0.71	1.24	2.25
Jiangsu	24.16	25.36	29.43	34.24	0.49	1.11	1.89	4.13
Zhejiang	14.97	18.72	21.89	29.06	0.38	0.70	1.34	2.62
Fujian	14.13	18.28	24.49	31.48	2.40	4.97	9.03	12.89
Guangdong	147.74	180.62	221.26	269.44	18.44	35.33	54.80	79.24
Hainan	2.62	3.27	5.37	6.25	0.06	0.25	0.38	0.53
Guangxi	5.53	6.33	8.06	7.73	0.09	0.22	0.39	0.58
Beijing	9.77	10.22	11.21	13.08	0.26	0.50	0.86	1.50
Provincial total	444.20	503.86	586.57	685.17	24.48	48.47	78.13	120.53
PRC total	475.20	525.40	620.90	719.10	–	–	–	–

Notes:
The figures refer to exports by the 'foreign trading units' of the provinces, opened coastal cities and SEZs. *Sanzi* (three-foreign-funded) enterprises cover equity joint ventures, co-operative joint ventures and wholly foreign-owned ventures. Figures in brackets refer to the sum total for all the 15 OCCs and 11 OCPs including Shanghai and Tianjin. PRC total includes centrally controlled exports, in addition to the total provincial exports.
Sources:
CLES (part 2), (January 1989), pp. 45–51; (January 1990), pp. 52–59; (January 1991), pp. 45–55; and (February 1992), pp. 32–42. PRC total for 1988–90 is from *ZGTJNJ* 1991, p. 615; and for 1991 *CLES* (part 1) (January 1992), p. 21.

TABLE A9. *Total Import and the* Sanzi *Share in the* Econocoas *Areas in China, 1988–91 (100 million US$)*

	Total				Sanzi share			
	1988	1989	1990	1991	1988	1989	1990	1991
SEZs	56.61	64.51	73.66	93.10	16.37	21.50	39.78	49.10
Shenzhen	37.64	42.44	47.68	56.64	11.54	14.00	24.63	32.42
Zhuhai	7.59	7.90	9.17	12.51	1.96	3.03	8.33	6.07
Shantou	7.19	7.67	9.01	12.60	1.07	1.67	2.39	3.97
Xiamen	4.18	6.50	7.80	11.35	1.79	2.79	4.42	6.64
OCCs	62.65	76.12	67.15	75.41	11.94	20.05	23.86	36.23
	(65.92)	(81.54)	(72.34)	(82.23)	(13.19)	(21.62)	(26.55)	(41.40)
Dalian	3.57	3.95	4.62	8.29	2.17	1.45	2.32	5.11
Tianjin	8.40	9.85	7.34	8.96	1.11	2.06	2.10	3.02
Qingdao	1.12	2.22	2.06	2.86	0.33	0.83	0.63	1.07
Shanghai	32.04	42.55	34.95	30.98	5.07	9.76	10.40	13.59
Guangzhou	17.52	17.55	18.18	24.32	3.27	5.94	8.40	13.44
OCPs	217.78	244.19	262.01	346.57	43.03	62.73	100.49	128.65
	(258.22)	(296.59)	(304.30)	(386.51)	(49.20)	(74.55)	(112.98)	(145.26)
Liaoning	10.71	12.42	11.50	16.99	2.61	2.19	3.32	6.44
Hebei	3.73	3.97	3.67	3.78	1.40	1.02	1.56	1.28
Shandong	8.83	10.59	8.62	10.74	0.86	1.83	2.21	3.64
Jiangsu	10.28	13.04	11.92	18.75	1.26	2.45	4.34	8.35
Zhejiang	4.94	6.32	5.82	9.39	0.47	0.83	1.12	2.37
Fujian	14.13	15.85	18.90	26.00	6.11	7.58	11.45	16.44
Guangdong	158.39	172.52	194.99	250.67	29.39	45.02	74.37	87.29
Hainan	3.34	6.34	4.36	7.23	0.43	1.12	1.52	2.10
Guangxi	3.44	3.14	2.23	3.02	0.51	0.68	0.59	0.74
Beijing	9.66	9.75	10.03	13.10	4.98	6.39	5.30	6.87
Provincial total	297.30	341.20	348.46	447.43	79.24	116.18	125.68	169.38
PRC total	552.70	591.40	533.50	637.94	–	–	–	–

Notes and Sources:
As Table A8.

Chinese Foreign Trade*

Nicholas R. Lardy

China's opening to the outside world was perhaps the most visible of its reforms of the 1980s. China's international trade volume grew dramatically, it attracted tens of billions of dollars of foreign direct investment and it became an active borrower in international financial markets. In contrast to the pre-reform era, foreign trade grew more rapidly than the domestic economy and in some regions of the country it appeared that it had become a powerful engine of growth, accelerating not only the speed of domestic development but the pace of structural and technical transformation as well.

What has been less clear to outside observers is the degree to which the domestic economy has adjusted both to accommodate and to benefit from this expanding volume of foreign trade. Has the expansion of foreign trade been achieved largely through a state-driven export strategy in which sales on the international market are viewed simply as a means of financing much needed imports? This would imply, as in the pre-reform era, that exports were selected without much consideration of China's comparative advantage and that, as a result, expanding exports might contribute little or nothing to economic growth.

Or has the growth of exports come from a new industrial system, largely unconnected with the domestic economy? That is sometimes the image presented by the rapid development of export processing, particularly in south China. Foreign parts and components are brought in, assembled or processed using relatively low-cost Chinese labour, and then exported to world markets. This capitalizes on China's comparative advantage in labour-intensive activities and thus contributes to economic growth. But the funding and management of these export processing firms, whether in the special economic zones or not, is largely foreign and it is not immediately obvious that this dynamic sector has provided much economic stimulus to indigenous manufacturing firms.

Or has the vastly expanded volume of foreign trade been accompanied by the type of changes in the domestic economy that are likely to bring China a larger share of the potential economic gains resulting from its increased participation in world trade? Development economists have long argued that countries pursuing externally-oriented development strategies achieve

* I am indebted to participants at the workshop in Hong Kong in September 1991 for helpful comments on a draft of this paper and to Scott Cameron for his work on the empirical analysis of Chinese exports.

higher rates of economic growth,[1] both because they attain higher rates of savings and investment and because of more efficient use of scarce resources. These efficiency gains in such countries stem from two distinct sources. The first is that marginal factor productivities are typically higher in export than in non-export oriented activities. As a larger share of the resources of an economy is shifted to the higher productivity export sector, the overall efficiency of the economy necessarily rises.

The second source of efficiency gains is less obvious. Even those portions of the economy not producing for the international market are likely to become more efficient when an inwardly-oriented development strategy is replaced with a policy of greater openness to the international market. More efficient management and production techniques, better access to imported inputs, and so forth, initially stimulate productivity in the tradeable goods sector, in response to competitive forces that are unleashed by increased openness.[2] But these improvements then spread to stimulate the non-tradeable goods sector of the economy. The latter also benefits from lower cost imported inputs. According to one estimate, these indirect effects in the non-tradeable goods sector contribute more to increased economic growth than the direct gains from shifting resources into the higher productivity export sector.[3]

While this analysis is customarily made for developing countries that have replaced inwardly-oriented development strategies with more externally-oriented policies, there is every reason to believe that it should also be relevant for reforming centrally-planned economies. Many of the features of inwardly-looking trade regimes can be found in centrally-planned economies, including, most importantly, a high degree of protection of domestic industries. In most developing economies this is achieved through high tariffs and other forms of protection. Essentially the same result is achieved even more directly in centrally-planned economies when the variety and quantity of imported commodities are determined by the state foreign trade plan.

A high degree of protection of domestic industry is usually combined with an overvalued domestic currency (too few units of domestic currency per unit of foreign currency) and a rigid system of control of foreign exchange. This provides a mechanism that can in effect tax exports, typically agricultural products, raw materials, and so on, while subsidizing those

---

[1] Anne O. Kreuger, *Foreign Trade Regimes and Economic Development: Liberalization Attempts and Consequences* (Cambridge, Mass.: Ballinger Publishing Company, 1978). World Bank, *World Development Report 1987* (New York: Oxford University Press, 1987). Michael Michaely, Demetris Papageorgiou and Armeane M. Choksi, *Liberalizing Foreign Trade: Lessons of Experience in the Developing World* (Cambridge, Mass.: Basil Blackwell, 1991).

[2] Tradeable goods are goods that are actually traded or goods that would be traded if it were profitable to do so.

[3] Gershon Feder, "On exports and economic growth," *Journal of Development Economics*, Nos. 1–2 (1983), pp. 59–73.

imports that state bureaucrats designate high priority. Traditional exports are taxed because the official exchange rate, which over-values the domestic currency, gives producers of these goods fewer units of domestic currency per dollar's worth of goods sold in the international market. The same overvaluation means that importers favoured by the state pay a lower price, in terms of domestic currency, than they would with an equilibrium exchange rate. Exchange control is required to wrest foreign exchange receipts from exporters, who would not voluntarily part with foreign currency at such an exchange rate. Similarly, on the demand side the artificially low price requires the intervention of the authorities to ration foreign exchange in the face of excess demand.

Before reform, China's foreign exchange regime had these features, in common with other centrally planned economies. The domestic currency, the *renminbi*, was highly over-valued and the Bank of China acted as the agent of the state, exercising a monopoly over the control of foreign exchange on behalf of the planning authorities.

A central theme of this article is that from roughly the mid-1980s onward the pace of domestic economic reforms accelerated, making it more likely that increased foreign trade would be economically beneficial. That forms the basis of the prediction that China's foreign trade will probably expand considerably in the 1990s and play an even more positive role in contributing to economic growth. However, before analysing the reforms of the domestic economy that have facilitated the expansion of foreign trade, it is useful to examine how rapidly China's trade has grown in the reform period.

China's Trade Volume

Table 1 sets out the trade data published by two different agencies – the Ministry of Foreign Economic Relations and Trade and the General Customs Administration. The two series differ primarily in their treatment of export processing and compensation trade activities. The Customs data include on the import side the value of imported parts and components used in processing activities, and on the export side the full value of processed and assembled exports. By contrast, the Ministry data on exports include in principle only the value added in such processing activities, and imported parts and components used in processing are not included in the import figures. Similarly, the Customs data on imports include the value of machinery brought into China under compensation trade contracts and their export data include all the exports produced using the machinery. The Ministry data do not include either, for imports, the value of the imported machinery or, for exports, the value of the portion of the goods produced

TABLE 1. *China's Foreign Trade, 1978–91 (US$ billions)*

	Ministry Data			Customs Data		
	Total	Imports	Exports	Total	Imports	Exports
1978	20.6	10.9	9.7	–	–	–
1979	29.3	15.7	13.7	–	–	–
1980	37.8	19.6	18.3	38.1	20.0	18.1
1981	40.4	19.5	20.9	44.0	22.0	22.0
1982	39.3	17.5	21.9	41.6	19.3	22.3
1983	40.7	18.5	22.2	43.6	21.4	22.2
1984	49.8	25.4	24.4	53.6	27.4	26.1
1985	60.3	34.3	25.9	69.6	42.3	27.4
1986	60.1	33.1	27.0	73.9	42.9	30.9
1987	68.1	33.4	34.7	82.7	43.2	39.4
1988	80.5	39.9	40.6	102.8	55.3	47.5
1989	82.6	39.2	43.4	111.6	52.5	59.1
1990	84.1	32.4	51.7	115.4	53.4	62.1
1991	99.5	38.5	60.9	135.7	63.8	71.9

Note:
– indicates data not available.
Sources:
   Ministry data: Editorial Board of the Almanac of China's Foreign Economic Relations and Trade, *Almanac of China's Foreign Economic Relations and Trade 1989* (English edition) (Hong Kong: China Resources Advertising Company Ltd., 1989), p. 353; Yao Jianguo, "Foreign trade increase in 1989," *Beijing Review*, No. 7 (1990), p. 43; "News in brief," *Beijing Review*, No. 5 (1991), p. 43. Customs data: State Statistical Bureau, *Zhongguo tongji zhaiyao 1991* (*Chinese Statistical Abstract 1991*) (Beijing: Statistical Publishing House, 1991), p. 97; Jing Ji, "New trade record set because of import rise," *China Daily Business Weekly*, 12–18 January 1992, p. 1.

with this machinery that is exported to provide payment in kind to its foreign supplier.[4]

Because the net foreign exchange earnings from processing activities are a relatively low share of the total value of processed exports, the Customs data overstate the growth of China's foreign trade,[5] and in this sense the data released by the Ministry appear to provide a better guide. However, most developing countries' trade data include processing and activities such as compensation trade on a gross basis so the Customs data are probably the preferred source when comparing the growth of China's foreign trade with other countries.[6]

[4] The two series also differ in other minor aspects.
[5] Sung Yun-wing estimates that value added constitutes 20% of the gross value of export receipts earned in processing activities. "Explaining China's export drive: the only success among command economies," unpublished paper, 1990, p. 19.
[6] The General Agreement on Tariffs and Trade (in the annual *International Trade*), the

TABLE 2. *China's Foreign Trade Growth, 1980–91*

	Average annual growth rate (%)
China's trade:	
Ministry data	9.2
Customs data	12.3
Memo items:	
China's growth of gross national product	8.8
World trade growth	5.5

Notes:
 Rates of growth of trade are calculated from current price data. Rates of growth of output are expressed in terms of "comparable prices."
Sources:
 Table 1; State Statistical Bureau, *Zhongguo tongji zhaiyao 1991* (*Chinese Statistical Abstract 1991*) (Beijing: Statistical Publishing House, 1991), pp. 3, 5; "Guanyu 1991 nian guomin jingji he shehui fazhan de tongji baogao," ("Statistical report on China's social and economic development in 1991"), *Renmin ribao* (*People's Daily*), 29 February 1992, p. 2; General Agreement on Tariffs and Trade, *International Trade 1989–90* (Geneva: GATT, 1990), p. 15; GATT Press Release 19 March 1991, p. 7; "U.S. takes lead back in exports," *The New York Times* (National edition), 18 March 1992, pp. C1, C19.

The differences between the two series affect any assessment of China's foreign trade. The Ministry data show that China's trade more than doubled in the period 1980–91 while the Customs data show that it more than tripled. However, even the former mean that China's foreign trade grew significantly more rapidly than world trade. As shown in Table 2, between 1980 and 1991 the average annual rate of growth of China's trade was more than 9 per cent according to the Ministry data and over 12 per cent according to the Customs data. By comparison the rate of growth of world trade between 1980 and 1991 was 5.5 per cent per annum. Thus China's share of world trade, though small, expanded rapidly. According to the General Agreement on Tariffs and Trade, in the period 1979–89 China's ranking as a trading country increased more than any other country in the world.[7]

Explaining China's Export Growth

Although the pace of China's trade expansion is clear, its sources are not. Has the growth of exports been the result of decentralized decisions by firms and/or trading companies responding to economic incentives? Or has

International Monetary Fund (in the annual *Direction of Trade Statistics Yearbook*), and the World Bank (in the annual *World Development Report*) all use data of the Chinese Customs Administration as the basis for the statistical tables reporting China's trade data.

 [7] GATT, *International Trade 1989–90*, Vol. I (Geneva: GATT, 1990), pp. 28–30.

TABLE 3. *Chinese Exports of Crude Oil and Refined Petroleum Products, 1977–90*

	Millions of tons	*Billions of US$*
1977	11.1	1.0
1978	13.6	1.3
1979	16.4	2.4
1980	17.5	4.3
1981	18.4	4.9
1982	20.5	4.9
1983	19.9	4.5
1984	27.6	5.2
1985	36.24	6.7
1986	33.95	3.2
1987	32.17	3.9
1988	30.84	3.3
1989	29.13	3.5
1990	29.25	4.3

Sources:
1977–84: Kenneth Lieberthal and Michel Oksenberg, *Policy Making in China: Leaders, Structures, and Processes* (Princeton: Princeton University Press, 1988), pp. 262–3. 1985–90: State Statistical Bureau, *Zhongguo tongji zhaiyao* (*Chinese Statistical Abstract*) (Beijing: Statistical Publishing House, various years), 1987, p. 90; 1988, p. 86; 1990, p. 99; 1991, p. 99.

the rapid expansion of trade occurred largely within the traditional system of central planning? Are increased exports identified primarily through export planning and managed through nationally-run monopolistic foreign trade companies? What is the role of foreign-invested firms?

The central theme of this article is that the sources of China's trade growth have changed significantly over the past dozen years. The surge in the value of exports in the late 1970s and early 1980s came largely from decisions of the state at the central level. A major source was increasing exports of petroleum, one of the key products identified by Deng Xiaoping in 1975 as having the potential to finance China's outward turn. As shown in Table 3, between 1977 and 1985 China's exports of crude oil and refined petroleum products grew from 12 to 36 million metric tons and the value of petroleum exports rose by almost $6 billion. Thus a single product category accounted for one-third of China's incremental export earnings.

More significantly, despite evidence that a growing shortage of energy was crippling the pace of domestic economic expansion, exports of crude oil and refined petroleum products absorbed a very large share of these products. Between 1977 and 1985 incremental exports of crude oil absorbed 98 per cent of all additional output.[8] Once the decision was made to rely on this source, exports grew dramatically in both volume and value terms.[9] This occurred despite significant domestic challenges to its economic rationality, and the fact that domestic oil production grew less rapidly than originally anticipated, with the search for offshore deposits by multinational oil companies falling far short of initial "optimistic expectations of an oil bonanza which would finance China's foreign purchases."[10]

After 1985 this pattern began to change. Petroleum and a small number of other products under the tight control of the central state planning and trade apparatus no longer served as significant sources of export growth. The commodity composition of China's exports began to change in ways that suggest that trade decision-making was becoming more decentralized and increasingly sensitive to economic factors.

The change in the sources of export growth is reflected in the evolving composition of exports. As shown in Table 4, in the first half of the 1980s primary products (including agricultural products and minerals) regularly comprised from 45 to 50 per cent of China's exports. This was little changed from the period from the mid-1960s to 1980 when they accounted for just over half.[11] Primary products are essentially commodity exports – homogeneous goods sold on international markets at world prices, and little marketing knowledge is needed to sell them.

After the mid-1980s, the share of primary commodities in Chinese exports fell continuously and the share of manufactured goods rose from half in 1985 to over three-quarters by 1991. Only a small part of this can be accounted for by the decline in the price of petroleum on world markets in the second half of the 1980s.[12] Rather, it was due to the rapid growth of exports of textiles and other light manufactured goods,[13] to reach an all-

[8] Kenneth Lieberthal and Michel Oksenberg, *Policy Making in China: Leaders, Structures, and Processes* (Princeton, New Jersey: Princeton University Press, 1988), p. 262.

[9] Nicholas R. Lardy, *Foreign Trade and Economic Reform in China, 1978–1990* (Cambridge: Cambridge University Press, 1992), pp. 95–96.

[10] Lieberthal and Oksenberg, *Policy Making in China*, p. 260.

[11] Editorial Board of the Almanac of China's Foreign Economic Relations and Trade, *Almanac of China's Foreign Economic Relations and Trade 1989* (English edition) (Hong Kong: China Resources Advertising Co. Ltd., 1989), p. 361.

[12] The average price China received per ton fell 21% from $185 in 1985 to $146 in 1990. State Statistical Bureau, *Zhongguo tongji zhaiyao 1991* (*Chinese Statistical Abstract 1991*) (Beijing: Statistical Publishing House, 1991), p. 99. The change in the price of oil alone would have reduced the primary product share of exports to 47.8%, thus accounting for only one-tenth of the shrinkage of the share of primary product exports between 1985 and 1990. However, its influence was more significant in the short run. For example, the price per ton fell by 50% in 1986 to $92, contributing significantly to the sharp decline in the share of primary product exports in 1986 compared to the previous year. State Statistical Bureau, *Zhongguo tongji zhaiyao 1987* (*State Statistical Abstract 1987*) (Beijing: Statistical Publishing House, 1987), p. 90.

[13] Since the data in Table 4 are derived from Customs statistics in some sense they may overstate the rising share of manufactured goods in total exports. The Customs data on exports, as explained above, include the gross value of processed and assembled exports. These exports grew dramatically in the second half of the 1980s.

TABLE 4. *The Commodity Composition of Chinese Exports, 1980–91(%)*

	Primary products	*Manufactured products*
1980	50.2	49.8
1981	46.6	53.4
1982	45.0	55.0
1983	43.3	56.7
1984	45.7	54.3
1985	50.5	49.5
1986	36.4	63.6
1987	33.6	66.4
1988	30.4	69.6
1989	28.6	71.4
1990	25.6	74.4
1991	22.5	77.5

Notes:
 Primary product exports include five categories: foodstuffs, beverages and tobacco, non-food raw materials, minerals and fuels, and animal and vegetable oils and fats.
Sources:
 States Statistical Bureau, *Zhongguo tongji zhaiyao* (*Chinese Statistical Abstract*) (Beijing: Statistical Publishing House, various years), 1983, p. 73; 1985, p. 90; 1986, p. 96; 1987, p. 89; 1988, p. 85; 1990, p. 98; 1991, p. 98. Zhu Mincai, 'Zhongguo duiwai jingmao chixu fazhan,' ('China's foreign economic and trade relations continue to develop'), *Renmin ribao*, 31 January 1992, p. 7.

time high by the late 1980s. These goods are more heterogeneous than primary commodities and selling them in large quantities on international markets requires a more sophisticated understanding of consumer tastes, quality standards, and so forth. Moreover, the production of textiles and other light manufactured goods tends to be much more labour-intensive than the production of primary goods, suggesting that the composition of exports was shifting to reflect China's underlying comparative advantage in labour-intensive products.

This hypothesis is confirmed by an analysis of more disaggregated trade data released by the Chinese Customs Administration and a detailed 1985 industrial census carried out under the auspices of the State Council. The latter provides data on the value of fixed and working capital, the number of staff and workers, and output value for 510 uniquely-identified industries.[14] By establishing a correspondence between these industries and the

[14] State Council National Industrial Census Leading Small Group Staff Office, *Zhonghua renmin gongheguo 1985 nian gongye pucha ziliao* (*1985 Industrial Census of the People's Republic of China*) (Beijing: Chinese Statistical Publishing House). The data used came from volume 3, pp. 90–121, 128–39, 204–35, published in March 1988. They cover all manufacturing

63 distinct categories of exports that are identified at the two-digit level of disaggregation in the Standard International Trade Classification System used by the Chinese Customs Administration, one can investigate the production characteristics of China's exports.[15]

The most striking empirical result is that there is a strong inverse correlation between the growth of exports during 1985–90 and the ratio of capital to labour used in production. In short, Chinese exports were increasingly labour-intensive after 1985. This result is borne out at several levels. First, the data confirm the view that primary products are more capital intensive to produce than are manufactured goods. Total assets per worker in the production of primary product exports averaged more than one-third more than in the production of manufactured goods exports. The most obvious capital intensive category is crude oil and refined petroleum products where assets per worker, almost 45,000 *yuan*, were more than four times the average for all manufactured exports.[16]

Secondly, looking at all the export categories there is a strong inverse correlation between export performance in 1985–90 and capital intensity in production.[17] Table 5 provides the data for the five export categories that experienced the largest absolute increases in exports. These expanded by US$12 billion, more than 40 per cent of China's export expansion.[18] The ratio of capital to labour in production in four of these five categories was substantially below the mean of all categories. Thirdly, by contrast, in the first half of the 1980s there appears to be little correlation between relative capital intensity in production and export growth.[19] As already noted, ex-

establishments classified as independent accounting units regardless of the form of ownership. In 1988 these enterprises accounted for 85% of manufactured goods output. Thomas G. Rawski, "How fast has Chinese industry grown?" Research Paper Series No. 7, Socialist Economies Reform Unit, World Bank, March 1991, p. 2.

[15] Copies of the concordance are available from the author. It should be noted that the SITC scheme includes category S9, commodities not elsewhere classified, which includes mostly export processing and assembly activities. They cannot be assigned to specific industries. Thus the analysis below does not include them.

[16] The only one of the 63 categories of exports more capital intensive was electric power, also classified as a primary product.

[17] The correlation coefficient is –0.29. Regressing the capital/labour ratio in production on the changes in exports of all categories produces a negative coefficient that is statistically different from zero at the 5% level. This relationship would be even stronger if processed and assembled exports, which are highly labour-intensive, could be taken into account. By 1990 re-exports of processed and assembled imports rose to $10.453 billion. The absolute increase in these exports between 1985 and 1990 exceeded that of any of the two-digit export categories analysed.

[18] The share of China's export expansion accounted for by these five categories of exports is calculated on the basis of the export data reported by the Ministry of Foreign Economic Relations and Trade. This is the appropriate basis for measurement since, as noted above, the disaggregated export data being analysed excluded processing and assembly activities.

[19] Disaggregated analysis cannot be done for the whole period since detailed trade data of the Chinese Customs Administration for the years before 1982 have not been publicly released. For 1982–84 for all export categories the correlation between export performance and capital intensity in production is positive but very weak. The correlation coefficient is +0.08.

TABLE 5. *Capital Intensity in Production of China's Largest Incremental Export, 1985–90*

SITC	Trade category description	Change in exports 1985–90 (US$ billions)	Assets per worker (yuan)
D84	Apparel	4.31	5,222
D65	Textile yarn and fabrics	3.49	8,621
D89	Miscellaneous manufactures	1.47	6,832
D76	Telecommunications and sound recording and reproducing equipment	1.41	20,277
D85	Footwear	1.36	6,178
Mean of all export categories		0.45	13,991

Notes:
  Assets include both fixed capital (valued at original prices) and working capital.
Sources:
  General Administration of Customs of the People's Republic of China, *Chinese Customs Statistics* (Hong Kong: Economic Information and Agency), various issues; State Council National Industrial Census Leading Small Group Staff Office, *Zhonghua renmin gongheguo 1985 nian gongye pucha ziliao* (*1985 Industrial Census of the People's Republic of China*) Vol. 3 (Beijing: Chinese Statistical Publishing House, 1988).

ports of very capital intensive primary products such as crude oil and refined petroleum products grew rapidly. But so did exports of textiles and apparel. The difference in the second half of the decade is that exports from capital intensive sectors that had generated significant growth of exports in the first half of the decade shrank in relative and sometimes absolute terms.[20] In addition to crude oil and refined petroleum products, which registered the sharpest drop of any export category, these included chemical fibres, railway equipment and ships.

The evolving commodity composition of Chinese exports was the consequence of three critical developments: decentralization of decision-making

The estimated coefficient on the capital/labour ratio in a linear regression on changes in exports is positive but not significant, even at the 10% level.

[20] Similar findings – that China's trade specialization in the early 1980s was not based on comparative advantage but that by the late 1980s China was exploiting its comparative advantage more fully – have been reported by Zhang Xiaogang and Peter G. Warr, "China's trade patterns and comparative advantage," in *China: Trade and Reform* (Canberra: Australian National University National Center for Development Studies, 1991), pp. 46–72. Their study is based on China's 1981 input-output table, which contains 14 sectors producing traded goods; estimates of relative Chinese domestic prices and world prices for these 14 sectors; and World Bank estimates of the shadow prices of primary factors. Compared to the present study the main advantage is that it takes into account the intermediate goods used in the production of exports. Its disadvantages are that it is based on far more aggregated trade data and that the World Bank estimates of shadow prices are "rough."

in foreign trade, reforms in the pricing of traded goods, and the abandonment of an over-valued exchange rate.

Decentralization of foreign trade

In the pre-reform era China's planners determined imports and exports largely via the system of material balances that was used to construct the basic economic plan. They thus co-ordinated the flow of raw materials and intermediate goods among major state enterprises and ensured that the production of each good was sufficient to meet both inter-industry demand and final demand for consumption, investment and export. Planners used imports to fill the difference between planned demand and domestic production capability for high priority capital goods where the alternative of scaling back final demand would have meant reducing the level of investment. Exports sufficient to pay for these imports were then identified, starting with goods for which domestic supplies exceeded planned demands. The foreign trade plan incorporating these commodity flows was quite comprehensive. The export plan specified the quantities of 3,000 individual commodities that were to be procured by the state for export,[21] and the import plan incorporated more than 90 per cent of all imports.

Bureaucratically, by the mid-1950s foreign trade was a complete monopoly of the central government. A handful of specialized foreign trade corporations, some created as early as March 1950, was responsible for implementing the plan. The key feature of this arrangement was a lack of competition since each of the foreign trade corporations was responsible for carrying out trade in specified, non-overlapping product areas. For example, the China National Metals and Minerals Import and Export Corporation managed international trade in steel, non-ferrous metals, coal and coke, building and refractory materials, and other metal products. The continued dominant role of these firms in the early years of reform is reflected in their share of China's exports and imports. In 1981 national foreign trade companies subordinate to the Ministry of Foreign Economic Relations and Trade accounted for 91 per cent of exports and 87 per cent of imports. By 1984 their shares were 79 per cent and 65 per cent respectively.[22]

Trade reforms in the mid-1980s substantially altered the arrangements summarized above. This is shown most clearly by two indicators: the growing number of foreign trade corporations and the declining scope of the foreign trade plan. The State Council, in a major foreign trade reform document promulgated in September 1984, called for an end to the mo-

[21] Sun Wenxiu, "A review and forecast of the reforms of the foreign trade system," *Jihua jingji yanjiu* (*Planned Economy Research*), No. 8 (1989), p. 53.

[22] World Bank, *China: External Trade and Capital* (Washington, D.C.: The World Bank, 1988), pp. 102–3.

nopoly power of the specialized national foreign trade companies. This was to be achieved by creating a large number of small and medium-sized trading companies.[23] Within two years the Ministry of Foreign Economic Relations and Trade had approved the creation of more than 800 separate import and export corporations. Initially many of these were created by converting the provincial branches of the national foreign trade companies into local companies carrying out trade in the same product lines. However, later provinces and municipalities established many general trading companies authorized to handle a much broader range of goods. As a result, by the late 1980s the number of companies had soared to more than 5,000. This created new problems. China had long enjoyed a high reputation for fulfilment of trade contracts. Some of the newly-created companies, however, lacked adequate experience and funding or were not able to acquire domestically the goods they had contracted to export. Non-performance of trade contracts became a matter of growing concern to China's trade partners.[24]

The State Council took steps in May 1988 and March and November 1989, first to reassert central control over the process of approving the creation of new trading companies and, subsequently, to dissolve or merge existing companies found to be unqualified or illegal. However, the resulting cutback still leaves substantial room for competition among these firms. By the spring of 1990 roughly 70 per cent of all foreign trade corporations had been examined and only 800 had been either closed or forced to merge with another corporation. When the campaign to examine the foreign trade companies ended in August 1991, 1,402 had been closed or forced to merge, leaving China with 3,673 foreign trade corporations.[25]

Just as important as the expansion in the number of trading companies was the reduced scope of the foreign trade plan. The number of planned export commodities fell from 3,000 in the pre-reform era to 112 by 1988.[26] The share of exports specified in the annual foreign trade plan fell to 45 per

[23] State Council, "Notice concerning the report of opinions on reforming the foreign trade system," in Bank of China Staff Office, *Yijiubasi nian waihui gongzuo zhongyao wenjian xuanbian* (*A Compilation of Important Documents in 1984 Foreign Exchange Work*) (Beijing: Chinese Banking Publishing House, 1986), pp. 173–4. Extracts of this document, which omit much important material, have been published in both Chinese and English, Editorial Board of the Almanac of China's Foreign Economic Relations and Trade, *Almanac of China's Foreign Relations and Trade 1986* (Beijing: Ministry of Foreign Economic Relations and Trade Publishing House, 1986), pp. 29–32 and 388–92.

[24] Stanley Lubman, "Investment and export contracts in the People's Republic of China," *Brigham Young University Law Review*, No. 3 (1988), p. 557.

[25] Reporter, "We must firmly grasp and carry out the work of rectifying the various kinds of foreign trade corporations," *Guoji shangbao* (*International Business*), 21 March 1990, p. 1; "The national work of rectifying foreign trade corporations is almost completed," *ibid.* 1 September 1991, p. 1. Of the companies eliminated, 1,083 (36.6% of the original number) were under provincial, municipal or other local jurisdiction, 200 (15.4%) under the jurisdiction of special economic zones, and 119 (14.4%) subordinate to various national ministries.

[26] Sun Wenxiu, "A review and forecast of the reforms of the foreign trade system," *Jihua jingji yanjiu* (*Planned Economy Research*), No. 8 (1989), pp. 53–4.

cent in the same year. The scope of import planning fell even more rapidly, from more than 90 per cent of total imports at the beginning of the 1980s to 40 per cent by 1988.[27] In the same year only 17 import commodities fell into the planned category. Moreover, from 1985 the foreign trade plan was divided into mandatory and guidance portions. Mandatory plan imports and exports were specified in quantitative terms and were usually the responsibility of the head offices of the national foreign trade companies. In 1988 the mandatory export plan covered 21 specific commodities, only about 20 per cent of China's total exports. Fifteen of these were the sole responsibility of the national foreign trade companies, with the responsibility for the other six shared between national and local foreign trade corporations. The remaining 91 planned export commodities were in the guidance category. On the import side there were nine mandatory plan commodities under the control of the national foreign trade companies and eight guidance plan commodities.[28] Guidance plan imports and exports were generally specified in value terms, giving local trading corporations more flexibility. This allowed them to take economic factors into account when determining the precise mix of imported and exported products within each category.

Pricing of traded goods

In the pre-reform trade regime world market prices had little or no effect on the Chinese domestic prices of tradeable goods. It was this that led the World Bank to characterize China's traditional trade regime as an "airlock system."[29] Foreign trade corporations purchased goods specified by the plan from domestic producers at officially established prices. Thus producers received the same price whether goods were sold domestically or in the international market. Moreover, they received none of the foreign exchange income from the sale of the goods abroad nor did they have any direct claim on it to purchase goods abroad for their own use. Under these circumstances producers had little economic incentive either to sell on the international market or to expand production of goods for which there was strong international demand.

Domestic prices of imported goods also tended to be unconnected to the world market since after 1964 the prices of 80 per cent of China's imports were set at levels comparable to similar domestic goods.[30] Only when there

[27] Working Party on China's Status as a Contracting Party, "China's foreign trade regime: note by the Secretariat," (Geneva: General Agreement on Tariffs and Trade, 1988), p. 21.

[28] Zhang Yuqing and Wang Hejun, "China's laws and regulations on foreign trade management," *Intertrade* (March 1990), p. 7.

[29] World Bank, *China: Long-Term Issues and Options* (Baltimore: The Johns Hopkins University Press, 1985), p. 17.

[30] Contemporary China Series Editorial Board, *Dangdai zhongguo de wujia* (*Contemporary China Commodity Prices*) (Beijing: Social Sciences Publishing House, 1989), p. 226.

was none or when the volume of domestic production was extremely limited was the price of an imported good based on the world price.

These procedures substantially distorted trade decisions because the domestic price of imports diverged from the world price. In some cases China's domestic industry was highly protected since foreign goods with relatively low production costs had their prices marked up to the level of Chinese goods. The tendency was compounded by liberal adjustments upward from the price of the "comparable" Chinese goods to account for differences in quality. In other cases imports were sold at prices significantly below world prices. For example, imported grain and chemical fertilizer were sold at the same prices as domestically produced output, which were artificially low, so that imports of these products were highly subsidized.

Reforms of the past decade, particularly those of the latter half of the 1980s, transformed the pricing of traded goods. Domestic sale prices of a growing share of imported goods began to be based on the world market price. This trend accelerated after the State Council's 1984 foreign trade reform document called for the widespread adoption of the "agency system" in which foreign trade corporations undertake transactions on behalf of domestic firms and charge them a commission. When the agency system applies to imports the importing firm pays the world market price (converted to domestic currency at the official exchange rate) plus shipping and port fees, a commission, and any tariffs that apply. This procedure is referred to as "foreign trade agent price formation" (*waimao daili zuojia*). By 1986, the domestic prices of four-fifths of all imports were based on import cost with only 28 commodities continuing to be priced according to comparable domestic goods.[31] After 1988 this list was reduced even further, including, during 1989, the removal of two of the most important commodities: from January timber and plywood,[32] and from November most imported steel and nonferrous metals.[33] By the end of 1989 the list contained only 14 commodities so that the domestic prices of 90 per cent of all China's imports were based on world market prices. In late April 1990 there were only eight commodity categories left: chemical fertilizer, wood pulp, alkyl benzene, five sodium compounds, nonionic surface active agents, grain, phosphorous

[31] Chen Jiaqin, "Marxist exchange rate theory and China's exchange rate policy," *Jingji lilun yu jingji guanli* (*Economic Theory and Economic Management*), No. 6 (1989), p. 54. State Bureau of Commodity Prices, Ministry of Foreign Economic Relations and Trade, and Ministry of Finance, "Notice on issues in the domestic price formation of centrally financed imports," in State Bureau of Commodity Prices Foreign Price Office, *Zhongguo shewai jiage fagui yu zhengce zhinan* (*A Handbook of China's Policy and Laws on Foreign Prices*) (Hong Kong: Hong Kong Main Culture Company, Ltd., 1988), p. 117.

[32] State Bureau of Commodity Prices, *Zhongguo wujia nianjian 1990* (*Chinese Commodity Price Yearbook 1990*) (Beijing: Chinese Commodity Price Publishing House, 1990), pp. 343–44.

[33] State Bureau of Commodity Prices Foreign Price Office, "Foreign prices," in State Bureau of Commodity Prices, *Zhongguo wujia nianjian (1989)* (*Chinese Commodity Price Yearbook 1989*) (Beijing: Chinese Commodity Price Publishing House, 1989), p. 162.

ore, and titanium dioxide and intermediates for producing agro-chemicals.[34] And the shrinkage of the list continued with the elimination of sodium tripolyphosphate with effect from 1 January 1991.[35] The domestic prices of well over 90 per cent of all goods imported into China in 1991 were based on world market prices. The old pricing regime, which provided a high degree of protection to some import competing industries or a high degree of subsidy to domestic users of some imported commodities, had largely faded away.

The initial pace of change in the domestic pricing of export goods appears to have been somewhat slower than that for imports. But by the late 1980s, the state used the pre-reform pricing system for only 21 export goods. These planned exports accounted for only 20 per cent of the value of China's total exports in 1988. At the other extreme in the same year, 55 per cent of total exports fell outside the plan, meaning that producers were not compelled to deliver them to trading corporations at state-fixed prices but could take advantage of the proliferation of competing foreign trade companies to bargain for the most favourable price. Initially these corporations sought to exploit the producers' lack of knowledge of world market conditions by paying them low prices for their goods.[36] But over time, with the growing number of trading companies, the degree of competition increased, tending to move domestic prices closer to world market prices. Even producers of the 21 commodities that fell within the export plan could take advantage of this competition by producing quantities of goods above the planned level. Over-plan production could be sold internationally on a decentralized basis and producers bargained with foreign trade corporations for more favourable domestic prices for that portion of their output.

Thus, as the scope of the foreign trade plan shrank and competition among a growing number of foreign trade corporations increased, the influence of international prices on domestic prices of exports rose.

The exchange rate and exchange control

Just as international prices had only the most modest influence on Chinese decisions on import and export commodities, the price of foreign exchange had little effect on the volume of either imports or exports in the pre-reform era. Thus, as in other centrally-planned economies, the exchange rate was a largely passive policy instrument.[37] China's domestic currency was highly

---

[34] Lardy, *Foreign Trade and Economic Reform in China, 1978–1990*, p. 163.

[35] "Regulations concerning price issues," *Jiage lilun yu shijian* (*Price Theory and Practice*), No. 1 (1991), p. 64.

[36] Yang Peixin, "Reform the foreign exchange system to stimulate foreign trade," *Shijie jingji daobao* (*World Economic Herald*), 28 March 1988, p. 3.

[37] Josef M. van Brabant, *Exchange Rates in Eastern Europe: Types, Derivation and Application*, World Bank Staff Working Papers No. 778 (Washington, D.C.: The World Bank, 1985), p. 5.

over-valued in the pre-reform era and the resulting excess demand for foreign exchange was handled through a rigid system of exchange control. The domestic currency cost of earning foreign exchange was persistently higher than the official exchange rate, making most exports financially unprofitable.[38] The Ministry of Foreign Trade reallocated the profits that were made by some foreign trade corporations on their sale of imports on the domestic market to offset or compensate for the losses incurred by other foreign trade corporations on their sale of export goods. In practice this meant that the effective exchange rate varied from corporation to corporation and sometimes even on a product-by-product basis. This phenomenon, which has been called the "price-equalization mechanism," was common in centrally-planned economies. Unfortunately, compensating for the divergences between domestic and foreign prices undermined the incentive for trading companies to exploit comparative advantage trade opportunities.[39]

Reforms of the exchange rate and relaxation of exchange control were among the most dramatic changes in China during the last decade. As shown in Table 6, the Chinese authorities devalued the currency from a rate that averaged 1.6 *renminbi* per U.S. dollar in the late 1970s to an average of 5.3 *renminbi* in 1991.

Changes in the official exchange rate appear to have had only a modest effect on trade in the first half of the 1980s for two reasons. First, as already noted, since the reform of traded goods pricing was just beginning, the exchange rate had little effect either on the domestic currency earnings of most export producers or on the prices paid by most consumers of imports. Secondly, changes in the official exchange rate did not really affect the foreign trade corporations which were responsible for most trade transactions. In their transactions with the Bank of China they cleared their accounts at exchange rates that differed from the official rate but did not necessarily change when the latter changed. Moreover, foreign trade corporations frequently received financial subsidies to cover domestic currency losses from foreign trade transactions.

From 1985, however, changes in the exchange rate had a greater effect on trade. This was partly because changes in the pricing of traded goods meant that exchange rate adjustments had a direct effect on the domestic prices of an increasing number of imports and exports. In addition, the value of the currency fell significantly in the second half of the 1980s. By the end of 1990 the official rate had fallen to 5.22 *yuan* per dollar. Even when the official rate remained at 3.72, from the middle of 1986 to near the end of 1989, the

[38] Y. Y. Kueh and Christopher Howe, "China's international trade: policy and organizational change and their place in the 'economic readjustment'," *The China Quarterly*, No. 100 (December 1984), pp. 844–5. Lardy, *Foreign Trade and Economic Reform in China, 1978–1990*, pp. 25–6.

[39] Josef M. van Brabant, *The Planned Economies and International Economic Organizations* (Cambridge: Cambridge University Press, 1991), pp. 78, 93, 107.

TABLE 6. *The* Yuan-*Dollar Exchange Rate, 1978–91*

Year	Yuan per dollar
1978	1.68
1979	1.55
1980	1.50
1981	1.71
1982	1.89
1983	1.98
1984	2.33
1985	2.94
1986	3.45
1987	3.72
1988	3.72
1989	3.76
1990	4.78
1991	5.32

Note:
Rate is the average of the average annual selling and buying rates.
Sources:
People's Bank of China Research and Statistics Department, *Zhongguo jinrong tongji 1952–1987* (*Chinese Financial Statistics 1952–1987*) (Beijing: Chinese Financial Publishing House, 1988), pp. 156–57; State Statistical Bureau, *Zhongguo tongji zhaiyao 1990* (*Chinese Statistical Abstract 1990*) (Beijing: Statistical Publishing House, 1990), p. 101; *Zhongguo tongji Zhaiyao 1991* (*Chinese Statistical Abstract 1991*) (Beijing: Statistical Publishing House, 1991), p. 101; *Zhongguo tongji zhaiyao 1992* (*Chinese Statistical Abstract 1992*) (Beijing: Statistical Publishing House, 1992), p. 105.

average exchange rate received by exporters improved significantly since they could convert a rising share of their export earnings to domestic currency at a more favourable swap market rate, explained below. By the end of 1990 the real value (i.e. adjusted for relative inflation in China and the rest of the world) of the Chinese currency was 61 per cent of that in 1985 when the value is calculated on a trade weighted basis.[40] Combined with the reform of the pricing of traded goods this devaluation reduced substantially the bias against exports and the subsidy to imports of the pre-reform foreign trade and payments regime.

The resulting reduction in the excess demand for foreign exchange made possible a significant reduction in the rigidity of the exchange control sys-

[40] Department of the Treasury, "Report to the Congress on international economic and exchange rate policy," (Washington, D.C.: Department of the Treasury, May 1991), p. 24.

TABLE 7. *Foreign Exchange Market Volume, 1987–91 (US$ millions)*

Year	Value of Transactions
1987	4,200
1988	6,264
1989	8,566
1990	13,164
1991, first 11 months	18,175
1991, estimate	20,000

Notes:
Estimate for 1991 is based on the assumption that the volume of transactions in December was roughly equal to the monthly average in the first 11 months of the year.
Sources:
Working Party on China's Status as a Contracting Party, "China's foreign trade regime: note by the secretariat" (Geneva: General Agreement on Tariffs and Trade, 1988) p. 27; Reporter, "Initial steps in the establishment of China's foreign exchange market," *Jinrong shibao* (*Banking News*), 15 February 1989, p. 1; Zhang Guanghua and Wang Xiangwei, "Swap centers will be updated," *China Daily Business Week*, 7 May 1990, p. 1; Han Guojian, "Foreign exchange market opens wider," *Beijing Review*, 3–9 June 1991, p. 38. Shi Mingshen, "Woguo waihui xingshi haozhuan" ("China's foreign exchange situation changes for the better"), *Renmin ribao*, 23 January 1992, p. 2.

tem. The process of relaxation began as early as 1979 with a modest foreign exchange retention system that provided firms producing export goods with a claim to use a small share of the foreign exchange earnings their products generated. The scheme expanded steadily in two dimensions. First, the average share of retained earnings grew from less than 10 per cent of export earnings in 1979 to more than 40 per cent by 1988.[41] Secondly, the opportunity to trade these foreign exchange use rights, which was introduced in 1980, grew. Formal parallel markets existed as early as 1985 and by 1988 there were parallel auction markets for foreign exchange in about 40 Chinese cities. More importantly, the volume of trading in foreign exchange steadily expanded over the decade. As shown in Table 7, the volume of transactions soared from $4.2 billion in 1987 to $13.2 billion by 1990.[42] In the first 11 months of 1991 it grew by more than 50 per cent to reach $18.175 billion.[43]

[41] Lardy, *Foreign Trade and Economic Reform in China, 1978–1990*, p. 54.
[42] *Ibid.* p. 61.
[43] Shi Mingshen, "Wo guo waihui xingshi haozhuan" ("China's foreign exchange situation changes for the better"), *Renmin ribao*, 23 January 1992, p. 2.

Initially there was a substantial gap between the official exchange rate and the market price of foreign exchange, reflecting the continued over-valuation of the domestic currency at the official exchange rate. In 1988, for example, buyers of foreign exchange in the market paid an average of 6 *yuan* per dollar, a premium of two-thirds over the then official rate of 3.7 *yuan* per dollar. However, as the volume of transactions on the parallel market for foreign exchange expanded and the State Administration of Exchange Control devalued the official exchange rate further in December 1989 and November 1990, excess demand for foreign exchange at the official rate ebbed. In late 1990, when the official rate was 5.2 *yuan* per dollar, the parallel market rate was only 5.4 *yuan* per dollar.[44] In 1991 the State Administration Exchange Control began a policy of frequent but small adjustments in the official exchange rate. These adjustments, which led to an official exchange rate of 5.4 by the end of the year, appear to be partly guided by developments in the foreign exchange market. For example, by the third quarter of 1991 the parallel market rate had increased to 5.83. But because the official rate had been devalued further, this represented a premium of under 10 per cent over the official rate at the time.

The role of the swap market in allocating foreign exchange grew as a result of reforms of the foreign exchange retention system introduced in 1991. Before this each province had a fixed quota of foreign exchange to be delivered to the centre and was allowed to retain 80 per cent of all foreign exchange earnings above this amount. For the other 20 per cent, they were paid in *renminbi* at the official exchange rate. Retained foreign exchange could be used to finance imports outside the plan or could be sold on the swap market for domestic currency. The 1991 reform of the foreign trade contract system abolished the distinction between quota and over-quota foreign exchange earnings, substituting instead a requirement that half of all foreign exchange must be remitted to the centre. This effectively raises the marginal rate of remission from 20 per cent to 50 per cent. However the centre agreed to pay for the increased flow at the swap market rate rather than the official exchange rate, that is it will buy two-fifths of remitted foreign exchange at the official exchange rate and three-fifths at the swap market rate. As a result the swap market price has become even more important. Before the 1991 reform, approximately half of all foreign exchange was priced, either implicitly or explicitly, at the swap market rate. From 1991 this fraction rose to four-fifths. According to one prediction made early in 1991, the total amount of foreign exchange priced explicitly at the swap market rate in 1991, including that which the centre would pay for at the swap rate, would reach $25 billion.[45]

[44] Xinhua, "Central bank increases export oriented loans," Foreign Broadcast Information Service, *China: Daily Report*, 22 January 1990, p. 2.

[45] Hu Fengying, "A brief account of China's new foreign trade system," *Shijie jingji yanjiu* (*World Economy Study*), No. 3 (1991), p. 33. Hu also estimated that the volume of market

The net result of these reforms was to erode substantially the bias against exporting. Exporters on average received a much more favourable exchange rate for that share of their earnings they were still compelled to hand over to the foreign exchange authorities and they received the remainder in the form of a use right. That use right either could be sold for domestic currency in a market where the degree of official intervention appears to have diminished significantly in the past five years or could be used to buy foreign goods. On the import side, the implicit subsidy available to users of planned imports shrank dramatically as more and more goods were imported on a decentralized basis and priced according to the world market price converted to *yuan* at a more realistic official exchange rate or at the parallel market price for foreign exchange.[46]

In short, China appears to be within striking distance of achieving internal convertibility of the *renminbi* in trade transactions. Among the socialist and former socialist states, only Poland matches this pace of reform. Moreover, unlike Poland, China's reform was not backed with a massive programme of rescheduling and writing off existing foreign debt or a multi-hundred million dollar standby loan agreement with the International Monetary Fund.

Regional and sectoral export trends

The three reforms analysed briefly above created the conditions in which decentralized trade based on economic incentives could flourish. This is evident in the kinds of enterprises that became the most successful exporters by the late 1980s. Particularly significant is the growing share of China's exports produced by rural township and village enterprises and joint venture enterprises. As shown in Table 8, this trend was most obvious in the second half of the 1980s when the three reforms really began to take hold. Rural enterprise exports jumped from about four to more than 12 billion dollars between 1985 and 1990 and joint venture exports from around a quarter of a million dollars in 1985 to 12 billion dollars in 1991. In short, these two decentralized sectors of the Chinese economy accounted for a large share of the growth of exports in the second half of the 1980s when the opportunities for decentralized exporting clearly emerged.

Additional evidence of the new conditions comes from an examination of

transactions in foreign exchange for the year would be $16 billion, implying an estimate of central government purchases of foreign exchange at the market price but not through the market of $9 billion. Hu's estimate turned out to be low.

[46] In the absence of other forms of protection, that provided to domestic producers of goods that compete with imports would have been reduced in many cases since the reforms of import pricing (i.e. shifting to pricing based on the world market) would have more than offset the effect of the higher domestic currency price of foreign exchange. However, in many sectors tariffs, quotas and other barriers still provide significant protection to Chinese import competing industries.

TABLE 8. *Exports of Rural and Joint Venture Enterprises, 1985–91 (US$ billions)*

	Rural enterprises	Joint venture enterprises
1985	3.9	0.3
1986	4.5	0.5
1987	5.1	1.2
1988	8.0	2.5
1989	10.1	4.9
1990	12.5	7.8
1991	–	12.1

Sources:
For rural enterprise exports: Xinhua, "China sees good years in rural industry," *China Daily*, 7 December 1990, p. 1; Wang Ping and Che Delong, "Enhanced export role envisaged for coastal township enterprises," *Jingji yu guanli yanjiu* (*Research on Economics and management*), No. 5 (1989), p. 13; Wu Yunhe, "Townships told to develop exports," *China Daily*, 25 October 1989, p. 1; David Zweig, "Internationalizing China's country-side: the political economy of exports from rural industry," *The China Quarterly*, No. 128 (December 1991), p. 718. For joint venture exports: Qu Yingpu, "Foreign funds flow in," *China Daily Business Weekly*, 24 December 1990, p. 1; Staff reporter, "Exports boom for foreign-funded firms," *China Daily*, 21 January 1991, p. 1; State Statistical Bureau, "Guanyu 1991 nian guomin jingji he shehui fazhan de tongji baogao," ("Statistical report on China's social and economic development in 1991"), *Renmin ribao*, 29 February 1992, p. 2.

the regional pattern of export growth within China. Perhaps the most notable example is Guangdong province. At the outset of reform in 1978, Guangdong was a second-tier exporter selling $1.4 billion in world markets, about half the level of Shanghai.[47] Up to the middle of the 1980s Guangdong's share of China's total exports actually fell slightly. That is not surprising: Guangdong is not a significant producer of crude oil, refined petroleum products or the capital-intensive manufactured goods that were the main sources of China's export growth up to the mid-1980s.

However, after 1985 Guangdong's share rose significantly. Exports more than quadrupled from just under $3 billion in 1985 to $13.69 billion in 1991. The average annual rate of growth of Guangdong's exports over this period was 29 per cent compared to 13 per cent for the rest of the country.[48] As a

[47] Most published provincial trade data, including that for Guangdong, is compiled on the same principles as those used by the Ministry of Foreign Economic Relations and Trade. Thus in the analysis below where the growth of the province's exports is compared to the nation as a whole and where the province's exports are expressed as a share of national exports the calculations are based on the Ministry data in Table 1.

[48] Guangdong Statistical Bureau, *Guangdong tongji nianjian 1991* (*Statistical Yearbook of Guangdong 1991*) (Beijing: Chinese Statistical Publishing House, 1991), p. 303. State Statistical

result Guangdong's share of China's exports rose from 11 per cent in 1985 to 21 per cent in 1991. In the process Guangdong eclipsed Shanghai to become China's largest exporter. Exports of Shanghai-produced goods rose only 10 per cent between 1981 and 1988.[49]

It would be tempting to attribute Guangdong's success entirely to its proximity to Hong Kong and its large share of China's foreign-invested enterprises. Indeed, exports of foreign-invested firms in 1990 did account for a third of the province's earnings with processing and compensation trade bringing another 6 per cent. But half the growth between 1985 and 1990 was due to expanded international sales by indigenous firms in the region, so other factors must be involved. Several can be suggested. First, Guangdong manufacturing firms were on average only half the size of Shanghai's and they were much less likely to be state-owned. In 1988 the two regions produced almost identical levels of industrial output, measured by gross value,[50] but the number of firms in Guangdong was twice that in Shanghai. Guangdong firms were smaller and capable of responding more quickly to changing international market conditions.

The advantage of smaller size was reinforced by the modest role of the state in the ownership of Guangdong's industry. Only one-quarter of firms were state-owned. Three-quarters, producing by 1988 60 per cent of manufactured goods output, were urban collective, township and village, private, or joint venture firms. They were far more entrepreneurial than state-owned firms, purchasing most of their inputs and selling most of their output on the market rather than working through the state's material distribution and wholesaling systems. In Shanghai, by contrast, entrepreneurial firms in 1988 produced only one-third of industrial output. Large-scale, state-run establishments dominated the municipality's manufacturing sector.

The second critical difference was that Guangdong, having had a low priority in the state's plans for economic development since the 1950s, had a more market-oriented economy than Shanghai, even before reform.[51] With fewer state-owned firms tied to the state's system of material distribution, enterprises in the province were more likely to buy raw materials,

Bureau, *Zhongguo tongji nianjian 1991* (*Chinese Statistical Yearbook 1991*) (Beijing: Statistical Publishing House, 1991), p. 97. Xu Dezhi, "Guangdong foreign trade rises to all-time high," *China Daily Business Weekly*, Spring Trade Fair supplement, 15 April 1992, p. 3. Xu is the director of the Guangdong Provincial Foreign Economic Relations and Trade Commission.

[49] Ezra F, Vogel, *One Step Ahead in China: Guangdong under Reform* (Cambridge, Mass.: Harvard University Press, 1989), pp. 372–84. Lardy, *Foreign Trade and Economic Reform in China 1978–1990*, pp. 126–36, 168.

[50] The gross value of industrial output in 1988 in Guangdong was 105.077 billion *yuan*, in 1980 prices. In Shanghai it was 108.270 billion *yuan*, also in 1980 prices, Guangdong Statistical Bureau, *Guangdong tongji nianjian 1991*, p. 53. Shanghai Statistical Bureau, *Shanghai tongji nianjian 1989* (*Shanghai Statistical Yearbook 1989*) (Beijing: Statistical Publishing House, 1989), p. 127.

[51] Ezra F. Vogel, *Canton under Communism: Programs and Politics in a Provincial Capital, 1949–1968* (Cambridge, Mass.: Harvard University Press, 1969), pp. 128–32.

machinery and other producer goods on the market. By 1991 this had expanded further and more than 80 per cent of all producer goods (i.e. machinery, equipment and other capital goods) used in the province were purchased on the market,[52] whereas nationally the figure was only about half.[53] Many of the capital goods used in Guangdong came from other provinces. The development of markets and the use of marketing agents with well-developed extra-provincial ties were critical to the success of Guangdong's firms.

In contrast, Shanghai's industries were dependent largely on the state's system of material distribution. As this system eroded in the 1980s, some state-run industries declined as they lost their primary source of raw material supplies and were unable or unwilling to develop alternative sources through the market. This was particularly noticeable in the textile industry. As central government's deliveries of raw cotton to the city's factories fell sharply in the second half of the 1980s, the industry fell into a slump from which it has yet to recover.[54]

Coal is another commodity that illustrates the significant differences between Shanghai and Guangdong, neither of which has any major local deposits. In 1989 the central government provided three-quarters of Shanghai's coal requirements through the system of planned allocation. The municipality purchased the remainder on the open market. But in Guangdong in the same year, the central government's allocations provided only 32 per cent of requirements and 68 per cent had to be purchased on the market outside the province.[55] As a result Guangdong paid substantially more for its coal, and passed on the cost to its customers in higher electricity rates.[56] While Guangdong suffered power shortages, they appeared modest given the pace of industrial development in the region.[57] Guangdong developed reliable extra-provincial supplies of coal through market channels and

[52] "Guangdong takes lead in economic reform," *China Daily*, 14 February 1992, p. 4.

[53] Li Hong, "Big firms to be forced into market mechanism," *China Daily*, 28 February 1992, p. 1.

[54] The value of output (measured in constant prices) in the textile and clothing industries fell 1% between 1985 and 1989 in Shanghai, Shanghai Statistical Bureau, *Shanghai tongji nianjian 1990* (*Shanghai Statistical Yearbook 1990*) (Beijing: Chinese Statistical Publishing House, 1990), pp. 96–7. By contrast the value of output of these industries nationally more than tripled from 22.1 billion *yuan* to 76.8 billion *yuan* between 1985 and 1989. State Statistical Bureau, *Zhongguo tongji zhaiyao 1991* (*Chinese Statistical Abstract 1991*) (Beijing: State Statistical Publishing House, 1991), p. 66. The national data are in current prices so overstate the growth of output somewhat. However, there is no doubt that national output grew substantially over this period and the relative role of Shanghai in the industry shrank dramatically.

[55] Liu Shujie, "A research report on the issue of dual track pricing of coal," *Zhongguo wujia* (*China Price*), No. 1 (1991), p. 29.

[56] Guangdong and Shanghai respectively paid 148.0 and 39.9 *yuan* per ton for state allocated coal and 252.0 and 210.0 *yuan* per ton for coal purchased on the market. *Ibid.* p. 30.

[57] In the mid-1980s, foreign invested firms in Guangdong typically included stand-by power generation equipment in their plants. By the late 1980s local supplies of power were sufficiently reliable that such facilities were not usually included in new joint venture plants in South China.

built additional thermal-powered generating capacity financed largely by local resources.[58] Thus it more than doubled its output of electric power between 1985 and 1990, meeting rapidly rising demand both from industry and from domestic consumers as electric appliances became common in both urban and rural areas.[59] Shanghai's electric power output rose only 10 per cent over the same period.[60] Guangdong was able to compensate for what initially appeared to be a disadvantage, its low priority in the state's plan for the distribution of key industrial commodities, by increasing its reliance on the market.

The rapid growth of Guangdong's trade contributed to a structural change of the province's industry as well as an acceleration of its economic growth. Between 1978 and 1990 industrial output in the province expanded by an average of 16.3 per cent per annum in real terms, more than 4 percentage points per annum over the national average. But Guangdong's light industry grew even more rapidly, on average 18.8 per cent per year, so that its share of total industrial output rose from 57 to 69 per cent.[61] This structural change was largely a result of the province's rapidly growing exports and evolving export structure. Guangdong's traditional exports were predominantly live pigs, vegetables and other agricultural goods sold primarily to Hong Kong. As recently as 1985, 41 per cent of the exports of indigenous local firms (excluding joint venture firms and firms engaged in processing and compensation trade) were agricultural and processed agricultural products. By 1990 this had fallen to only 25 per cent, mirroring a 15 percentage point increase in the share of light and textile industry exports. The dramatic rise in the latter reflected huge increases in the exports of shoes (rising 41 times between 1985 and 1990), garments (up six-fold), cotton piece goods (up seven-fold), silk piece goods (quadrupling), plastic items (up 18-fold), toys (quadrupling), and tools (up five-fold).[62]

---

[58] Among other local sources were bonds specifically issued by Guangzhou municipality to finance electric power projects. Christine I. Wallich, "Recent developments in China's financial sector: financial instruments and markets," in James A. Dorn and Wang Xi (eds.), *Economic Reform in China: Problems and Prospects* (Chicago: University of Chicago Press, 1989), pp. 140–1.

[59] Guangdong's annual electric power output rose from 16.7 billion kilowatt hours in 1985 to 34.4 billion kilowatt hours in 1990. Guangdong Statistical Bureau, *Guangdong tongji nianjian 1991*, p. 161. In addition Guangdong imported electric power from Hong Kong.

[60] Shanghai's production rose from 25.63 billion kilowatt hours in 1985 to 28.4 billion kilowatt hours in 1990. Shanghai Municipal Statistical Bureau, *Shanghai Statistical Yearbook 1991* (Concise edition) (Beijing: China Statistical Publishing House, 1991), p. 73. The municipality may have been able to draw on the East China regional grid to bring in electric power generated in adjacent provinces. Booming industrial production in some of these provinces, notably Jiangsu, may have limited these transfers.

[61] Guangdong Statistical Bureau, *Statistical Yearbook of Guangdong 1991*, p. 53. State Statistical Bureau, *Chinese Statistical Yearbook 1991* (Beijing: Statistical Publishing House, 1991), p. 55.

[62] Guangdong Statistical Bureau, *Guangdong Statistical Yearbook 1990*, p. 384; *Statistical Yearbook of Guangdong, 1991*, pp. 304, 309.

In contrast there is no evidence that trade played a similar role in trans-forming Shanghai's industry over the same period. Industrial output grew by only 6.9 per cent per annum, little more than half the national average. Between 1978 and 1990 light industry advanced only marginally more rap-idly than heavy industry, and indeed for the period 1981–90 heavy industry slightly outperformed light industry. Thus after 1981 the share of heavy industry increased almost three percentage points to reach 45.3 per cent of industrial output in 1990, proportionately half again as great as in Guangdong.[63]

The pace of trade reform

While the analysis above emphasizes the growing influence of markets and prices, including the price of foreign exchange, in determining the pattern of China's imports and exports, this reform process was slowed down or even set back in two periods, from the second quarter of 1985 until 1987, and from mid-1989 into 1991. Liberalization of foreign trade, particularly of imports, in the fourth quarter of 1984 led to a growing trade imbalance. As shown in Table 9, China framed the foreign trade liberalization passed by the State Council in September 1984 from a position of a trade surplus. However, in the fourth quarter imports grew at an astounding rate of 50 per cent and the trade balance turned sharply negative. That trend accelerated throughout 1985 leading to an all-time record annual trade deficit of $14.9 billion.

The second period of significant trade imbalance began in 1988. As previous administrative measures had brought the merchandise account closer to balance by the end of 1987, controls on imports were relaxed. An upsurge of consumer expenditure in 1988 led to rapidly rising imports. Although the government moved to reduce domestic credit expansion from the fourth quarter of 1988 to cool down an overheated economy, the flow of imports was not interrupted. Indeed increased imports of consumer goods, particularly durables, may have been seen as a means of mopping up excess purchasing power that was contributing to an unusually high rate of infla-tion in the latter half of 1988. As a result in the 12-month period ending in June 1989, the trade deficit reached $12.3 billion, almost matching the previous record 12-month deficit in calendar year 1985.[64]

In both periods the state adopted a variety of administrative measures to restrict imports and promote exports in order to reduce the trade imbal-ance. In 1985 a major way of cutting back on decentralized imports was a freeze on the use of retained foreign exchange. Localities and export-

---

[63] Shanghai Statistical Bureau, *Shanghai Statistical Yearbook 1990*, pp. 91–2; *Shanghai Sta-tistical Yearbook 1991*, p. 64.

[64] World Bank, *China: Between Plan and Market* (Washington, D.C.: The World Bank, 1991), pp. 21–2.

producing enterprises were subject to "quota controls on the use of retained foreign exchange" that drastically reduced their right to use a fraction of the foreign exchange they had earned. By the end of 1986, $19.1 billion in retained foreign exchange had been "borrowed" by the central government, which used it in part to finance its own trade deficit.[65] When the system of retained foreign exchange returned to normal, it appears that the foreign exchange "borrowed" by the centre was never repaid.

In response to the second period of a burgeoning deficit, the central authorities imposed substantially increased restrictions on imports, particularly after mid-1989. There was a ban on the import of many types of consumer goods, an expansion of the scope of import substitution restrictions on imports, and a recentralization of control of decision-making on some types of imports. For example, imports of foreign luxury cars, cigarettes, alcohol and canned beverages were banned from the first half of 1989. The list of import substitute products, which cannot be imported without the permission of the Ministry supervising domestic production of competing goods, expanded significantly. That led to de facto bans on some imports even when the foreign goods were cheaper than or technologically superior to the domestic product. The state also took measures to reassert central control of imports of a broad range of products, including wool, some types of steel products, plywood, colour television components, scientific measuring devices, various types of building materials and chemical fertilizer.[66]

At the same time the state stepped up efforts to provide preferred access both to raw materials and to credit to assure the continued growth of exports. Assured credit supplies for exporters were particularly important in the fourth quarter of 1988 and in 1989 because the central monetary authority was pursuing an overall restrictive credit policy in order to help control inflation. Without preferred access to credit, exports would have been severely restricted.

The effect of these measures on the trade balance was dramatic. By the third quarter of 1989 imports were falling in absolute terms, reducing the quarterly trade deficit to $700 million, less than a fifth of the deficit in the second quarter. In the final quarter of 1989, the deficit was only $100 million. In 1990 China achieved trade surpluses that grew greater in each quarter. For the year as a whole, imports fell $5.8 billion, exports rose $9.5 billion, and the trade surplus was $8.74 billion. By the end of 1990 Chinese foreign exchange reserves had risen to $28.6 billion, more than twice the level of mid-1989.[67]

[65] Song Hai, "Macroperspective reflections on the reform of China's foreign exchange management system," *Jingji yu guanli yanjiu* (*Research on Economics and Management*), No. 1 (1988) reprinted in *Caizheng, jinrong* (*Finance, Banking*), No. 3 (1988), p. 143.
[66] *The Chinese Economy in 1990 and 1991: Uncertain Recovery* (Washington, D.C.: Central Intelligence Agency, 1991), pp. 27–31.
[67] *Ibid.* p. 5.

If the previous pattern held, the reduction of the deficit should have set the stage for a renewed relaxation of controls on imports. Indeed imports did begin to grow in the last quarter of 1990 and continued to do so at double-figure rates in the early months of 1991. But exports moved up even more rapidly leading to substantial monthly trade surpluses. In the first half of 1991 the trade surplus grew almost 50 per cent compared to the first half of 1990. The continued cumulation of such large surpluses led a United States government analysis written at mid-year to conclude that China's trade strategy had changed fundamentally from a genuine policy of opening up and trade liberalization toward a policy of "continued emphasis on export growth without import liberalization."[68] However, as the data in Table 9 show, compared with the same period a year earlier, China's balance of trade surplus fell sharply in the second half of 1991. The surplus for the year as a whole was down significantly in 1991 and it appears likely that this trend will accelerate in 1992.

Chinese trade practices became a matter of growing concern in the United States since what was a modest bilateral trade deficit with China in the mid-1980s grew to $6.2 billion in 1989 (the sixth largest American deficit on a world-wide basis) and then to $10.4 billion (the third largest) in 1990 and $12.76 billion (the second largest) in 1991.[69] These deficits were related to a dramatic shift in the direction of China's trade, particularly on the export side, with the United States becoming an increasingly important market. The United States' share of China's exports went from 6 per cent in 1979 to 14 per cent in 1985 and 26 per cent in 1991.[70]

In contrast the share of China's exports going to Japan actually declined during the 1980s. Japan absorbed $4 to $5 billion annually in Chinese products in 1980–82, approximately 24 per cent of all Chinese exports. By 1988–90 Japanese imports from China were $10–$12 billion annually, but that was only 19 per cent of China's then much larger export volume. Japanese exports to China plunged from a peak of $12.5 billion in 1985 to only $6.1 billion in 1990. Thus from the late 1980s Japan too incurred a deficit in its trade with China.

[68] *Ibid.* p. 12.

[69] Department of the Treasury, "Report to the Congress on international economic and exchange rate policy," p. 25.

[70] Erin McGuire Endean, "China's foreign commercial relations," in *China's Economic Dilemmas in the 1990s: The Problems of Reforms, Modernization, and Interdependence*, Study Papers submitted to the Joint Economic Committee, Congress of the United States, Vol. 2 (Washington, D.C.: United States Government Printing Office, 1991), p. 769 and official U.S. Department of Commerce data on imports from China and data on China's total exports from the General Customs Administration. Chinese data on sales to the United States are of little value since they exclude Chinese goods re-exported to the United States through Hong Kong. In 1989, for example, Chinese data show sales of $4.39 billion whereas the Department of Commerce reported imports from China of $11.989 billion. For more discussion of this problem in analysing bilateral imbalances in U.S.–China trade see Nicholas R. Lardy, "Redefining U.S.-China economic relations," Analysis Monograph Series No. 5. (Seattle, Washington: National Bureau of Asian and Soviet Research, June 1991).

TABLE 9. *China's Balance of Trade, 1983–91 (US$ billions)*

		Quarterly	Annually
1983			+0.8
1984	I	+0.3	−1.3
	II	+1.1	
	III	−0.2	
	IV	−1.9	
1985	I	−2.8	−14.9
	II	−3.7	
	III	−3.8	
	IV	−4.8	
1986	I	−3.1	−12.0
	II	−3.5	
	III	−2.5	
	IV	−3.0	
1987	I	−1.1	−3.8
	II	−0.9	
	III	−0.7	
	IV	−1.1	
1988	I	−0.7	−7.7
	II	−0.5	
	III	−2.3	
	IV	−4.2	
1989	I	−1.9	−6.6
	II	−3.9	
	III	−0.7	
	IV	−0.1	
1990	I	+0.8	+8.7
	II	+1.7	
	III	+2.3	
	IV	+3.8	
1991	I	+2.3	+8.1
	II	+1.4	
	III	+2.6	
	IV	+1.8	

Notes:
The balance of trade is exports minus imports, as reported by the Chinese Customs Administration. The quarterly and the annual data are not always fully consistent for two reasons. First, the annual figures apparently incorporate revisions in the underlying data, but the corrections for the quarters are not published. Secondly, the quarterly data for the years 1980–86 have been published only in domestic prices and thus must be converted to dollars, so the results depend on the exchange rate used – either the average annual rate published in the *Statistical Yearbook* or the quarterly rates published in *International Financial Statistics* by The International Monetary Fund.
Sources:
General Administration of Customs, *Chinese Customs Statistics* (Hong Kong: Economic Information and Agency), various issues.

However, this deficit differed from that of the United States in two respects. First, even at its peak in 1990 of $5.9 billion Japan's deficit was only about half that of the United States. Secondly, Japan's deficit narrowed to $5.6 billion in 1991 because of a 40 per cent increase in exports combined with an 18 per cent increase in imports (Japan's share of China's total exports stabilized),[71] while the United States' deficit continued to widen.

Because of its growing bilateral trade deficit, the United States initiated formal bilateral discussions on market access issues in mid-1991 with the expectation that the Chinese authorities would reduce the number and severity of administrative barriers they imposed on imports. These included import licensing requirements; selective quantitative restrictions on imports; onerous technical barriers, mainly product testing and certification requirements; and a lack of transparency (i.e. many internal regulations not available to foreigners) in China's trade regime. Bilateral negotiations on China's protection of intellectual property rights also began around the same time, in late May 1991. The United States government believed that if copyright and patent protection provided by China were raised to world standards American firms would be more willing to sell computer software, chemicals, pharmaceuticals and so forth. That would increase American sales to China, thus reducing the deficit.

The first two rounds of bilateral discussions on market access took place in Beijing in June and in Washington in August 1991. President Bush promised to initiate trade sanctions against Chinese imports into the United States market if these efforts were not successful.[72] In October the United States administration launched an investigation of China's trade practices under section 301 of the United States Trade Act of 1974. Under the provisions of the law China had until 10 October 1992 to satisfy specific American complaints or face prohibitive tariffs on some of its exports to the United States. Only a few weeks later the United States Trade Representative announced that negotiations to improve China's protection of intellectual property had failed and that the United States would impose prohibitive tariffs on specified Chinese exports. This step is allowed under the special 301 provision of United States trade law dealing with foreign violations of American patents and copyrights. Although many observers predicted that China would not respond to the threat of sanctions, an agreement was reached in mid-January 1992, only hours before a final deadline for the imposition of punitive tariffs. Under the agreement China undertook to provide stronger protection of patents and copyrights, particularly for pharmaceuticals and other chemical products, computer software and sound recordings.

---

[71] Japanese External Trade Organization, *China Newsletter*, No. 61 (March–April 1986), pp. 23–4; No. 91 (March–April 1991), pp. 23–4; No. 97 (March–April 1992), pp. 22–3.

[72] George Bush, letter to Senator Max Baucus, 19 July 1991, p. 3.

Conclusion

China's foreign trade has made stunning advances since economic reform began in the late 1970s. Initially trade expansion was heavily state directed. However, from the mid-1980s onward this was gradually displaced by a more market determined pattern of trade. The proliferation of new trading companies that could compete with the handful of national foreign companies – which had once enjoyed a monopoly on trade transactions – and far-reaching reforms in the pricing of traded goods and the *renminbi* created the economic environment in which decentralized trade decision-making based on economic incentives became increasingly important. The growing role of trade after 1985 in regions such as Guangdong province, where the system of state-owned firms and their associated supply and marketing is relatively modest, highlights the character of China's trade reforms. However, the emergence of large trade deficits, once in the middle of the decade and once near the end, led to some retrogression as the centre increased its reliance on administrative intervention to curtail imports.

These episodes underline the main limitation on China's trade reforms – the partial nature of domestic economic reform. Periodic burgeoning trade deficits reflect the centre's difficulty in exercising macroeconomic control of a semi-reformed domestic economy. The traditional system of controlling aggregate demand has atrophied significantly and the development of market-oriented fiscal and monetary policy instruments has just begun.[73] Moreover, the sources of export growth, particularly in the second half of the 1980s and early 1990s, underline the limitations of domestic reform. State-owned industrial enterprises account for a disproportionately small share of China's export growth.

If China can address these problems successfully there seems little doubt that the reforms of the second half of the 1980s will provide the basis for the continued growth of Chinese exports and thus of imports as well.

[73] Lardy, *Foreign Trade and Economic Reform in China, 1978–1990*, pp. 136–41.

Consumption and Living Standards in China

Joseph C. H. Chai

The future of the reforms in China ultimately depends on whether, and if so to what extent, reforms introduced in the recent past have improved the consumption and the standard of living of the Chinese people. It also depends on whether any such gains in the standard of living have been widely spread among the whole population. Since 1978 real per capita consumption in China has risen at an average annual rate of 7 per cent which is more than three and a half times that of the preceding 21 years. As a result, the standard of living of the average Chinese citizen in 1990 was more than double that of 1978. However, the growth of consumption and the living standards was rather uneven during the reform period. During the first phase of the reforms (1978–85) the consumption standard increased rapidly without widening existing income disparity. During the second phase (1985–90), however, improvements in consumption standards slowed significantly amidst rising inflation and growing income inequality. The question is whether the recent trend of a relatively slow rise in the standard of living and greater income disparity will continue in the 1990s. The purpose of this article is to examine the recent trends and changes in the level, structure and differentials of Chinese consumption and living standards, and to assess their prospects for the 1990s.

Measurement of a country's living standard is a hazardous undertaking as there is no commonly agreed set of criteria and in any case the criteria are constantly shifting. Measuring the Chinese living standard is even more difficult because of the problematic nature of Chinese consumption and income data[1] as well as the paucity of data on the qualitative aspects of living standards. The following analysis of trends from 1978 to 1990 considers first the quantitative and then the qualitative aspects. In view of the limited data and the lack of objective criteria for measurement of the living standard the work is exploratory in nature and the conclusions should be treated as tentative. They will need empirical confirmation when more data and objective criteria of measurement become available.

Quantitative Aspects

The quantitative aspects of consumption and living standard are usually measured in terms of per capita income and consumption. Table 1 presents

---

[1] See Nicholas R. Lardy, "Consumption and living standards in China, 1978–83," in *The China Quarterly*, No. 100 (December 1984), pp. 849–65.

TABLE 1. *Material Consumption per Capita*

Year	Yuan in 1980 prices	Index (1978 = 100)
1957	141	65
1978	216	100
1979	236	109
1980	256	119
1981	273	126
1982	289	134
1983	310	144
1984	349	162
1985	398	184
1986	422	195
1987	449	208
1988	478	221
1989	475	220
1990	486	225

Average Annual Growth (per cent)

1957–78	2.0
1978–85	9.1
1985–90	4.1
1978–90	7.0

Note and Sources:
  Material consumption per capita in 1980 prices are estimated from material consumption per capita in current prices as given in *ZGTJNJ* 1991, pp. 42 and 79, deflated by price deflator derived from Chinese linked index (index in current prices/index in comparable prices) as given in *ZGTJNJ* 1991, p. 43.

estimates of per capita material consumption for selected years between 1957 and 1990, expressed in 1980 prices. It is worth noting that this statistical series may not accurately reflect the real consumption standard of the Chinese people. This is, first, because material consumption data are derived from the methodology of Chinese national income accounting and include only material components of personal and collective consumption, [2] and secondly, because the price deflator used to derive real consumption is derived from the Chinese linked index of "comparable prices." Table 1 shows that, as already mentioned, Chinese material consumption from 1978 to 1990 grew at an annual average rate of 7 per cent which is more than three and a half times that of the previous 21 years, and by 1990 the level of Chinese consumption was more than double that of 1978. However, consumption growth was rather uneven during this period. In the first phase of

[2] *2000 nian Zhongguo de renmin xiaofei (2000 China's People Consumption)* (Beijing: Zhongguo shehui kexue chubanshe, 1988), p. 108.

reforms (1978–85) it was relatively high, averaging 9 per cent, but during the second phase (1985–90) it declined to only 4 per cent, less than half the previous rate.

This trend is corroborated by data on the per capita disposable income taken from the household survey sample (see Table 2). Disposable income is defined as "income available" for the urban household and "net income" for the rural household. Disposable income of the worker and peasant household are deflated by the cost of living index and rural retail consumer price index, to obtain real disposable income in constant (1980) prices. The estimates of national average disposable income per capita in column 3 are a weighted average of those of worker and peasant households, with the weights being the respective shares of the non-agricultural and agricultural population in the total population. As indicated in the table, the average annual growth of per capita real disposable income in 1978–90 was 7.2 per cent which is four and a half times that achieved in 1957–78. Again, by 1990, Chinese real disposable income per capita was

TABLE 2. *Per Capita Disposable Income (yuan in 1980 prices)*

Year	Urban	Rural	Nation-wide total
1957	294	90	129
1978	346	145	181
1979	–	170	–
1980	439	191	238
1981	447	219	261
1982	473	261	300
1983	493	298	335
1984	555	338	380
1985	558	352	394
1986	631	353	411
1987	642	363	420
1988	650	365	424
1989	629	340	401

Average Annual Growth (per cent)			
1957–78			1.6
1978–90			7.2
1978–85			11.7
1985–90			1.2

Note:
    See text for data estimation.
Sources:
    ZGTJNJ 1983, p. 499; 1984, pp. 462 and 471; 1985, p. 551; 1990, pp. 250, 263, 289, 296 and 312; 1991, pp. 230, 243 and 269.

TABLE 3. *Sources of Growth of Material Consumption per Capita*

	Material consumption per capita (1980 yuan)	NMP per capita (1980 yuan)	Rate of accumulation (1980 prices)	Rate of consumption (1980 prices)
1978	216	337	35.9	64.1
1979	236	355	33.4	66.6
1980	256	374	31.4	68.6
1981	273	387	29.3	70.7
1982	289	412	29.8	70.2
1983	310	447	30.6	69.4
1984	349	501	30.3	69.7
1985	398	561	29.0	71.0
1986	422	594	29.0	71.0
1987	449	645	30.4	69.6
1988	478	706	32.3	67.7
1989	475	721	34.1	65.9
1990	486	745	34.8	65.2
Average Annual Growth				
1978–80	8.9	5.3		3.5
1981–85	9.9	9.7		0.2
1985–90	4.1	5.8		−1.7

Note:
NMP per capita in 1980 prices is estimated according to the procedure in the note to Table 1.
Sources:
ZGTJNJ 1991, pp. 32, 33 and 79.

more than double that of 1978. But the rate of growth was also uneven. Most of the growth occurred during the first phase of the reform (1978–85) with a significant slowing-down in the second phase (1985–90).

To discover what caused Chinese per capita consumption to grow so fast during the earlier period and then slow down, its growth can be divided into the growth in the rate of consumption or the share of consumption in NMP and the growth of NMP per capita.[3] Table 3 presents estimates of these

[3] Since

$$\frac{C}{P} = \frac{C}{Y} \times \frac{Y}{P}$$

where C stands for consumption, Y, national income, NMP, net material product and P, population, hence

$$\frac{\overset{\circ}{C}}{P} = \frac{\overset{\circ}{C}}{Y} + \frac{\overset{\circ}{Y}}{P}$$

together with the rate of accumulation in 1980 prices. It reveals that during the initial years of the reforms (1978–80) the rapid increase of per capita consumption was due to the increase in both the rate of consumption and NMP per capita. The increase in the former was made possible by a significant fall in the rate of accumulation from 35.9 per cent to 31.4 per cent between 1978 and 1980. Between 1981 and 1985 the rate of accumulation changed very little, and hence, most of the rapid increase of per capita consumption was due to the rapid increase of NMP per capita. Finally, during the later period of the reforms in 1985–90, the rate of accumulation rose once again from 29 to 34.8 per cent. Consequently there was a drop in the rate of consumption. This, together with the slowdown of the rate of growth of NMP per capita, contributed to the slower growth of per capita consumption during this period.

Qualitative Aspects

The level of welfare of the Chinese people is determined not only by the amount of material consumption but also by qualitative aspects of life which are hard to quantify and very often can be inferred only indirectly. These include changes in consumer satisfaction, access to health and education services, availability of social and economic security, the extent of income inequality and the degree of environmental degradation.

Consumer satisfaction

Consumer satisfaction can be significantly increased, even with a set amount of consumer goods, if means can be found to improve their allocation and distribution.[4] In the past freedom of exchange among consumers was severely limited because of widespread non-price rationing. The reforms brought about a significant reduction in the number of rationed goods and the development of a free market system which has enhanced consumers' freedom of exchange and hence enabled them to achieve a more efficient consumption pattern.

In the past the separation of consumer prices and producer prices and the lack of enterprise autonomy in output decision-making meant that producers either did not know or were not allowed to respond to consumer demand. The introduction of the two-track pricing system brought a greater alignment of producer and consumer prices which, together with the newly-gained greater autonomy in output decisions, helped producers to provide the kinds of goods demanded by consumers. There was also a marked

[4] F. L. Pryor, *A Guidebook to the Comparative Study of Economic Systems* (London: Prentice Hall, 1985), pp. 56, 58.

improvement in product design, colour and quality, encouraged by increased competition among producers under marketization.

Finally, Chinese consumer satisfaction was significantly enhanced by improvements in the distribution system. Thanks to the promotion of the service sector in general, and the encouragement of private enterprises in particular, the number of establishments in the retail, catering and service trades per 10,000 population soared from 13 in 1978 to 104 in 1989.[5] This reduced the average shopping time of Chinese consumers and increased their leisure time.

Health and education

Improvement in people's longevity and knowledge depends on the ease of access to health and education services and can be indicated by life expectancy at birth and the adult literacy rate. These, together with per capita income, are considered the basic indicators for human development by the United Nations.[6] As the data in Table 4 show, average life expectancy increased only slowly between 1980 and 1989, from 68 to 70 years, compared with a 25-year rise between 1950 and 1975. For the adult literacy rate the figures are even worse. Illiteracy fell from 38.1 to 23.5 per cent during 1962–82, but has suffered a resurgent increase in the more recent period. A plausible explanation of the lack of improvement in health and education is the demise of the commune system, which, while extremely inefficient in production, did provide wider access to health and education services, especially for the poor and elderly. With the disappearance of communes access has been increasingly unequal because certain services which they previously provided without charge now have to be paid for by the consumer.[7]

Economic security

The well-being of an individual is also affected by the degree of economic security. This can be threatened by inflation and unemployment, both of which lead to a substantial decline in real income. Table 5 presents official estimates of annual changes in indexes of Chinese worker and employee cost of living, rural retail prices and free market prices. Such price indicators show that China had little or no open inflation before the reforms. After the introduction of market-orientation the average annual increase in prices was significantly more than that of the pre-reform period. In fact, it is

[5] ZGTJNJ 1991, p. 269.

[6] United Nations, Human Development Report (New York: Oxford University Press, 1990), p. 13. The author is grateful to D. Doessel for drawing his attention to this reference.

[7] Deborah Davis, "Chinese social welfare policies: policies and outcomes," The China Quarterly, No. 119 (September 1989), pp. 577–97.

TABLE 4. *Human Development Indicators*

	Life expectancy at birth (years)	Adult illiteracy rate (per cent)
1950	40[1]	–
1960	47[2]	–
1962	–	38.1[3]
1975	65[2]	–
1981	68[3]	–
1982	–	23.5[3]
1987	70[2]	26.8[3]
1989	70[4]	–

Notes and Sources:
  [1] Nick Eberstadt, "Material poverty in the PRC in international perspective," in U.S. Congress, Joint Economic Committee, *China's Economy Looks Towards the Year 2000* (Washington, D.C.: U.S. Government Printing Office, 1986), Vol. I, p. 293.
  [2] United Nations, *Human Development Report* (New York: Oxford University Press, 1990), pp. 45 and 134.
  [3] SSB, *Zhongguo shehui tongji ziliao* (*Chinese Social Statistical Materials*), 1985, pp. 28 and 137; *ZGTJNJ* 1991, p. 852.
  [4] World Bank, *World Development Report 1991*.

TABLE 5. *Average Annual Increases in Consumer Prices (%)*

	1957–78	1978–90
Worker cost of living	0.7	6.9
Rural retail prices	0.1	5.9
Free market prices	3.5	6.9

Source:
  ZGTJNJ 1991, pp. 230, 243 and 248.

generally agreed that the official price indexes tend to underestimate the true rate of inflation so it may have been even higher in recent years than is suggested by these figures. The greater price instability is a manifestation of the growing difficulties experienced by the government in achieving a balance between aggregate demand and supply under increased decentralization and marketization of the economy.[8]

  [8] D. H. Perkins, "Reforming China's economic systems," *Journal of Economic Literature* (June 1988), pp. 624–5.

With the demise of rural communes, the abandonment of guaranteed state jobs and the introduction of a contract worker system in the cities, job insecurity has increased in recent years. Enterprises under pressure to make their operations profitable have informally shed many of their former employees. As previous social aims have to some extent given way to economic considerations, the relatively large amount of disguised unemployment has also diminished and contributed to the growing number of unemployed.

Before the reforms a social security system financed by the communes in rural areas and by urban enterprises in the cities reduced the economic insecurity caused by inflation, unemployment, industrial accidents, illness, old age and so on. With the end of the communes, financial problems have caused access to social security in rural areas to diminish. In the cities, the enterprises still provide social security for tenured workers but not for unemployed migrants from rural areas or contract workers – the latter accounting for an increasing share of the urban workforce.[9] The enterprise-financed system is disintegrating but state-financed social security is still not in place.[10] Thus Chinese workers and peasants are caught in the descending part of the U-curve of economic and social security as observed in other market economies.[11]

Income differentials

Individuals tend to judge their own level of economic well-being by the standard of living enjoyed by their neighbours. Thus, if income is distributed fairly evenly, people are less likely to feel deprived than if distribution is uneven.

The issue of whether market-oriented reforms are likely to generate increased income inequality cannot be settled by a priori reasoning. On the one hand, income inequality may rise with the re-introduction of the distribution principle "to each according to his/her contribution," as well as the deliberate attempt by government to widen income differentials in order to provide work incentives. On the other hand, the deregulation of economic activities and the reduction in barriers to the movement of production factors under the reforms should enable individuals to gain more equal access to job opportunities and capital, and so encourage specialization in accordance with the principle of comparative advantage. Under such conditions production factor returns would be expected to be much more equal, reducing income inequality. Thus, the net effects of the reforms on income

[9] S. J. Burki, "Development strategies for poverty alleviation," *Asian Development Review*, No. 1 (1990), p. 17.

[10] Wang Zhongmin, "Wo guo manzu jiben xuqiu de zhidu xuanze" ("The choice of basic needs satisfaction system in our country") *Jingji yanjiu ziliao*, No. 3 (1989), pp. 1–18.

[11] C. A. Tisdell, *Economic Development in the Context of China: Policy Issues* (London: Macmillan, forthcoming).

distribution can only be settled empirically. The increased availability of data from China enables us to establish, with some confidence, the trend in income distribution during the reform era. As the survey of these data later in this article shows, there was a slight reduction in income inequality and in the incidence of poverty during the first phase of the reforms, but a rise in both during the second phase.

Environmental degradation

It is reasonable to expect an increase in environmental degradation under the reforms. Its commonly identified indirect causes are rapid economic growth, industrialization and urbanization. China's GDP during the reform era grew almost twice as fast as it had done previously. The annual growth rate of industrial output during 1978–90 was 1.24 times higher than that during 1957–78. Between 1957 and 1978 official data suggest that the proportion of the total population living in cities and towns rose only modestly from 15.4 to 18 per cent, whereas between 1978 and 1990 it jumped from 18 to 26 per cent (see Table 13, below). However, these data overestimate the pace of urbanization of China during the reform era due to a change in the definition of "cities and towns" in 1984. A more accurate measure is the share of the non-agricultural population in the total population. As indicated in Table 13, while this share declined during 1957–78, it increased from 18 to 21 per cent between 1978 and 1990. Since all three indicators grew much faster during the reform era compared with the earlier period environmental degradation must also have increased at a faster rate under the impact of reforms.

Another commonly identified cause of environmental degradation is inadequate specification of ownership rights. Under the contract responsibility system most resources in China, including land, have been contracted out to individuals, but they are formally still publicly owned and their transferability is normally restricted. Moreover, the responsibility and rights of the contractee over resource use are not clearly delineated, and the contracts are not long or secure enough to encourage private investment and conservation. The reforms have shifted the level of decision-making from the central to local and individual levels, which increasingly rely on price signals as the basis of their decision. Yet most of the common resources, such as air and water, either have no price or are underpriced because of the absence or underdevelopment of markets for them. Insecurity of ownership induces individuals to maximize short-term instead of long-term profit. This behaviour together with the undervaluation of most resources leads to their overuse and lack of maintenance and conservation.

Unfortunately empirical data on the stock of pollutants in air, water, and so on for recent years are patchy. Those for the pre-reform period are virtually non-existent. Hence it is impossible to form a firm judgment on these matters.

To sum up, the quantitative aspects of life in China, as measured in terms of per capita consumption and income, have made significant gains in recent years. Improvements in the qualitative aspects of life, however, have been mixed. On the one hand, consumer satisfaction has increased considerably with greater freedom of consumer choice and more efficiency in the distribution and allocation of consumer goods. On the other hand, there is evidence of growing inequality in access to education and medical care. There is also evidence of increased economic insecurity, income inequality and environmental degradation.

Changes in the Pattern of Consumption

Changes in the consumption pattern of rural and urban households during the 1980s are presented in Table 6. The data are based on the urban and rural household survey. The former covers non-agricultural households such as those of workers and other employees, and the latter covers agricultural or peasant households. "Consumption" in the surveys includes not only commodities or services purchased but also those produced by households.

As Table 6 shows, the consumption *structure* has changed markedly because of the rapid rise in the *level* of consumption. Between 1981 and 1990, the nominal share of basic necessities (such as staple food, clothing and fuel) in total expenditure declined for both groups of households, whereas that of non-basic items (non-staple foods, housing, daily goods and others) as well as services, increased. For urban households, the nominal share of expenditure on staple food fell by almost half from 1981 to 1990. A similar pattern is also observable for rural households. The decline in expenditure for clothing for both groups was less dramatic during the same period. The share of fuel appears to have been fairly stable for both groups.

For rural households the nominal share of expenditure on non-staple food increased by more than 30 per cent from 1981 to 1990. The rate of increase was more modest for urban households during the same period. This difference in the rate of increase appears to be related to income differential between the two groups. A similar pattern is discernible for service expenditure. Whereas the nominal share of service expenditure of rural households increased by 208 per cent between 1981 and 1990, it rose by only 39 per cent for urban households. This difference reflects the relatively high level of service consumption already enjoyed by urban households at the beginning of the reform period.

In the case of housing expenditure, a reverse pattern is observable. De-

TABLE 6. *Changes in Consumption Structure (%)*

	1981	1985		1990	
		Current prices	1981 prices*	Current prices	1981 prices*
Rural Households					
Material Expenditure	97.6	97.1	97.3	92.6	93.1
Food	59.7	57.8	55.4	54.9	51.7
Staple	32.1	26.2	24.8	18.4	18.0
Non-staple	27.6	31.5	30.6	36.5	32.3
Clothing	12.4	9.9	11.6	8.4	11.0
Housing	9.8	12.4	11.7	12.9	12.0
Fuel	5.6	5.7	6.0	4.5	4.5
Daily goods and others	10.2	11.4	12.5	11.9	14.0
Services Expenditure	2.4	2.9	2.8	7.4	6.9
Total (*yuan*)	190.8	317.4	276.0	538.1	282.0
Urban Households					
Material expenditure	93.4	93.3	93.5	90.8	91.3
Food	56.7	52.3	46.8	54.2	46.6
Staple	13.0	9.0	10.3	5.6	9.0
Non-staple	43.7	43.3	37.0	47.6	37.6
Clothing	14.8	14.6	17.1	13.4	17.0
Housing	1.4	1.0	1.1	2.3	2.7
Fuel	1.9	1.7	1.9	1.6	1.8
Daily goods and others	18.6	23.8	26.7	19.3	23.2
Services Expenditure	6.6	6.7	6.5	9.2	8.8
Total (*yuan*)	456.8	673.2	585.5	1,278.9	650.4

Note:
  * Estimated by deflating individual expenditure items in current prices by their respective consumer price indexes (rural retail consumer price index and worker cost of living index) as given in *ZGTJNJ* 1991, pp. 235–7, 239–41, 243 and 250.
Sources:
  ZGTJNJ 1991, pp. 298, 280–1; Lin Baipeng, *Zhongguo xiaofei jieguo xue* (Beijing: Economic Science Publishing Co., 1987), pp. 106, 154; *Zhongguo nongcun jingji tongji daquan 1949–1987*, p. 563.

regulation and privatization of the urban housing market was advocated by Deng Xiaoping as early as 1978 and was officially sanctioned by the State Council in 1980. However, the implementation of this policy took place on a narrow experimental basis in selected cities. Due to the low-rent policy and the high price of the average housing unit, individuals had little incentive to purchase their own units. Thus, deregulation made little progress until 1988, when a Housing Reform Working Conference was called by the State Council to formulate an "implementation scheme" for the privatization of urban housing. According to this scheme, housing reform was to be extended to 80 major cities in 1988 and another 150 to 2,000 cities, as well as to 6,000 counties and townships, by 1989; by 1990 it was to be implemented by most cities and towns.[12] With accelerated deregulation of the housing market after 1988 the share of housing expenditure of urban households rose rapidly. In contrast, the share of housing expenditure of rural households rose less dramatically, housing deregulation having started much earlier in the countryside.

It is of interest to examine the consumption composition in *real* terms, since the high rate of inflation in the late 1980s might significantly change the relative prices and so distort real consumption patterns. Table 6 shows that consumption patterns in real terms do differ significantly from those in nominal terms. For urban households, it is interesting to note first that while in nominal terms there was an increase in the Engel coefficient between 1985 and 1990, in real terms it had declined. Thus the perverse behaviour of the Engel coefficient observed in nominal terms is apparently due to price distortions. Secondly, while the urban sector's nominal share of non-staple food expenditure increased, the real share actually declined during 1981–90. The decline is apparently due to the derationing of non-staple food, the increased purchase of these goods at higher prices on the free market and the high rate of inflation in the late 1980s. According to the 1988 urban household survey data, urban households purchased 80, 57, 60, 76, 63 and 69 per cent of their fresh vegetables, pork, beef and mutton, chicken, eggs, and fish, respectively, in free markets.[13] Thirdly, while there appears to be a decline in the share of clothing in nominal terms, its share actually increased in real terms. For rural households, the real consumption pattern also differs significantly from the nominal one. The decline of the Engel coefficient and the share of staple food in total household expenditure in real terms is more drastic, compared with nominal measures. But the reverse is true for the share of non-staple food consumption.

To study the change of response of consumer demand to changes in income, income elasticity for two time intervals, 1981–85 and 1985–90, are presented in Table 7.[14] As indicated, elasticities of food expenditure were

---

[12] "Zhufang zhidu gaige shizai bixing" ("Housing reform is inevitable"), *Jingji yanjiu ziliao*, No. 16 (1988), pp. 7–9.

[13] *China's Urban Household Income and Expenditure Survey Data, 1988* (Beijing: Zhongguo tongji chubanshe, 1989), p. 21.

[14] Income elasticity estimates are based on Engel function

$$e_i / p_i = A(E/p)^a (P_i/p)^b$$

where e_i and E stands for ith expenditure items and total expenditures per capita respectively, and p_i and P are the corresponding price deflators. Since b is relatively small when e_i is defined as a broad category in Table 6, income elasticity between year t and t-1 can be directly estimated as

$$a = \left[\log e_{i(t)} - \log e_{i(t-1)} \right] / \left[\log E_{(t)} - \log E_{(t-1)} \right].$$

See T. Mizoguchi, "Statistical indicators defining poverty levels using Japanese examples," *The Philippine Economic Journal*, No. 2 (1980), p. 101.

TABLE 7. *Times Series Elasticities of Expenditures*

| | Rural | | Urban | |
	1981–85	1985–90	1981–85	1985–90
Food	0.8016	−2.2431	0.2321	0.9497
Staple	0.3038	−14.9579	−0.1077	0.1641
Non-staple	1.2813	5.9684	0.3278	1.1488
Clothing	0.8334	−1.5368	1.5868	0.9365
Housing	1.4803	2.0211	−0.0641	9.6608
Fuel	1.1996	−11.9474	0.8115	0.7090
Daily goods and others	1.5483	6.1158	2.4475	−0.3151
Services	1.3406	43.0105	0.9313	3.8490

Source:
  Table 6.

less than unity for both groups of households, while those of staple food were negative and declined steadily for rural households. It is interesting that the elasticities of food of rural households became negative in the period 1985–89. One possible explanation is that Chinese peasants squeezed food consumption in order to make cash available for building new houses, acquiring consumer durables and purchasing services.[15] The elasticity for clothing also declined and remained at a low level between 1985 and 1990. Elasticities for housing and services rose significantly for both groups. For urban households the biggest jump is recorded for housing expenditure, whereas for rural households services displayed the largest increase. While elasticities for daily goods and other consumer durables for rural households increased steadily and remained high, those for urban households declined and became negative during 1985–90, indicating either that consumption of some basic durable goods had reached saturation point, or the diversion of expenditures for private housing construction and ownership.

Despite the shift in the pattern of consumption, the rank order of the major consumption categories in the urban household budget remained fairly stable during 1981–90. Food remained the largest expenditure item, absorbing just under half of the total real expenditure by 1990 (see Table 6). The next major category is daily goods and other consumer durables, accounting for about one-quarter. The third is clothing, taking up less than one-sixth, followed by services, housing and fuel. In future, with the abolition of state subsidies on many of these items and the deregulation of the housing market, their shares can be expected to increase substantially.

For rural households there have been more dramatic changes in con-

[15] Y. Y. Kueh, "Food consumption and peasant incomes in the post-Mao era," *The China Quarterly*, No. 116 (December 1988), pp. 634–70 at p. 652.

sumption patterns. Food remained the largest item, accounting for half the family budget in real terms. Clothing, which was ranked second, has dropped to fourth. Second place, as in the urban household budget, has been assumed by daily goods and other consumer durables. Housing rose from fourth to third. Finally, services have come to outrank fuel as the fifth most important item. The rank order of major consumption categories in the rural family budget has thus become closer to that of the urban households.

International Comparisons

A comparison between the Chinese consumption pattern and that of other comparable Asian-Pacific countries helps, first, to identify whether and to what extent China has succeeded in narrowing its consumption gap with neighbouring countries in recent years, and secondly, to predict the direction of change in China's consumption pattern in the near future. At the same time, any international comparison of consumption patterns is fraught with difficulties. A major problem lies in the choice of an appropriate exchange rate. In order to compare the pattern of Chinese consumption with that of other countries at a similar stage of development it is necessary to measure China's per capita income in U.S. dollars. But the official exchange rate of the *yuan* is a non-equilibrium rate which undervalues its real value. The use of purchasing power parity (PPP) exchange rate estimated from price comparisons on a product-by-product basis between China and the United States is also problematic, as Chinese prices may not be strictly comparable with American prices.

Another difficulty in placing the Chinese consumption structure in an international perspective is that the budget of urban households is heavily subsidized, particularly with respect to the basic and biggest expenditure items such as food, housing, medicine, fuel and other services.[16] The total value of these subsidies, together with other transfer income, accounted for about 82 per cent of the average wage packet of the urban worker in 1978.[17] The significance of subsidies in urban income and consumption has increased since then as the average subsidies appear to have grown faster than nominal wages.[18] The distortion effect of these subsidies on the urban household consumption pattern is evident from Table 8, which presents a modified budget of urban households, in 1981, adjusted for subsidies. Compared with the unadjusted budget, the share of food and housing expenditures is significantly higher, while those of clothing and daily goods and

---

[16] Lardy, "Consumption and living standards," pp. 853–6.
[17] Yang Shengmin, *Zhongguo xiaofei moshi de xuanze (Choice of Chinese-style Consumption Model)* (Beijing: Zhongguo shehui kezue chubanshe, 1989), p. 157.
[18] Lardy, "Consumption and living standards," pp. 862–3; *ZGTJNJ* 1990, pp. 113 and 815.

TABLE 8. *Urban Household Consumption Structure Adjusted for Subsidies, 1981*
(yuan *per capita*)

	Expenditures unadjusted	Subsidies	Expenditures adjusted for subsidies	Unadjusted expenditure structure in %	Adjusted expenditure structure in %
Material expenditure	35.56	10.93	46.49	93.40	94.84
Food	21.57	8.82	30.39	56.66	62.00
Clothing	5.63	0.02	5.65	14.79	11.53
Housing	0.59	1.84	2.43	1.55	4.97
Fuel	0.74	0.21	0.95	1.94	1.94
Daily goods and others	7.03	0.06	7.09	18.46	14.46
Service expenditure	2.51	0.02	2.53	6.59	5.16
Total	38.07	10.95	49.02	100.00	100.00

Source:
  Hu Jian, *Dongdan de xiaofei jieguo* (*Fluctuating Consumption Structure*) (Beijing: Xueyuan Publishing, Co., 1989), p. 57.

other consumer durables are lower. This indicates that the unadjusted urban family budget data systematically distort the significance of the individual budget items because of the effect of state subsidies.

A third difficulty in comparing China's consumption structure with those of other countries is that Chinese consumer behaviour is distorted by the effects of administered prices and quantity rationing. Chinese consumers may increase their consumption of a good simply because it is impossible to spend money on more desirable goods which are in short supply. Hence, in comparison to otherwise similar countries, some goods in China may be relatively over- or underconsumed.[19]

In Table 9 the Chinese consumption pattern during 1985–90 is compared with that of Taiwan and Japan at a comparable stage of development (Japan in 1955–60 and Taiwan in the late 1960s), measured in terms of per capita GNP based on official exchange rates. With respect to food consumption Table 9 indicates that the Chinese Engel coefficient during 1985–90 was much higher than that of either Taiwan in 1969 or Japan in 1955–60. According to international standards the consumption level is considered poor when the Engel coefficient is as high as 50–59 per cent and moderately comfortable (*xiaokang*) with a coefficient of 40–50 per cent. The relatively high level of the Chinese Engel coefficient, however, should not be inter-

[19] L. Podkammer, "Estimates of disequilibria in Poland's consumer markets, 1965–1978," *The Review of Economics and Statistics*, 1982, pp. 423–31.

TABLE 9. *International Comparison of Consumption Levels: China, Taiwan and Japan*

	China 1985–90	Taiwan 1969	Japan 1955–60
GNP per capita	311[1]	343[2]	349[4]
Engel coefficient	56.0[3]	43.6[2]	50.2[5]
Nutrition (per capita daily intake)			
Calories	2,628[6]	–	2,100[5]
Protein (g)	62.0[6]	–	69.7[5]
Fat and oil (g)	41.4[6]	–	22.5[5]
Meat (kg)	18.1[7]	23.8[8]	–
Fish (kg)	5.7[7]	29.0[8]	–
Housing			
m² per capita	14.8[9]	12.1[10]	7.28[11]
% urban home with piped water	77.4[12]	–	81.8[5]
with own toilet	39.0[12]	–	88.4[5]
Clothing[13]	121.7	–	100
Durable and semi-durable consumer goods[13]			
Daily goods	96.8	–	100
Culture and recreation goods	96.3	–	100
Service expenditure[13]	29.9	–	100
Overall total[13]	79.1	–	100

Notes and Sources:

[1] *ZGTJNJ* 1991, p. 31, official estimates of GNP and exchange rate in current prices.

[2] SSB, *Taiwan, Hong Kong, Singapore, South Korea and Thailand, Economic and Social Statistical Data* (Beijing, 1988), pp. 9, 36.

[3] Weighted average of rural and urban household coefficient in current prices.

[4] SSB, *Guomin shouru tongji ziliao huibian 1949–1985* (*National Income Statistical Data Collection, 1949–1985*) (Beijing: Zhongguo tongji chubanshe, 1987), p. 429.

[5] T. Mizoguchi, "Statistical indicators defining poverty levels, using Japanese examples," *The Philippine Economic Journal*, No. 44 (1980), pp. 99, 108, 115.

[6] 1984–86, FAO, *Production Yearbook* (1988), pp. 292–6.

[7] *ZGTJNJ* 1991, p. 273.

[8] Average for 1965–69: USDA, *Pacific Rim Agriculture and Trade Report* (August 1989), p. 42.

[9] Weighted average of urban and rural households in 1990: *ZGTJNJ* 1991, p. 306.

[10] 1975 figure: T. Mizoguchi, "Socioeconomic characteristics of poverty: macro and micro aspects," *Asian Development Review*, No. 1 (1990), p. 29.

[11] 1958–63 figure: Mizoguchi, "Statistical indicators defining poverty levels, using Japanese examples," p. 115.

[12] SSB, *1988 nian zhongguo chengzhen jumin jiating shouzhi tiaocha ziliao* (*1988 China's Urban Household Income Expenditure Survey Data*) (Beijing: Zhongguo tongji chubanshe, 1989), p. 20.

[13] T. Mizoguchi *et al.*, "A comparison of consumption level between Japan and PRC," *Hitotsubashi Journal of Economics*, No. 30 (1989), pp. 23, 26.

preted as an indication of a comparatively poor living standard in China, for it may have been caused by overconsumption of food under disequilibrium conditions in the consumer market.

A comparison of nutritional standards between China and Japan shows that the calorie, fat and oil daily intake was higher in China than in Japan in the late 1950s. However, the protein intake was somewhat lower. Though the level of Chinese food consumption was relatively high in relation to per capita income, the quality of diet still leaves much to be desired as plant sources supply more than half the Chinese calorie, protein and fat intake. In 1983 it was estimated that the percentage intake of these three items from animal sources was 7.8, 7.5 and 47 per cent respectively.[20] This is borne out by the relatively low per capita consumption of meat and fish. Compared with 1965–69 Taiwan, Chinese per capita consumption of meat and fish in 1985–90 was only 76 and 20 per cent respectively.

Housing conditions, on the other hand, have greatly improved in China in recent years, especially with relaxation of restrictions on housing construction in the countryside. Per capita floor space rose sharply during 1978–90 from 8.1 to 17.8 square metres per capita for rural households, and from 3.6 to 6.7 square metres per capita for urban households.[21] By 1990, average floor space for all households had reached 14.8 square metres, which was considerably higher than that of Japan in the late 1950s and even exceeded that of Taiwan in 1974. Thus, it appears that housing is a budget item that has been overconsumed in China in relation to the prevailing level of per capita income, especially in the countryside.

In spite of the increased floor space per head, the quality of housing remains relatively poor, especially in urban China. The 1988 urban household survey reveals that around 20 per cent of the dwellings were privately owned. However, the percentage of urban dwellings which had their own toilets and piped water was lower than that achieved by Japan in the late 1950s. Data on the quality of rural housing in China are not available, but there is no doubt that the percentage of dwellings with such facilities is still considerably lower in the countryside.

Clothing also seems to be considerably overconsumed in urban households in China. Table 9 indicates that the real consumption of total clothing in the Chinese urban households in 1985 was 1.2 times that of Japan in 1960. The real consumption of durable and semi-durable consumer goods by urban households in China was comparable to that of Japan in the late 1950s. The real services expenditure of the Chinese urban household in 1985 was much lower than that of their Japanese counterparts in the late 1950s, indicating an underconsumption due to limited supply. It approached only about 30 per cent of the Japanese level.

The overall consumption level of Chinese urban households in 1985

---

[20] Yang Shengmin, *Choice of Chinese-style Consumption Model*, p. 224.
[21] *ZGTJNJ* 1990, p. 324.

amounted to about 86 per cent of that of Japan in 1960. Since the rural consumption standard was only about half that of urban residents in China, whereas in Japan the consumption standard of rural households was not significantly different from that of urban households, the average consumption level of all Chinese households in 1985 must have been considerably less than 86 per cent of that of 1960 Japan.

Differentials and Poverty

Consumption and living standard differentials within a nation are primarily determined by consumption disparities within the urban and rural households, and the urban-rural consumption gap. Consumption disparity within the rural households can be inferred from rural income inequality. The Gini coefficient calculated by the State Statistical Bureau reveals that rural income inequality rose during the first phase of the reform (see Table 10). For the second phase, 1985–90, the officially estimated Gini coefficient is not available. No estimate of the Gini coefficient for this period from the incomplete rural income data published has been attempted here, since the calculation would require assumptions about average household size and income for each income group to be made which might significantly bias the result. However, since most of the rural disparity is accounted for by regional differences in the rural income distribution, the trend of rural disparity can be inferred from that of regional disparity.

Table 11 shows that there is a significant disparity between the provinces in rural per capita nominal income.[22] For example, per capita income of Shanghai peasants in 1985 was more than three times that of peasants in the poorest province, Gansu. By 1990 the income gap between the two had risen to a ratio of more than four to one. The rising trend of the interprovincial rural income inequality is also evident from the estimated population-weighted coefficient of variation which rose from 0.7389 in 1985 to 0.75563 in 1990.

Similarly, the consumption disparity amongst urban households can also be inferred from the urban income distribution. Published data, based on the urban household income and expenditure survey, are more detailed and an estimate of the Gini coefficient is therefore possible without having to rely on too many assumptions. As indicated in Table 10, urban income inequality declined between 1977 and 1984, but rose again between 1984 and 1990.

Trends in the rural-urban consumption disparity appear to follow the same path as urban income differentials. As the data in Table 12 indicate, the urban-rural real consumption gap narrowed from 2.9 to 1 in 1978 to 2.2

---

[22] Nominal instead of real per capita income is considered here because of the unavailability of price indexes for most of the poorest provinces (Yunnan, Guizhou, Gansu and Qinghai).

TABLE 10. *Rural and Urban Income Distribution: Gini Coefficient*

	Rural[1]	*Urban*[2]
1977	–	0.186
1978	0.2124	–
1980	0.2336	–
1981	0.2388	–
1982	0.2318	–
1983	0.2459	–
1984	0.2577	0.168
1985	0.2636	–
1989	–	0.174
1990	–	0.180

Notes and Sources:
[1] SSB, *Zhongguo nongmin shouru yanjiu* (*Chinese Peasant Income Studies*) (Taiyuan: Renmin chubanshe, 1987), pp. 4–7.
[2] Estimated from urban household income and expenditure survey data. *ZGTJNJ* 1990, p. 298; 1991, p. 278; *2000 nian zhongguo de renmin xiaofei* (*2000 China's People's Consumption*) (Beijing: Zhongguo shehui kezue chubanshe, 1987), p. 75.

to 1 in 1985. This was mainly caused by the rapid growth of peasant consumption, which rose more than twice as fast as in the urban sector. Since 1985 the growth of rural real consumption has, however, slowed, whereas that of the urban household has accelerated. Thus the urban-rural consumption gap has widened again. However, as Lardy points out, the gap is anyway an underestimation since urban households receive huge subsidies which increased even after 1978.

The overall consumption disparity depends also on the percentage share of the urban population or, more accurately, of the non-agricultural population since with a given urban-rural consumption gap, the shift of population from a relatively low rural consumption standard to a higher urban standard will contribute to the overall increase in consumption disparity until the time that half of the population lives in urban areas.[23] As the data in Table 13 show, the share of the "real" urban population, namely the non-agricultural population, did increase, but at a low rate.

Piecing together the evidence of rural and urban income inequality, the urban-rural consumption gap and the share of the real urban population, the overall consumption disparity appears to have remained relatively stable or even declined slightly in the first phase of reform, mainly due to the reduction of the urban-rural consumption gap and urban income inequality. But from 1985, with a widening urban-rural consumption gap, and increas-

[23] Perkins, "Reforming China's economic systems," p. 639.

TABLE 11. *Regional Disparities in per Capita Net Income of Chinese Peasants, 1985 and 1990 (in yuan)*

Provinces/ municipalities	Agricultural population (1986) in million	as %	Per capita net income 1985	1990
Nation average	848.2	100.0	398	630
East:				
Beijing	3.9	0.5	775	1261
Tianjin	3.7	0.4	565	1069
Shanghai	4.3	0.5	806	1665
Liaoning	22.2	2.6	468	776
Shandong	68.0	8.0	408	645
Jiangsu	51.2	6.0	493	884
Zhejiang	34.1	4.0	609	1045
Fujian	22.9	2.7	397	764
Guangdong	50.0	5.9	495	952
Hebei	48.4	5.7	385	592
Central:				
Heilongjiang	19.7	2.3	398	671
Jilin	14.6	1.7	414	717
Henan	68.9	8.1	329	482
Shanxi	21.0	2.5	358	560
Anhui	44.6	5.3	397	517
Hubei	39.1	4.6	421	602
Hunan	48.9	5.8	395	546
Jiangxi	28.7	3.4	377	580
Sichuan	88.3	10.4	315	505
Shaanxi	25.0	3.0	295	460
West:				
Guangxi	34.6	4.1	303	500
Ningxia	3.3	0.4	321	534
Xizang	1.8	0.2	353	437
Xinjiang	9.3	1.1	394	623
Neimenggu	14.4	1.7	360	607
Yunnan	30.5	3.6	338	490
Guizhou	26.4	3.1	288	435
Gansu	17.5	2.1	255	399
Qinghai	2.9	0.3	343	514
Coefficient of variation, population weighted:				
			0.7389	0.7556

Sources:
Population: PRC's Ministry of Agriculture's Department, *Zhongguo nongcun jingji tongji daquan 1949–1986* (*China's Comprehensive Rural Economics Statistics 1949–1986*) (Nongye chubanshe, 1989), pp. 12–13. Per capita net income: *ZGTJNJ* 1991, p. 297.

TABLE 12. *Urban and Rural Real Personal Consumption per Capita* (yuan *in 1980 prices*)

	Rural (1)	Urban (2)	Ratio (3) = (2)/(1)
1978	147	419	2.85
1979	158	437	2.77
1980	173	468	2.71
1981	187	508	2.72
1982	200	502	2.51
1983	218	512	2.35
1984	245	545	2.23
1985	280	592	2.11
1986	286	635	2.22
1987	298	694	2.33
1988	316	744	2.35
1989	313	723	2.31
1990	310	750	2.42

Source:
    ZGTJNJ 1991, pp. 270–71. Estimation: see note to Table 1.

TABLE 13. *Urban and Rural Population Data (%)*

	Cities and towns[1]	Villages[1]	Share of	
			Agricultural[2]	Non-agricultural[2]
1957	15.4	84.6	80.7	19.3
1978	17.9	82.1	82.1	17.9
1979	19.0	81.0	81.8	18.2
1980	19.4	80.6	81.1	18.9
1981	20.2	79.8	81.8	18.2
1982	21.1	78.9	81.4	18.6
1983	21.6	78.4	81.2	18.8
1984	23.0	77.0	80.7	19.3
1985	23.7	76.3	79.5	20.5
1986	24.5	75.5	79.3	20.7
1987	25.3	74.7	79.5	20.5
1988	25.8	74.2	79.3	20.7
1989	26.2	74.0	78.9	21.1
1990	26.4	74.0	78.6	21.4

Notes and Sources:
    [1] *ZGTJNJ* 1991, p. 79.
    [2] Derived from agricultural and non-agricultural population total and per capita personal consumption data, *ZGTJNJ* 1991, pp. 42, 79 and 270.

TABLE 14. *Poverty Incidence*

	1981[1]	*1985*[1]	*1990*[2]
Rural			
Poverty line (*yuan*)	169	200	338
Households (%)	44.3	12.3	13.1[3]
Urban			
Poverty line (*yuan*)	314	375	572
Households (%)	11.2	9.9	3.4[4]

Notes and Sources:
  [1] Medium scenario estimates of the World Bank cited in S.J. Burki, "Development strategies for poverty alleviation," *Asian Development Review*, No. 1 (1990), p. 16.
  [2] Poverty line adjusted for inflation by using worker cost of living index for urban households and unweighted average of free market and rural consumer retail price index for rural households.
  [3] Percentage of households with a per capita annual net income below 300 *yuan* only. See *ZGTJNJ* 1991, p. 294.
  [4] Percentage of households with a per capita annual disposable income of 632. See *ZGTJNJ* 1991, p. 278.

ing income inequality within the urban and rural sectors, as well as a rise in the share of the non-agricultural population, the overall consumption disparity has been rising again.

The trend in the incidence of poverty (the percentage share of rural and urban households falling below the poverty line) also follows the same pattern as overall income and consumption inequality. In 1985 the official poverty line was 200 *yuan* for the rural population, and 375 *yuan* for the urban population, regarded as reasonable approximations of the cost of a minimum basket of food and other basic needs sufficient to maintain a subsistence existence for an average rural and urban resident. Correcting for inflation, it is possible to estimate the changes in the percentage of rural and urban households falling below the poverty line in recent years. As the data in Table 14 indicate, the incidence of rural poverty has been much higher than that of urban areas. During the first phase of the reform (between 1981 and 1985) both the rural and urban incidence of poverty declined. But since 1985, while urban poverty continued to fall, rural poverty rose again.

The rate of poverty can be reduced by either increased average income or reduced income disparity. A study of poverty in Japan during 1963–77 reveals that the elasticities of the poverty rate with respect to the average income and the Gini coefficient were –2.90 and 1.95 respectively.[24] Thus the

[24] D.K. Nanto, "Poverty incidence in Japan," *The Philippine Economic Journal*, No. 2 (1980), p. 153.

rapid decline of poverty incidence in the rural sector in China during the first phase of the reform was mainly due to the rapid growth of the rural household income. In the urban sector the reduction of the poverty rate during the first phase of the reform was due to both increased income and decreased income disparity.

A closer look at the profile of the absolute poor in China reveals that most of the rural poor reside in the remote and mountainous terrain of its central and western regions. Table 15 shows the regional incidence of poverty measured in terms of percentage share of counties with average per capita rural income below 300 *yuan* in 1989. It indicates that the western and central regions contained the largest percentages of poor counties. The relative incidence of poverty was highest in the western region. Provinces with the highest relative incidence of poverty are Yunnan, Guizhou, Shaanxi, Gansu, Neimenggu and Guangxi. The urban poor, on the other hand, are characterized by large families, a low employment rate and a relatively large number of dependents.[25]

Outlook for the 1990s: per Capita Consumption

Prospects for continuing improvement of living standards in the 1990s depend on an assessment of the likely development of those factors which determine the level of per capita consumption. Since this is defined as consumption fund divided by population, and the level of the consumption fund is the difference between national income and accumulation, growth of per capita consumption depends on the growth of national income, the growth of population and changes in the rate of accumulation.

The "Ten-Year Economic Programme" merely reiterates the goal of quadrupling China's 1980 national income by the year 2000 and achieving a 6 per cent growth rate of GNP in the 1990s and a "relatively comfortable" (*xiaokang*) consumption standard for Chinese consumers by the end of the century. Unfortunately, it provides very few clues on the exact level of Chinese consumption and how its pattern is expected to change as China achieves a per capita income of US$1,000. The following discussion therefore has to rely on projections made under the "2000 China" project made earlier by a group of scholars affiliated to the influential State Council's Economic, Technological and Social Development Research Centre.

According to this projection national income is expected to rise at 6.5 per cent for the 1980s and at about 7 per cent in the 1990s (see Table 16). The annual average growth of the population is projected at about 1.2 per cent. NMP per capita is scheduled to reach 1,144 *yuan* or US$763 (1980 prices) by

---

[25] *Urban Household Income and Expenditure Survey Data*, p. 23.

TABLE 15. *Regional Rural Poverty Profile, 1989*

	% Distribution of counties (1)	% Distribution of poor counties (2)	Relative incidence of poverty (3) = (2)/(1)
East:	26.1	8.1	0.31
Beijing	0.6	0	0
Tianjin	0.5	0	0
Shanghai	0.4	0	0
Liaoning	3.0	1.7	0.57
Shandong	5.2	0	0
Jiangsu	3.1	0	0
Zhejiang	3.4	0.8	0.24
Fujian	3.0	0	0
Guangdong	4.5	0	0
Hebei	6.6	5.5	0.83
Central:	42.4	42.1	0.99
Heilongjiang	3.1	1.9	0.61
Jilin	2.2	0	0
Henan	5.6	5.8	1.04
Shanxi	4.4	5.8	1.32
Anhui	3.2	2.2	0.69
Hubei	3.5	3.1	0.89
Hunan	4.3	3.9	0.91
Jiangxi	3.7	0	0
Sichuan	8.2	11.1	1.35
Shaanxi	4.2	8.3	1.98
West:	31.5	49.8	1.58
Guangxi	3.5	5.5	1.57
Ningxia	0.8	1.1	1.38
Xizang	2.9	1.4	0.48
Xinjiang	3.3	0.8	0.24
Neimenggu	3.4	5.5	1.59
Yunnan	5.0	19.1	3.82
Guizhou	3.4	10.0	2.94
Gansu	3.4	5.8	1.71
Qinghai	1.6	0.6	0.38

Source:
ZGNYNJ 1990, p. 415.

the year 2000. The rate of accumulation is expected to decline from 31.5 per cent in 1980 to 29 per cent in the 1980s and 1990s. Real per capita consumption by the year 2000 is expected to be triple that of 1980. Finally, the urban–rural consumption gap is expected to narrow from 2.71 to 1 in 1980 to 1.86 to 1 in the year 2000. As Table 16 indicates, the projected income

TABLE 16. *Projection of Chinese Consumption Levels and Differential in the 1990s*

| | "2000 China" projection | | Reported achievement in 1990 (3) | (3)/(1) in % (4) | Required growth rate (1990–2000) in % (5) | Actual rate of growth (1985–90) in % (6) |
	1990 (1)	2000 (2)				
NMP growth rate (in %)	6.5[1]	7[2]	8.7[2]	134		7.5
NMP[3]	6,923	14,271	8,513	123	5.3	1.5
Population (100 million)	11.19	12.48	11.43	102	0.9	5.8
NMP per capita[4]	619	1,144	745	120	4.4	3.7
Rate of accumulation (in %)	29	29	35	121	-1.8	5.7
Total material consumption[3]	4,915	10,132	5,559	113	6.2	5.0
Personal consumption[3]	4,292	8,714	4,612	108	6.6	4.1
Per capita material consumption[4]	439	812	486	111	5.3	3.3
Per capita personal consumption[4]	384	698	403	105	5.6	
of which:						
agricultural population	315	573	310	98	6.3	2.1
non-agricultural population	684	1,066	750	110	3.6	4.9
Ratio of agricultural to non-agricultural pop.	2.17	1.86	2.42	112	-2.6	2.8

Notes:
[1] 1980–90.
[2] 1990–2000.
[3] 100 million 1980 *yuan*.
[4] 1980 *yuan*.

Sources:
Columns 1 and 2: Medium scenario, see *2000 China's People's Consumption*, pp. 106–14; column 3: Tables 1, 3 and 12.

and consumption targets for 1990 appear to have been too conservative inasmuch as they have already been significantly overfulfilled in 1990. With regard to the projected income and consumption targets for the year 2000, the picture is mixed. The projected income target appears to be conservative, since the rate of growth required to achieve it is fairly modest compared with the actual rate of growth in recent years (1985–90). However, the projected consumption targets for 2000 appear somewhat ambitious as the required rates of growth are significantly higher than those achieved in the last few years. This over-optimistic assessment of the level of Chinese consumption in 2000 is mainly due to underestimates of population growth and the rate of accumulation. As Table 16 indicates, recent population growth was higher than the projected 1.2 per cent rate of increase; moreover, the rate of accumulation has not declined (as was projected) but has risen, indicating a declining investment productivity. Thus the growth of Chinese consumption in the 1990s depends critically on the future population growth rate and rate of accumulation. If the rising trend of the latter can be arrested and the income growth of the recent past can be sustained over the next decade, then China should be able to double its living standard between 1990 and 2000. If the population growth rate is brought under control and the rate of accumulation is curbed by increasing investment productivity, China's consumption standard in the year 2000 may well be more than double its 1990 level. However, China is likely to face an uphill task in controlling its population and the rate of accumulation growth under the existing population structure and economic system.[26]

The projected decline of the urban–rural consumption gap made by Chinese economists is also too optimistic. To reverse the widening gap of recent years, the growth of urban consumption would have to be brought into line with that of rural consumption, and the enormous subsidies provided to urban consumers would have to be reduced drastically – a move that seems politically unacceptable.

Consumption Pattern

Changes in real consumer expenditure in different categories of consumer goods depend both on income growth, and income and price elasticities of demand. The difficulty of predicting change in Chinese consumption pattern is that the Chinese consumer market in the past was in disequilibrium. Thus, any income and price elasticities estimated solely on the basis of the observed disequilibrium prices, quantities consumed and expenditure cannot be regarded even as an approximation of actual Chinese consumer behaviour. Neither can they be used as the basis for future predictions.

[26] See the assessment of China's population growth and accumulation rate in the articles by Robert Ash and K. C. Yeh in this issue.

Projections of future Chinese consumption patterns are numerous. One was made by the above-mentioned "China 2000" project. Another uses the Extended Linear Expenditure Systems (ELES), as presented by Lluch, Powell and Williams.[27] Both projections obtain their Chinese consumer behaviour parameters from data on the disequilibrium prices, expenditures and quantities observed in the early 1980s. The resulting projections in consequence differ markedly from the levels actually achieved.

A more promising method, suggested by Podkammer, is to resort to an international comparison.[28] The average Chinese consumer's behaviour under equilibrium can be inferred from the consumption of other countries which have enjoyed persistent equilibrium conditions in the consumer's market and which are comparable with China in terms of their level of development, climatic and cultural conditions. In the following discussion we choose Taiwan in the 1975–79 period and Japan in 1967 as our reference base for projecting Chinese consumption patterns in the late 1990s. Both Taiwan and Japan had achieved a per capita income of US$1,000 during the periods used for the comparison. Comparing the current Chinese consumption structure with that of Taiwan and Japan during the reference period, it is possible to identify meat consumption, consumer durables, urban housing and services as potential growth areas and bottlenecks.

As mentioned earlier, the current Chinese diet is still very deficient in animal calories and protein, and its per capita real consumption level is very low compared with Taiwan at the same level of development. The growth of income in the 1990s is likely to increase the demand for meat (international studies indicate that the income elasticity of demand for meat is very high). Since the grain–meat conversion rate is also high, growth of income in the 1990s is likely to increase substantially the demand for grain. If it is assumed that the Chinese consumption of meat, eggs, fish, milk and direct grain in the year 2000 matches the levels of Taiwan during 1975–79 – namely 34.1, 6.6, 36.1, 20.2 and 153 kilograms per capita respectively – with an average conversion rate of 2.2 to 1,[29] the total requirement of grain, including seed, in the year 2000 would amount to 468 million tons per annum.[30] Grain output is projected to increase from an annual average of 404 million tons during 1985–90 to 500 million tons by the year 2000 implying an annual growth rate of 2 per cent. Allowing for a milling rate of 0.87, the availability of Chinese grain would then reach 435 million tons. Compared with the projected requirement, China would face a deficit of 33 million tons in the

[27] See Lin Baipeng et al., Zhongguo xiaofei jiegouxue (Studies of Chinese Consumption Structure) (Beijing: Jingji kexue chubanshe, 1987), and C. Lluch et al., Patterns in Household Demand and Saving (New York: Oxford University Press, 1977).

[28] Podkammer, "Estimates of disequilibrium," p. 425.

[29] This conversion rate is derived from 2000 China's People's Consumption, p. 223.

[30] The seed rate used to derive the demand for seed is taken from F.W. Crook, "China's grain production to the year 2000," USDA, China: Agriculture and Trade Report, June 1988, p. 31.

TABLE 17. *Comparison of Coverage Rate of Consumer Durables (per 100 house-holds), China and Japan*

	China[1]	Japan[2]	
	1990	1964	1967
Television set	74	90.3	96.4
Washing machine	38	61.0	84.8
Refrigerator	12	38.0	77.6
Motor car	negl.	–	13.1
Air conditioner	negl.	–	3.9
Vacuum cleaner	negl.	27.0	53.8

Notes and Sources:
 [1] *ZGTJNJ* 1991, p. 274.
 [2] *2000 China's People Consumption*, p. 135.

year 2000. Thus grain imports would have to be almost two and a half times that of 1990. Such imports would have to be even higher if the targeted rate of 2 per cent annual output growth of grain were not achieved or if the population growth were to exceed the targeted 1.2 per cent growth rate during the 1990s.

Apart from meat, another rapidly-growing category of consumption is likely to be "new" consumer durables such as refrigerators, washing machines, air conditioners, vacuum cleaners and motor cars. In general, growth of demand for these items is inversely related to their current coverage rate. As Table 17 indicates, the coverage rate of these items in China in 1989, with the exception of television sets, was significantly lower than that of Japan in 1964. Thus, pending the increased availability of piped water and electricity, the demand for washing machines, refrigerators, vacuum cleaners and even air conditioners is likely to soar. However, to catch up with the coverage rate of 1967 Japan by the year 2000, starting from China's low base level and given its enormous population, would require an enormous expansion in the output of these goods. Such a high rate of output growth is likely to be severely constrained by scarce invest-ment resources and foreign exchange constraints.

Urban housing is another potential area of very fast growth. Though rural housing conditions have improved greatly, urban housing conditions still remain relatively poor and basic. The average living space available per person in the urban areas was only 6.7 square metres in 1990 – well below the minimum housing norm of 8 square metres per person. Moreover, the goal of matching the number of housing units with the number of house-holds so that each household has a dwelling place of its own has not yet been achieved. Many households still live communally. With the lifting of the rural–urban migration ban and the surge in the number of newly-weds, the number of households looking for self-contained units is likely to soar rapidly. At the same time, as income grows, the demand for more living space will also increase. There is little doubt that the Chinese construction industry is capable of meeting this challenge in the 1990s. But since housing construction is relatively capital intensive and most housing construction so far has been financed by the state, a major question is whether the government will be prepared to tolerate an increased share of these so-called "non-productive" investments in its annual investment budget. If not, the government's policy response is likely to be either to restrain urban housing demand (through price increases or a slowing down in income growth), or to step up the pace of housing reforms and encourage individuals to invest in co-operative and private housing.

Finally, the service sector is a consumer area likely to experience a major expansion in the 1990s. The point has already been made that services are currently "underconsumed" because of their limited supply, especially in rural areas, and a significant service consumption gap exists between China and Japan at a comparable level of development. The income elasticity of demand for services is very high, especially for transport and communications (which averaged 2.7 to 3.2 and 1.4 to 1.7 for the non-agricultural and agricultural household respectively in Japan during 1960 to 1965).[31] As Japan approached and exceeded the threshold of US$1,000 per capita during the 1965–70 period, the share of service expenditures reached almost one-quarter of the family budget for both non-agricultural and agricultural households. In contrast, services made up less than 10 per cent of the Chinese urban and rural family budget in 1990. Some services, such as retail trade, catering, repairs and personal services, are highly labour intensive, and are therefore unlikely to face severe resource constraints. According to the "Ten-Year Economic Programme" the share of services in China's GNP is planned to increase from the current one-quarter to around one-third by the year 2000. Other services, however, such as transport, health and education are relatively capital-intensive and are likely to face severe resource constraints. To fill the gap between the growing capital demand of the service sector and the meagre supply of state capital, it is again likely that the government will have to increase private activity significantly in these areas.

Summary

Since 1978 real per capita material consumption in China has risen at an average annual rate of 7 per cent and more than doubled the standard of living of the average citizen. Nevertheless, China has made only limited

[31] For the prospects of achieving the planned target of food grain production in 2000 see the article by Robert Ash in this issue.

progress in improving the qualitative aspects of life. While consumer satisfaction has significantly increased, thanks to much greater freedom of consumer choice, as well as improved distribution and allocation of consumer
goods and services, the welfare of the average citizen is still adversely
affected by widening income disparity, a rising rate of rural poverty, dimin-
ishing economic security, increased environmental degradation and unequal access to education and medical care.

During a decade of reforms and under the impact of the open door
strategy, the quality of the structure of Chinese consumption also improved
markedly. The shares of most of the basic necessities, such as staple food,
clothing and fuel, in total household expenditures were significantly reduced, whereas those of mostly non-basic goods, such as non-staple food,
housing, consumer durables and services, rose. Despite these changes, Chinese real consumption level has not yet reached the level of "moderate
comfort" (*xiaokang*) and its gaps with the neighbouring Asian-Pacific countries at comparable stages of development have still not been bridged. The
Engel coefficient remains relatively high and the percentage share of animal
sources in daily Chinese nutrient intake, as well as the per capita consumption of services, are still rather low.

Growth of per capita consumption slowed significantly in the second
phase of the reforms (1985–90) and was less than half of that achieved in the
first phase. This was due to a slowdown of NMP growth, accompanied by a
rising rate of accumulation. Thanks to the high rate of inflation even real
per capita disposable income stagnated during these years.

Looking ahead in the 1990s, the prospect of accelerating improvements
in Chinese living standards depends on the overall economic growth, the
growth of population, the rate of accumulation and the continuation of the
market-oriented reforms. If population growth is brought under control
and the rate of accumulation is curbed, and barring political instability
which might result from the leadership succession crisis and the impact of
recent developments in the Soviet Union, China's real consumption standard by the year 2000 may well more than double its 1990 level. However,
income disparity is expected to increase as well. Non-staple foods, especially meat, the "new" consumer durables, urban housing and services are
likely to face the fastest-growing demand. Growth in this sector, however,
is likely to be increasingly limited by investment and foreign exchange
constraints. To ease the resource constraint, the Chinese government is
likely either to restrain consumer demand by way of price increases or a
slowdown of income growth or significantly to enlarge private sector participation in the production of these goods and services.

Index